The American Exploration and Travel Series

[Complete list on page 397]

THE
COLUMBIA
RIVER

THE COLUMBIA RIVER

Or scenes and adventures during a
residence of six years on the western side of
the Rocky Mountains among various tribes
of Indians hitherto unknown; together with
"A Journey across the American Continent"

by ROSS COX

Edited and with an Introduction by
EDGAR I. STEWART AND JANE R. STEWART

NORMAN : UNIVERSITY OF OKLAHOMA PRESS

BY EDGAR I. STEWART

Custer's Luck (Norman, 1955)

The Field Diary of Lieutenant Edward S. Godfrey
(editor, with Jane R. Stewart) (Portland, Oregon, 1957)

Ross Cox, *The Columbia River*
(editor, with Jane R. Stewart)
(Norman, 1957)

Library of Congress Catalog Card Number: 57–11191
Copyright 1957 by the University of Oklahoma Press,
Publishing Division of the University.
Composed and printed at Norman, Oklahoma, U.S.A.,
by the University of Oklahoma Press.
First printing.

FOR
FRED AND BERTHA
RAVENSCROFT

Editors' Acknowledgments

The late Frederic L. Paxson used to remark that the book which could be written under one roof was not worth writing, and similarly it might be said that no book can be written, or edited, without the assistance of many persons. For aid in preparing this edition of Ross Cox, *The Columbia River,* we are grateful to Professor Charles H. Hunter, head of the department of history in the University of Hawaii, who helped in identifying the persons and places mentioned in the Sandwich Islands, and to Mr. W. Kaye Lamb, Dominion archivist, Dominion of Canada, who answered our questions about "who and where" in Cox's journey across the continent. Professor Erna Gunther of the department of anthropology in the University of Washington furnished valuable information about the Indian tribes; while the Reverend J. Neilson Barry, of Portland, Oregon, to whom this and subsequent generations of historians will be forever indebted, gave generously of his time and counsel, despite a severe illness. Mrs. Edith Shaw of the Eastern Washington College Library and Mrs. Elizabeth Gilbert of the Spokane Public Library gave that generous and unselfish help that is the trade-mark of the professional reference librarian; while Mr. Jerome Peltier of Spokane and Mr. Robert Hitchman, two zealous and dedicated historical amateurs, by their aid and encouragement, and the loan of books and materials, contributed far more than they will ever know. Virginia Walton of the Montana State Historical Society furnished valuable information about Saleesh House. To each and all of these we are deeply and sincerely grateful.

Cheney, Washington

Edgar I. Stewart
Jane R. Stewart

ix

Contents

Chapter 4

Chapter 5

Chapter 6

Chapter 7

Chapter 8

Chapter 9

Contents

Chapter 10

Chapter 11

Chapter 12

Chapter 13

Chapter 14

Chapter 15

Chapter 16

Chapter 17

Chapter 18

Contents

Chapter 19

Author placed in charge of Oakinagan—Erects new buildings there—Musquitoes—Sagacity of the horses—Rattlesnakes good food—Sarsaparilla—Black snakes—Climate—Whirlwinds—Handsome situation—Character of the tribe—Manner of trading—Extraordinary cures of consumption

Chapter 20

Author nearly blinded by hawks—Foxes—Great number of wolves—Their method of attacking horses—Lynxes—Bears—Anecdote of a kidnapping bruin—Ingenious plan of getting off bear-skins—Account of the horses on the Columbia—Great feat performed by one

Chapter 21

Letter from the proprietors—Author winters at Oakinagan—Letter from Mr. Mackenzie—A number of horses stolen—Successful plan to recover them—Description of soil, climate, productions, &c., of the lower part of the Columbia

Chapter 22

Description of climate, soil, &c., above the rapids—Sketch of various tribes—The Chohoptins—Yackamans—Oakinagans—Sinapoils—Spokans—Anecdote—Pointed Hearts—Cause of war—Cootonais—Kettle Indians—Kamloops, &c.

Chapter 23

Ascent of the Columbia—Its lakes—Dangerous navigation—High water—Arrive at the mountains—Melancholy detail of the death of six of the party

Chapter 24

Canoe Valley and River—Appearance of mountains—M'Gillivray's Rock—Dangerous situation of party on a raft—Arrive at Rocky Mountain House—Volcanic appearances—Animals, &c.—Indian tradition respecting the mammoth—Difference in size of trees

Contents

Cruelty to relatives—Horrible treatment of prisoners—Sanguinary quarrels—Extraordinary ceremonies attending the dead
—Barbarities practised on widows, &c.—Table of population   367

List of Illustrations

Maps

Editors' Introduction

When Captain James Cook, on his third voyage to the Pacific Ocean, stopped briefly on the northwest coast of North America and permitted his men to barter a few furs from the natives, mostly for the purpose of repairing their own clothing, he quite unconsciously set in motion a train of events destined to be of world-wide significance. Although not acquired with any intention of resale, some of these furs were later sold in the Chinese market at a fantastic price and a fabulous profit, the selling price in some instances being one hundred times the amount paid, a fact which led to a near mutiny since the crew not unnaturally voiced a demand to return to the northwest coast for the purpose of obtaining more furs.

Although the fur trade was of great antiquity, had already been responsible for much of the exploration of North America, and was to be responsible for much more, here was a literally untouched source of supply; and there was no other place where furs existed in such quantity, were of such high quality, and could be obtained so cheaply as on the northwest coast. Here the sea otter, which ultimately became the royal fur of China, existed in abundance, and there was nothing else in the economy of Europe that could be obtained so cheaply and sold so advantageously. The news of this great fur bonanza did not reach Europe for several years, but the result, considering the difficulties in communication and transportation at the time, was a regular stampede to the region where fortunes were to be made overnight. One member of Cook's crew, serving as a corporal of marines, was a young American from Connecticut, John Ledyard, a veritable American Marco Polo. Arriving back in Boston and Philadelphia at the close of the American Revolution, he attempted to interest the merchants and shipowners of those cities in this new enterprise. But he found no success, for the depression that followed the winning of independence, when the Thirteen Colonies lost their preferred trade position within the British Empire, lay heavy on the land, and capital for investment was almost nonexistent. Ledyard then journeyed to France, where he brought the idea to the attention of Thomas Jefferson, who had succeeded Benjamin Franklin as the American representative in Paris. Jefferson, one of the most many-sided men in American public life, was interested, but no capital was forthcoming.

In 1788, however, probably as a direct result of Ledyard's efforts, a firm of Boston merchants started the first American ships toward the waters of the Pacific Northwest. These were the *Columbia Redivia*, better known as the *Columbia,* under the command of Captain John Kendrick, and the sloop *Lady Washington,* commanded by Captain Robert Gray. The American ships were at Nootka Sound when the Spanish commandant seized several British ships for trespassing and brought the two countries to the verge of war, but they were not molested in any way. After a few months of trading along the coast, the two captains exchanged ships, and Gray, in the *Columbia,* returned to Boston by way of China, thus becoming the first American ship and the first American commander to circumnavigate the globe. After only a short stay in Boston, Gray returned to the northwest coast and by 1792 was again coasting along its shores trading for furs. Since the best bargains were to be made with natives who had little or no idea of the value that the white man put upon the commodity for which he was trading, all the ships engaged in the trade constantly sought previously untouched areas and ran the prows of their ships into every promising cove and inlet, continually seeking villages whose inhabitants had never before seen a white man, were not familiar with his ways or goods, and would have a large stock of accumulated furs to trade. It was this search for bargains in peltry that resulted in the discovery by Captain Gray of the Columbia River and of what is today Grays Harbor. Although the existence of this great river of the West had been suspected for many years, and even actually reported by the Spaniard Bruno Heceta in 1776, Gray, in 1792, was the first white man to enter its estuary, even though the question of whether he actually ever saw the river itself is still a matter of dispute.

But in the meantime other forces were at work, and the contest for the political and economic control of the Pacific Northwest developed into a race for empire, with the fur trappers and traders as its agents and instrumentalities. In 1670, the Hudson's Bay Company had been chartered by Charles II and given almost monopolistic rights in the region of present French Canada, despite the fact that the French were already in effective possession of the St. Lawrence Valley and that their enterprising traders were pointing ever westward. French activity centered in Montreal; and following the expulsion of the French from America in 1763, the merchants of that city continued their trade in furs (despite the alleged monopoly of the Hudson's Bay Company). Gradually a number of small groups of independent traders came into existence and finally, in 1783, found formal organization as the North West Company.

In 1793, Alexander Mackenzie, in the employ of the North West Company, crossed the continent and on July 22 inscribed, with a mixture of vermillion and grease, the record of the successful completion of his exploration on the southeast face of a large rock overlooking Dean Channel, into which the Bella Coola River empties. It had been explored only a few weeks before by the boats from George Vancouver's ships. Vancouver had been sent out to negotiate a final settlement of the Nootka Sound controversy with Spain and to explore the coast. The year previous, hearing of Gray's discovery of the Columbia River, about whose existence he had expressed doubt, Vancouver had sent his lieutenant, Broughton, in the tender *Chatham* across the bar at the entrance and up the stream to a point several miles above the site of present Vancouver, Washington.

On his return to civilization, Mackenzie, owing to disagreements among the partners, separated himself from the fur trade and returned to England, where he published the account of his travels in a volume which was nothing if not a blueprint of the plans for British imperial expansion. This volume, coming to the attention of President Jefferson, reinforced the earlier influence of John Ledyard and brought the President to an acute awareness of the Pacific Northwest's importance to the future destiny of the American Republic and of the inherent danger in the British advance toward the mouth of the Columbia River.

The result was the Lewis and Clark expedition, which journeyed to the mouth of the Columbia River and back in the years 1804–1806, and which was designed to lay the foundation for the subsequent challenge by the United States to Great Britain for the control of the fur trade of the Far West. The traders were already beginning to push into the area west of St. Louis. On their way up the Missouri River the party of explorers met several parties of traders and trappers returning from the upriver country, and on their return they met many more traveling up the Missouri on their way into the interior in search of furs and peltries. The race for empire was on.

Nor was the North West Company idle. Mackenzie's work had been only a beginning, and in succeeding years other officials of the company followed up the work that he had begun. This was not immediate, for the ruling hierarchy of the company felt that fur trading rather than exploration was the true business of the concern and frowned upon enterprises such as that of Mackenzie. But in 1799, the autocratic procedures of Simon McTavish led to a revolt on the part of some of the younger partners, a movement that was led by Alexander Mackenzie in person and resulted in the organization of the XY Company, which fought the Northwesters on their own grounds and with their own weapons. So lawless did the struggle for supremacy become that a special act of Parliament, the Canada Jurisdiction Act, was passed in order to put an end to the disorders. But in 1804, the death of McTavish resulted in a reunion of the two companies, and the rejuvenated organization now carried the quest for furs as far as the Arctic Ocean and the Rocky Mountains; while David Thompson, who had earlier served an apprenticeship with and then entered the service of the Hudson's Bay Company, now left the employ of that concern and carried the banner of the Northwesters as far as the Pacific.

But in the meantime a new and formidable rival had entered the field. John Jacob Astor came from Germany to the United States to seek his fortune shortly after the close of the American War of Independence. It was only a short time after his arrival, tradition says, that he decided to enter the fur trade as the surest and quickest way to a fortune, having learned of the profits to be made in it from a fellow German emigrant, who had been in America before, while his ship was icebound in Baltimore Harbor. That his decision was not unsound is shown by the fact that within sixteen years he had become one of the leading figures in the American fur trade and had also incurred the bitter hatred and enmity of his rivals.

In 1808, Astor chartered the American Fur Company with the

open and avowed intention of exploiting the fur resources of the newly acquired Louisiana Territory. This idea led inevitably to another, a similar exploitation of the resources of the Columbia River Valley, the advantages of which had been described by Lewis and Clark. In this later scheme the main post or fort was to be established at the mouth of the river, with various subsidiary posts located in the interior. Every year a supply ship would be sent to the main post with a year's supply of provisions and trade goods. There it would take on board the accumulated catch of furs or peltries and transport them to China, where they would be disposed of. There the ship would take on board a cargo of tea and other Oriental commodities and return to New York. In the meantime the interior posts would have been supplied by canoes and other light craft from the main depot and their accumulated peltries taken to the mouth of the river to await the next visit of the supply ship.

It was a program imperial in its conception and universal in its implications, and Astor, perhaps a little dubious of his ability to bring it to full realization singlehandedly, approached the North West Company with a view to securing their co-operation. But the Northwesters refused to go along, and in 1810 the Pacific Fur Company was organized. Astor was a businessman with little or no actual field experience in the fur trade, so he induced a number of former North West Company men to become partners in the new organization, although he provided all the capital and agreed to cover all the losses incurred during the first five years.

In September of 1810, the *Tonquin,* the first supply ship, sailed from New York under the command of Captain Jonathan Thorn, a naval officer who secured a furlough in order to take command of the ship. There were several of the Canadian partners on board, and the result was a tempestuous voyage, at least in so far as the personal relations of the captain and the partners were concerned, and it sowed the seeds of subsequent disaster. After touching at the Hawaiian Islands, where the services of a number of islanders were secured, the *Tonquin* arrived at the mouth of the Columbia River in March, 1811. Here, after some delay in which the antagonism between the captain and the partners again came to the surface, the site for the main trading post was selected and construction begun. Having landed the necessary construction materials and a part of the supplies, the *Tonquin* sailed on a trading voyage to the north, from which it never returned.

In the same month that the *Tonquin* arrived at the mouth of the Columbia River, the overland party of Astorians under the command of Wilson Price Hunt, who, like Astor, was without practical experience in the fur trade, left its winter camp near present St. Joseph and started up the Missouri River. After leaving that river at the Arikara villages near the present site of Pierre, South Dakota, owing to reports of danger from the Blackfeet, the party struck out across country and, after a trip of incredible hardship and privation, finally straggled into Fort Astoria in small detachments during the months of January and February, 1812. In May, 1812, the second supply ship, the *Beaver,* on which Ross Cox was one of the passengers, arrived at Astoria. Despite losses, suffering, and hardships experienced by all the various expeditions, the outlook seemed cheerful and promising. But it was to be rudely dissipated shortly afterward by the news that war had broken out between the United States and Great Britain and by the further information that a British warship was on the way to force the capitulation of the establishment. Under these circumstances Duncan McDougall, the senior partner on the ground, sold the post to representatives of the North West Company, in a transaction the necessity for and the ethics of which have been hotly disputed ever since. A short time afterward, the British sloop of war *Raccoon* arrived, and despite the fact that the British flag flew over the post, Captain Black, who possibly was drunk, landed and went through the ceremony of taking possession for Great Britain. This was an action that under the terms of the later Treaty of Ghent, which ended the War of 1812, justified the United States in demanding its restitution. With the sale of Astoria, some of the partners and clerks, Ross Cox included, took advantage of a very favorable offering made to them and proceeded to join the Canadian concern. Others, for whom the glamour of the fur trade had grown thin, or who had abandoned their hopes of making a fortune in a short time, took advantage of the opportunity to return to the East.

In the meantime other events had been transpiring, and the North West Company had been threatened with disaster from a new and unexpected quarter. The Hudson's Bay Company, which had claimed a monopoly of the fur trade in Canada since 1670, the date of its charter, had become so decrepit and moribund that a proposal made by Alexander Mackenzie that the North West Company buy out its rival failed of approval by the other partners. They not unnaturally objected to spending good money for the purchase of a concern that they felt would in any case fall into their hands within a few years. That this did not happen was the result of the revitalizing of the Hudson's Bay Company by the energy and enthusiasm of a single individual, the Earl of Selkirk, who, oddly enough, was not interested in the fur trade but in the foundation of an agricultural colony.

Thomas Douglas, fifth Earl of Selkirk, was born in Scotland, on St. Mary's Isle at the mouth of the River Dee, the twentieth of June, 1771. When he was only seven years old a raid on his ancestral home by John Paul Jones in the *Ranger* terrified the boy and gave him a deep and lasting hatred for the United States. In the course of his life this antipathy took the form of an opposition to continued emigration of British subjects to the United States, where sturdy English and Scotch families could become the sinews of strength to a nation that he felt might in time develop into a great rival of the British Empire. Although a Lowlander, he was particularly sympathetic toward the economic plight of the Scotch Highlanders, whose whole scheme of existence had been demolished by the substitution of large-scale sheep raising for small-scale agriculture. Their economic condition was such that they were virtually forced to migrate, but Lord Selkirk did not propose to see them go to the United States if he could help it.

In 1801, the appearance of Alexander Mackenzie's book called his attention to the agricultural possibilities of the Canadian West. The next year he attempted to interest the British government in a proposal to establish a colony of Highland Scots in the region of the present province of Manitoba, but without success. In 1803, he did succeed in establishing such a colony on Prince Edward Island, and following a visit to his colony, he went on to Montreal. There he was cordially, and somewhat lavishly, entertained by the ruling powers of the North West Company, although some of the partners were suspicious of him at the time, feeling that he was too inquisitive and asked too many questions.

In 1807, following his return to England, Lord Selkirk married the daughter of James Wedderburn-Colvile, one of the largest shareholders in the Hudson's Bay Company, and began to buy stock in that almost-bankrupt concern with the object of gaining control and translating his great colonization dream into reality. Somewhere he came under the influence of a very remarkable and capable individual.

Colin Robertson had been employed by the North West Company and stationed at Green Lake on Beaver River south of Lake Île-à-la Crosse, which was under the supervision of John McDonald of Garth. For some cause, McDonald discharged Robertson, and, whatever his reasons may have been, this action proved to be a colossal mistake and tragic in its consequences, for it was Robertson who had convinced Lord Selkirk of the desirability of establishing an agricultural colony in the valley of the Red River. By 1810, Lord Selkirk had acquired control of the Hudson's Bay Company, and in February of the next year he requested the company to grant him 110,000 square miles of territory lying along the "Red River of the North," in what is now the states of North Dakota and Minnesota and the Canadian provinces of Saskatchewan and Manitoba.

The North West Company had adopted what might seem to be a modern technique in that several of the partners had purchased stock in the Hudson's Bay Company, thereby keeping themselves informed of what the opposition was doing or planning to do. News of the Selkirk grant was received in Montreal with consternation and dismay not unmixed with resentment at what might have been considered an abuse of hospitality. But there was no thought of surrender or retreat, only a determination to fight. The whole Selkirk scheme was impractical and absurd, and the Northwesters knew it, for they realized how impossible it would be to supply an agricultural colony situated in the middle of the American continent. They knew from experience how difficult it was to supply some of their more isolated posts, and Lord Selkirk's problem was infinitely more complex. But, absurd or not, the colony would lie across their best canoe routes from Montreal to the interior and would cut their vital arteries of communication. So well developed was the North West Company's system of waterways that a trader could leave Cumberland House on the Saskatchewan River, or, for that matter, any other post in the interior, and reach the Arctic Ocean, the Atlantic, or the Gulf of Mexico without making a portage of more than a day's duration. The same was almost true of the Pacific, although here the crossing of Athabaska Pass entailed more time and more hardship. The Selkirk colony, if allowed to prosper, would also deprive the company of its best region for the supply of pemmican. Labor in the canoes was hard and arduous, and space was precious, two factors that demanded a food small in bulk but great in nutritive qualities. This demand was admirably met by pemmican, which can be said to have constituted an essential ingredient of the fur trade.

Pemmican was generally made from the flesh of the buffalo, although any lean meat such as deer or elk could have been used. The flesh was first cut into very thin slices and dried either in the sun or before a fire. It was then reduced to a powder by being pounded with a wooden mallet or pestle, then mixed with melted buffalo tallow, and the whole thing poured into a bag made from the hide of the buffalo. Each bag generally weighed about ninety pounds, and much meat went into surprisingly little pemmican, one buffalo providing enough lean meat for one bag of pemmican. The better grades of pemmican were sometimes mixed with dried berries, but there was nothing appetizing or delectable about any pemmican. In more than one sense a little went a long way. It could be eaten cold, fried, or boiled with flour, but in any case it could only be described as unappetizing, although some methods of preparation were less distasteful than others.

The farmer, the agricultural settler, was the great enemy of the fur trader, and this project of Lord Selkirk, if allowed to succeed, meant disaster to the far-flung empire of the North West Company. And the traders fought back with all the means at their command, viciously and bitterly, not only with economic weapons but with military as well, until a true civil war between the partisans of the Hudson's Bay Company and the North West Company was being waged in the wilderness of North America. Prices out of all proportion were paid for furs, the natives were debauched with liquor, rival forts and posts were attacked, captured, and pillaged, and even murder of opponents resorted to. This struggle culminated in the famous Seven Oaks Massacre on June 19, 1816, in which Robert Semple, governor of the Hudson's Bay territories in North America, and a group of twenty-one of Lord Selkirk's colonists were brutally murdered. The affair, which took place at what is now a park in the city of Winnipeg, was committed by a group of metis, Bois Brûlés, or Red River half-bloods, under the leadership of Cuthbert Grant, himself a mixed blood of Scotch-Cree ancestry.

Although the surviving settlers abandoned the colony and fled for their lives, Lord Selkirk re-established the settlement and displayed a determination to fight fire with fire. But this time things had gone too far; the British Colonial Office, acting under the statute of 1803, intervened, and it was obvious that some kind of a settlement had to be made. By this time both companies, forced almost into bankruptcy, realized that the struggle could not be continued, and the deaths of both Alexander Mackenzie and Lord Selkirk, within a few months of each other, smoothed the way for the inevitable merger.

This was the larger picture in which Ross Cox operated as a very small figure. He went out to Astoria on the *Beaver* as a member of the Astor company. Later, after the surrender of the post, he joined the North West Company and had many thrilling adventures, which, we may be sure, lost nothing in the telling. Finally, he made the long journey overland from Fort George, on the Columbia River, to Montreal, on the St. Lawrence, almost at the height of the "war" between the rival companies.

Of Cox himself we know little besides what he tells us in his book. He was born in Dublin in the year 1793 and was, therefore, a youth of eighteen when he joined the Pacific Fur Company in 1811. How long he had been in the United States or what he was doing we do not know, but it is fair to assume that he was another young man who was seeking his fortune. Either he was exceedingly eager to accompany the expedition or his qualifications were not too highly thought of, for he signed on as a clerk at a salary of $100 a year, while all the other clerks received $150 or more. Henry Willets, whose death at sea is recorded by Cox, was signed on as a hunter at $150. That his services were not considered too valuable is shown by the fact that at a meeting of the resident partners on June 25, 1813, when the fort at Astoria was short on supplies for the interior posts and had more clerks than were needed, it was agreed and resolved "that if it meet their own approbation their engagements shall be delivered up to Donald McLennan, Donald McGillis and Ross Cox with full permission to engage elsewhere provided they give their notes for any balances they may owe to the concern." The resolution was signed by Duncan McDougall, Donald McKenzie, David Stuart, and John Clark.[1] In other words, these three clerks were considered the least valuable to the company and were, if they so desired, to be released from their contracts and allowed to make other arrangements for themselves. In other words, Cox was not as essential to either the Pacific Fur Company or the North West Company as he apparently

[1] See T. C. Elliott, "The Sale of Astoria, 1813," *Oregon Historical Quarterly,* Vol. XXXIII, p. 45.

thought he was. But all three of the clerks elected to remain with the company, and when the North West Company purchased Astoria, Cox transferred his allegiance to the Canadian corporation, although both McLennan and McGillis took advantage of the opportunity to return to Montreal with the overland express. Cox remained on the Columbia River until he made the overland journey. It was during this time that he described himself as having a "cropped head, John-Bullish face, low, and somewhat corpulent person." In 1818, he returned to Ireland and the next year married Miss Hannah Cumming. He was employed for many years as a clerk in the head police office in Dublin, and until 1837, he served as the Dublin correspondent of the *London Morning Herald,* which accounts for his journalistic style.

His account was one of three published by clerks who had been with the Astor expeditions. In 1820, Gabriel Franchère published his *Voyage,* but being in French it did not attract the attention it deserved until a translation was published in New York in 1840. In 1831, Cox published his book in London, and it was so successful that by the next year it was in a third edition, while an American edition was published in New York. Internal evidence indicates that Cox was familiar with Franchère's book; in fact, it may have been the appearance of the latter's work that was responsible for his decision to put his own experiences into print. In 1849, Alexander Ross published his *Adventures of the First Settlers on the Oregon or Columbia River,* to be followed by *The Fur Hunters of the Far West* and *The Red River Settlement.* While all three writers have much in common since their books are about the same thing, they present different points of view, and perusal of all three is necessary for a complete picture of the trade and the period that they describe. Cox's worst faults are that he apparently wrote largely from memory and that much of what he relates was nothing more nor less than hearsay of which he had no direct knowledge. His chronology is often badly mixed, and he constantly attributes to himself an importance in the general scheme of things to which he was not entitled. In common with many writers of the day, he often interrupts his narrative of events with quotations and literary allusions that more often serve as a means of displaying his own erudition than as an illuminant for the text. In some cases they are literally "dragged in," while in others there is the suspicion that the text was made to fit the quotation, rather than the reverse. But however annoying this may be to the modern reader, it must be remembered that Cox was writing for a British audience of the early nineteenth century, by which it was apparently expected. And the cardinal historical sin is to judge one age by the standards of another; therefore, Cox cannot be censured for doing what was expected of him.

But there is much that is good in Cox's volume. He presents an illuminating picture of the business end of the fur trade, of how the companies operated in the field, of the vicissitudes and hardships that were endured, and of the loneliness and the boredom that were the lot of the various functionaries at their posts for the winter, relieved only by an occasional visit from another trader or by the dangers and hazards of the trade. His discussion of the ways and habits of the Indians, their native customs, and their reactions to the ways of the white man are not without interest. His more or less between-the-lines account of the progressive and largely unconscious deterioration of character that resulted from close contact and association with a barbaric race only slightly above the Stone Age called attention to a little-known aspect of the price that the white man paid for the furs obtained in the wilderness. His matter-of-fact comments on the circumstances of daily life—the working conditions, especially the food, the use of horse and dog meat, the attempts at cultivating gardens—could not have helped but be of interest to his readers, and today they serve to remind us of a part of the price at which the West was won.

All in all, the Ross Cox volume presents a thrilling narrative. Even when due allowance is made for the author's romanticizing and exaggerations, we must appreciate the sacrifices that were necessary in the quest for furs and the conquest of a continent. It is a tale told by an individual who was very human, and who was not inclined to minimize his own importance in the scheme of things. It is a drama of toil and hardship not unmixed with gaiety, of success and failure, of dreams come true, and of hopes turning to ashes, all played by relatively humble, obscure men who did not realize the significance of their roles. It is played against the backdrop of a struggle for empire between two Anglo-Saxon nations, which, despite sharing a common heritage and tradition, had differing political and economic philosophies. The prize for the winner was control of the great river whose existence had become almost a legend before it became an established fact, and whose control was known to be essential to the domination, both political and economic, of the region that men then knew as the "Oregon country." As a part of the presentation of that drama Ross Cox's *The Columbia River* deserves to be eternally remembered.

THE
COLUMBIA
RIVER

To The Right Honourable
Lord Francis Leveson Gower, &c. &c.
These Volumes Are Respectfully Dedicated,
As a Slight Tribute of Respect for his Lordship's
Character as a Man, His Talents as a Poet,
and His Consistency as a Statesman;
by His Lordship's Obedient Humble Servant,
The Author

Author's Preface

The following Narrative embraces a period of six years, five of which were spent among various tribes on the banks of the Columbia River and its tributary streams; and the remaining portion was occupied in the voyage outwards, and the journey across the continent.

During this period the Author ascended the Columbia nine times, and descended it eight, wintered among various tribes, was engaged in several encounters with the Indians, was lost fourteen days in a wilderness, and had many other extraordinary escapes.

He kept journals of the principal events which occurred during the greater part of this period, the substance of which will be found embodied in the following pages. Those who love to read of "battle, murder, and sudden death," will, in his description of the dangers and privations to which the life of an Indian trader is subject, find much to gratify their taste; while to such as are fond of nature, in its rudest and most savage forms, he trusts his sketches of the wild and wandering tribes of Western America may not be found uninteresting.

They cannot lay claim to the beautiful colouring which the romantic pen of a Chateaubriand has imparted to his picture of Indian manners; for the Author, unfortunately, did not meet with any tribe which approached that celebrated writer's splendid description of savage life. He has seen many of them before the contamination of white men could have deteriorated their native character; and, while he records with pleasure the virtues and bravery of some, truth compels him to give a different character to the great majority.

The press has of late years teemed with various "Recollections," "Reminiscences," &c. of travels, scenes, and adventures in *well known* countries, but no account has been yet published of a great portion of the remote regions alluded to in this work. They are therefore new

5

to the world; and, if the Author's unpretending narrative possesses no other claim to the public favor, it cannot at least be denied that of novelty.

Author's Introduction

In the year 1670 a charter was granted by Charles the Second to the Hudson's Bay Company, whose first governor was Prince Rupert, by which the Company was allowed the exclusive privilege of establishing trading factories on the shores of that noble bay and its tributary rivers. Owing to this charter, the fur-trade, which forms an important and extensive branch of American commerce, was for a long period monopolised by the Company; but, from the peculiar nature of its constitution, little progress was made by its officers in extending its trading posts, or exploring the interior, until the year 1770, when Mr. Hearne was sent on an expedition to the Arctic Sea, for an account of which I beg to refer the reader to that gentleman's simple and interesting narrative.[1]

While Canada belonged to France the Canadian traders had advanced many hundred miles beyond Lake Superior, and established several trading posts in the heart of the country, some of which the *voyageurs* still call by their original names; such as Fort Dauphin,[2] Fort Bourbon,[3] and others.

---

[1] Samuel Hearne, *A Journey From the Prince of Wales's Fort in Hudson's Bay to the Northern Ocean* (London, A. Strahan and T. Cadell, 1795). This book has been reprinted with an introduction and notes by J. B. Tyrell, as Vol. VI of the Publications of the Champlain Society (Toronto, 1911).

[2] Fort Dauphin was an old French fort on the northwest shore of Lake Manitoba. It was built by the sons of the Sieur de la Vérendrye in 1741, on what is now known as Mossy River, which flows into the lake from the west. See *Historic Forts and Trading Posts of the French Regime and of the English Fur Trading Companies,* compiled by Ernest Vorhis (Ottawa, National Development Bureau, Department of the Interior, 1930), 58. (Hereinafter cited as Vorhis, *Historic Forts.*)

[3] Fort Bourbon was also a French fort built by Pierre Gaultier de Varennes, one of the sons of La Vérendrye, in 1741. It was located on what is now Fort Island near the mouth of the Saskatchewan River. See Vorhis, *Historic Forts,* 42–43.

The conquest of that province opened a new source of trade to British enterprise; and while the officers of the Hudson's Bay Company fancied their charter had secured them in the undisturbed possession of their monopoly, an active and enterprising rival was gradually encroaching on their territories, and imperceptibly undermining their influence with the Indians; I allude to the North-West Fur Company of Canada, which originally consisted of a few private traders, but subsequently became the first commercial establishment in British America.

It is not here necessary to enter into a detail of the formation and increase of this Company. Its first members were British and Canadian merchants; among whom Messrs. Rocheblave,[4] Frobisher,[5] Fraser,[6] M'Tavish,[7] Mackenzie,[8] and M'Gillivray[9] were the most prominent. Their clerks were chiefly younger branches of respectable Scottish families, who entered the service as apprentices for seven years; for which period they were allowed 100 pounds, and suitable

[4] Pierre Rastel de Rocheblave (1764?–1840) was born in Illinois of French ancestry. In 1804, he became a wintering partner of the North West Company and retired in 1821. See *Documents Relating to the North West Company,* edited by William Stewart Wallace (Toronto, The Champlain Society, 1934), 494–95. (Hereinafter cited as Wallace, *Documents.*)

[5] Joseph Frobisher (1740–1810), an original member of the North West Company, who became one of its greatest figures. See Wallace, *Documents,* 446.

[6] Simon Fraser (1760?–1830) appears to have become a partner of the North West Company about 1795 and to have retired in 1800. He is not to be confused with the man of the same name who discovered the Fraser River in present British Columbia. See Wallace, *Documents,* 445.

[7] Simon McTavish (1750–1804). In 1779, he became one of the partners of the original sixteen-share North West Company. In 1787, he formed a partnership with Joseph Frobisher, known as McTavish, Frobisher and Company, which became the supply house and virtual directorate of the North West Company. See Wallace, *Documents,* 485–86.

[8] Sir Alexander Mackenzie (1764–1820), one of the most famous names in the history of the fur trade, was born in Stornoway, Outer Hebrides, and in 1787 became a partner in the North West Company, after having been associated with one of its smaller rivals, Gregory, McLeod and Company. In 1788, he took over the western department of the enlarged company, and the next year he reached the Arctic Ocean by way of the Mackenzie River. In 1793, he headed the expedition that reached the Pacific Ocean overland. See Wallace, *Documents,* 474. The journal of the expedition has been edited by Milo Milton Quaife: *Alexander Mackenzie's Voyage to the Pacific Ocean in 1793* (Chicago, The Lakeside Press, 1931).

[9] William McGillivray (1764?–1825). In 1790, he became a partner in the North West Company, and in the firm of McTavish, Frobisher and Company three years later. In 1804, he became the chief director of the former company. Fort William, the company headquarters on Lake Superior, was named in his honor. See Wallace, *Documents,* 471.

clothing. At the expiration of their apprenticeship they were placed on yearly salaries, varying from 80 to 160 pounds, and according to their talents were ultimately provided for as partners; some, perhaps, in a year or two after the termination of their engagements; while others remained ten, twelve, or sixteen years in a state of probation.

This system, by creating an identity of interest, produced a spirit of emulation among the clerks admirably calculated to promote the general good; for, as each individual was led to expect that the period for his election to the proprietory depended on his own exertions, every nerve was strained to attain the long-desired object of his wishes.

Courage was an indispensable qualification not merely for the casual encounters with the Indians, but to intimidate any competitor in trade with whom he might happen to come in collision. Success was looked upon as the great criterion of a trader's cleverness; and provided he obtained for his outfit of merchandise what was considered a good return of furs, the partners never stopped to inquire about the means by which they were acquired.

The Hudson's Bay Company, on the contrary, presented no such inducements to extra exertion on the part of its officers. Each individual had a fixed salary, without any prospect of becoming a proprietor; and some of them, whose courage was undoubted, when challenged to single combat by a Nor-Wester, refused; alleging as a reason, that they were engaged to trade for furs, and not to fight with fellow-subjects!

Independently of the foregoing circumstances, the North-West Company, in the selection of its canoe-men, or, as they are called, *engagés,* had another great advantage over its chartered rival. These men were French Canadians, remarkable for obedience to their superiors; and whose skill in managing canoes, capability of enduring hardship, and facility of adapting themselves to the habits and peculiarities of the various tribes, rendered them infinitely more popular in the eyes of the Indians than the stubborn, unbending, matter-of-fact Orkney men, into whose ideas a work of supererogation never entered.[10]

The diminished amount of their imports, joined to the increased demand of goods from their factories, at length opened the eyes of

[10] The chief part of the boatmen and several of the officers of the Hudson's Bay Company were, formerly, natives of the Orkney Islands.—R. C. (The Original Ross Cox footnotes are signed "R. C."—eds.)

9

the Hudson's Bay directors to the success of their formidable opponents, and induced them to attempt, when too late, to arrest their career. By their charter they now laid claim to the exclusive privilege of trading, not merely on the English River and its various branches, but also on the Saskachawan, Red River, and all the other streams which empty themselves into the great Lake Winepic,[11] the waters of which are carried to Hudson's Bay by the rivers Nelson and Severn.

This territorial claim, unsupported by any physical power, had but little weight with their persevering rivals. They were far beyond the reach of magisterial authority; and an injunction could not be easily served, nor obedience to it enforced, in a country fifteen hundred or two thousand miles beyond the limits of any recognised jurisdiction.

After establishing opposition trading posts adjoining the different factories of the Hudson's Bay Company in the interior, the indefatigable Nor-Westers continued their progress to the northward and westward, and formed numerous trading establishments at Athabasca, Peace River, Great and Lesser Slave Lakes, New Caledonia,[12] the Columbia, &c.; to none of which places did the officers of the Hudson Bay attempt to follow them. By these means the North-West Company became undisputed masters of the interior. Their influence with the natives was all-powerful; and no single trader, without incurring imminent danger from the Indians, or encountering the risk of starvation, could attempt to penetrate into their territories.

A few independent individuals, unconnected with either company, the chief of whom was Mr. John Jacob Astor, a wealthy merchant of New York, still carried on a fluctuating trade with the Indians, whose lands border Canada and the United States; but their competition proved injurious to themselves, as prices far above their value were frequently given to the natives for their furs.

With the interior thus inaccessible, and the confines not worth disputing, Mr. Astor turned his thoughts to the opposite side of the American continent, and accordingly made proposals to the North-West Company to join with him in forming an establishment on the Columbia River. This proposition was submitted to the consideration

[11] Lake Winnipeg.
[12] New Caledonia was the name applied to the interior of present British Columbia, the region of the upper Fraser and Stuart rivers, because of its geographical resemblance to the Highlands of Scotland.

of a general meeting of the wintering proprietors; and, after some negotiations as to the details, rejected.

Mr. Astor therefore determined to make the attempt without their co-operation; and in the winter of 1809 he succeeded in forming an association called the "Pacific Fur Company," of which he himself was the chief proprietor. As able and experienced traders were necessary to ensure success, he induced several of the gentlemen connected with the North-West Company to quit that establishment and join in his speculation. Among these was Mr. Alexander M'Kay,[13] an old partner, who had accompanied Sir Alexander Mackenzie in his perilous journey across the continent to the Pacific Ocean.

It was intended in the first instance to form a trading establishment at the entrance of the Columbia, and as many more subsequently on its tributary streams as the nature and productions of the country would admit. It was also arranged that a vessel laden with goods for the Indian trade should sail every year from New York to the Columbia, and after discharging her cargo at the establishment, take on board the produce of the year's trade, and thence proceed to Canton, which is a ready market for furs of every description. On disposing of her stock of peltries at the latter place, she was to return to New York freighted with the productions of China.

The first vessel fitted out by the Pacific Fur Company was the *Tonquin,* commanded by Capt. Jonathan Thorne, formerly a lieutenant in the service of the United States. She sailed from New York in the autumn of 1810, and had on board four partners, nine clerks, with a number of mechanics and *voyageurs,* with a large and well assorted cargo for the Indian and Chinese trades. Much about the same period a party under the command of Messrs. W. P. Hunt,[14] and Donald Mackenzie,[15] left Saint Louis on the Missouri, with the

[13] Alexander McKay (d. 1811) entered the North West Company's service before 1791 and later became a partner in the concern. He retired in 1808 and two years later joined the Pacific Fur Company. See Wallace, *Documents,* 473.

[14] Wilson Price Hunt (1782–1842) was born in Hopewell, New Jersey, but early in life he moved to St. Louis, where he engaged in the mercantile business. In 1822, he was appointed postmaster at St. Louis, a position that he held for eighteen years. He was a leading citizen of the city and was held in high esteem, although he was not popular. The article by William J. Ghent in the *DAB* is adequate.

[15] Donald McKenzie (1783–1851) was born in Scotland and in 1800 came to Canada, where he entered the service of the North West Company. In 1809, he joined the Pacific Fur Company and in 1811 made the overland journey with Hunt. Later, after the sale of Astoria, he became a partner in the North West Company and began the

intention of proceeding as nearly as possible by Lewis and Clarke's route across the continent to the mouth of the Columbia. This party consisted, besides the above gentlemen, who were partners, of three clerks, and upwards of seventy men.

The following year, 1811, another vessel, the *Beaver,* of 480 tons, commanded by Captain Cornelius Sowles,[16] sailed for the Columbia. She had on board one partner, six clerks, and a number of artisans and *voyageurs,* with a plentiful supply of every thing that could contribute to the comfort of the crew and passengers.

The exaggerated reports then in circulation relative to the wealth to be obtained in the Columbia induced merchants of the first respectability to solicit for their sons appointments in the new Company; and many of their applications were unsuccessful. The Author, who was at this period in New York, captivated with the love of novelty, and the hope of speedily realising an independence in the supposed *El Dorado,* exerted all his influence to obtain a clerkship in the Company. He succeeded, and was one of those who embarked on board the *Beaver.*

With what success his golden anticipations were crowned, together with all his "travels' history," will be amply detailed in the following Narrative.

---

development of the Snake River fur trade. After the merger he became a chief factor in the Hudson's Bay Company and retired in 1833. See Wallace, *Documents,* 477.

16 This name is given as both *Sowle* and *Sowles.* He was born in October, 1769, in the town of Tiverton, Rhode Island, also the birthplace of Captain Robert Gray. Little is known of his early life, but, like many New Englanders, he followed the sea and engaged in trade in the Pacific and the Far East. As a result he was much better prepared for service with the Astor company than was Captain Thorn. His disposition, in contrast with that of Thorn, was almost timid. See F. W. Howay, "Captain Cornelius Sowle on the Pacific Ocean," *Washington Historical Quarterly,* Vol. XXIV, pp. 243–49, and Kenneth W. Porter, *John Jacob Astor, Business Man* (2 vols., Cambridge, Harvard University Press, 1931), I, 199.

A Six Years' Residence
on the Banks of The Columbia River, &c.

Chapter 1

Singularly luminous appearance of the ocean—The Equator—Magellanic clouds—Falkland Islands—Storm, and loss of two men—Cape Horn— Dreadful storm—Islands of Juan Fernandez and Massafuero—Trade winds in the Pacific—A shark—Arrival at Sandwich Islands

On Thursday the 17th of October, 1811,[1] we sailed from New York, with a gentle breeze from the northward, and in a few hours lost sight of the high lands of "Never Sink."[2] Our cabin passengers were, Messrs. Clarke,[3] Clapp,[4] Halsey,[5] Nicolls,[6] Seton,[7] Ehninger,[8] and

[1] Although Cox gives the date of sailing as the seventeenth, Coues says that it actually sailed a week earlier, on the tenth, and accounts for the discrepancy by the fact that since both days were Thursdays, Cox's memory played him false. See *New Light on the Early History of the Greater Northwest: The Manuscript Journals of Alexander Henry and of David Thompson, 1799–1814*, edited by Elliott Coues (3 vols., New York, Francis P. Harper, 1879), II, 763. (Hereinafter cited as *Henry-Thompson Journals.*) Porter, *John Jacob Astor*, I, 200, gives the date as the seventeenth but says that the ship cleared on the thirteenth and that owing to contrary winds it did not get out of the harbor until four days later.

[2] These are the range of hills along the northeast coast of New Jersey, west of Sandy Hook.

[3] John Clarke (1781–1852) was born in Montreal and entered the service of the North West Company at the age of nineteen. In 1810, he joined the Pacific Fur Company and in 1811 was in charge of the expedition that went out in the *Beaver*. Later, after the failure of the Pacific Fur Company, he joined Lord Selkirk's Red River colony, and after the merger of 1821, he became a chief factor in the Hudson's Bay Company. See Wallace, *Documents*, 432–33. It might be noted that Franchère says that Clarke was American born and that he entered the North West Company's service at the age of sixteen. See Gabriel Franchère, *Narrative of a Voyage to the Northwest Coast, 1811–1814,* translated and edited by J. V. Huntington, in Vol. VI of Reuben Gold Thwaites (ed.), *Early Western Travels* (Cleveland, Arthur H. Clark, 1904), 273. Franchère's book is one of the most valuable sources for the history of the Pacific Northwest in this period.

[4] Benjamin Clapp. He married a Chinook woman and later left with Hunt in the

13

self; with Captain Sowles, and Messrs. Rhodes, Champenois, and Dean, officers of the ship.

Nothing particular occurred until the night of the 7th of November, when we were gratified with observing the ocean assume that fiery appearance mentioned by several of our circumnavigators; to account for which has not a little perplexed the most erudite inquirers into marine phenomena. During our passage through these liquid flames we had what sailors term a "smacking breeze" of eight knots. The captain declared that he had never witnessed so luminous an appearance of the sea; and so great was the light afforded by the waves, that we were thereby enabled to peruse books of a moderate sized print!

On the following day, the 8th, we made the Cape de Verds,[9] at which place it was the captain's intention to stop for a day or two; but the wind being favourable he relinquished the idea, and kept under way. We had fine gales and pleasant weather until the 17th, on which day we crossed the Equator, in longitude 30° west, with a light northerly breeze, which on the following day subsided into a dead calm. This calm continued eight days, during which period we did not advance ten miles.

On the 26th a smart breeze sprang up, which drove us on nobly at the rate of from seven to ten knots an hour. The 28th we spoke a Portuguese brig bound from Rio Grande to Pernambuco. The captain and crew of this vessel were all negroes, the lowest of whom was

Albatross, in August, 1813. He served in the American commerce raider *Essex* under Commodore David Porter. See Franchère, *Narrative,* 405, and also J. Neilson Barry, "What Became of Benjamin Clapp?", *Washington Historical Quarterly,* Vol. XXI, pp. 13–17.

[5] J. C. Halsey, after the surrender of Astoria, went with Hunt to Sitka, where he was left as Astor's representative in that region. See Franchère, *Narrative,* 406.

[6] C. A. Nicolls, or Nichols. The information in Cox is all that we know of him.

[7] Alfred Seton was the highest paid of the clerks, receiving $200 a year, while most of the others received $150. See Porter, *John Jacob Astor,* I, 478. After the surrender of Astoria, he left with Hunt in the *Pedlar.* His adventures, which constitute an epic in individual heroism, are outlined in Franchère, *Narrative,* 407. He continued his interest in the fur trade and in 1832 furnished financial backing for Captain Bonneville. See Franchère, *Narrative,* 273.

[8] George Ehninger was a nephew of John Jacob Astor. See Franchère, *Narrative,* 273.

[9] The Cape Verde Islands were a regular stopping place for ships sailing around Cape Horn. Another reason for not stopping was that the impressment controversy was then raging, and since the islands were Portuguese and in close alliance with England, Captain Sowle, having a number of British subjects on board, did not care to risk encountering a British warship in the harbor.

six feet high. We inquired from the sable commander what was his longitude; but he could not give us any information on the subject! After setting this unfortunate navigator right we pursued our course; and the wind still continuing fresh, we were quickly emancipated from the scorching influence of a vertical sun.

On the 10th of December, in latitude 39°, we spoke the American ship *Manilla*, Captain M'Lean, on her return from a whaling voyage, and bound to Nantucket, Rhode Island. The captain came on board, and politely waited till we had written a few letters, of which he took charge. A few days after this we lost sight of the celebrated Magellanic clouds,[10] which had been visible almost from the time we crossed the Equator. That these nebulae should be so immutable in their form and station, has been a source of no trifling perplexity to our natural philosophers. As so much ink has already been consumed in speculations respecting these phenomena, and such various and conflicting opinions elicited from the most learned astronomers of the last and present age, I conceive it would be presumptuous in me to offer a single word on the subject. These clouds are white, and in shape nearly resemble an equilateral triangle, rounded at each angular point.

On the 21st of December, at five A. M., land was discovered on our weather bow. The captain pronounced it to be the coast of Patagonia; and acting on this opinion, we kept along-shore, in order to pass between the Falkland Islands and the mainland; but, strange to tell! at noon, when he obtained a meridian observation, he discovered that what he previously conceived to be the Patagonian coast was in reality a part of the Falkland Islands. To account for this mistake, it is proper to mention, that during the preceding ten days the haziness of the weather precluded the possibility of our obtaining either a solar or lunar observation; we therefore were compelled to sail entirely by dead reckoning. To this may be added, the effect of a strong westerly current; and had the obscure weather continued but a day longer, the consequences might have proved fatal.

As the wind was fair, and we had proceeded so far, the captain abandoned his original intention, and determined to sail round the eastern extremity of the islands, and from thence to shape his course for Cape Horn. We coasted along the shore until the 24th, with light

---

[10] Franchère speaks of these as "the clouds of Magellan" and says that they were "three little white spots that one perceives in the sky almost as soon as one passes the equator," and that they were located in the south-southwest. See *Narrative*, 200.

15

westerly and south-westerly breezes. Albatrosses, penguins, and pintado birds were very numerous around the ship. We shot several, and took others with a hook and bait. One albatross which we caught in this manner received but little injury. It had an enormously large bill, measured eleven feet from wing to wing when extended, and kept a fierce English bull-dog at bay for half an hour.

Although the Falkland Islands occupy in the southern hemisphere a similar degree of latitude to that of Ireland in the northern, still they possess none of the characteristic fertility of the "Emerald Isle." Of grass, properly so called, there is none in those islands. In vegetable and animal productions they are also deficient; and the climate, generally speaking, is cold, variable, and stormy. Yet for such a place the British empire was on the point of being involved in a war, the preparations for which cost the nation some millions![11]

On the 24th we took leave of the islands with a gentle breeze right aft, but this changed ere we had cleared the Sea-lion rocks to a violent head-gale. All the lighter sails were instantly furled; in the hurry of doing which, the gaskets or small ropes which bound the flying jib gave way, and two sailors were sent out to adjust it. While they were in the act of performing this hazardous duty a tremendous wave struck the forepart of the ship, carried away the jib-boom, and with it the two unfortunate men who were securing the sail. The ship was immediately hove to, and every piece of timber, empty barrel, or hencoop on deck was thrown over to afford the unfortunate men a chance of escape. Unhappily all our efforts were unavailing; the poor fellows

[11] It may be remembered that our ejection from these islands by Buccarelli, a Spanish officer, brought the celebrated Samuel Johnson in collision with Junius.—R. C. (In 1771, Dr. Samuel Johnson published a political pamphlet entitled "Thoughts on the late Transactions respecting Falkland's Islands," the material for which was furnished by the government. In this he attempted to prove that it was wise and laudable to suffer the question of right to the islands to remain undecided, rather than involve the country in another war. Some of his critics said that he put the value of the islands too low. "Junius" was the champion of the opposition. See James Boswell, *The Life of Samuel Johnson, LL.D* [3 vols., London, The Macmillan Company, 1912], I, 470–71.—eds.)

In 1776, England founded a colony in the Falkland Islands under the name of Port Egmont, but the colonists were dislodged by an expedition sent out by Bucareli, the Spanish governor of Buenos Aires. For a time war threatened to be the result, but the Spaniards ultimately backed down, and in 1771, Great Britain took possession for the second time. But there was a definite stipulation by the Madrid government that the act allowing Great Britain to take possession did not in any way constitute a waiver of Spain's claims to the islands.—eds.

remained in sight about ten minutes, when they disappeared amidst the raging billows. When the accident occurred, two of the ship's company jumped into the jolly-boat, and with all the thoughtless good-nature of sailors, were about cutting away the lashings to go to the assistance of their ill-fated messmates, when the captain observing them, ordered them out of the boat, exclaiming, "D——n you, have you a mind to go to hell also?"

This was the most gloomy Christmas eve I ever spent. The above melancholy accident had thrown a cloud over every countenance; and when to this was added the darkness of the cabin (the dead-lights being all in), with the loud roaring of the storm, and the Alpine waves threatening every instant to ingulph us, our situation may be more easily imagined than described. Home, with all its mild and social endearments at this season of general festivity, involuntarily obtruded itself on our recollections. The half-expressed wish of being once more on *terra firma* was unconsciously communicated from one to another. But when we looked upon the weather-beaten face of our veteran captain, and observed the careless, if not contented air of his officers and crew; when we felt that they were enduring the "peltings of the pitiless storm" unmoved and without a murmur; and when we reflected on the immense expanse of ocean through which we had to plough our way, and how fruitless would be the indulgence of unmanly apprehension,—"to the wind we gave our sighs," ascended to the deck, and tendered our feeble assistance to the captain.

The gale continued with much violence until the 29th; when, at two P. M., we made Staten Land. At four P. M. we perceived the "snow-topt" mountains of Terra del Fuego, rearing their majestic heads above the clouds, and surveying with cold indifference the conflict of the contending oceans that on all sides surround them. As we approached Cape Horn the weather moderated, and the captain ordered all the lighter masts and yards again to be rigged.

January 1st, 1812, at two P. M., on this day, we bade adieu to the Atlantic, and sailed round the long-dreaded southern extremity of America, with a gentle breeze from the N.N.W., at the rate of one mile per hour, and under top gallant studding-sails; a circumstance I believe unparalleled in the history of circumnavigation.

Toward evening the wind died away; and

Not a breeze disturb'd the wide serene.

17

Our entrance into the great Pacific was marked by none of those terrible concussions of the "vasty deep," the frequency of which have given such a fearful celebrity to Cape Horn. It seemed as if the two mighty oceans had ceased for a period their dreadful warfare, and mingled their waters in the blessed calm of peace. On our right rose the wild inhospitable shores of Terra del Fuego; on the left lay the low desert islands of Diego Ramarez; while all around myriads of whales, porpoises, and other marine monsters, emerging at intervals from the deep, and rolling their huge bodies over the placid surface of the surrounding element, agreeably diversified the scene.

This calm was of short duration. On the following day the wind shifted once more ahead, and drove us as far as 61° S. before we cleared Cape Noire, the south-western point of Terra del Fuego. During this period we had a succession of cold boisterous weather, and occasionally came in collision with large masses of floating ice, from which we however escaped without injury.

It is unnecessary to mention to my geographical readers that the period at which we doubled the cape is the summer season in the high southern latitudes; and if such be its attractions in the balmy season of the year, what a region must it be on the arrival of

Barren Winter, with his nipping colds!

We are informed by the early geographers, that Terra del Fuego was so called from several volcanoes which contrasted their vivid flames with the surrounding icy wastes; and from the same authority we learn that Patagonia, which is on the opposite side of the Straits of Magellan, was inhabited by a race of people of immense stature. Modern travellers, however, have obtained a more correct knowledge of that country, and have reduced the wonderful altitude of the supposed giants to the common standard of humanity. Young travellers should not make rash assertions, particularly if opposed to the received opinions of the world. I cannot however avoid saying, that it is my belief there is no better foundation for the volcanoes than there was for the accounts of the giants. For several days that we were in sight of this supposed land of fire, we did not observe the smallest appearance of smoke; and our captain, who had made many voyages round Cape Horn, declared he had never perceived the slightest volcanic appearance in its neighbourhood.

On the 12th of January the wind veered in our favour, and enabled

18

us to proceed with brisk southerly breezes till the 19th, on which day, in lat. 52°, long. 79° W., nearly abreast of the Straits of Magellan, we encountered a most dreadful gale from the eastward, which lasted eighteen hours. Our ship was a stout strong-built vessel, notwithstanding which she sustained considerable damage. The bulwarks were completely washed away, the head carried off, the mainmast and bowsprit sprung, and the foresail, which was the only one set, was blown to a thousand shivers. We shipped several heavy seas in the cabin, and for some time all our trunks were floating. The violence of the storm however moderated on the 20th, and enabled us once more to bring the vessel under control. Had it continued twelve hours longer, we should inevitably have been dashed to pieces on the iron-bound shores of Terra del Fuego; for, at the period the hurricane broke, we were not twenty-five leagues from shore; and owing to the unmanageable state of the vessel, the wind was driving us with unopposed force in that direction. The billows made sad havock among the remainder of our live stock. The sheep, poultry, and most of our hogs, were carried away; and a few only of the last, fortunately for us, escaped drowning, to die by the hands of the butcher.

On the 27th a young man named Henry Willets, who had been engaged as a hunter in the Company's service, died of the black scurvy, a disease which it is supposed he had contracted previous to his embarkation, as no other person on board had any scorbutic affection. As many of my readers may not be acquainted with the melancholy ceremony of consigning the body of a fellow being to the deep, I shall mention it. The deceased was enveloped in his blankets, in which two large pieces of lead were sewed and placed immediately under his feet. The body was then laid on a plank, one end of which rested on the railing, and the other was supported by his comrades, the crew and passengers forming a circle about it. The beautiful and sublime burial service of the Church of England was then read in an audible and impressive manner by Mr. Nicolls, who officiated as chaplain, after which the plank was raised, the body with the feet downwards slided gently into the ocean, and in a moment we lost sight of it for ever.

On the 4th of February, at two P. M., we made the island of Juan Fernandez, and at six, that of Massafuero,[12] at the latter of which

[12] Juan Fernández is four hundred miles and Más Afuera five hundred miles off the coast of Chile.

the captain determined to touch for a supply of wood and water. It was on the former island in the beginning of the eighteenth century, that Alexander Selkirk, a Scotchman, resided for several years, and from whose rude undigested story the ingenious De Foe, by adding the fictitious Friday, &c., has given to the world the delightful romance of *Robinson Crusoe*.

On the morning of the 5th we stood in to about five miles off shore, when the ship was hove to; and at six o'clock we proceeded for the island in the pinnace and jolly-boat, with twenty-four empty water-casks. Our party, including mates, passengers, and sailors, amounted to twenty-three. A heavy surf broke along the beach, and after searching in vain for a fair opening to disembark, we were reduced to the disagreeable necessity of throwing ourselves through the surf, and succeeded in accomplishing a landing at the imminent risk of our lives. After making a cheering fire to dry our clothes, we divided into two parties, for the purpose of exploring the island. Messrs. Clarke, Clapp, and Seton, formed one; and Messrs. Nicolls, Halsey, and myself, the other; Messrs. Rhodes, Dean, and Ehninger, remained in the boats, and at the landing-place, to superintend the watering and fishing business.

The island appears to be one vast rock split by some convulsion of nature into five or six parts. It was through one of these chasms that our party determined to proceed; and accoutred each with a fowling-piece, horn, and pouch, we set forward in quest of adventures. The breadth of the aperture at its entrance did not exceed fifty feet, and it became narrower as we advanced. Through the bottom meandered a clear stream of fine water, from which the boats were supplied, and which proved of great service to us in the course of our excursion. We had not proceeded more than half a mile, when we encountered so many difficulties in climbing over steep rocks, passing ponds, waterfalls, &c., that we were compelled to leave our guns behind us. Thus disembarrassed, we continued our course for upwards of two miles up a steep ascent, following the different windings of the stream, which, at intervals, tumbling over large rocks, formed cascades which greatly impeded our progress.

In proportion as we advanced the daylight seemed to recede, and for some time we were involved in an almost gloomy darkness, on account of the mountain tops on each side nearly forming a junction. We now regretted the want of our guns, as we observed a great number of goats on the surrounding precipices, and the dead bodies of several, in a more or less decayed state, which we supposed must have fallen in bounding from cliff to cliff, and ascending the slippery and almost perpendicular hills among which they vegetate. A little farther on, on turning the point of a projecting rock, we were agreeably relieved by the bright rays of the sun, which shone with great splendour on the chaotic mass of rocks by which we were encompassed. Reanimated by the presence of this cheering object, we redoubled our pace, and were already congratulating ourselves with being near the summit of the mountain (which from the height we had ascended must have been the case), when our progress was arrested by a large pond, upwards of twenty feet deep; and from the steepness of the rocks on each side, it was impossible to pass it except by swimming. We therefore determined to return before night overtook us in such a dreary place; and after encountering fifty hairbreadth escapes, reached the watering place about seven o'clock, hungry as wolves, and almost fatigued to death. Here we found the other party, who had arrived a short time before us. Messrs. Clarke and Clapp shot two fat goats; and Mr. Dean, who with three men remained in the boats, caught between three and four hundred excellent fish, out of which we succeeded in making an excellent supper.

Sixteen of the casks being now filled, Mr. Rhodes judged it expedient to proceed with them to the ship, and to return the following day for the remainder. Ten were made fast to the pinnace, and six to the jolly-boat, and at one o'clock, A. M., on the morning of the 6th, after some hours' hard rowing, we reached the ship amidst a storm of thunder, lightning, and rain. During that day it blew too fresh to permit the boats to return, and we kept standing off and on till the 7th, when the breeze moderated, and enabled us to bring off the remaining casks.

Massafuero rises abruptly from the sea, and has but a narrow strip of beach. It was formerly well stocked with seals, but these animals have been nearly destroyed by American whalers. The goats are numerous, but too rancid to be used for food, except in cases of necessity. The island also appears to be devoid of wood. The carpenter who went on shore for the purpose of procuring some that could be used in building a boat, found only a few pieces with a close grain, very hard, and in colour resembling box; it was fit only for knees. Mr. Clapp's party in their tour, which was along the beach, round the western extremity of the island, saw none of this necessary article; and in the cleft of the mountain through which our party proceeded, we observed only a few trees of the kind found by the carpenter, growing among inaccessible rocks. The most valuable production of Massafuero is undoubtedly its fish, of which there is a great variety. No one on board was able to appropriate names to all we took. The smallest is a species of whiting, and very delicate when fried. The largest bears a strong resemblance to cod, and by some of our people was deemed superior. There are also several kinds of bass, herrings, crabs, &c. We caught a few conger eels, the most disgusting I ever saw; but, as a counterbalance, the Massafuero lobster, for largeness of size, beautiful variety of colours, and deliciousness of taste, is, I believe, unrivalled.

With the exception of the fish, there is nothing to induce a vessel to touch at this place, while the fruitful island of Juan Fernandez is so near, but a desire, as was our case, of concealing the object of its voyage from the inquisitive and jealous eye of the Spanish authorities, who were stationed at the latter island.[13]

A few days after leaving Massafuero we got into the trade winds, which wafted us on at an even steady rate, varying from four to seven knots an hour. A curious incident occurred on Sunday the 23rd of February, early on the morning of which day a hog had been killed; a practice which had been generally observed every Sabbath morning during the voyage.

After breakfast, the weather being calm, a number of the crew and passengers amused themselves by bathing around the vessel. Some of them had returned on board, when a sailor on the forecastle discovered a large shark gliding slowly and cautiously under the starboard bow. With great presence of mind, he instantly seized a small rope called a clew-line, and with characteristic dispatch made a running knot, which he silently lowered into the water. The monster unwarily passed the head and upper fin through the noose; on observing which, the sailor jerked the rope round the cat-head, and, with the assistance of some of his messmates, succeeded in hauling it on deck. In the mean time, those who were still sporting in the water were

[13] While Spain held possession of South America, every vessel touching at Juan Fernandez was subjected to a rigorous search; and from the number of our guns, joined to the great quantities of warlike stores on board, the captain did not deem it prudent to run the risk of an inquisitorial inspection. I should hope the officers of the Chilian republic stationed here have adopted a more liberal policy.—R. C.

almost paralysed on hearing the cry of "a shark! a shark!" and not knowing on which side of them lay the dreaded danger, some made for the ship, and others swam from it; each momentarily expecting to come in contact with

His jaws horrific, arm'd with threefold fate,

when their fears were dissipated by announcing to them the welcome intelligence of his caption. On dissecting him, the entire entrails of the hog which had been killed in the morning were found in his belly! so that he must have been alongside during the whole of the forenoon, and was doubtless intimidated by the number of the swimmers, from attacking any of them individually.

On the 4th of March we crossed the Equator, for the second time this voyage, with a brisk south-easterly breeze; and on the 25th, at daybreak, we made the island of Owhyee, the largest in the group of the Sandwich Islands.[14] It was the captain's original intention to stop at this place for his supplies; but on approaching Karakakooa[15] Bay we were informed by some natives, who came off in canoes, that Tamaahmaah,[16] the king, then resided in Whoahoo. As we were anxious, for several reasons, to have an interview with his majesty, the captain relinquished the idea of stopping here, and stood about for the latter island.

As we sailed along Owhyee, with a fine easterly breeze, nature and art displayed to our view one of the finest prospects I ever beheld. The snow-clad summit of the gigantic Mouna Roah,[17] towering into the clouds, with its rocky and dreary sides, presented a sublime *coup d' oeil*, and formed a powerful contrast to its cultivated base, and the beautiful plantations interspersed along the shore. Eternal winter reigned above, while all beneath flourished in the luxurance of perpetual summer. The death, too, of the ill-fated and memorable Cook will attach a melancholy celebrity to this island; as it was here that that great navigator was sacrificed in a temporary ebullition of sav-

[14] The island of Hawaii. The Sandwich Islands are now known as the Hawaiian Islands.

[15] Kealakekua Bay.

[16] King Kamehameha I, called the "Napoleon of the Pacific," and whose reign marked the beginning of law and order in the Hawaiian group. See Franchère, *Narrative*, 216, n. 27.

[17] Mauna Loa.

age fury, and closed a brilliant career of services, which reflect honour on his country, and will perpetuate his name to his latest posterity.

As the wind continued fresh, we soon cleared Owhyee, and passed in succession the islands of Mowee,[18] Ranai,[19] Morotoi,[20] and in the evening came in sight of Whoahoo. While we sailed along this interesting group of islands several Indians boarded us, from whom we purchased a few hogs, some melons, plantains, &c. It being too late to attempt anchoring this evening, we stood off and on during the night.

[18] Maui.
[19] Lanai.
[20] Molokai.

Chapter 2

Whoahoo—Visit from a chief—Nocturnal excursion—King and queens—Invasion of the ship—White men—Gardens—Foot race, and summary justice—Throwing the spear—Royal residence, and body guard—Mourning for a chief's wife—Billy Pitt, George Washington, &c.

On Thursday the 26th of March, at noon, we came to anchor outside of the bar in Whytetee Bay,[1] about two miles from shore, and nearly abreast of a village from which the bay is named.

A short time after anchoring we were visited by an eree or chief, named Tiama, in a double canoe, who was sent by the king to learn from whence the ship came, whither bound, &c. After obtaining the necessary information, and taking a glass of wine, he returned, and was accompanied by the captain, who went on shore in order to acquaint his majesty with the particular object he had in touching here. Tiama informed us that a *taboo*[2] was then in force, which accounted for our not being visited by any of the natives. At ten o'clock the captain came back with Tiama. He had met with a favourable reception from Tamaahmaah, who promised to expedite his departure as soon as possible.

Mr. Nicolls observing the chief preparing to return, and being impatient to go on shore, proposed that the passengers should accompany him. This was opposed by others; upon which it was put to the vote, when four appearing in its favour, the motion was of course carried. The ayes were Messrs. Nicolls, Clapp, Halsey, and myself; the minority chose to remain on board. The weather was calm, and we took with us a couple of flutes. Our canoe went on briskly until we passed

---

[1] Waikiki.
[2] See Cook, Vancouver, &c.—R. C.

the channel of the bar, when a most delightful nocturnal prospect opened on us. The serenity of the sky, and the brightness of the moon enabled us to discern objects distinctly on shore. The village of Whytetee, situated in an open grove of cocoa-nut trees, with the hills rising gently in the rear, presented a charming perspective by moonlight, while the solemn stillness of the night, interrupted at intervals by the hoarse murmurs of the surges, as they broke over the bar, rendered the scene in the highest degree romantic. On landing we found the beach covered with a concourse of natives, whom the sound of our flutes had attracted thither. They came pressing on us in such crowds, that were it not for the chief's authority, we should have had considerable difficulty in forcing a passage through them. About midnight we reached the village, and Tiama conducted us to his house, where we experienced a hospitable reception from his family, which consisted of three strapping wives, two handsome daughters, and a brother, about twenty years of age. A young pig lost its life by our arrival, on which, with some cocoa-nuts and bananas, we made an excellent supper. Tiama's brother was our *major domo;* he attached himself particularly to Nicolls, who called him Tom; and as a compensation for his trouble and obliging attention to us, made him a present of his stockings, which, unfortunately for poor Tom, were silk ones. He was so proud of the gift, that he immediately put them over his olive-coloured calves, and without any shoes, he continued walking and working about the house. This was usage to which silk stockings were not accustomed, and the consequence was that before morning their soles had vanished. Our repast being finished, the chief ordered a bevy of young females, who since our arrival had been hovering about the house, to entertain us with one of their native airs. They at once complied, and having formed themselves into a semicircle, sang in rather an harmonious manner; their languishing eyes, and significant pauses, evidently showed, without the aid of an interpreter, that the subject was amatory. This over, Tom conducted us to a neat lodge which Tiama had allotted for our use, and in which we enjoyed the remainder of the night in undisturbed repose on soft beds of island cloth.

On the following morning we arose early, and took a refreshing walk on the sea-shore, after which we returned to the ship in Tiama's canoe. Our appearance was a subject of merriment to those on board. One bare-legged, another without his cravat, the coat of a third closely buttoned up to conceal the absence of his vest, all in fact lighter than when we set out; but nothing was purloined. We had been hospitably entertained by the chieftain and his family; gratitude demanded a return, and as we had omitted to furnish ourselves with trinkets, we could only supply the deficiency by parting with a portion of our least useful clothing.

As the taboo had ceased to operate this day, we found the vessel crowded with natives bartering their produce with our people. At noon we were honoured by a visit from their majesties, the king, and four queens, attended by Krimacoo,[3] the prime minister, and several of the principal chiefs, together with Messrs. Maninna[4] and Hairbottle,[5] two white men; the former a Spaniard, who held the office of chief interpreter to the king, and the latter an Englishman, and head pilot of his majesty's fleet.

The king and queens came in a large double canoe, which was formed by lashing two canoes together, separated by bars of two and a half feet in length from each other. Each canoe had fourteen chosen men. On the bars was raised a kind of seat on which the queens reposed, and above all was placed an arm-chest well stored with muskets, on which the king

> *Above the rest*
> *In shape and gesture proudly eminent*
> *Sat like—a tailor.*

Immediately before his majesty was a native who carried a handsome silver-hilted hanger, which was presented to him by the late emperor of Russia, and which on state occasions he had always carried before him, in imitation as we supposed of European sword-bearers. Behind the royal personage sat another native who carried a large and highly-polished bowl of dark-brown wood, into which his majesty ever and anon ejected all his superabundant saliva.

After he had arrived on the deck, Tamaahmaah shook hands in the most condescending manner with every one he met between the cabin and the gang-way, exclaiming to each person, *"Aroah, Aroah nuee"*[6]

---

[3] This name is also given as *Kalaimoku*. The modern spelling is *Kalanimoku*.

[4] This was Don Francisco Marín de Paula. He had arrived in the islands in 1791 and had a large plantation on Oahu.

[5] The correct spelling is *Harbottle*. He had been the mate of a British ship.

[6] *Aloha,* a form of greeting and farewell. The famous song *"Aloha Oe"* had not been composed at this time.

(I love you, I love you much). There was a degree of negligent simplicity about his dress, which strongly characterized the royal philosopher. His head was crowned with an old woollen hat; the coat was formed of coarse blue cloth in the antique shape, with large metal buttons; the waistcoat, of brown velvet, which in its youthful days had been black; a pair of short, tight, and well-worn velveteen pantaloons displayed to great advantage coarse worsted stockings and thick-soled shoes, all admirably adapted for the tropics; while his shirt and cravat, which had formerly been white, seemed to have had a serious misunderstanding with their washerwoman. Such, gentle reader, was the costume of Tamaahmaah the First, king of the Sandwich Islands, hereditary prince of Owhyee, and protector of a confederation of escaped convicts from New South Wales![7]

The royal party remained on board to dine. The king only sat at table, and was placed at the right hand of the captain, with the attendant who carried his saliva reservoir behind him. He ate voraciously, and in a very commendable manner washed down the solids with a fair quantum of Madeira, to the virtues of which he appeared by no means to be a stranger. On filling the first glass he drank our healths individually; after which he plied away nobly, and apparently unconscious of the presence of any of the company. He did not touch the port, but finished between two and three decanters of the Madeira. As the ladies are prohibited from eating with the men, we were of course deprived of the pleasure of their society at our repast; but after we had quitted the table they were graciously permitted to occupy our seats. Their dinner had been dressed on shore by their own cooks, and was brought by them on board; it consisted of small raw fish, roasted dogs, and a white mixture called *pooah*,[8] of the consistency of flummery. This last they take by dipping the two forefingers of the right hand into the dish which contains the *pooah*, and after turning them round in the mixture until they are covered with three or four coats, they raise the hand, and giving the fingers a dexterous twist, to shake off the fag-ends, bring them forward rapidly to the mouth, which is ready open for their reception, and by a strong labial compression, they are quickly cleared of their precious burden!

---

[7] Tamaahmaah was hereditary king of Owhyee only; he subsequently conquered all the other islands. A number of convicts are at Whoahoo, who escaped from Botany Bay by means of American vessels, and who reside here in security.—R. C.

[8] Poi.

But in plain, unadorned simplicity of dress, they far exceeded their royal consort. It merely consisted of a long piece of their country cloth wrapped in several folds round the waist, and reaching only to the knees, leaving the breasts and legs exposed to the criticisms of amateurs in female beauty; to this they occasionally add a scarf of the same material, which is negligently thrown over the shoulders, and falls behind. They are very corpulent: the favourite measured nearly nine feet in circumference round the waist; and the others were not much inferior in size. We may say of the royal taste, that

They were chosen as we choose old plate,
Not for their beauty, but their weight.

Still they possess mild engaging countenances, with that "soft sleepiness of the eye" by which Goldsmith distinguishes the beauties of Cashmere. Their conduct is under strict surveillance. Mr. Hairbottle informed us, that a few days previous to our arrival an intrigue had been discovered between the favourite queen and one of the king's body guard. As their guilt admitted of no doubt, the unfortunate paramour was strangled on the same night; but as Tamaahmaah still cherished a lingering affection for his frail favourite, he pardoned her, with the short but pithy expression, "If you do it again. . . ."

During the afternoon the king employed himself in taking the dimensions of the ship, examining the cabins, state-rooms, &c. Scarcely an object escaped the royal scrutiny. Observing Mr. Seton writing, he approached him, and began to examine the various little nic-nacs with which the desk was furnished. Seton showed him a handsome penknife of curious workmanship, containing a number of blades, *not* with an intention of bestowing it; with this he appeared particularly pleased, and putting it into one of the pockets of his capacious vest, said, *"Mytye, nue nue mytie"* (good, very good), and walked away. It was in vain for Seton to expostulate; his majesty did not understand English, and all entreaties to induce him to return the penknife were ineffectual. On the following day, however, a chief brought Seton a handsome present from the king, of mats, cloth, and other native productions, with two hundred fine cocoa-nuts.

In the course of the evening the queens played draughts with some of our most scientific amateurs, whom they beat hollow; and such was the skill evinced by them in the game, that not one of our best players succeeded in making a king.

Late in the evening our illustrious guests took their departure, accompanied by all their attendants; but they had scarcely embarked in their canoes when the ship was boarded on all sides by numbers of women, who had come off in small canoes paddled by men or elderly females, and who, after leaving their precious cargo on deck, returned quickly to the island, lest the captain should refuse his sanction to their remaining in the vessel. They crowded in such numbers about the crew as to obstruct the performance of their duty, and the captain threatened to send them all on shore in the ship's boats if they did not behave themselves with more propriety. This had the desired effect, and while they remained on board they gave no farther cause for complaint.

On the following morning, the 28th, we weighed anchor, and worked the ship a few miles higher up, exactly opposite the village of Honaroora,[9] where the king resided. We spent the day on shore, at the house of a Mr. Holmes,[10] a white man, and a native of the United States, by whom we were sumptuously entertained. He had been settled here since the year 1793, and at the period I speak of was, next to the king, the greatest chief on the island. He had 180 servants, or under-tenants, whom he called slaves, and who occupied small huts in the immediate vicinity of his house. He had also extensive plantations on Whoahoo, and on the island of Morotoi, from whence he derived a considerable income. He was married to a native wife, by whom he had several children. The eldest was a most interesting girl, aged about fifteen years, with a peculiarly soft and expressive countenance. Nature, in her freaks, had bestowed upon this island beauty an extraordinary profusion of hair, in which the raven tresses of the mother were strangely intermingled with the flaxen locks of the father. She spoke tolerably good English, and always sat near him. He appeared to watch her conduct with all the parental solicitude of a man who, from long experience, well knew the danger to which she was exposed from the general demoralization of manners that prevailed about her. Mr. Holmes is greatly respected by the natives, by whom he is entitled *Eree Homo,* or the Chief Holmes.

As we met here several other respectable white men, I shall mention their names, and, first, Mr. Maninna. This gentleman had been a Spanish officer, and in consequence of having while stationed at

[9] Honolulu.
[10] Oliver Holmes. He was, for a time, governor of the island of Oahu.

30

Mexico killed a superior officer in a quarrel, he fled to California, from whence he escaped to the Sandwich Islands, where, having acquired the language with wonderful facility, he was appointed to the office of chief interpreter. He was a man of general information, spoke French and English fluently, and from his easy manners, and insinuating address, shortly became a general favourite. He had built a handsome stone house, the only one on the island, in which he resided with his wife, who was the daughter of a chief. Her sister lived also in the same house; and the busy tongue of scandal, which even here has found an entrance, did not hesitate to say that the two sisters equally participated in his affections. His drawing-room was decorated with a number of Chinese paintings, which he obtained from Canton, of the crucifixion, the Madonna, different saints, &c.; but on removing a sliding pannel from the opposite side, subjects of a far different nature were represented!

Mr. Davis,[11] the king's gardener, was a Welshman, and at this period had been settled on the island twelve years. He had also considerable plantations, and had a native wife, who was a most incontinent jade. He had just returned from a distant part of the island, whither he had been in pursuit of his faithless *cara sposa*, who had eloped a few days before with one of her native beaux. Poor Davis felt rather sore on being bantered by old Holmes on this affair. "Tam the strap," said he, "I cot her snug enough to be sure with her sweetheart; but I think she'll remember the pasting I gave her all the tays of her life." We were informed he might have easily parted from her, and procured a more suitable match, but he was unfortunately too much attached to her to think of taking another.

Mr. Hairbottle, the chief pilot, is a native of Berwick, and was formerly boatswain of an English merchant ship. He had resided upwards of fourteen years on the different islands, and had been married to a native wife, who was dead for some years. He was a quiet, unassuming old man, whose principal enjoyments consisted in a glass of rum grog and a pipe of tobacco.

Mr. Wadsworth, an American. This gentleman had been chief mate of a ship which had touched here about six years before. Having quarrelled with his captain, they separated, and he took up his residence in the island. The king, who gave particular encouragement to

[11] This man is not to be confused with Isaac Davis, a survivor of the American ship *Fair American* who died prior to Cox's arrival. They were two different men.

white men of education to settle here, immediately presented Wadsworth with a *belle brunette* for a wife, together with a house and some hogs.

Here we also found a gentleman from New York, under the assumed name of Cook; but who was recognized by Mr. Nicolls as a member of a highly respectable family in that city, named S——s. He had, like Wadsworth, been also chief officer of an American East Indiaman, which had touched here about three months previous to our arrival; and in consequence of a misunderstanding with the captain, he left the ship, and took up his abode with Mr. Holmes. On hearing of this circumstance, Tamaahmaah, as an encouragement to his settling permanently on the island, gave him the daughter of a principal chief for a wife, some land, and a number of hogs. S——s, however, did not appear to relish his situation: he had been too long accustomed to the refinements of civilization, at once to adapt himself to Indian habits, and received with apathy the fond caresses of his olive-coloured spouse. He expressed a desire to return in our ship, but the captain's arrangements could not permit it.

While on this subject I may as well mention that the example of Wadsworth and S——s seemed to be contagious; for a few days after our arrival, Mr. Dean, our third officer, had a serious altercation with the captain, which ended in his quitting the ship; and on its coming to the king's knowledge, he sent for him, and told him if he would remain, and take charge of his fleet, he would give him a house and lands, plenty of hogs, and a beautiful daughter of a chief for a wife. Dean told him he had not yet made up his mind on the subject, and requested time to consider the offer. The king did not object, and the interview ended. I believe however that Dean subsequently quitted the island, and returned to New York.

Mr. Holmes gave us a plentiful dinner of roast pork, roast dog, fowl, ham, fish, wine, and rum, with a profusion of excellent tropical fruit. A number of native servants attended at table, each holding a napkin; they performed their duty in a very expert manner, and appeared to be well acquainted with all the domestic economy of the table. Their livery was quite uniform, and consisted merely of a cincture of country cloth round the waist, from which a narrow piece of the same stuff passed between the legs, and was fastened to the belt, leaving the remainder of the body totally uncovered! Our noble commander was vice-president, and undertook to carve the dog; which duty he performed in a manner quite unique. He was the only one of our party who partook of it. The idea of eating so faithful an animal without even the plea of necessity, effectually prevented any of us joining in this part of the feast; although, to do the meat justice, it really *looked* very well when roasted. The islanders esteem it the greatest luxury they possess; and no one under the dignity of an eree of the first class is permitted to partake of this delicious food. However singular their taste may be regarded in this respect by modern civilization, my classical readers may recollect that the ancients reckoned dogs excellent eating, particularly when young and fat; and we have the authority of Hippocrates for saying that their flesh is equal to pork or mutton. He also adds, that the flesh of a grown dog is both wholesome and strengthening and that of puppies relaxing. The Romans, too, highly admired these animals as an article of food, and thought them a supper in which the gods themselves would have delighted!

Independently of the white men whose names I have mentioned, there were about fourteen others, belonging to all nations, the majority of whom were convicts who had effected their escape from Botany Bay, and were held in no estimation by the natives. They are supremely indolent, and rum and women seemed to constitute their only enjoyment.

On the 29th we made an excursion into the interior with Davis. His gardens were extensive, and pleasantly situated at the foot of the hills, between four and five miles from Honaroora. They were laid out with taste, and kept in excellent order. Exclusive of the indigenous productions of the country, with which they were plentifully stocked, he planted a few years before some *Irish* potatoes, and the crop more than equalled his expectations. We also observed some prime plantations of sugar cane. A few of those we measured had fourteen feet eatable, and were one foot in circumference, which, I am informed, far exceeds the best Jamaica canes. The climate of the Sandwich Islands is, however, more propitious to the growth of the cane than that of the West Indies, at which latter place it has, besides, many enemies to encounter which are strangers to the islands in the Pacific; such as monkies, ants, bugs, the blast, &c., one or other of which often destroys the fairest hopes of the planter. The islanders distil an inferior spirit from it, which the resident white people have dignified by the title of "country rum." It is weak, and has a smoky, insipid taste, and does not produce intoxication except taken in large quantities.

On our way back we visited the king's gardens, which were contiguous to Davis's. They were much more extensive than his, although far inferior in neatness, and contained nothing particularly deserving notice. Davis was the only white man who superintended his own plantations: the others were left to the management of their servants, and were seldom visited by the proprietors; and as he was a good practical agriculturist, his gardens were superior to any we saw on the island. In the course of this tour we did not observe a spot that could be turned to advantage left unimproved. The country all around the bay exhibits the highest state of cultivation, and presents at one view a continued range of picturesque plantations, intersected by small canals, and varied by groves of cocoa-nut trees; the whole bounded on the back ground by gently sloping hills, and in the front by the ocean. We returned late in the evening, highly delighted with our day's excursion, and sat down to an excellent dinner prepared for us by the worthy Cambrian, in whose hospitable mansion we spent the night.

On the 30th we were present at a grand pedestrian racing match, between Krikapooree, the king's nephew, and an American black named Anderson, who was his armourer; the latter won, after a well contested struggle. The race-course presented a novel and striking appearance. At the upper end was erected a covered platform about twenty feet from the ground, on which the king sat cross-legged, and without any covering whatever, save the waistband commonly worn by the natives. His guards armed with muskets paraded around the platform; while on each side, and close to the guards, were assembled an immense concourse of natives of all classes, mingled together without any regard to rank, age, or sex. The two favourite queens were richly dressed: one wore a light-blue satin gown, trimmed with broad gold lace; the other had on a cream-coloured riding-habit of cassimere, ornamented with silver lace, and a profusion of sugar-loaf buttons, &c. These dresses were made for them in England, fitted them admirably, and set off their persons to great advantage. They walked through the crowd along with several chiefs' wives, and seemed in a high degree to enjoy the bustling scene before them. Betting was very spirited on the issue of the race. Money of course was out of the question; but among the lower classes its place was supplied by axes, beads, knives, scissors, handkerchiefs, and various kinds of trinkets; and among the erees of the first and second grades we could distinguish scarlet and blue cloths, silks, Chinese shawls, calicoes, ribbons, &c. Several quarrels occurred among the men, which were settled *à l' Anglaise* by the fist. One of the natives had a dispute about a bet with an English sailor who had been left here a short time before by his captain for mutiny. The Indian felt he was right, and refused to yield to the chicanery of the sailor, who, in order to intimidate him, drew from his pocket a small pistol, which he cocked, and presented in a menacing manner at the islander's breast, swearing if he did not submit he would shoot him. This however was disregarded by the other, who seemed determined not to flinch; but the king, who had observed the whole transaction from his elevated position, ordered the sailor to be brought up to him, which was instantly complied with. He then took the pistol, and delivered it to one of his attendants to be placed in the royal armoury, and addressing the sailor, told him the only punishment he should then inflict on him would be the forfeiture of the pistol; but in case he ever offended in the same manner again, he would have him put to death. We were quite delighted with this summary administration of justice, for the sailor appeared to be a quarrelsome rascal, and bore an infamous character among his associates.

After the race was over, several wrestling and boxing matches took place, on which there was also considerable betting. Some of our party who were amateur pugilists declared their style of hitting to be admirable; but as I unfortunately never studied the noble science of self-defence, I am quite incompetent to hazard an opinion on the subject. I will however say, that no unfair play was used, and that no blow was struck while a man was down. At the termination of these encounters a large space was formed, for two natives to display their skill in throwing the spear. A full account of this wonderful performance is given in Cook's voyages; and I can only add, that the amazing activity evinced in avoiding each other's weapons, by leaping to the right or left, or allowing them to pass under their arms, between their legs, &c. and their surprising dexterity and self-possession in a situation in which an European would be transfixed ere he had time to look about him, must be seen to be credited. This exercise forms the amusement of their earliest years, and is the *ne plus ultra* of their education. No islander can take a wife until he is able to withstand the attacks of any old warrior whom the chief of his tribe may appoint to try him; so that this condemnation to celibacy, among a people so notoriously amorous, contributes, I should imagine, more than any other cause, to the wonderful perfection at which they have arrived in this exercise.

In front of the royal residence there are planted thirty pieces of cannon, fifteen on each side, chiefly six and nine pounders. A body guard of handsome athletic young men are stationed close to the house; two of whom are placed as sentinels at the door, and are relieved with as much regularity as at any garrison in England. In the day-time their muskets generally remain piled before the door, but are taken in at night. These *gardes-du-corps* have no particular dress to distinguish them from civilians; and after the amusements just mentioned had ended, the king ordered them to go through the manual and platoon exercises; which, considering the limited means they have had for learning, they performed with tolerable precision.

Shortly after quitting this noisy and bustling scene of mirth and festivity we were attracted by the sounds of mourning voices to a large house in a retired corner of the village; in front of which sat eight women, in a circle, all in a state of intoxication. At times their voices died away to a low mournful tone; when, suddenly changing, they vented the wildest and most frantic cries, tearing their hair, beating their breasts, and gnawing the ends of their fingers. In the intervals they moistened their parched throats from a bottle which was passed round from one to the other; and after all had partaken of the libation they renewed their cries with redoubled vigour. Their hanging breasts, dishevelled hair, and fiery eyes, presented more the appearance of furies than of human beings; and we were at first afraid to approach them, apprehensive of an attack in the height of one of their paroxysms. We were told, however, there was no danger, and they would injure no one save themselves. On inquiry, we ascertained that the dead body of a chief's wife of the second class lay in an adjoining house, and that these women were her friends and relatives mourning her death. This ceremony, although possessing a degree of rude lachrymose comicality, had nothing peculiarly interesting, and we quickly left the scene.

Several of the chief's have punctured on their arms the names of celebrated English and American statesmen, captains of ships, &c. At the race-course I observed Billy Pitt, George Washington, and Billy

Cobbett, walking together in the most familiar manner, and apparently engaged in confidential conversation; while in the centre of another group, Charley Fox, Thomas Jefferson, James Maddison, Bonaparte, and Tom Paine, were to be seen on equally friendly terms with each other. They seem to be proud of these names, and generally prefer them to their own. Krimacoo, the prime minister, is called Billy Pitt, from the great influence he possesses. He is consulted by the king on all subjects of importance; and in cases of particular emergency Mr. Holmes is sent for to give his advice.

Chapter 3

*Tamaahmaah—The Eooranee—Curious custom—Fickleness in dress—
Character of natives—Important position of the islands—Cow hunting—
Complete our supplies—Take a number of natives—Departure—New dis-
covery—Arrival at the Columbia*

From this period until our departure we were honoured with several
visits from the royal family, principally connected with the business
of procuring our supplies. The king was a hard bargain maker, and
although he had several pipes of Madeira in his stores, he would not
barter a single article until he obtained a quarter-cask of that wine,
of which he was passionately fond. He was by no means as generous
as many of his subjects, and he seldom committed an act of liberality
without having a particular object in view. He had upwards of forty
small schooners built by the natives, which were quite useless to him
from their ignorance of navigation; and when he made the presents
which I have already mentioned to the officers who had quarrelled
with their captains, he had in view their settling on the island, and
availing himself of their services in teaching the natives to navigate
these vessels. The taboos of Tamaahmaah were often influenced by
his dreams; one of which gave rise, while we remained here, to an
extraordinary proclamation, which ordered, that during the space of
one day "no native should leave the island; and that no dogs should
bark, hogs grunt, or cocks crow!" This whimsical prohibition was
strictly complied with by the islanders; but I need scarcely state, that
the three last-mentioned classes of his majesty's subjects did not yield
it the same ready obedience. This was called a "dreaming taboo," to
distinguish it from the established ones, which occur at stated periods,
and are regulated by the high priest.

At this time Tamaahmaah had only three children living, two sons and one daughter. They were rather homely in their appearance, and afforded a bad specimen of royal beauty. The eldest son was about twenty years of age, and was called the *Eooranee*.[1] He possessed considerable authority, and was more feared than his father, though not so much beloved. The following anecdote will show the dread in which he was held by the natives. Some of the men engaged in the Company's employment had received permission to spend a day on shore. As they did not return that night, I accompanied Mr. Clarke the following morning in search of them; and after wandering about for some time, we discovered the party descending a hill near the village, each with a lass under his arm, their hats decorated with flowers, ribbons, and handkerchiefs, and a fifer and fiddler at their head, playing away merrily. They were all nearly "half-seas over," and were on their way to the ship when they perceived us. They insisted in an humble good-natured manner on our taking the lead; and as we were anxious to get them on board, we accordingly joined them, and marched on at their head. We had not proceeded far when the Eooranee met us, and he appeared so much pleased with the procession, that he fell into the ranks. As we approached the wharf, several of the natives, who had been drawn by the sound of the music to the party, retired on seeing the young prince; but one unfortunate rascal, who was quite drunk, annoyed us as we passed him, by pushing us and pulling our clothes; and as the king's son was dressed like an European, he treated him in the same manner; but I never saw consternation so strongly depicted as when the poor wretch looked up, and beheld the frowning countenance of the dreaded Eooranee. The effect was instantaneous; he fell prostrate, as if thunderstruck, and remained perfectly motionless until we lost sight of him. We however did not part with the prince until he had promised that no punishment should be inflicted on the offending islander.

The male branches of the royal family are held in peculiar veneration, more particularly their heads. No individual, with the exception of domestics specially appointed for that purpose, is permitted to touch that part of their sacred person, or any covering that has ever been on it, upon pain of death. My ignorance of this law was near embroiling me in a serious scrape. A few days after our arrival, while strolling on the outskirts of the village, I observed an individual walking before

[1] The Crown Prince. The present spelling is *Iolani*.

39

me dressed in a handsome green frock-coat, well-made pantaloons, and Hessian boots, followed by a native carrying the tail of a white cow, which he used in driving away the flies that annoyed his master. As I was given to understand that I had been introduced to all the white men of respectability on the island, I felt anxious to ascertain who this important personage was, and therefore took a circuitous turn in order to have a front view of him. It was the Eooranee. He called me to him, and we sat down under the shade of some plantain trees. He then began to examine my clothes very minutely, and took off my hat, which was a handsome one of Portuguese willow. While this examination was going on, I felt a desire to look at his, which was of a peculiarly fine texture, and therefore uncovered the head of his highness with as little ceremony as he had observed towards me; but I had scarcely touched the forbidden covering when I received a warm *soufflet* on the right cheek from the attendant. Not knowing the cause of this aggression, I determined on instant retaliation, and seizing a stone, was in the act of hurling it at the fellow's head, when my arm was arrested by the Eooranee, who begged of me, in broken English, to desist, and at the same time turned to his domestic, whom he reprimanded with marks of evident displeasure, after which he ordered him to retire.

While this was going on, I observed Anderson the armourer pass, to whom I related the circumstance. The king's son then spoke to him for some time, after which Anderson told me that if any islander had committed such an offence, instant death would have followed, and added, that the prince begged him to assure me that he deeply regretted the conduct of his domestic, who should have distinguished between a stranger and a native, and that he had dismissed him with disgrace. When Anderson had finished, the Eooranee grasped my hand in the most friendly manner; and as I felt satisfied with the explanation he had given, I returned its pressure with equal warmth. At this period the resident white people looked to his succession with considerable apprehension, as he was supposed to entertain views hostile to their interests. They might have been led to form this conclusion from his distant habits, and capricious tyranny towards his immediate followers; but I am happy to state, their fears were groundless; for on his accession to the supreme power at his father's death, he treated them with marked indulgence, and held out the greatest encouragement to white people to settle on the island. The day after the circumstance above detailed, I met him near the king's house in a state of nudity, conversing with some of the guards, and the same evening I again saw him in the loose light dress of a West India planter. His father and himself were very fickle in their clothing. I saw the old man one day in the full dress of an English general, which had been sent to him by his late majesty George III; but he felt so awkward in the cocked-hat, boots, &c., that he quickly got rid of them, and a few hours afterwards we saw him lounging about the village, sans hat, sans coat, sans shirt, sans culottes, sans every thing! On the death of the old king the Eooranee succeeded by the title of Tamaahmaah the Second.[2] At the period of our visit they knew nothing of the Christian religion; and the white professors of it who were resident among them, were badly calculated to inculcate its divine precepts. Since then, however, thanks to the indefatigable and praiseworthy exertions of the missionaries, this rude, but noble-hearted race of people, have been rescued from their diabolical superstitions, and the greater part of them now enjoy the blessings of Christianity.

Cook, Vancouver, Perouse,[3] and others, have already written so ably on the manners, customs, amusements, laws, religion, and natural productions of these islands, that I might very probably subject myself to the charge of plagiarism, or book-making, if I touched on them. To those therefore who feel anxious for farther information on these subjects, I would recommend the above authorities, in which they will have their curiosity amply gratified.

The vice of thieving attributed to the male inhabitants is rather exaggerated. It is certainly true, that numbers of those who visit trading ships are not scrupulous in appropriating to their own use every trifling article on which they can conveniently lay their hands;

[2] This unfortunate prince is the same who, with his young queen, lately fell victims to misjudged British hospitality, joined to a climate to which they were unaccustomed. —R. C. (In 1823, King Kamehameha II and his queen had sailed for England, supposedly to seek a British protectorate for his kingdom. They arrived at Portsmouth in May of the next year, and in July both of them died following an attack of measles. See Ralph S. Kuykendall, *The Hawiian Kingdom, 1778–1854* [Honolulu, University of Hawaii, 1938], 76–80.—eds.)

[3] These books are: James Cook and James King, *A Voyage to the Pacific Ocean* (3 vols., London, G. Nicol and T. Cadell, 1784); George Vancouver, *A Voyage of Discovery to the North Pacific Ocean, and Round the World* (6 vols., London, J. Stockdale, 1801); Jean François de Galaup, Comte de la Pérouse, *A Voyage Round the World in the Years 1785, 1786, 1787, and 1788* (3 vols., London, J. Johnson, 1798).

but it should be observed, they do not consider such abstractions in the same light as if they robbed each other. This circumstance I think it necessary to mention, without attempting to justify it; for were we to consider all their petty thefts in the same point of view that we are accustomed to regard such offences in civilised countries, we should form a very poor opinion of their honesty.

The women, too, have been generally accused of lasciviousness; but from what I saw, joined to the information I obtained, I am induced to think the charge too general. It must, indeed, be admitted, that the deportment of those who are in the habit of frequenting trading ships is not calculated to impress a stranger with a high idea of their virtue; but why make the censure general? If a native of Owhyee were to form his opinion of the morality of our countrywomen from the disgusting conduct of the unfortunate females who crowd our sea-ports and ships, I should imagine he would entertain a very poor estimate of English chastity. In the interior of the islands, and at a distance from sea-ports, I am informed that in the relative situation of wife and mother, their conduct is irreproachable. It is true, that in the places at which ships are accustomed to touch, a universal depravity seems to pervade all classes; for it is no uncommon sight to see parents bring their daughters, brothers their sisters, and husbands their wives, to earn the wages of prostitution. These vices cannot, I fear, be totally eradicated; but it is pleasing to learn, that through the active agency of the missionaries, their frightful predominancy has been greatly diminished. In other respects, the natives are brave, active, hospitable, true to their word, confiding, cleanly in their domestic economy, easily satisfied at their meals, obedient to proper authority, excellent agriculturalists, quick in learning, with an aptitude for improvement that is really astonishing; and on the whole I would say, that their character presents a fairer field for success to the exertions of the moral cultivator than that of any untutored people whom I ever met.

Recent events seem destined to place the Sandwich Islands in a much more important situation on the political map of the world, than they occupied fifteen or twenty years ago. While Spain had possession of Mexico, California, and the southern continent, they were seldom visited but by fur traders, for the purpose of refitting, or obtaining fresh provisions, and were regarded by the world more as objects of curiosity than as places from which any political advantages were

42

likely to be derived. But now that the Mexicans and Southern Americans have succeeded in emancipating themselves from the slothful despotism of their ancient rulers, the native energies of their character will shortly begin to develope themselves; and uncontrolled by the trammels which so long fettered their commercial prosperity, a few years may see their fleets, in imitation of their bold and enterprising brethren of the northern continent, ploughing their way through the Pacific, and, in exchange for their precious metals, bringing back to their country the luxurious productions of China and the Indies. The Sandwich Islands are nearly equidistant from the western coast of Mexico and the eastern boundaries of China, and consequently lie nearly in the track of vessels passing between the two continents. But the circumstance of all others calculated to raise them to the highest degree of importance is the stupendous enterprise lately set on foot of forming a junction between the Pacific and Atlantic, by cutting a canal through the Isthmus of Darien.[4] If this magnificent undertaking succeed, the long and dangerous voyages round Cape Horn and the Cape of Good Hope will be avoided, and comparatively short and safe passages made to the western coast of America, Japan, China, our East Indian possessions, &c.

In the course of these voyages, particularly to the East, the Sandwich Islands must be touched at for fresh supplies, or, at least, closely passed. In either case, they will become an important acquisition to a maritime power. With the assistance of science, they can be rendered impregnable; and when we take into consideration their great natural capabilities of defence, their noble harbours, productive soil, and temperate climate, joined to the inoffensive deportment of the inhabitants, we may safely conclude that their present state of independence will not be of long duration. It is probable they will ultimately become tributary to Great Britain, Russia, or America; and in the event of war between any of these nations, the power in possession of the islands, from their commanding position, will be able, during the continuation of hostilities, not only to control the commerce of the Pacific, but also neutralise, in a great degree, the advantages likely to be derived from the Grand Junction Canal.

Several of our domestic quadrupeds are now reared on the islands;

---

[4] Several projects had been advanced for a canal across the isthmus. Cox possibly has reference to the plan advanced by Aaron Palmer and a New York syndicate in 1824. Such a feat was beyond the engineering technique and the financial resources of that day.

such as cows, sheep, goats, and horses. The last are brought from California, and are a small hardy race. The cows at Whoahoo are the descendants of those left there by our navigators, and are perfectly wild. We purchased two of them from the king; and he ordered upwards of one hundred men of his body guard, with several chiefs, to proceed to the place where the animals were grazing, to assist us in catching those we had bought. It was situated a few miles from the village, in a handsome valley, studded with cocoa-nut trees. A couple of hundred additional natives volunteered to join us. They proceeded cautiously in the first instance, until they surrounded the herd, which they succeeded in driving to an inclosure. One more expert than the rest then advanced, under the cover of some trees, with a long rope, at the end of which was a running noose. Having quietly waited for some time until a proper opportunity offered, he at length threw the rope, and succeeded in catching a young cow. On feeling the noose round her neck, she became quite furious, and made a desperate plunge at him, which he skilfully avoided by running up a cocoa-nut tree, having previously fastened one end of the rope round the trunk. We had intrenched ourselves with the chiefs behind a stone wall, close to the herd; and being apprehensive that the captive might break loose, we fired, and shot her. Upon hearing the report, the herd rushed furiously out of the inclosure, and ran at the natives; but as they had anticipated such a result, each man secured a retreat behind a tree; and in a moment after the furious animals had gained their freedom three hundred cocoa-nut trees might have been seen, each manned with a native, who looked down with the full confidence of security on the enraged herd below. Finding it impossible to catch another, we were obliged to fire among them, and killed a second. A few shots without ball were then discharged, which drove them to their old pasture, and enabled the natives to descend. The king preserved these cattle for the purpose of bartering with ships touching there for provisions; and though he killed none for the royal table, he very condescendingly accepted from us a present of a sirloin.

As we intended to engage some of the natives for the Company's service at the Columbia, and as the captain also required some to assist in working the ship (several of the crew being indifferent sailors), he demanded permission from Tamaahmaah to engage the number that should be deemed necessary. This was at once granted; and Messrs. Holmes and Maninna were requested to act as recruiting sergeants on the occasion, which duty they kindly undertook to perform. On the intelligence being announced, the vessel was crowded with numbers, all offering to "take on." With the assistance of the above gentlemen we selected twenty-six of the most able-bodied of these volunteers: sixteen for the Company's service, and ten for the ship's. We agreed to pay each man ten dollars a month, and a suit of clothes annually. An old experienced islander, who was called Boatswain Tom, and who had made several voyages both to Europe and America, was engaged to command them. He got fifteen dollars a month, and was to have the sole control of his countrymen. Several of the females also volunteered to accompany us, but we were obliged to decline their kind offers. Mr. Wadsworth, of whom I have already spoken, was also engaged for the Company's service, to act as an officer on sea or land, as occasion should require. He brought his lady with him, not being accustomed, as he declared, to live in a state of single blessedness.

On the 5th of April we got all our supplies on board. They consisted of sixty hogs, two boats full of sugar-cane to feed them, some thousand cocoa-nuts, with as much bananas, plantains, taro, melons, &c., as could be conveniently stowed in the ship. The same evening we took leave of the king and royal family, and bade adieu to our kind white friends; after which we embarked; and on the following morning, Tuesday, April the 6th, we weighed anchor, and set sail for the Columbia. Krikapooree, the king's nephew, and several young chiefs, accompanied us three or four leagues from land, and took leave of us with tears in their eyes. The addition we received to our numbers in live stock, joined to the cargo of fruit, &c., lumbered our deck greatly, and annoyed the crew in working the ship. When any number of the natives were wanted to perform a particular duty, word was passed to Bos'n Tom; who, to do him justice, betrayed none of the softer feelings of national partiality to his countrymen. The moment he gave "the dreadful word" it was followed by a horrid yell; and with a rope's end he laid on the back and shoulders of every poor devil who did not happen to be as alert as he wished, accompanied by a laughable *mélange* of curses in broken English, and imprecations in his own language.

We had tolerably good easterly breezes, and nothing particular occurred until the 18th, at four P. M., when a man ahead cried out "Land on the weather-bow!" As we were then not more than half way between the islands and the American continent, we eagerly rushed on deck to feast our eyes with a view of our new discovery.

After looking at it for some time very attentively through his glass, the captain pronounced it to be an island, with a dark-brown soil, and apparently destitude of vegetation, and added, with marks of evident exultation, that he always felt certain we should fall in with unknown islands in these latitudes (about 35° north), and in that expectation had diverged materially from the usual course of vessels proceeding to the north-west coast. We now sounded, but got no bottom with one hundred fathoms; and while this was going on we were all busy in forming conjectures respecting this *terra incognita*. The first thing to be decided on was the name. One thought that Mr. *Astor,* being the owner of the ship, and the founder of the company, had the best claim, and therefore moved that it be called *"Astor's* Island." This having been seconded, an amendment was moved by another person, who argued that the ship had a prior right to the honour, and stated he would have it called *"Beaver* Island." The amendment having been seconded, it was about to be put, when the captain declared that, fond as he was of his ship, and highly as he respected his owner, he thought the claims of their immortal president superior to either, and that he would therefore, without consulting the wishes of any one, call it *"Maddison's* Island."[5] Although there were few admirers of the "immortal" president on board, the captain's decision settled the controversy; for on such occasions he is always the high priest. Mr. Clarke said, if it proved any way fruitful, he would colonize it, and appoint Wadsworth, with his island beauty, king and queen. Some hoped the inhabitants would not be afraid of white men; while others cursed the inhabitants, particularly the females, and expressed a wish that the new discovery would contain some cooling simples. In the mean time, we kept standing under easy sail for this unknown paradise; but in proportion as we advanced the hills seemed to ascend, and blend their craggy summits with the passing clouds. A pale bright opening appeared to divide the land; and the sad conviction was at length forced on us, that Maddison's Island was, like his immortality, based on a nebulous foundation. In fact, it turned out what sailors call "a cape fly-away island"; and all our glorious speculations dissolved literally *in nubibus*.

This disappointment chagrined us much; but none felt it more

[5] The misspelling is obvious.

46

sensibly than the captain, who was quite chapfallen on the occasion. However, on the 1st of May, we made the real *terra firma*, in lat. 41° N., Cape Orford in sight.[6] We coasted along-shore until the 5th, when we had the happiness of beholding the entrance of the long-wished-for Columbia, which empties itself into the Pacific in lat. 46° 19′ N., and long. 129° W. Light baffling winds, joined to the captain's timidity, obliged us to stand off and on until the 8th, on which day we descried a white flag hoisted on Cape Disappointment, the northern extremity of the land at the entrance of the river. A large fire was also kept burning on the cape at night, which served as a beacon. A dangerous bar runs across the mouth of the Columbia; the channel for crossing it is on the northern side close to the cape, and is very narrow, and from thence to the opposite point on the southern side, which is called Point Adams, extends a chain or reef of rocks and sand-banks, over which the dreadful roaring of the mighty waters of the Columbia, in forcing their passage to the ocean, is heard for miles distant.

Early on the morning of the 9th Mr. Rhodes was ordered out in the cutter, on the perilous duty of sounding the channel of the bar, and placing the buoys necessary for the safe guidance of the ship. While he was performing this duty we fired several guns; and, about ten o'clock in the morning, we were delighted with hearing the report of three cannon from the shore in answer to ours. Towards noon an Indian canoe was discovered making for us, and a few moments after a barge was perceived following it. Various were the hopes and fears by which we were agitated, as we waited in anxious expectation the arrival of the strangers from whom we were to learn the fate of our predecessors, and of the party who had crossed the continent. Vague rumours had reached the Sandwich Islands from a coasting vessel, that the *Tonquin* had been cut off by the Indians, and every soul on board destroyed; and, since we came in sight of the river, the captain's ominous forebodings had almost prepared the weaker part of our people to hear that some dreadful fatality had befallen our infant establishment. Not even the sound of the cannon, and the sight of the flag and fire on the cape, were proofs strong enough to shake his doubts. "An old bird was not to be caught with chaff": he was too well acquainted with Indian cunning and treachery to be deceived by such appearances. It was possible enough that the savages might have

6 Now Cape Blanco.

surprised the fort, murdered its inmates, seized the property, fired the cannon, to induce us to cross the bar, which, when once effected, they could easily cut us off before we could get out again. He even carried his caution so far, as to order a party of armed men to be in readiness to receive our visitors. The canoe arrived first alongside. In it was an old Indian, blind of an eye, who appeared to be a chief, with six others, nearly naked, and the most repulsive looking beings that ever disgraced the fair form of humanity. The only intelligence we could obtain from them was, that the people in the barge were white like ourselves, and had a house on shore. A few minutes afterwards it came alongside, and dissipated all our fearful dreams of murder, &c., and we had the delightful, the inexpressible pleasure of shaking hands with Messrs. Duncan M'Dougall[7] and Donald M'Lennan,[8] the former a partner, and the latter a clerk of the Company, with eight Canadian boatmen. After our congratulations were over, they informed us, that on receiving intelligence the day before from the Indians that a ship was off the river, they came down from the fort, a distance of twelve miles, to Cape Disappointment, on which they hoisted the flag we had seen, and set fire to several trees to serve in lieu of a lighthouse.

The tide was now making in, and as Mr. Rhodes had returned from placing the buoys, Mr. M'Lennan, who was well acquainted with the channel, took charge of the ship as pilot; and at half-past two P. M. we crossed the bar, on which we struck twice without sustaining any injury; shortly after which we dropped anchor in Baker's Bay,[9] after a tedious voyage of six months and twenty-two days. Mr. M'Dougall informed us that the one-eyed Indian who had preceded

[7] Duncan McDougall (d. 1817) joined the Pacific Fur Company in 1810. There is some dispute concerning whether he had previously been in the service of the North West Company. He took part in the founding of Astoria and in 1813 married a daughter of Comcomly. See Wallace, *Documents,* 466; and also *Henry-Thompson Journals,* II, 759.

[8] Donald McLennan was a clerk who came out in the *Tonquin.* In 1811, he was with David Stuart's party and in 1812 with Clarke's party, which built Fort Spokane. In 1813, he entered the service of the North West Company. See *Henry-Thompson Journals,* II, 899.

[9] Baker's Bay is just inside Cape Disappointment and was named for Captain Baker of the ship *Jenny* of Bristol, which Broughton found at anchor there on October 21, 1792. Baker claimed that he had been there before, which raises the possibility that Captain Robert Gray was not the first person to enter the estuary of the Columbia River. See T. C. Elliott (ed.), "Log of the Captain of H. M. S. *Chatham,*" *Oregon Historical Quarterly,* Vol. XVIII, p. 238.

him in the canoe was the principal chief of the Chinook nation, who reside on the northern side of the river near its mouth; that his name was Comcomly,[10] and that he was much attached to the whites. We therefore made him a present, and gave some trifling articles to his attendants, after which they departed.

[10] On Chief Comcomly see J. F. Santee, "Comcomly and the Chinooks," *Oregon Historical Quarterly,* Vol. XXXI, pp. 271–78.

Chapter 4

Account of the Tonquin—*Loss of her chief mate, seven men, and two boats— Extraordinary escape of Weekes—Erection of Astoria—Mr. Thompson of the N. W. Company—Arrival of Messrs. Hunt and Mackenzie, and sketch of their journey overland*

After the vessel was securely moored Captain Sowles joined our party, and we took our leave of the good ship *Beaver;* in which, after a voyage of six months and three weeks, we had travelled upwards of twenty thousand miles.

In the evening we arrived at the Company's establishment,[1] which was called Fort Astoria in honour of Mr. Astor. Here we found 5 proprietors, 9 clerks, and 90 artisans and canoe-men, or, as they are commonly called in the Indian country, *voyageurs.* We brought an addition of 36, including the islanders; so that our muster-roll, including officers, &c., amounted to 140 men.

The accounts which we received from our friends at Astoria were highly discouraging as to our future prospects, and deeply melancholy as to the past. But, that my readers may understand the situation of affairs at the time of our arrival, it will be necessary to take a short retrospect of the transactions that occurred antecedent to that period.

The ship *Tonquin,* to which I have alluded in the introduction, sailed from New York on the 6th September, 1810. She was commanded by Captain Jonathan Thorne,[2] a gentleman who had been

[1] On the contrary, Franchère says that Clarke, Seton, and Ehninger came ashore on the tenth, shortly after the arrival of the *Beaver,* but that the others, including Cox, did not land until two days later. See *Narrative,* 273, 276.

[2] Captain Jonathan Thorn had been commissioned as a midshipman in 1800. He served in the war against the Barbary pirates and was cited by Stephen Decatur for conspicuous gallantry. In February, 1807, he was promoted to the rank of lieutenant, and in May 1810, he was given a furlough for the purpose of commanding the *Tonquin,*

formerly a first lieutenant in the navy of the United States, and while in that service, during their short war with Algiers, had distinguished himself as a bold and daring officer. His manners were harsh and arbitrary, with a strong tincture of that peculiar species of American *amor patriae,* the principal ingredient of which is a marked antipathy to Great Britain and its subjects.

Four partners, namely, Messrs. Alexander M'Kay, Duncan M'Dougall, David[3] and Robert Stuart,[4] embarked in her, with eight clerks, and a number of artisans and *voyageurs,* all destined for the Company's establishment at the Columbia.[5] These gentlemen were all British subjects, and, although engaged with Americans in a commercial speculation, and sailing under the flag of the United States, were sincerely attached to their king and the country of their birth. Their patriotism was no recommendation to Captain Thorne, who adopted every means in his power to annoy and thwart them. To any person who has been at sea it is unnecessary to mention how easy it is for one of those nautical despots to play the tyrant, and the facilities which their situation affords, and of which they too often avail themselves, of harassing every one who is not slavishly subservient to their wishes.

Messrs. M'Kay, M'Dougall, and the Stuarts, had too much Highland blood in their veins to submit patiently to the haughty and uncivil treatment of the captain; and the consequence was, a series of quarrels and disagreeable recriminations, not merely in the cabin but on the quarter-deck.

an indication of the importance that the United States government attached to the enterprise, or of Astor's influence, or of both. It is probable that, despite his reputation as a martinet, in Captain Thorn's death the United States lost a naval officer of "unusual ability and integrity." The voyage of the *Tonquin* is well covered in Franchère, *Narrative,* 193, n. 18, 196–242; and Alexander Ross, *Adventures of the First Settlers on the Oregon or Columbia River, 1810–1813,* in Vol. VII of Reuben Gold Thwaites (ed.), *Early Western Travels* (Cleveland, Arthur H. Clark, 1904), 43–47.

[3] David Stuart (1765–1853) became a partner of the Pacific Fur Company and was one of the most zealous of Astor's supporters. He remained with the American Fur Company until 1833. See Wallace, *Documents,* 500.

[4] Robert Stuart (1785–1848) was a nephew of David Stuart, a partner of Astor, and one of the founders of Astoria. He is best known for his transcontinental journey in 1812–13, in the course of which he may have discovered South Pass. See Wallace, *Documents,* 500; and also *On the Oregon Trail: Robert Stuart's Journey of Discovery (1812–1813),* edited by Kenneth A. Spaulding (Norman, University of Oklahoma Press, 1953).

[5] The complete list of passengers and crew is given in Franchère, *Narrative,* 194–95.

They touched at the Falkland Islands for a supply of water; and while Mr. David Stuart and Mr. Franchère, with a party, were on shore, the captain, without any previous intimation, suddenly gave orders to weigh anchor, and stood out to sea, leaving the party on one of the most desert and uninhabitable islands in the world. The gentlemen on board expostulated in vain against this act of tyrannic cruelty, when Mr. Robert Stuart, nephew of the old gentleman who had been left on shore, seized a brace of pistols, and presenting one at the captain's head, threatened to blow out his brains if he did not instantly order the ship to lay to and wait for his uncle's party. Most part of the crew and officers witnessed this scene; and as they appeared to sympathise deeply with young Stuart, the captain thought it more prudent to submit, and gave orders accordingly to shorten sail, and wait the arrival of Mr. Stuart's party.

The determined resolution evinced by young Mr. Stuart on this occasion, and the apparent apathy of his officers, who stood quietly by while a pistol was presented to his head, were never forgiven by Captain Thorne.

The *Tonquin* doubled Cape Horn in safety, and arrived in the middle of February at the Sandwich Islands, from which place they took ten natives for the establishment, and sailed for the coast on the 1st of March.

On the 23rd of March they arrived at the mouth of the Columbia; and although it blew a stiff breeze, the captain ordered Mr. Fox, the chief mate, with two American sailors and two Canadian *voyageurs*, to proceed in the long-boat towards the bar, for the purpose of sounding the channel.

From the threatening appearance of the sky and the violence of the gale, Mr. M'Kay thought this a most hazardous undertaking, and implored Captain Thorne to postpone it until the weather became more moderate. His orders however were peremptory; and finding all remonstrance useless, Mr. Fox with his little crew embarked, and proceeded to fulfil his instructions. That unfortunate officer seemed to have a presentiment of his approaching fate, for on quitting the vessel he took an affectionate farewell of all his friends; to some of whom he mentioned he was certain they would never see him again. His prediction was verified; but we could never ascertain correctly the particulars of their fate. It is supposed however that the tide setting in, joined to the violence of the wind, drove the boat among the breakers, where it and its unfortunate crew must have been dashed to pieces.

The ship stood off and on during the 24th, and on the 25th, the wind having moderated, she stood in for Cape Disappointment. Mr. Aikin, one of the officers, accompanied by Weekes, the smith, Coles, the sailmaker, and two Sandwich Islanders, were sent ahead in the jolly-boat to ascertain the lowest depth of water in the channel; the ship in the mean time following after, under easy sail. Aiken reported by signal that there was water sufficient; upon which the captain ordered all sail to be crowded, and stood in for the bar. The jolly-boat was now ordered to fall back and join the ship; but having unfortunately got too far to the southward, it was drawn within the influence of the current, and carried with fearful rapidity towards the breakers. It passed within pistol shot of the vessel, its devoted crew crying out in the wildest accents of despair for assistance. This however was impossible, for at that moment the *Tonquin* struck on the bar; and the apprehension of instant destruction precluded the possibility of making any attempt to save the jolly-boat, which by this time was carried out of sight. The wind now moderated to a gentle breeze; but owing to the tide setting out strongly, the water became so low, that the ship struck several times; and to add to the horror of the situation, they were quickly surrounded by the darkness of night. During an awful interval of three hours, the sea beat over the vessel; and at times some of the crew imagined they heard the screams of their lost companions, borne by the night winds over the foaming billows of the bar. A little after twelve o'clock however the tide set in strongly, with a fresh breeze from the westward; and all hands having set to work, they providentially succeeded in extricating themselves from their perilous situation, and worked the ship into Baker's Bay, inside Cape Disappointment, where they found a safe asylum. It blew a perfect gale the remainder of the night.

On the morning of the 26th, some of the natives came on board. They appeared to be very friendly, and betrayed no symptoms of fear or distrust. Parties were immediately dispatched towards the northern shore, and round the cape, in order to ascertain, if possible, the fate of the two boats.

Shortly after one of them returned accompanied by Weekes, who gave the following account of his miraculous escape from a watery grave. "When we passed the vessel, the boat, owing to the want of a rudder, became quite unmanageable, and notwithstanding all our exertions, we were carried into the northern edge of the great chain of breakers. The tide and current however were setting out so strongly, that we were absolutely carried through the reef without sustaining any injury, but immediately on the outer edge a heavy sea struck us, and the boat was upset. Messrs. Aikin and Coles disappeared at once, and I never saw them afterwards. On recovering my first shock, I found myself close to the Sandwich islanders, who had stripped off their clothes with extraordinary dispatch. We all seized the boat, and after much difficulty succeeded in righting it. We then got out a little of the water, which enabled one of the islanders to enter the boat, and he quickly baled out the remainder. His companion also recovered the oars, and we then embarked. I endeavoured to persuade the two poor islanders to row, well knowing the exertion would keep them alive; but it was quite useless, they were so spent from fatigue, and be-numbed by the cold, that they refused to do any thing, and threw themselves down in the boat, apparently resigned to meet their fate. I had no notion, however, of giving up my life in that manner, and therefore pulled away at the oars with all my strength. About midnight one of my unfortunate companions died, and his surviving country-man flung himself on the body, from which I found it impossible to dislodge him. I continued hard at work during the night, taking care to keep to the northward of the bar, and at daylight found myself close to a sandy beach, on which the surf beat heavily. I was nearly exhausted, and therefore determined to run all risks to get ashore. I fortunately succeeded, and ran the boat on the beach. I then assisted the islander, who had some signs of life still in him, to land; but the poor fellow was too weak to follow me. I was therefore obliged to leave him, and shortly after fell on a well-beaten path, which in a few hours brought me in sight of the ship, when I met the party who conducted me on board. Thanks to the Almighty for my wonderful escape!"

The people who went in search of the surviving islander did not find him until the following morning, when they discovered him in a deplorable state, close to some rocks. They carried him to the ship; and in a few days, by the proper and humane treatment of Mr. Fran-chère, he was perfectly restored to his health.

Some time was occupied after their arrival in looking out for a proper place to build their fort; and at length, on the 12th of April, they selected a handsome and commanding situation, called Point George, twelve miles from the cape, and on the south side of the river. The keel of a schooner of thirty tons' burden was also laid at the same time, the skeleton of which had been brought out from New York.

During the month of May, Messrs. M'Kay, Stuart, Franchère,[6] and Matthews,[7] made several excursions up the river as far as the first rapids, in which they were well received by the natives, from whom they collected a quantity of furs.

It having been arranged that the *Tonquin* was to make a coasting excursion as far as Cook's River, and touch at the various harbours between that place and the Columbia, she weighed anchor on the 1st of June, and dropped down to Baker's Bay. Mr. M'Kay, and Mr. Lewis,[8] one of the clerks, embarked in her for the purpose of obtaining a correct knowledge of the various tribes on the coast, it being intended that after her cruise to the northward, the ship was to return to the Columbia, take what furs they might have purchased during her absence, which the captain was to dispose of in Canton, from whence he was to return to New York with a cargo of Chinese goods.

Mr. Mumford, the chief mate, in consequence of a dispute with Captain Thorne, refused to proceed farther with him, and was engaged by the Company to take the command of the little schooner when finished.

The *Tonquin* took her final departure from Columbia on the 5th of June, with a fair wind, and passed the bar in safety.

In the month of July Mr. David Thompson,[9] astronomer to the

---

[6] Gabriel Franchère (1786–1863) was born at Montreal, and in 1810, he joined the Pacific Fur Company as a clerk. He made the voyage on the *Tonquin* and was present at the founding of Astoria. After the surrender of that place he took service with the North West Company, but only long enough to enable him to return to Montreal overland. See Wallace, *Documents,* 443.

[7] This was William W. Matthews, who joined the expedition in New York, and who later joined the North West Company. See "Matthews' Adventures on the Columbia," edited by Jesse S. Douglas, *Oregon Historical Quarterly,* Vol. XL, pp. 105–48.

[8] James Lewis, who on the voyage out had acted as the captain's clerk. See Franchère, *Narrative,* 199. He has been made the subject of a historical novel, *I, James Lewis,* by Gilbert W. Gabriel (Garden City, Doubleday, Doran and Company, 1932).

[9] David Thompson, who was one of the most remarkable men in the history of the Pacific Northwest, arrived at Astoria on the fifteenth of July and took his departure on the twenty-second. See "Journal of David Thompson," edited by T. C. Elliott, *Oregon Historical Quarterly,* Vol. XV, pp. 63, 106. The definitive account is *David Thompson's Journals Relating to Montana and Adjacent Regions, 1808–1812,* edited by

North-West Company, of which he was also a proprietor, arrived with nine men in a canoe at Astoria, from the interior. This gentleman came on a voyage of discovery to the Columbia, preparatory to the North-West Company forming a settlement at the entrance of the river. He remained at Astoria until the latter end of July, when he took his departure for the interior, Mr. David Stuart, with three clerks and a party of Canadians, accompanying him, for the purpose of selecting a proper place on the upper parts of the river for a trading establishment.

Early in the month of August a party of Indians from Gray's Harbour arrived at the mouth of the Columbia for the purpose of fishing. They told the Chinooks that the *Tonquin* had been cut off by one of the northern tribes, and that every soul on board had been massacred. This intelligence was not at first believed; but several other rumours of a similar nature having reached Astoria, caused considerable uneasiness, particularly as the month passed away without any news of a satisfactory nature having been received.

During the month of September the people at the fort were kept in a state of feverish alarm by various reports of an intention on the part of the natives to surprise and destroy them. October commenced, and the period fixed for the return of the *Tonquin* had long since elapsed, still no intelligence of her arrived, with the exception of farther reports of her destruction, accompanied by additional evidence, of a nature so circumstantial as to leave little doubt but that some dreadful fatality had occurred.

On the 5th of October, Messrs. Pillet[10] and M'Lennan, two of the clerks who had gone to the interior with Mr. D. Stuart, returned to Astoria, accompanied by a free hunter named Bruguier,[11] and two Iroquois hunters. They stated that Mr. Stuart had chosen a place

M. Catherine White (Missoula, Montana State University Press, 1950). There is little reason to doubt that he had been sent to the region to take possession of the mouth of the Columbia River for the North West Company but that he had been forestalled by the arrival of Astor's men. See Ross, *First Settlers,* 101.

[10] In Franchère's list of passengers the name is given as Pillot. Little is known of him except what is given in the volumes by Ross and Cox. He was a Canadian who had joined the expedition in New York. After the sale of Astoria he returned overland with the party that left Fort George on April 4, 1814. See Franchère, *Narrative,* 276, n. 76.

[11] This was apparently Régis Brugier whom Franchère had known in Canada. A trader, who had lost his outfit, he had become a free trapper. See Franchère, *Narrative,* 260.

for a trading post about seven hundred miles up the Columbia, at the mouth of a river called Oakinagan,[12] and among a friendly tribe, who appeared to be well furnished with beaver. About this period the schooner was completed and launched. She was called the *Dolly*, in honour of Mrs. Astor; and as provisions at the fort became scarce, she was despatched up the river for a supply, under the command of Mr. R. Stuart and Mr. Mumford.

The dark and dismal months of November and December rolled over their heads without bringing them any certain intelligence of the *Tonquin*. During this period it rained incessantly; and the Indians had withdrawn themselves from the banks of the Columbia to their winter-quarters in the sheltered recesses of the forests, and in the vicinity of springs or small rivulets.

They continued in this state of disagreeable anxiety until the 8th of January, 1812, when their drooping spirits were somewhat raised by the arrival of Mr. Donald Mackenzie with two canoes from the interior. This gentleman was accompanied by Mr. M'Lellan,[13] a proprietor, Mr. Read,[14] a clerk, and ten men. He had left St. Louis in the month of August, 1810, in company with Mr. Hunt. They passed the winter of that year at a place called Nadwau,[15] on the banks of the Missouri, where they were joined by Messrs. M'Lellan,

[12] The present Okanogan River, a tributary of the Columbia, which rises in British Columbia. The post was established on the east bank of the stream just above its entrance into the Columbia. It was one of the most famous and profitable of all the Northwest posts. See Judge William C. Brown, "Old Fort Okanogan and the Okanogan Trail," *Oregon Historical Quarterly*, Vol. XV, pp. 1–38.

[13] Robert McClellan (1770–1815) had had a varied career as a soldier and a trader. He had been a partner of Ramsay Crooks and had traded independently before joining Hunt's party in its camp near the mouth of the Nodaway River. At Astoria he became dissatisfied with his position in the company, and after one ineffectual attempt to make his way east, he joined the party of Robert Stuart. See Stella M. Drumm, "More About Astorians," *Oregon Historical Quarterly*, Vol. XXIV, pp. 347–49.

[14] This was John Reed, although Cox regularly spells it *Read*. He was a clerk of Irish extraction, the only clerk with the overland expedition and more mature and active than the other clerks. In 1813, he was sent with a party to the Snake River to round up the stragglers that had been left there and with his party was massacred in January of 1814. See Kenneth W. Porter, "Roll of the Overland Astorians," *Oregon Historical Quarterly*, Vol. XXXIV, pp. 110–11.

[15] The present Nodaway River, which enters the Missouri River from the north. It is some five hundred miles from the mouth of the Missouri and a short distance above the city of St. Joseph. See *John Bradbury's Travels in the Interior of America, 1809–1811,* in Vol. V of Reuben Gold Thwaites (ed.), *Early Western Travels* (Cleveland, Arthur H. Clark, 1904), 37.

Crooks,[16] and Miller,[17] three American traders, connected with Mr. Astor.

In the spring of 1811 they ascended the Missouri in two large barges, until they arrived on the lands of a powerful tribe named the Arikaraws.[18] Here they met a Spanish trader, Mr. Manuel Lisa,[19] to whom they sold their barges and a quantity of their merchandise.

Having purchased 130 horses from the Indians, they set off in the beginning of August on their land journey, to cross the Rocky Mountains. Apprehensive of coming in contact with the Black-feet, a warlike and savage tribe, who have a strong antipathy to the white men, they were obliged to proceed as far south as the latitude of 40°, from whence they turned into a north-west course. This brought them to an old trading post, situated on the banks of a small river;[20] and

[16] Ramsay Crooks was a native of Scotland and an early fur trader. He was one of those whom Lewis and Clark met while descending the Missouri River in 1806. He had served with the North West Company and had been in partnership with Robert McClellan. He joined Astor in 1810. Like McClellan, he became disgusted with affairs at Astoria and returned east with Robert Stuart's party. Later, as a prominent American businessman, he was influential in attracting the attention of John Floyd of Virginia to the importance of the Oregon country to the United States. The account of his life by William J. Ghent in the *DAB* is adequate.

[17] Joseph Miller had been an army officer but resigned in 1805 and took to trading and trapping. In 1810, he joined the overland Astoria expedition under Hunt, and his reputation in and around St. Louis was such that his accession greatly strengthened the prestige of the expedition. But at Henrys Fork of the Snake River he became disgusted with the conduct of the enterprise, threw up his partnership, and with four men remained in the mountains to trap. Later he fell in with Robert Stuart's party of returning Astorians and with them returned to St. Louis. See *Henry-Thompson Journals*, II, 885 n.

[18] The Arikara Indians were bold and brave warriors, who, because of their sedentary habits and the fact that they practiced agriculture, were known as the "Corn Indians." But in temperament they were somewhat mercurial, and their friendship could not be depended upon. Also known as the Rees, their principal villages were located on the Missouri River near present Pierre, South Dakota.

[19] Manuel Lisa was one of the pioneers of the early fur trade on the upper Missouri and Yellowstone rivers. As early as 1807 he had established a post at the confluence of the Big Horn and Yellowstone rivers. Subsequently, an attempt to expand into the area of the Three Forks of the Missouri was thwarted by the hostility of the Blackfeet, and the trappers decided to abandon the country. Cox is incorrect in saying that they "met" Lisa. Actually, both expeditions were traveling up the Missouri River, Hunt ahead and Lisa trying to overtake him so that they might travel together through the dangerous Indian country. There had been much opposition to the Astor enterprise in St. Louis, and Hunt was suspicious of Lisa's motives and intentions and tried to keep from being overtaken. Lisa finally caught up with Hunt just before reaching the Arikara villages. Learning of the Blackfoot danger ahead, Hunt traded his boats to Lisa for horses, purchased other animals from the Indians, and started overland.

[20] Andrew Henry, who had been associated with Lisa in the Missouri Fur Com-

as they had no doubt it would bring them to the Columbia, they immediately set about making canoes, for the purpose of descending that river.

Mr. Miller, not liking the aspect of affairs at this place, requested permission to return to the United States, which was granted; and a few men were allowed to accompany him on his way back.[21]

The party, which now consisted of about sixty people, commenced their voyage downwards; but from the rapidity of the current, and the number of dangerous rapids, they determined, after having lost one man and a portion of their baggage, to abandon such a perilous navigation, and undertake the remainder of their journey on foot.

In pursuance of this resolution they divided into four parties, under the commands of Messrs. Mackenzie, Hunt, M'Lellan, and Crooks, still keeping in view their original intention of following the course of the river. Messrs. Mackenzie and M'Lellan took the right bank, and Messrs. Hunt and Crooks the left. They were under a strong impression that a few days would bring them to the Columbia, but they were miserably disappointed. For three weeks they followed the course of the river, which was one continued torrent; and the banks of which, particularly the northern, consisted of high precipitous rocks, rising abruptly from the water's edge. The greater part of this period was one of extreme suffering. Their provisions became shortly exhausted, and they were reduced to the necessity of broiling even the leather of their shoes to sustain nature; while, to complete their misfortunes, they were often unable to descend the steep declivities of the rocks for a drink of the water which they saw flowing beneath their feet.

From the tormenting privations which they experienced in following the course of this stream, they called it "Mad River"; and in speaking of it afterwards, the Canadians, from the bitterness of their recollections, denominated it *la maudite rivière enragée.* Mr. Hunt's party did not suffer so much as those on the right bank, in consequence

pany, had led a small party of men from the fort at the mouth of the Big Horn River up the Madison River and across the Continental Divide to Henrys Fork of the Snake River. Here, in 1810, near the present town of St. Anthony, Idaho, they built Fort Henry, the first American establishment in the Pacific Northwest. They were not molested by the Blackfeet, but game was scarce and the winter severe, so the fort was abandoned in the spring.

[21] As previously noted, Miller was disgusted at the way things were going. However, he did not return to St. Louis immediately but remained in the mountains to trap.

of occasionally meeting some of the natives, who, although they always fled on perceiving them, left their horses behind. The party were obliged to kill a few of these animals, and in payment for them, left some goods near their owners' huts.

After a separation of some days the two parties came in sight of each other; and Mr. Hunt had a canoe made out of the skin of a horse, in which he sent some meat over to his famishing friends. He also suggested the idea of their crossing over in the canoe one by one to the south side, where they would, at all events, have a better chance of escaping death by starvation. This was readily agreed to; but the attempt was unfortunately unsuccessful. One of the best swimmers embarked in the canoe, but it had scarcely reached the centre of the river when, owing to the impetuosity of the current, it upset, and the poor *voyageur* sunk to rise no more.

Finding the impracticability of their reunion by this means, they continued to pursue their respective courses, and in a few days after Mr. Mackenzie's party fell on a considerable river, which they subsequently ascertained to be Lewis' River.[22] Here they met a tribe of friendly Indians, from whom they purchased several horses, and with renovated spirits they pursued their journey along the banks of the principal river. Among this tribe they found a young white man in a state of mental derangement. He had, however, lucid intervals, and informed them that his name was Archibald Petton,[23] and that he was a native of Connecticut; that he had ascended the Missouri with Mr. Henry, an American trader, who built the house our people saw at the upper part of Mad River; that about three years ago the place was attacked by the savages,[24] who massacred every man belonging to the establishment with the exception of himself; and that having escaped unperceived, he wandered about for several weeks, until he met the friendly tribe with whom we found him. The dreadful scenes he had witnessed, joined to the sufferings he had gone through, pro-

[22] This name was often applied to the lower reaches of the Snake and Clearwater rivers.

[23] This was Archibald Pelton, rather than Petton, who was found near the site of present Lewiston, Idaho. He had come west with Andrew Henry. He was taken to Astoria, where his name became a word in the Chinook jargon signifying mental derangement. See J. Neilson Barry, "Archibald Pelton, the First Follower of Lewis and Clark," *Washington Historical Quarterly*, Vol. XIX, pp. 199–201.

[24] Cox is in error here; Fort Henry was never attacked by the Indians, let alone destroyed. Pelton probably had reference to the attack on the party at the Three Forks.

duced a partial derangement of his intellect. His disorder was of an harmless nature; and as it appeared probable that civilized companionship would, in the course of time, restore him to his reason, Mr. Mackenzie very humanely brought him along with the party.

On arriving at the entrance of Lewis' River, they obtained canoes from the natives in exchange for their horses, and meeting with no obstruction from thence downwards, arrived at Astoria on the 18th of January, 1812. Their concave cheeks, protuberant bones, and tattered garments, strongly indicated the dreadful extent of their privations; but their health appeared uninjured, and their gastronomic powers unimpaired.

From the day that the unlucky attempt was made to cross in the canoe, Mr. Mackenzie had seen nothing of Mr. Hunt's party, and he was of opinion they would not be able to reach the fort until the spring was far advanced. He was, however mistaken; for on the 15th of February, Mr. Hunt, with thirty men, one woman, and two children,[25] arrived at Astoria.

This gentleman stated that shortly after his last separation from the northern party he arrived among a friendly tribe, whose village was situated in the plains. They treated him and his party with great hospitality; in consequence of which he remained ten days with them, for the double purpose of recruiting his men and of looking for one of his hunters, who had been lost for some days. Having received no intelligence of the man, Mr. Hunt resumed his journey, leaving Mr. Crooks, with five men, who were much exhausted, among the Indians, who promised to pay every attention to them, and conduct them part of the way downwards on their recovery.

Mr. Hunt, in the mean time, fell on the Columbia, some distance below its junction with Lewis' River, and having also obtained canoes, arrived safely on the day above mentioned. The corporeal appearance of his party was somewhat superior to that of Mr. Mackenzie's, but their outward habiliments were equally ragged.

The accession of so many hungry stomachs to the half-starved garrison at Astoria, would have produced serious inconvenience had not the fishing season fortunately commenced earlier than was antici-

[25] This was Mme Dorion and her two children. Another child, born en route, had died shortly after birth. See J. Neilson Barry, "The Trail of the Astorians," *Oregon Historical Quarterly,* Vol. XIII, pp. 227–39; and the same author's "The First-Born on the Oregon Trail," *Oregon Historical Quarterly,* Vol. XII, pp. 164–70.

pated, and supplied them with abundance of a small delicious fish resembling pilchard,[26] and which is the same mentioned by Lewis and Clarke as anchovy.

On the 30th of March the following departures took place: Mr. Read for New York, charged with dispatches to Mr. Astor, accompanied by Mr. M'Lellan, who quitted the country in disgust. This gentleman had fancied that a fortune was to be made with extraordinary celerity in the Columbia; but finding his calculations had exceeded the bounds of probability, he preferred renewing his addresses to the fickle jade in a country less subject to starvation and fighting.

Messrs. Farnham[27] and M'Gillis,[28] with a party, also embarked for the purpose of proceeding to the head of Mad River,[29] for the trading goods which Mr. Hunt had deposited there *en cache;* and Mr. Robert Stuart set off at the same time, with a fresh supply for his uncle's establishment at Oakinagan.

[26] Probably the smelt, the spring run of which is still something of a phenomenon along the lower Columbia and its tributaries, especially the Sandy River.

[27] Russell Farnham, from Massachusetts. He was characterized by Alexander Ross as "a bustling, active and enterprising fellow." See Ross, *First Settlers,* 211. There is a summary of his career in Stella M. Drumm, "More About Astorians," *Oregon Historical Quarterly,* Vol. XXIV, pp. 338–44.

[28] Donald McGillis, (1786–1817), a Canadian clerk. He was probably born on Cape Breton and came out in the *Tonquin.* Later he joined the North West Company but did not remain long in its service. See Wallace, *Documents,* 469.

[29] This was a name applied by the Canadians, with sufficient justification, to the upper reaches of Snake River, especially around and above Caldron Linn, which was near the present Milner, Idaho.

Astoria in 1811

From Tacoma Edition of Irving's Astoria
(New York, G. P. Putnam's Sons, 1897)

Cape Disappointment

from a painting by Captain Henry James Warre

Courtesy Oregon Historical Society

Chapter 5

Particulars of the destruction of the Tonquin *and her crew—Indians attack a party ascending the river—Description of fort, natives, and the country*

It is now time to return to the *Tonquin,* of which no news had been heard during the winter, with the exception of the flying rumours already alluded to. That vessel, as mentioned in the preceding chapter, sailed from the Columbia on the 5th of June, 1811, on a trading speculation to the northward; and Mr. M'Kay took on board, as an interpreter, a native of Gray's Harbour, who was well acquainted with the various dialects of the tribes on the coast. From this Indian the following melancholy particulars were learned.[1]

A few days after their departure from the Columbia they anchored opposite a large village, named "New Whitty," in the vicinity of Nootka,[2] where Mr. M'Kay immediately opened a smart trade with the natives. He went on shore with a few men, was received in the most friendly manner, and slept a couple of nights at the village. During this period several of the natives visited the vessel with furs. The harsh and unbending manners of the captain were not calculated to win their esteem; and having struck one of their principal men whom he had caught in a petty theft, a conspiracy was formed by the friends of the chief to surprise and cut off the vessel. The faithful in-

[1] There are other descriptions of the destruction of the *Tonquin,* but they are all based on the same original account, that of the Indian interpreter, who could have had reasons for telling the story as he did. Alexander Ross says that the name of this Indian was Kasiascall but that he was called Lamazu by the Chinooks. Ross also casts some doubt on the accuracy of the interpreter's story. See *First Settlers,* 163–73; and Franchère, *Narrative,* 288–94.

[2] Nootka, one of the most famous places in the history of the Northwest fur trade, is on the west shore of Vancouver Island. It is north of Clayoquot Sound. The village known as New Whitty was located on Templar Channel of Clayoquot Sound.

terpreter, having discovered their designs, lost no time in acquainting Mr. M'Kay, who instantly hurried on board for the purpose of warning the captain of the intended attack. That evening Mr. M'Kay told the interpreter that the captain only laughed at the information, and said he could never believe that a parcel of lazy thieving Indians would have the courage to attack such a ship as his. The natives, in the mean time, apprehensive from Mr. M'Kay's sudden return that their plans were suspected, visited the ship in small numbers, totally unarmed, in order to throw our people off their guard. Even the chief who had been struck by Captain Thorne, and who was the head of the conspiracy, came on board in a manner seemingly friendly, and apparently forgetful of the insult he had received.

Early in the morning of the day previous to that on which the ship was to leave New Whitty a couple of large canoes, each containing about twenty men, appeared alongside. They brought several small bundles of furs, and, as the sailors imagined they came for the purpose of trading, were allowed to come on deck. Shortly after, another canoe, with an equal number, arrived also with furs; and it was quickly followed by two others, full of men carrying beaver, otter, and other valuable skins. No opposition was made to their coming on board; but the officer of the watch perceiving a number of other canoes pushing off, became suspicious of their intentions, and warned Captain Thorne of the circumstance. He immediately came on the quarter-deck, accompanied by Mr. M'Kay and the interpreter. The latter, on observing that they all wore short cloaks or mantles of skins, which was by no means a general custom, at once knew their designs were hostile, and told Mr. M'Kay of his suspicions. That gentleman immediately apprised Captain Thorne of the circumstances, and begged him to lose no time in clearing the ship of the intruders. This caution was however treated with contempt by the captain, who remarked, that with the arms they had on board they would be more than a match for three times the number. The sailors in the mean time had all come on the deck, which was crowded with Indians, who completely blocked up the passages, and obstructed the men in the performance of their various duties. The captain requested them to retire, to which they paid no attention. He then told them he was about going to sea, and had given orders to the men to raise the anchor, that he hoped they would go away quietly, but if they refused, he should be compelled to force their departure. He had scarcely finished, when, at a signal given by one of the chiefs, a loud and frightful yell was heard from the assembled savages, who commenced a sudden and simultaneous attack on the officers and crew with knives, bludgeons, and short sabres, which they had concealed under their robes.

Mr. M'Kay was one of the first attacked. One Indian gave him a severe blow with a bludgeon, which partially stunned him; upon which he was seized by five or six others, who threw him overboard into a canoe alongside, where he quickly recovered, and was allowed to remain for some time uninjured.

Captain Thorne made an ineffectual attempt to reach the cabin for his fire-arms, but was overpowered by numbers. His only weapon was a jack-knife, with which he killed four of his savage assailants by ripping up their bellies, and mutilated several others. Covered with wounds, and exhausted from the loss of blood, he rested himself for a moment by leaning on the tiller wheel, when he received a dreadful blow from a weapon called a *pautumaugan*,[3] on the back of the head, which felled him to the deck. The death-dealing knife fell from his hand; and his savage butchers, after extinguishing the few sparks of life that still remained, threw his mangled body overboard.

On seeing the captain's fate, our informant, who was close to him, and who had hitherto escaped uninjured, jumped into the water, and was taken into a canoe by some women, who partially covered his body with mats. He states that the original intention of the enemy was to detain Mr. M'Kay a prisoner, and, after securing the vessel, to give him his liberty, on obtaining a ransom from Astoria; but on finding the resistance made by the captain and crew, the former of whom had killed one of their principal chiefs, their love of gain gave way to revenge, and they resolved to destroy him. The last time the ill-fated gentleman was seen, his head was hanging over the side of a canoe, and three savages, armed with *pautumaugans,* were battering out his brains.[4]

In the mean time the devoted crew, who had maintained the unequal conflict with unparalleled bravery, became gradually overpowered. Three of them, John Anderson, the boatswain, John Weekes, the carpenter, Stephen Weekes, who had so narrowly escaped at the Co-

[3] A species of half sabre, half club, from two to three feet in length, six inches in breadth, and double edged.—R. C.

[4] McKay's widow later became the wife of John McLoughlin, for many years chief factor of the Hudson's Bay Company at Fort Vancouver. There is a possibility that the McKays had separated before his death.

lumbia, succeeded, after a desperate struggle, in gaining possession of the cabin, the entrance to which they securely fastened inside. The Indians now became more cautious, for they well knew there were plenty of fire-arms below; and they had already experienced enough of the prowess of the three men while on deck, and armed only with hand-spikes, to dread approaching them while they had more mortal weapons at their command.

Anderson and his two companions seeing their commander and the crew dead and dying about them, and that no hope of escape remained, and feeling moreover, the uselessness of any farther opposition, determined on taking a terrible revenge. Two of them, therefore, set about laying a train to the powder magazine, while the third addressed some Indians from the cabin windows, who were in canoes, and gave them to understand, that if they were permitted to depart unmolested in one of the ship's boats, they would give them quiet possession of the vessel without firing a shot, stipulating, however, that no canoe should remain near them while getting into the boat. The anxiety of the barbarians to obtain possession of the plunder, and their disinclination to risk any more lives, induced them to embrace this proposition with eagerness, and the pinnace was immediately brought astern. The three heroes having by this time perfected their dreadful arrangements, and ascertained that no Indian was watching them, gradually lowered themselves from the cabin windows into the boat, and, having fired the train, quickly pushed off towards the mouth of the harbour, no obstacle being interposed to prevent their departure.

Hundreds of the enemy now rushed on deck to seize the long-expected prize, shouting yells of victory; but their triumph was of short duration. Just as they had burst open the cabin door, an explosion took place,[5] which in an instant hurled upwards of two hundred savages into eternity, and dreadfully injured as many more. The interpreter, who had by this time reached land, states he saw many mutilated bodies floating near the beach, while heads, arms, and legs, together with fragments of the ship, were thrown to a considerable distance on the shore.

[5] There is also the story that the *Tonquin* was blown up by a mortally wounded survivor who locked himself in the powder magazine. The best summary of the evidence with regard to the destruction of the ship is in a note by Huntington on page 294 of Franchère, *Narrative*.

Destruction of the Tonquin

The first impression of the survivors was, that the Master of Life had sent forth the Evil Spirit from the waters to punish them for their cruelty to the white people. This belief, joined to the consternation occasioned by the shock, and the reproaches and lamentations of the wives and other relatives of the sufferers, paralysed for a time the exertions of the savages, and favoured the attempt of Anderson and his brave comrades to escape. They rowed hard for the mouth of the harbour, with the intention, as is supposed, of coasting along the shore to the Columbia; but after passing the bar, a head wind and flowing tide drove them back, and compelled them to land late at night in a small cove, where they fancied themselves free from danger; and where, weak from the loss of blood, and the harassing exertions of the day, they fell into a profound sleep.

In the mean time, the terror of the Indians had in some degree subsided, and they quickly discovered that it was by human agency so many of their warriors had been destroyed. They therefore determined on having the lives of those who caused the explosion; and being aware, from the state of the wind and tide, that the boat could not put to sea, a party proceeded after dark cautiously along the shore of the bay, until they arrived at the spot where their helpless victims lay slumbering. Bleeding and exhausted, they opposed but a feeble resistance to their savage conquerors; and about midnight, their heroic spirits mingled with those of their departed comrades.

Thus perished the last of the gallant crew of the *Tonquin;* and in reflecting on their melancholy fate, it is deeply to be regretted that there was no person of sufficient influence at Astoria to bring about a reconciliation between Captain Thorne and Mr. M'Kay; for were it not for the deplorable hostility and consequent want of union that existed between these two brave men, it is more than probable this dreadful catastrophe would never have occurred.[6]

On the morning of the 11th of May, the day after our arrival, while walking with some of my companions in front of the fort, indulging in gloomy reflections on the fate of the *Tonquin*, and the unpromising appearance of our general affairs, we were surprised by the arrival of two canoes with Messrs. Robert Stuart, M'Lellan, Read, and Farnham, together with Messrs. David Stuart, and R. Crooks.[7]

[6] From the particular description given by our informant of the dress and personal appearance of Anderson and the two Weekeses, we had no doubt of their identity.—R. C.

[7] Franchère says that these men returned before Cox landed from the *Beaver*. For other accounts of the incident at the falls see Franchère, *Narrative,* 274–76; and Ross, *First Settlers,* 187–88.

The unexpected return of the four first individuals, who had only left the fort on the 30th March, was caused by a serious rencontre which they had with the natives in ascending. On arriving at the portage of the falls, which is very long and fatiguing, several of the Indians in a friendly manner tendered their horses to transport the goods. Mr. Stuart, having no suspicion of their dishonesty, gladly accepted the offer, and entrusted a few of them with several small packets of merchandise to carry. On arriving, however, in a rocky and solitary part of the portage, the rascals turned their horses' heads into a narrow pathway and galloped off with the goods, with which they escaped. Their comrades on foot in the mean time crowded about the *voyageurs* who were carrying the packages, and as Mr. Stuart observed the necessity of greater precaution, he took his post at the upper end of the portage, leaving Messrs. Read and M'Lellan in charge of the rear-guard. Mr. Read was the bearer of the dispatches, and had a tin case, in which they were contained, flung over his shoulders. Its brightness attracted the attention of the natives, and they resolved to obtain possession of the prize. A group, therefore, patiently watched his motions for some time, until they observed he had separated himself from M'Lellan, and gone ahead a short distance. The moment they supposed he was alone they sprung on him, seized his arms, and succeeded in capturing the tin case after a brave resistance, in the course of which he was knocked down twice, and nearly killed. Mr. M'Lellan, who had been an attentive observer of the whole transaction, instantly fired, and one of the robbers fell; upon which his companions fled, not however without securing the plunder. Mr. M'Lellan, imagining that Mr. Read had been killed, immediately joined Mr. Stuart, and urged that gentleman to fly from a place so pregnant with danger. This, however, he refused until he was satisfied respecting Mr. Read's fate; and taking a few men with him, he repaired towards the spot where Read had been attacked. The latter had in the mean time somewhat recovered from the effects of his wounds, and was slowly dragging himself along when Mr. Stuart's party came to his assistance, and conducted him to the upper end of the portage in safety. The loss of the dispatches determined Mr. Stuart to postpone Mr. Read's journey to New York, and the whole party proceeded to Oakinagan, the post established by Mr. David Stuart. They remained here only a few days, and early in May left it on their return to Fort Astoria. On their way down, near the entrance of the Shoshone River,[8] they fell in with Mr. R. Crooks and a Kentucky hunter, named John Day,[9] in a state of destitution.

I have already mentioned that this gentleman, with five of his men, owing to their inability to continue the journey from excessive fatigue, had been left by Mr. Hunt among a tribe of friendly Indians, supposed to be a branch of the extensive Snake nation. Finding, however, that they had nothing to expect from the strangers, these savages, shortly after the departure of Mr. Hunt, robbed them of every article in their possession, even to their shirts, in exchange for which they gave them a few old skins to cover their nakedness.

The miserable party, thus attired, and without any provisions, recommenced their journey to the Columbia, on the banks of which they arrived a few days previous to the descent of Mr. Stuart's party.

Here was a frightful addition to our stock of disasters. Fighting, robbery, and starvation, in the interior, with drownings, massacres, and apprehensions of farther attacks from the Indians on the coast, formed a combination sufficient to damp the ardour of the youngest, or the courage of the most enterprising. The retrospect was gloomy, and the future full of "shadows, clouds, and darkness." The scene before us, however, was novel, and for a time our ideas were diverted from the thoughts of "battle, murder, and sudden death," to the striking peculiarities connected with our present situation.

The spot selected for the fort was on a handsome eminence called "Point George," which commanded an extensive view of the majestic Columbia in front, bounded by the bold and thickly wooded northern shore. On the right, about three miles distant, a long, high and rocky peninsula covered with timber, called "Tongue Point," extended a

---

[8] Alexander Ross says that this encounter took place near the mouth of the Umatilla River. See *First Settlers*, 188. Drumm says that Crooks and Day were robbed and left naked near the mouth of the river that ever since has been known as John Day River. See Stella M. Drumm, "More About Astorians," *Oregon Historical Quarterly*, Vol. XXIV, p. 355. The John Day River enters the Columbia just east of the present town of The Dalles and considerably west of the Umatilla River. The name Shoshone River was another name for the Snake, which is obviously impossible here. Day and Crooks were probably robbed near the John Day and made their way upstream to the Umatilla, where they were rescued.

[9] John Day was a Kentucky hunter who had joined Hunt's party at the age of about forty. The statement that he later went insane at Astoria is impossible to verify. See Peter Skene Ogden's *Snake Country Journals, 1824–25 and 1825–26,* edited by E. E. Rich (London, Hudson's Bay Record Society, 1950), 29, 30 n., 98 n., 224; and also "The Last Will and Testament of John Day," edited by T. C. Elliott, *Oregon Historical Quarterly*, Vol. XVII, pp. 373–79.

considerable distance into the river from the southern side with which it was connected by a narrow neck of land; while on the extreme left, Cape Disappointment, with the bar and its terrific chain of breakers, were distinctly visible.

The buildings consisted of apartments for the proprietors and clerks, with a capacious dining-hall for both, extensive warehouses for the trading goods and furs, a provision store, a trading shop, smith's forge, carpenters workshop, &c. The whole surrounded by stockades forming a square, and reaching about fifteen feet over the ground. A gallery ran round the stockades, in which loop-holes were pierced sufficiently large for musketry. Two strong bastions built of logs commanded the four sides of the square; each bastion had two stories, in which a number of chosen men slept every night. A six-pounder was placed in the lower story, and they were both well provided with small arms.

Immediately in front of the fort was a gentle declivity sloping down to the river's side, which had been turned into an excellent kitchen garden; and a few hundred yards to the left, a tolerable wharf had been run out, by which *bateaux* and boats were enabled at low water to land their cargoes without sustaining any damage. An impenetrable forest of gigantic pine rose in the rear; and the ground was covered with a thick underwood of brier and huckleberry, intermingled with fern and honeysuckle.

Numbers of the natives crowded in and about the fort. They were most uncouth-looking objects; and not strongly calculated to impress us with a favourable opinion of aboriginal beauty, or the purity of Indian manners. A few of the men were partially covered, but the greater number were unannoyed by vestments of any description. Their eyes were black, piercing, and treacherous; their ears slit up, and ornamented with strings of beads; the cartilage of their nostrils perforated, and adorned with pieces of *hyaquau*[10] placed horizontally; while their heads presented an inclined plane from the crown to the upper part of the nose, totally unlike our European rotundity of cranium; and their bodies besmeared with whale oil gave them an

---

[10] This shell was white in color and of extreme hardness. It was tubular, shaped somewhat like a gamecock's spur, and varied from a quarter of an inch to four inches in length. It was used for money as well as for ornamentation. See *Fur Trade and Empire; George Simpson's Journal,* edited by Frederick Merk, in Vol. XXXI of the *Harvard Historical Studies* (Cambridge, Harvard University Press, 1931), 96 n.

appearance horribly disgusting. Then the women,—O ye gods! With the same auricular, olfactory, and craniological peculiarities, they exhibited loose hanging breasts, short dirty teeth, skin saturated with blubber, bandy legs, and a waddling gait; while their only dress consisted of a kind of petticoat, or rather kilt, formed of small strands of cedar bark twisted into cords, and reaching from the waist to the knee. This covering in calm weather, or in an erect position, served all the purposes of concealment; but in a breeze, or when indulging their favourite position of squatting, formed a miserable shield in defence of decency; and worse than all, their repulsive familiarities rendered them objects insupportably odious; particularly when contrasted with the lively eyes, handsome features, fine teeth, open countenance, and graceful carriage of the interesting islanders whom we had lately left.[11]

From these ugly specimens of mortality we turned with pleasure to contemplate the productions of their country, amongst the most wonderful of which are the fir-trees. The largest species grow to an immense size, and one immediately behind the fort at the height of 10 feet from the surface of the earth measured 46 feet in circumference! The trunk of this tree had about 150 feet free from branches. Its top had been some time before blasted by lightning; and to judge by comparison, its height when perfect must have exceeded 300 feet! This was however an extraordinary tree in that country, and was denominated by the Canadians *Le Roi de Pins*.[12]

The general size however of the different species of fir far exceeds any thing on the east side of the Rocky Mountains; and prime sound pine from 200 to 280 feet in height, and from 20 to 40 feet in circumference, are by no means uncommon.

Buffon asserts that "living nature is less active, less energetic in the new world than the old," which he attributes to the prevalence of moisture and deficiency of heat in America. This assertion was ably combated by the late Mr. Jefferson; but, without entering into the arguments of these celebrated philosophers, we may safely state, that

[11] Almost all writers are in agreement about the unprepossessing appearance of the Indian women. Despite this, many of the traders, such as Duncan McDougall, William Matthews, and Peter Skene Ogden, to mention only a few, contracted marriage alliances with daughters of some of the chiefs.

[12] A pine tree has been subsequently discovered in the Umpqua country, to the southward of the Columbia, the circumference of which is 57 feet; its height 216 feet without branches!—R. C.

if America be inferior to the old continent in the animal world, she can at least assert her superiority in the vegetable.

En passant, I may here remark, that although constant rains prevail eight months out of the twelve, and during the remaining four, which are the summer months, the heat is far from excessive, the large and stately elk, which are numerous about the lower shores of the Columbia, are equal, if not superior in size to those found in the hottest and driest parts of the world.

There are five or six different species of fir, with the peculiar qualities of which I am acquainted. They split even, make good canoes,[13] yield little ashes, scarcely produce any gum, and are excellent for building and other domestic purposes.

Our table was daily supplied with elk, wild fowl, and fish. Of the last, we feasted on the royal sturgeon, which is here large, white, and firm; unrivalled salmon; and abundance of the sweet little anchovy, which is taken in such quantities by the Indians, that we have seen their houses garnished with several hundred strings of them, dry and drying. We had them generally twice a day, at breakfast and dinner, and in a few weeks got such a surfeit, that few of us for years afterwards tasted an anchovy.

We remained upwards of six weeks at the fort, preparing for our grand expedition into the interior. During this period I went on several short excursions to the villages of various tribes up the river and about the bay. The natives generally received us with friendship and hospitality. They vary little in their habits or language; and the perfect uniformity in the shape of their heads would, I fancy, puzzle the phrenological skill of the most learned disciples of Gall or Spurzheim. I made a few midnight visits to their cemeteries, from which I abstracted a couple of skulls, which appeared totally devoid of any peculiar organic development. I regret that our travelling arrangements prevented me from bringing them across the mountains; for, without ocular proof, I fear the faculty could not be brought to believe that the human head was capable of being moulded to a shape so unlike the great mass of mankind. This however is dangerous ground; and I shall not pursue the subject farther, lest I might provoke the *gall* of the believers in the theory of craniology, among whom, I am

---

[13] Although Cox calls this a species of fir, it is probably the cedar from which the dugout canoes of the region were made.

aware, may be reckoned some of the most eminent men in the literary world.

We also visited Fort Clatsop, the place where Captains Lewis and Clarke spent the winter of 1805–1806; an accurate description of which is given in the journal of those enterprising travellers. The logs of the house were still standing, and marked with the names of several of their party.[14]

The most striking peculiarity of the immense forests which we observed in the course of these excursions was the total absence of the "wood notes wild" of the feathered tribe; and, except in the vicinity of a village, their deep and impervious gloom resembles the silence and solitude of death.

[14] Fort Clatsop, the wintering place of Lewis and Clark, was a little south of Astoria, near present Gearhart, Oregon. At this time the buildings were described as "piles of rough, unhewn logs, overgrown with parasite creepers." See Franchère, *Narrative,* 259.

Chapter 6

Departure from Astoria—Description of our party, landing, &c.—Appearance of river and islands—Fleas and musquitoes—First rapids, dangerous accident—Indian cemetery—Ugly Indians—Gibraltar—Cape Horn—The narrows and falls—Change in the appearance of the country—Attempt at robbery—Mounted Indians

In traveling through the Indian country several days must necessarily elapse devoid of interesting matter; and to the general reader a succinct detail of the diurnal proceedings of Indian traders would be rather dry. I do not profess to write a journal, and shall therefore make no apology for sparing my readers the trouble of perusing in every page the verbose accuracy which details, that in summer journeys we rise each morning between three and four o'clock, breakfast between nine and ten, and encamp between six and seven in the evening; and that, while on the water, few days elapse in which we are not obliged to put ashore several times to repair the damage sustained by our canoes in passing rapids, portages, or sunken trees.

On the 29th of June, 1812, all the necessary arrangements having been perfected, we took our departure from Astoria for the interior.[1] Our party consisted of three proprietors, nine clerks, fifty-five Canadians, twenty Sandwich Islanders,[2] and Messrs. Crooks, M'Lellan, and R. Stuart, who, with eight men, were to proceed with dispatches to St. Louis. Messrs. Hunt, M'Dougal, Clapp, Halsey, and Franchère remained at the fort. The *Beaver* had previously sailed for Canton, whence it was intended she should return to New York.

[1] For a less glamorous but more detailed, and undoubtedly more accurate, account of this journey see *Robert Stuart's Journey, 27–67.*

[2] The *Tonquin* had brought fifteen of the Sandwich Islanders from Whoahoo, which, joined with those we brought, amounted to thirty-one. Eleven remained at the fort. —R. C.

74

We travelled in *bateaux* and light-built wooden canoes. The former had eight, and the latter six men. Our lading consisted of guns and ammunition, spears, hatchets, knives, beaver traps, copper and brass kettles, white and green blankets, blue, green, and red cloths, calicoes, beads, rings, thimbles, hawk-bells, &c.; and our provisions of beef, pork, flour, rice, biscuits, tea, sugar, with a moderate quantity of rum, wine, &c. The soft and hard goods were secured in bales and boxes, and the liquids in kegs, holding on an average nine gallons. The guns were stowed in long cases. From thirty to forty of these packages and kegs were placed in each vessel, and the whole was covered by an oil-cloth or tarpaulin, to preserve them from wet. Each canoe and barge had from six to eight men rowing or paddling, independent of the passengers.

The Columbia is a noble river, uninterrupted by rapids for 170 miles; 100 of which are navigable for vessels of three hundred tons. It is seldom less than a mile wide; but in some places its breadth varies from two to five miles. The shores are generally bold and thickly wooded. Pine in all its varieties predominates, and is mixed with white oak, ash, beech, poplar, alder, crab, and cotton wood, with an undergrowth of briers, &c., through which our hunters made many ineffectual attempts to pass. The navigation is often obstructed by sandbanks, which are scattered over different parts of the river below the rapids, and are dry at low water. In the neighbourhood of these sandbanks the shores are generally low, and present some fine flat bottoms of rich meadow ground, bordered by a profusion of blackberry and other wild fruit shrubs; in the deep and narrow paths of the channel, the shores are bolder. The river, up to the rapids, is covered with several islands, from one to three miles in length; some of which are fine meadows, and others well wooded. Great caution is required to avoid sunken trees, called snags or planters, and by the Canadians *chicots*, which are generally concealed under the surface of the water; and which, if they come in contact with canoes, sailing rapidly, may cause them to sink if assistance be not at hand.

About three miles above the fort a long and narrow point of land, rather high, runs near half a mile into the river from the south side. It is called Tongue Point, and in boisterous weather is very difficult to double. On quitting Astoria it blew pretty fresh, and we took in a good deal of water in doubling this point. We stopped for the night about six miles above Tongue Point, on the south side, close to an old uninhabited village, but having no lack of animated beings of another description; I mean fleas, with which the place was completely alive; and we had not been on shore five minutes when we were obliged to strip, get a change of clothes, and drown the invaders of our late suit by dipping them in the river.[3] We had to pitch our tents on the sandy beach to avoid their attacks; but this was only "out of the frying-pan," &c.; for about midnight the tide came on us unawares; and the first intimation we received of our danger was the noise of the water beating against the canoes and baggage; and when the alarm was given, it was nearly up to our knees on the beach. It was a spring tide, on which the men did not calculate, and therefore kept no watch; added to which, every man was nearly drunk on quitting the fort.

We had immediately to set about getting the goods on the grass, and dressing ourselves. On examination the following morning, we found several bales were wet, which we were obliged to open for the purpose of drying. This detained us late, and we only made about ten miles on the second day, and landed on a small bottom, free from the tide, but somewhat infested by fleas and musquitoes. On the 1st of July it blew rather stiffly from the south-east, which retarded our progress considerably, and we did not make more than fifteen miles; but on the 2nd we had a good run, and encamped on a fine meadow island, where we hoped to spend a pleasant night, free from fleas. Our hopes were partly realised: none of the little agile backbiters attacked us; but their absence was more than amply compensated by myriads of musquitoes, from which we suffered the most painful torments all night; the face, ears, neck, and hands, were peculiar objects of their affection; and what between them and their brethren of the blanket, we scarcely had an unpunctured spot in our bodies. I was particularly honoured with their preference; and in the morning my eyes were completely closed up from the effects of their infernal stings.

We arrived on the evening of the 4th at the foot of the first rapids,[4] where we encamped. The Indians so far had been always friendly, and were in the habit of occasionally trading at Astoria; but as the tribe who resides at the rapids had previously manifested hostile feel-

---

[3] During the warm months of summer it is difficult to select a spot for an encampment free from these annoying insects.—R. C.

[4] A gorge cut directly across the mountain chain of the Cascades.

ings, it was deemed necessary to prepare for action. Each man was provided with a musket, and forty rounds of ball-cartridge, with pouch, belts, &c.; and over his clothes he wore leathern armour: this was a kind of shirt made out of the skin of the elk, which reached from the neck to the knees. It was perfectly arrow-proof; and at eighty or ninety yards impenetrable by a musket bullet. Besides the muskets, numbers had daggers, short swords, and pistols; and, when armed *cap-à-pié,* we presented a formidable appearance.

A council of war was then called, in which it was arranged that five officers should remain at each end of the portage, and the remainder, with twenty-five men, be stationed at short distances from each other. Its length was between three and four miles, and the path was narrow and dangerous, one part greatly obstructed by slippery rocks and another ran through a thick wood, from which a skilful enemy could have attacked us with advantage. We only made one half of the portage the first day, and encamped near an old village, with the river in front, a deep wood in the rear, at one end a natural intrenchment of rocks, and at the other a barrier formed by the canoes and *bateaux.* The whole brigade was divided into three watches, with five officers to each.

In the course of the day, in the most gloomy part of the wood, we passed a cemetery, materially different from those belonging to the lower tribes. There were nine shallow excavations, closely covered with pine and cedar boards, and the top boards sloping to let off the rain. Each place was about seven feet square, and between five and six feet in height. They contained numbers of dead bodies, some in a state of greater or less decomposition, and a few quite fresh. They were all carefully enveloped in mats and skins. Several poles were attached to these burial places, on which were suspended robes, pieces of cloth, kettles, bags of trinkets, baskets of roots, wooden bowls, and several ornaments; all of which the survivors believed their departed friends would require in the next world. Their veneration is so great for these offerings, that it is deemed sacrilege to pilfer one of them; and although these Indians are not remarkable for scrupulous honesty, I believe no temptation would induce them to touch these articles. Several of the boards are carved and painted with rude representations of men, bears, wolves, and animals unknown. Some in green, others in white and red, and all most hideously unlike nature.

About midnight we were thrown into a state of frightful confusion by the report of a gun, and the cries of Mr. Pillet, one of the clerks, that he was shot. Every one instantly seized his arms, and enquired on which side was the enemy; but our apprehensions were quickly appeased, on learning it was merely an accident.[5] One of the gentlemen, in examining the musket of a Sandwich Islander, to see if it was primed, handed it to him at full cock; and just as the islander had taken it, the piece went off, and the contents lodged in the calf of poor Pillet's leg, who naturally enough exclaimed he was shot. This was however, in our present circumstances, a disagreeable event, as it rendered Mr. Pillet not only incapable of fighting, but required three or four men to carry him in a litter over the various portages. The wound was dressed with friar's balsam and lint, the ball extracted the next day; and in about a month afterwards he was able to walk.

We commenced proceedings at four o'clock on the morning of the 6th, and finishing the portage about two in the afternoon. During our progress the Indians occasionally hovered about the loaded men, and made two or three trifling essays to pilfer them; but the excellent precautions we had adopted completely kept them in check, and deterred them from attempting any thing like forcible robbery. At the upper end of the portage, and while we were reloading the canoes, a number of the natives, several of whom were armed, assembled about us. They conducted themselves peaceably; but our numbers and warlike arrangements enforced respect. The dress of the men does not differ materially from that of the lower Indians; but they are incontestably more filthy and ugly. Their teeth are almost worn away. The greater number have very sore eyes; several have only one; and we observed a few old men and women quite blind. The men are generally naked; and the women merely wear a leathern belt, with a narrow piece of the same material joined to the front, which very imperfectly answers the purposes intended. Some wear leathern robes over the breast and shoulders; but others allow these parts to remain naked. We observed no one who appeared to assume the authority of a chief. Each seemed quite independent of the other, and complete master in his own house and family. Their unfeeling brutality

[5] Alexander Ross says that it was Cox who shot Pillett, the gun of the former "being held in some awkward and careless position, went off, and both balls passed through the calf of Mr. Pillett's right leg . . . ," but he puts the incident a year later. See *First Settlers*, 240.

to the few old blind people I have mentioned was really shocking; and I may safely say, a more unamiable race of democrats are not to be found in that country of republics. We distributed a quantity of tobacco among them, with which they appeared satisfied; after which we embarked, and proceeded on. The upper part of the chain of rapids is a perpendicular fall of nearly sixteen feet; after which it continues down nearly one uninterrupted rapid for three miles and a half. The river here is compressed by the bold shore on each side to about two hundred yards or less in breadth. The channel is crowded with large rocks, over which the water rushes with incredible velocity, and with a dreadful noise. Above the portage the river widens to about half a mile, and is studded for some distance with several rocky and partially wooded islands. We encamped above five miles from the portage, in a pretty little creek on the north side. The pine declines considerably in size above the rapids, and is more equally mixed with other trees; among which, on the left shore, from the portage up to our encampment, the hazel is predominant. We purchased some salmon on our way up, by which we were enabled to husband our own provisions with more economy. I omitted to mention that below the rapids we also got a quantity of excellent roots, called by the Indians *wappittoo*.[6] In size they resemble a small potatoe, for which it is a good substitute when roasted or boiled; it has a very slight tinge of bitterness, but not unpleasantly so, and is highly esteemed by the natives, who collect vast quantities of it for their own use and for barter. None of it grows above the rapids. On the evening of the 8th we reached the foot of the narrows, or, as the Canadians call them, *les dalles*. The river from the first rapids to the narrows is broad, deep, and rapid, with several sunken rocks, scattered here and there, which often injure the canoes. The Canadians, who are very fertile in baptizing remarkable places, called an island near our encampment of the 6th, "Gibraltar,"[7] from the rocky steepness of its shore; and about half way between the first rapids and narrows a bold promontory of high black rock stretches a considerable distance into the river, which, from the difficulty we experienced in doubling it, received the name of "Cape Horn."[8] The current here is very strong and full of whirlpools; so that except in calm weather, or with a fair wind, it is rather a dangerous undertaking

---

[6] The wapatoo. Despite Cox, it was found east of the Cascades.
[7] Gibraltar was probably the name given to present Dalles City Rock.
[8] Cape Horn is a name used by Cox for present Mitchell Point.

to "double the cape." The islands in the distance are crowded with great numbers of seals, which afforded excellent sport to our marksmen. As we approached the narrows the shores on each side were less covered with wood, and immediately close to them it had entirely disappeared. The land on the north side was bold and rocky, and about our encampment rather low, mixed with rocks, a sandy soil, and totally devoid of vegetation, except loose straggling bushes some distance inland. The Columbia, at the narrows, for upwards of three miles is compressed into a narrow channel, not exceeding sixty or seventy yards wide; the whole of which is a succession of boiling whirlpools. Above this channel, for four or five miles, the river is one deep rapid, at the upper end of which a large mass of high black rock stretches across from the north side, and nearly joins a similar mass on the south. They are divided by a strait not exceeding fifty yards wide; and through this narrow channel, for upwards of half a mile, the immense waters of the Columbia are one mass of foam, and force their headlong course with a frightful impetuosity, which cannot at any time be contemplated without producing a painful giddiness. We were obliged to carry all our lading from the lower to the upper narrows, nearly nine miles. The canoes were dragged up part of the space between the narrows. This laborious undertaking occupied two entire days, in consequence of the number of armed men we were obliged to keep as guards to protect those who carried the goods. It was a little above this place where our party had been recently attacked, and we were therefore obliged to be doubly cautious. The chief and several of the Indians kept about us during the portage. We gave them some tobacco and trifling presents to cultivate their friendship, in return for which they brought us some salmon. They had the discrimination to see from our numbers, and the manner we were prepared to receive them, that an attack would be attended with rather doubtful success, and therefore feigned an appearance of friendship, which we affected to believe sincere. The propriety of "assuming a virtue if we had it not," however questionable in morals, must be often practised among Indians; for they are such thorough-bred hypocrites and liars, that we found it often necessary to repose apparent confidence in them, when we well knew they were exerting their utmost skill to impose on and deceive us. Even here while the chief and some of his tribe were smoking with us at one of the resting places, a few of the gentlemen who were at the upper end of the portage, seeing no symptoms of danger, wandered a short distance among the rocks to view the narrows, leaving part of the goods unguarded. This was instantly observed by two fellows who were lurking close to the place, and who availed themselves of the opportunity to attempt carrying off an entire bale, but finding it rather heavy, were about rifling its contents when two of the loaded men arrived, and gave the alarm. The robbers had the audacity to attack the men, one of whom they knocked down; when the officers, on seeing what had occurred, returned back quickly, upon which the savages fled. A shot was fired at them by our best marksman, who was told merely to wing one, which he did with great skill, by breaking his left arm, at upwards of a hundred yards distance. The fellow gave a dreadful shout on receiving the ball, but still continued his flight with his comrade, until we lost sight of them. This piece of severity was deemed necessary, to prevent repetitions of similar aggressions. The chief, in strong terms, declared his ignorance of any previous intention on the part of these fellows to commit robbery, which we appeared not to doubt, at the same time giving him to understand, that in case any farther attacks were made, our balls would be directed to a more mortal part.

On the morning of the 11th we embarked, and proceeded a few miles with great labour, by dragging the canoes against the current, which is very strong between the upper narrows and the falls. The passengers all walked, and at some ugly rocky points part of the lading had to be taken out. This consumed the greater portion of the day; and we encamped that evening on the south side near the foot of the falls.[9] Here several Indians visited us; some armed and on horseback, others unarmed, and on foot. In language, dress, and manners, they appeared to belong to distinct nations. The horsemen were clean, wore handsome leathern shirts and leggings, and had a bold daring manner, which we did not observe with any of the tribes from the sea upwards. The more humble pedestrians were the natives of the place. They were nearly naked, and rather dirty in their persons, and professed to be friendly; but from several attempts they made at pilfering, we entertained strong doubts of their sincerity, and were obliged to order them to remove some distance from the camp. They seemed to regard the mounted Indians with a suspicious degree of apprehension, for which we were for some time at a loss to account; but

[9] This was the present Celilo Falls, long a favorite fishing resort of the tribes of that region.

81

which we subsequently learned was caused by their having been lately at war, in which they were vanquished, and several of their tribe killed by the equestrians. The latter remained on horseback most part of the time, making observations on our party, by which they apparently intended to regulate their future proceedings. They made no show of friendship, were rather cold and distant in their manners, and appeared to be a reconnoitring party sent out by the main body to watch our progress. As a precautionary measure, we judged it expedient to show them we were fully prepared for action, and accordingly assembled all the men in the evening, each encased in his coat of mail, and armed with a musket and bayonet. They remained looking at us very attentively, while our officers proceeded to examine each man's firelock with all due military solemnity. One-half of the men were then ordered to form a barrier with the canoes on our rear and flanks, which, with the river in front, effectually served to prevent a surprise during the night. The whole brigade was equally divided; and one half of the men having retired to rest, the remainder were posted as sentinels about the camp. Owing to the extreme heat, the Sandwich Islanders had thrown off their jackets and shirts during the day, and their swarthy bodies, decorated with buff belts, seemed to excite the particular attention of the Indians, who repeatedly pointed towards them, and then spoke to each other with considerable animation. Having completed our arrangements for the night, we offered them some tobacco, which they accepted, and then left us. It is necessary to observe, that in the course of the day a calumet was presented to some of the horsemen, which they refused; from which circumstance, joined to their general deportment, we were led to believe their visit was not of a pacific nature. We passed the night without any interruption to our repose, and commenced the portage of the falls early on the morning of the 12th; but as the ground over which the men were obliged to carry the baggage was covered with a deep bed of dry loose sand, which fatigued them extremely, they did not finish their laborious duty before night. We encamped late at the upper end of the falls, near a village of the Eneeshurs,[10] from whom we purchased some salmon. A few of the horsemen occasionally reconnoitred us during the day; but as our men made short resting-places, or pauses in the portage, by which the entire party were always in view of each other, the

[10] This tribe lived in the area near the mouth of the Deschutes River, the "river of the falls."

82

natives made no hostile attempt; and on observing the manner we had fortified our camp, and placed our sentinels for the night, they departed. The principal fall does not exceed fifteen feet in height; but at low water it is much higher. The descent of the Columbia from above this fall to the end of the lower narrows exceeds seventy feet, and throughout the whole distance (about ten miles) the river is strewed with immense masses of hard black rock, mostly honey-combed, and worn into a variety of fantastic shapes by the perpetual friction of the water in its fearful course downwards. The appearance of the country here is high, rocky, barren, and without timber of any kind. We found this a sensible inconvenience; for we were obliged to purchase some drift wood from the Indians for the purposes of cooking.

On quitting this place the following morning, a number of natives collected about us, among whom we distributed a quantity of tobacco. The river for some distance above this place is deep and rapid, and the banks steep and rocky. The canoes were dragged up several miles, and some of them damaged by the rocks. About four or five miles above the fall a high rocky island three miles in length lies in the centre of the river, on which the Indians were employed drying salmon, great quantities of which were cured and piled under broad boards in stacks. We encamped on the north side opposite the island, and were visited by some Indians, from whom we purchased salmon. They appeared friendly, and belonged to the Eneeshur tribe at the falls.

Here, and for several hundred miles farther upwards, the country assumes a new aspect. It is free from any rising grounds, or timber, and on each side nothing is to be seen but immense plains stretching a great distance to the north and south. The soil is dry and sandy, and covered with a loose parched grass, growing in tufts. The natives reside solely on the northern side. They have plenty of horses, and are generally friendly. Here also rattlesnakes are first seen, and are found for four or five hundred miles farther on. Between this place and Lewis' River the Columbia is interrupted by several rapids; some of which are trifling, others dangerous; but there are long intervals of smooth current which occasionally allowed us to hoist small sails, and thereby diminished the laborious duty of the canoe-men in paddling.

Chapter 7

Party commence eating horses—Remarkable escape from a rattlesnake—
Kill numbers of them—Arrive among the Wallah Wallah tribe—Description
of the country—The Pierced-nose Indians—Author's party proceeds up
Lewis' River—Purchase horses for land-travelling—Prickly pears—Awk-
ward accident—Leave the canoes, and journey inland

The day after quitting the encampment at the end of the rocky island
we stopped about one o'clock at a village, where we purchased five
horses. The value of the goods we paid for each in England would not
exceed five shillings. As these horses were intended for the kettle, they
were doomed to instant destruction. Our comparatively recent separation from the land o' "bread and butter" caused the idea of feeding
on so useful and noble an animal to be at first highly repugnant to
our feelings; but example, and above all, necessity, soon conquered
these little qualms of civilization; and in a few days we almost brought
ourselves to believe that the animal on which we fed once carried
horns, was divided in the hoof, and chewed the cud. A curious incident
occurred at this spot to one of our men named La Course, which was
nearly proving fatal. This man had stretched himself on the ground,
after the fatigue of the day, with his head resting on a small package
of goods, and quickly fell asleep. While in this situation I passed him,
and was almost petrified at seeing a large rattlesnake moving from
his side to his left breast. My first impulse was to alarm La Course;
but an old Canadian whom I had beckoned to the spot requested me
to make no noise, alleging it would merely cross the body and go away.
He was mistaken; for on reaching the man's left shoulder, the serpent
deliberately coiled itself, but did not appear to meditate an attack.
Having made signs to several others, who joined us, it was determined

84

that two men should advance a little in front, to divert the attention of the snake, while one should approach La Course behind, and with a long stick endeavour to remove it from his body. The snake, on observing the men advance in front, instantly raised its head, darted out its forked tongue, and shook its rattles; all indications of anger. Every one was now in a state of feverish agitation as to the fate of poor La Course, who still lay slumbering, unconscious of his danger; when the man behind, who had procured a stick seven feet in length, suddenly placed one end of it under the coiled reptile, and succeeded in pitching it upwards of ten feet from the man's body. A shout of joy was the first intimation La Course received of his wonderful escape, while in the mean time the man with the stick pursued the snake which he killed. It was three feet six inches long; and eleven years old, which I need not inform my readers we easily ascertained by the number of rattles. A general search was then commenced about the encampment, and under several rocks we found upwards of fifty of them, all of which we destroyed. There is no danger attending their destruction, provided a person has a long pliant stick, and does not approach them nearer than their length, for they cannot spring beyond it, and seldom act on the offensive except closely pursued. They have a strong repugnance to the smell of tobacco,[1] in consequence of which we opened a bale of it, and strewed a quantity of loose leaves about the tents, by which means we avoided their visits during the night. We had however nearly as bad visitors—the musquitoes, which from the falls upwards annoyed us dreadfully. We were obliged to make a slight fire of rotten wood in the *cul-de-sac* of our tents, which merely caused a smoke without flame, and which effectually drove them away; but the remedy was as bad as the disease, as we were nearly blinded and suffocated by the smoke.

Owing to the many accidents which befell our canoes in the rapids, and the time consequently employed in repairing them, and drying damaged goods, our progress was greatly retarded, and we did not reach the Wallah Wallah River until the 28th. During this period, we generally encamped on the northern banks of the river, purchased a number of horses for eating, and were several times without wood for cooking them. The Indians behaved in the most peaceable man-

---

[1] Rattlesnakes will sometimes, although not generally, take the offensive. This asserted repugnance for tobacco cannot be verified and is probably just another old wives' tale.

ner, and freely bartered with us such other provisions as they could spare. A few miles below the Wallah Wallah the land on the south side rises into rocky cliffs, near two hundred feet high, which extend some distance inland. There is a long and very dangerous rapid at their base, which, by way of pre-eminence, the Canadians call the *Grande Rapide*. We landed on the south side, up which the canoes were dragged with great difficulty. We observed immense numbers of rattlesnakes here, basking in the sun, and under the rocks, several of which we killed. Half a dozen of us fired together at a batch lying under one rock, and killed or wounded thirty-seven! Our guns were charged with goose shot. There was scarcely a stone in this place which was not covered with them. All the time we walked we were constantly on the *qui vive;* and I need not say, picked our steps very cautiously. From the friendly character of the natives, we had thrown by our armour for some days, which relieved us greatly, the heat, while we were obliged to wear it, being almost insupportable. Above this rocky eminence the country opened again into an extended plain. The river here, and for several miles lower down, is occasionally bordered with straggling clusters of willow, cotton wood, stunted red cedar, and sumach, with quantities of sarsaparilla. There is also abundance of furze bushes and wormwood, through which we observed several hares running, some of which we killed.

In the evening we encamped at the entrance of the Wallah Wallah River;[2] a number of that tribe visited us, and remained for some time smoking. We informed Tamtappam, their chief, that he wanted good horses fit to carry luggage, and others to eat, and requested he would procure for us as many as he could the following day. This he promised to do, and departed.

On the 29th we purchased twenty horses for Mr. Robert Stuart's party; which being deemed sufficient for them, he, with Messrs. Crooks and M'Lellan, and eight men, left us the next morning, under a salute of three cheers, to pursue their dangerous journey across the mountains, and thence by the Missouri to St. Louis. The Wallah Wallahs were decidedly the most friendly tribe we had seen on the river: they had an air of open and unsuspecting confidence in their manner that at once banished suspicion, and insured our friendship. There was a degree of natural politeness, too, evidenced by them on

[2] The Walla Walla River. Alexander Ross was later to build Fort Nez Percé near this point.

entering their lodges, which we did not see practised by any others. We visited several families in the village; and the moment we entered, the best place was selected for us, and a clean mat spread to sit on; while the inmates, particularly the women and the children, remained at a respectful distance, without manifesting any of the obtrusive curiosity about our arms or clothing by which we were so much annoyed amongst the lower tribes. The females, also, were distinguished by a degree of attentive kindness, totally removed from the disgusting familiarity of the kilted ladies below the rapids, and equally free from an affectation of prudery. Prostitution is unknown among them; and I believe no inducement would tempt them to commit a breach of chastity.

The Wallah Wallah is a bold, rapid stream, about fifty-five yards wide, and upwards of six feet deep; the water is clear, and rolls over a bed of sand and gravel. On the 31st we moved up to the north side of the mouth of Lewis' River,[3] which is about fourteen miles above the Wallah Wallah; its course is nearly due west, and at its junction with the Columbia it is upwards of six hundred yards wide. The current is very rapid; its waters deep, whitish, and slightly tepid, in which respect it forms a marked contrast to the Columbia, the waters of which are quite clear and cool. The latter river at this place is upwards of one thousand yards wide, and the current descends at an even rate of about four miles an hour. A little below the junction, however, it widens from a mile to a mile and a half, and has several islands, two of which are low and sandy, and are nearly three miles in length. Below these islands, a range of high hills are seen on each side of the river, running nearly from S.W. to N.E., and uncovered by any timber; but at an immense distance, in a southeasterly direction, a chain of high craggy mountains are visible, from which it is supposed the Wallah Wallah takes its rise. From their colour the Canadians call this chain *Les Montagnes Bleues*.[4] The banks of both rivers at their junction are low with a gentle rise on each side. The plains are covered with immense quantities of prickly pear, which was a source of great annoyance. Above Lewis' River the Columbia

---

[3] This is today's Snake River, which enters the Columbia opposite the city of Pasco, Washington.

[4] The Blue Mountains in southeastern Washington and northeastern Oregon. They constituted a formidable obstacle to early travelers over the Oregon Trail and still retain much of their primeval character.

runs in a northerly direction, below it in a westerly. We remained here three days purchasing horses for our journey inland. Mr. David Stuart and party proceeded in their canoes up the Columbia to the trading establishment which he had formed at Oakinagan River, which falls into the Columbia, from the northward, about two hundred and eighty miles above this place. Mr. Donald Mackenzie and his party proceeded up Lewis' River in order to establish a trading post on the upper parts of it, or in the country of the Snake Indians, his choice to be regulated according to the appearance of beaver in either place. The natives of this district are called the Pierced-nose Indians; but as French is the language in general use among traders in this country, owing to most part of their working men being Canadians, we commonly called them *Les Nez Percés*.[5] They do not differ much from the Wallah Wallahs in their dress or language, but are not so friendly, and demand higher prices for their horses. Their habitations are covered with large mats, fixed on poles; some are square, others oblong, and some conical; they are of various sizes, from twenty to seventy feet long, and from ten to fifteen feet broad. There are no interior divisions, and an opening in the top serves the double purpose of a window and chimney. These dwellings are pretty free from vermin, and are easily changed when occasion requires. The women wear leathern robes, which cover the shoulders, part of the arms, the breast, and reach down to their legs. The men have robes nearly similar, but not so long, with leggings which reach up half the thigh, and are fastened to a belt round the waist by leathern thongs. They are clean, active, and smart-looking, good hunters, and excellent horsemen. They enjoy good health, and with the exception of a few sore eyes, did not appear to have any disorder. They are fond of their children, and attentive to the wants of their old people. Their saddles are made of dressed deer-skin stuffed with hair; the stirrups are wooden, with the bottom broad and flat, and covered over with raw skin, which when dry becomes hard, and lasts a long time. The bridles are merely ropes made out of the hair of the horses' tails, and are tied round their under jaw. The women ride like the men: their saddles are high in front and rear, and formed something like the humps on

[5] The Nez Percé Indians are of Shahaptian stock and are one of the really great tribes of North America. Despite the name, they did not pierce the nose. A very good account is Francis Haines, *The Nez Percés: Tribesmen of the Columbia Plateau* (Norman, University of Oklahoma Press, 1955).

a camel's back; and they must bring their horses to a rock or old tree to enable them to mount. The men are hard and unfeeling riders: the rope bridles cut the corners of the poor horses' mouths; and the saddles generally leave their backs quite raw; yet in this state they ride them for several days successively without the least pity for the tortured animals.[6] We got plenty of salmon while we remained here, and some lamprey eels, the latter of which were oily and very strong. Having purchased twenty-five horses, we took our departure on the 3rd of August, and proceeded up Lewis' River, some on land with the horses, but the greater part still in the canoes. The water was very high, and rapid, and in many places the banks steep and shelving, which made the process of dragging up the canoes very difficult. Poling was quite impossible; for on the off, or outer side, the men could not find bottom with their poles. I remained on shore part of the time with the horses. In some places the path wound along the almost perpendicular declivities of high hills on the banks of the river, and was barely wide enough for one horse at a time. Yet along these dangerous roads the Indians galloped with the utmost composure; while one false step would have hurled them down a precipice of three hundred feet into the torrent below. Even walking along these dangerous declivities, leading my horse, I experienced an indescribable sensation of dread on looking down the frightful abyss.

On the 7th we reached a small stream which falls into Lewis' River from the north; the mouth is wide, and forms a kind of semicircular bay, but suddenly narrows to about ten or twelve yards.[7] A village of about forty mat-covered tents was situated at its junction with the main river. The inhabitants were busily employed in catching and drying salmon for their winter and spring stock; and as it was here we intended to leave the canoes and proceed to our destination by land, we encamped on the west side of the little bay, and immediately commenced a trade with the natives for horses. This place is not more than fifty miles from the Columbia; but owing to the rapidity of the current, and the many rapids with which it was interrupted, our progress was slow. The business of collecting and catching the horses, which generally occupied until eleven or twelve o'clock each

---

[6] The cruelty of Indians to their horses, and in fact to all dumb animals, is proverbial.

[7] The present Palouse River. In those days it was generally known as the Pavilion River. Lewis and Clark had called it "Drewyer's River," after one of their men.

day, also contributed to cause this delay. With the exception of small willow and cotton wood, there are no trees from the Columbia upwards. The ground is covered with loose grass, and abounds in great quantities of the prickly pear, the thorns of which are remarkably sharp, and strong enough to penetrate the leather of the thickest moccasins.

On the third day, while riding a short distance ahead of the men, my horse happened to stand on a bunch of the prickly pears, which pained him so much that he commenced plunging and kicking, and ultimately threw me into a cluster of them. My face, neck, and body, were severely pierced; and every effort to rise only increased the painfulness of my situation, for wherever I placed my hands to assist in raising my body they came in contact with the same tormenting thorns. In fact I could not move an inch; and to add to my disaster, I observed three rattlesnakes within a few feet of my head. The men who were in the rear driving the horses, hearing my cries, quickly came to my assistance, and with considerable difficulty disentangled me from my painful situation. The snakes in the mean time had disappeared. I immediately hailed the canoes, and resumed my old place on board, firmly resolved never again to ride while a prickly pear was visible.

The inhabitants of this fishing village were part of the Piercednose Indians. We remained here seven days, endeavouring to complete our number of horses, which we at length effected. The natives were hard to deal with, and we had to raise our prices. Several trifling articles were stolen from us, which the chief promised to recover; but he either made no attempt, or the means he used were ineffectual. He apologised for his want of success by saying that the thieves belonged to another tribe higher up the river, and that they had departed with the stolen property. In their dress, language, and dwellings these people differed little from those at the mouth of Lewis' River. On the evening of the 14th we laid up our *bateaux* and canoes in a snug spot covered with willow and loose shrubs, and recommended them to the care of the chief, who promised that they should be carefully preserved until our return the following spring. We made him a present of a fathom of blue cloth, an axe, and a knife; to his wife we gave a few strings of white and blue beads, and three dozen of hawk-bells for her *chemise de cuir;* and among the remainder we distributed a few heads of leaf-tobacco.

We purchased altogether fifty horses to carry the goods and baggage; and from the difficulty we experienced in procuring that number, we were not able to obtain enough for our own use. M'Lennan and I, however, succeeded in purchasing one for our joint use; and Farnham and Pillet got another. The men also obtained a few which occasionally served to relieve them in the progress of their journey. Our destination was fixed for the Spokan[8] tribe of Indians, whose lands lay about 150 miles from Lewis' River in a north-east direction, and among whom we were given to understand the North-West Company had already established a trading post from the east side of the Rocky Mountains. We also engaged an Indian guide to conduct us to the Spokan lands.

On the 15th of August, at five A. M., we took our departure from Lewis' River. Our party consisted of one proprietor, four clerks, twenty-one Canadians, and six Sandwich Islanders, with the Indian guide. We proceeded nearly due north along the banks of the small river for some miles through an open plain, which was bounded by a range of steep rugged hills, running from the westward over which we had to cross. In some places the path led over steep and slippery rocks, and was so narrow, that the horses which were loaded with large bales could not pass without running the risk of falling down the craggy precipices; and the men were obliged to unload them and place the bales singly on the top of the pack saddles. After we had passed as we imagined the most dangerous part of the pathway, and had commenced our descent into the plain, one of the horses missed his footing, and rolled down a declivity of two hundred feet, loaded with two cases of axes. The cases were broken, and their contents scattered about the rocks; but, with the exception of his sides, the skin of which was scraped off, the horse received no material injury. We arrived on the north side of these hills about eleven o'clock, when we stopped to breakfast on the banks of the river, which here turns to the eastward. We resumed our journey at two o'clock, and suffered severely during the day, from the intense heat, and the want of water. The country was a continued plain, with sandy and rocky bottom, mixed with loose tufts of grass. About seven in the evening we reached a cool stream, on the banks of which were a profusion of wild cherries, currants, and blackberries, which afforded us an unexpected and welcome treat. We encamped here for the night; and

[8] *Spokane* is the accepted spelling today.

did not hobble the horses,[9] as we were certain the luxurious herbage of the *prairie* would prevent them from wandering.

At four A. M. on the 16th we set off from our encampment, still pursuing a northerly course. The country was still champaign, and the grass long and coarse, but loosely imbedded in a sandy soil. About eight we came to a fine spring, at which we breakfasted, as our guide told us we should not find water beyond it for a great distance. After waiting here a few hours, we reloaded, and pursued our journey in the same direction. During the remainder of the day no "green spot bloomed on the desert" around us. The country was completely denuded of wood; and as far as the eye extended, nothing was visible but immense plains covered with parched brown grass, swarming with rattlesnakes. The horses suffered dreadfully, as well as their masters, from heat and thirst.[10] Two fine pointers belonging to Mr. Clarke were so exhausted that we were compelled to leave them behind, and never saw them afterwards. Several of the horses being on the point of giving up, and numbers of the men scarcely able to walk, Mr. Clarke sharply questioned the guide as to his knowledge of the country, and the probable time we might expect to fall in with water. The latter saw his doubts, and calmly replied, pointing to the sun, that when it should have gained a certain distance we might expect relief. We knew half an hour would not elapse before it should attain the desired point, and every watch was out to judge of the Indian's accuracy. He was right; and about half-past five P. M. we reached a small stream, by the side of which we encamped for the night. The guide gave us to understand we should find plenty of water the following day.

[9] When we were apprehensive that the horses might wander from an encampment, their two fore legs were tied together. This we called "hobbling."—R. C.

[10] The lack of water in this area is owing to the "rain shadow" cast by the Cascade Mountains to the west. A region of little precipitation, there are few streams, and many of these dry up during the summer. There are, however, a number of lakes.

Chapter 8

Author loses the party—Curious adventures, and surprising escapes from serpents and wild beasts during fourteen days in a wilderness—Meets with Indians, by whom he is hospitably received, and conducted to his friends

On the 17th of August we left our encampment a little after four A. M. During the forenoon the sun was intensely hot. Occasional bright green patches, intermixed with wild flowers, and gently rising eminences, partially covered with clumps of small trees, gave an agreeable variety to the face of the country, which we enjoyed the more, from the scorched and sterile uniformity of the plains through which we had passed on the two preceding days. We got no water, however, until twelve o'clock, when we arrived in a small valley of the most delightful verdure, through which ran a clear stream from the northward, over a pebbly bottom. The horses immediately turned loose to regale themselves in the rich pasture; and as it was full of red and white clover, orders were given not to catch them until two o'clock, by which time we thought they would be sufficiently refreshed for the evening's journey.

After walking and riding eight hours, I need not say we made a hearty breakfast, after which I wandered some distance along the banks of the rivulet in search of cherries, and came to a sweet little arbour formed by sumach and cherry trees. I pulled a quantity of the fruit, and sat down in the retreat to enjoy its refreshing coolness. It was a charming spot, and on the opposite bank was a delightful wilderness of crimson haw,[1] honeysuckles, wild roses, and currants. Its resemblance to a friend's summer-house, in which I had spent many happy days, brought back home with all its endearing recollections;

[1] The fruit of the hawthorn tree.

93

and my scattered thoughts were successively occupied with the past, the present, and the future. In this state I fell into a kind of pleasing, soothing reverie, which, joined to the morning's fatigue, gradually sealed my eyelids; and unconscious of my situation, I resigned myself to the influence of the drowsy god. But imagine my feelings when I awoke in the evening, I think it was about five o'clock, from the declining appearance of the sun! All was calm and silent as the grave. I hastened to the spot where we had breakfasted; it was vacant. I ran to the place where the men had made their fire; all, all were gone, and not a vestige of man or horse appeared in the valley. My senses almost failed me. I called out, in vain, in every direction, until I became hoarse; and I could no longer conceal from myself the dreadful truth that I was alone in a wild, uninhabited country, without horse or arms, and destitute of covering.[2]

Having now no resource but to ascertain the direction which the party had taken, I set about examining the ground, and at the northeast point of the valley discovered the tracks of horses' feet, which I followed for some time, and which led to a chain of small hills with a rocky, gravelly bottom, on which the hoofs made no impression. Having thus lost the tracks, I ascended the highest of the hills, from which I had an extended view of many miles around, but saw no sign of the party, or the least indication of human habitations. The evening was now closing fast, and with the approach of night a heavy dew commenced falling. The whole of my clothes consisted merely of a gingham shirt, nankeen trowsers, and a pair of light leather moccasins, much worn. About an hour before breakfast, in consequence of the heat, I had taken off my coat and placed it on one of the loaded horses, intending to put it on towards the cool of the evening; and one of the men had charge of my fowling-piece. I was even without my hat; for in the agitated state of my mind on awaking I had left it behind, and had advanced too far to think of returning for it. At some distance on my left I observed a field of high, strong grass, to which I proceeded; and after pulling enough to place under and over me, I recommended myself to the Almighty, and fell asleep. During the night confused dreams of warm houses, feather beds, poisoned arrows, prickly pears, and rattlesnakes, haunted my disturbed imagination.

On the 18th I arose with the sun, quite wet and chilly, the heavy

[2] Alexander Ross gives an entirely different version of how Cox came to be separated from the party. See *First Settlers*, 209.

The Massacre of the *Tonquin's* Crew
from a drawing by R. F. Zogbaum

From Tacoma Edition of Irving's Astoria
(New York, G. P. Putnam's Sons, 1897)

Indian Canoe, The Dalles
from a water color by A. J. Miller

The Voyageurs
from a painting by Charles Deas

dew having completely saturated my flimsy covering, and proceeded in an easterly direction, nearly parallel with the chain of hills. In the course of the day I passed several small lakes full of wild fowl. The general appearance of the country was flat, the soil light and gravelly, and covered with the same loose grass already mentioned; great quantities of it had been recently burned by the Indians in hunting the deer, the stubble of which annoyed my feet very much. I had turned into a northerly course, where, late in the evening, I observed, about a mile distant, two horsemen galloping in an easterly direction. From their dresses I knew they belonged to our party. I instantly ran to a hillock, and called out in a voice to which hunger had imparted a supernatural shrillness; but they galloped on. I then took off my shirt, which I waved in a conspicuous manner over my head, accompanied by the most frantic cries; still they continued on. I ran towards the direction they were galloping, despair adding wings to my flight. Rocks, stubble, and brushwood were passed with the speed of a hunted antelope—but to no purpose; for on arriving at the place where I imagined a pathway would have brought me into their track, I was completely at fault. It was now nearly dark. I had eaten nothing since the noon of the preceding day; and, faint with hunger and fatigue, threw myself on the grass, when I heard a small rustling noise behind me. I turned round, and, with horror, beheld a large rattlesnake cooling himself in the evening shade. I instantly retreated, on observing which he coiled himself. Having obtained a large stone, I advanced slowly on him, and taking a proper aim, dashed it with all my force on the reptile's head, which I buried in the ground beneath the stone.

The late race had completely worn out the thin soles of my moccasins, and my feet in consequence became much swoln. As night advanced, I was obliged to look out for a place to sleep, and, after some time, selected nearly as good a bed as the one I had the first night. My exertions in pulling the long, coarse grass nearly rendered my hands useless by severely cutting all the joints of the fingers.

I rose before the sun on the morning of the 19th, and pursued an easterly course all the day. I at first felt very hungry, but after walking a few miles, and taking a drink of water, I got a little refreshed. The general appearance of the country was still flat, with burned grass, and sandy soil, which blistered my feet. The scorching influence of the sun obliged me to stop for some hours in the day, during which I made several ineffectual attempts to construct a covering for my head. At times I thought my brain was on fire from the dreadful effects of the heat. I got no fruit those two days, and towards evening felt very weak from the want of nourishment, having been forty-eight hours without food; and to make my situation more annoying, I slept that evening on the banks of a pretty lake, the inhabitants of which would have done honour to a royal table. With what an evil eye and murderous heart did I regard the stately goose and the plump waddling duck as they sported on the water, unconscious of my presence! Even with a pocket pistol I could have done execution among them. The state of my fingers prevented me from obtaining the covering of grass which I had the two preceding nights; and on this evening I had no shelter whatever to protect me from the heavy dew.

On the following day, the 20th, my course was nearly north-east, and lay through a country more diversified by wood and water. I saw plenty of wild geese, ducks, cranes, curlews, and sparrows, also some hawks and cormorants, and at a distance about fifteen or twenty small deer. The wood consisted of pine, birch, cedar, wild cherries, haw-thorn, sweet-willow, honeysuckle, and sumach. The rattlesnakes were very numerous this day, with horned lizards, and grasshoppers; the latter kept me in a constant state of feverish alarm from the similarity of the noise made by their wings to the sound of the rattles of the snake when preparing to dart on its prey. I suffered severely dur-ing the day from hunger, and was obliged to chew grass occasionally, which allayed it a little. Late in the evening I arrived at a lake upwards of two miles long, and a mile broad, the shores of which were high, and well wooded with large pine, spruce, and birch.[3] It was fed by two rivulets, from the north, and north-east, in which I observed a quantity of small fish, but had no means of catching any, or I should have made a Sandwich-Island meal. There was however an abundant supply of wild cherries, on which I made a hearty supper. I slept on the bank of the nearest stream, just where it entered the lake; but during the night the howling of wolves and growling of bears broke

[3] While it is impossible to trace Cox's route with any degree of accuracy, since we do not know precisely from which point he started or how many miles he traveled during any one day, we do know that he was east of Lake Colville (present Sprague Lake) and that he probably became separated somewhere on Cow Creek. The trail to Spokane House crossed to the west of Cow Creek and the lake. This Cox did not know, so he kept to the east. The lake here mentioned could have been Downs Lake, to the east of the present town of Sprague.

in terribly on my slumbers, and "balmy sleep" was almost banished from my eyelids.[4] On rising the next morning, the 21st, I observed on the opposite bank at the mouth of the river, the entrance of a large and apparently deep cavern, from which I judged some of the preceding night's music had issued. I now determined to make short journeys for two or three days in different directions, in the hope of falling on some fresh horse-tracks, and, in the event of being unsuccessful, to return each night to the lake, where I was at least certain of procuring cherries and water sufficient to sustain nature. In pursuance of this resolution I set out early in a southerly direction from the head of the lake, through a wild, barren country, without any water or vegetation, save loose tufts of grass like those already described. I had armed myself with a long stick, with which during the day I killed several rattlesnakes. Having discovered no fresh tracks, I returned late in the evening hungry and thirsty, and took possession of my berth of the preceding night. I collected a heap of stones from the water side; and just as I was lying down observed a wolf[5] emerge from the opposite cavern, and thinking it safer to act on the offensive, lest he should imagine I was afraid, I threw some stones at him, one of which struck him on the leg. He retired yelling into his den; and after waiting some time in fearful suspense to see if he would reappear, I threw myself on the ground, and fell asleep. But, like the night before, it was broken by the same unsocial noise and for upwards of two hours I sat up waiting in anxious expectation the return of day-light. The vapours from the lake, joined to the heavy dew, had penetrated my frail covering of gingham; but as the sun rose, I took it off, and stretched it on a rock, where it quickly dried. My excursion to the southward having proved abortive, I now resolved to try the east, and after eating my simple breakfast, proceeded in that direction, and on crossing the two small streams, had to penetrate a country full of "dark woods and rankling wilds," through which, owing to the

---

[4] In this account Cox stretches credulity almost to the point of breaking. But if we remember that he was only nineteen, that he had been in the wilderness country only a few months, and that his experience might have dismayed much more experienced persons than he, he can be, at least partially, forgiven. But there were certainly not as many wild animals and dangerous reptiles in the region as he imagined. For a similar experience and description of the region only twenty-five years afterward see Samuel Parker, *Journal of an Exploring Tour Beyond the Rocky Mountains* (Ithaca, Mack, Andrus, and Woodruff, 1842), 293.

[5] This animal was probably a coyote.

immense quantities of underwood, my progress was slow. My feet too were uncovered, and, from the thorns of the various prickly plants, were much lacerated, in consequence of which, on returning to my late bivouack, I was obliged to shorten the legs of my trowsers to procure bandages for them. The wolf did not make his appearance; but during the night I got occasional starts, from several of his brethren of the forest.

I anticipated the rising of the sun on the morning of the 23rd, and having been unsuccessful the two preceding days, determined to shape my course due north, and if possible not return again to the lake. During the day I skirted the wood, and fell on some old tracks, which revived my hopes a little. The country to the westward was chiefly plains covered with parched grass, and occasionally enlivened by savannahs of refreshing green, full of wild flowers and aromatic herbs, among which the bee and humming bird banqueted. I slept this evening by a small brook, where I collected cherries and haws enough to make a hearty supper. I was obliged to make farther encroachments on the legs of my trowsers for fresh bandages for my feet. During the night I was serenaded by music which did not resemble "a concord of most sweet sounds," in which the grumbling bass of the bears was at times drowned by the less pleasing sharps of the wolves. I partially covered my body this night with some pieces of pine bark which I stripped off a sapless tree.

The country through which I dragged my tired limbs on the 24th was thinly wooded. My course was north and north-east. I suffered much from want of water, having got during the day only two tepid and nauseous draughts from stagnant pools, which the long drought had nearly dried up. About sunset I arrived at a small stream,[6] by the side of which I took up my quarters for the night. The dew fell heavily; but I was too much fatigued to go in quest of bark to cover me; and even had I been so inclined, the howling of the wolves would have deterred me from making the dangerous attempt. There must have been an extraordinary nursery of these animals close to the spot; for between the weak, shrill cries of the young, and the more loud and dreadful howling of the old, I never expected to leave the place alive. I could not sleep. My only weapons of defence were a heap of stones and a stick. Ever and anon some more daring than others approached me. I presented the stick at them as if in the act of levelling a gun,

[6] Perhaps present Rock Creek.

upon which they retired, vented a few yells, advanced a little farther, and after surveying me for some time with their sharp, fiery eyes, to which the partial glimpses of the moon had imparted additional ferocity, retreated into the wood. In this state of fearful agitation I passed the night; but as day-light began to break, Nature asserted her supremacy, and I fell into a deep sleep, from which, to judge by the sun, I did not awake until between eight and nine o'clock on the morning of the 25th. My second bandages having been worn out, I was now obliged to bare my knees for fresh ones; and after tying them round my feet, and taking a copious draught from the adjoining brook for breakfast, I recommenced my joyless journey. My course was nearly north-north-east. I got no water during the day, nor any of the wild cherries. Some slight traces of men's feet, and a few old horse tracks occasionally crossed my path; they proved that human beings sometimes at least visited that part of the country, and for a moment served to cheer my drooping spirits.

About dusk an immense-sized wolf rushed out of a thick copse a short distance from the pathway, planted himself directly before me, in a threatening position, and appeared determined to dispute my passage. He was not more than twenty feet from me. My situation was desperate, and as I knew that the least symptom of fear would be the signal for attack, I presented my stick, and shouted as loud as my weak voice would permit. He appeared somewhat startled, and retreated a few steps, still keeping his piercing eyes firmly fixed on me. I advanced a little, when he commenced howling in a most appalling manner; and supposing his intention was to collect a few of his comrades to assist in making an afternoon repast on my half-famished carcass, I redoubled my cries, until I had almost lost the power of utterance, at the same time calling out various names, thinking I might make it appear I was not alone. An old and a young lynx ran close past me, but did not stop. The wolf remained about fifteen minutes in the same position; but whether my wild and fearful exclamations deterred any others from joining him, I cannot say. Finding at length my determination not to flinch, and that no assistance was likely to come, he retreated into the wood, and disappeared in the surrounding gloom.

The shades of night were now descending fast, when I came to a verdant spot surrounded by small trees, and full of rushes, which induced me to hope for water; but after searching for some time, I was still doomed to bitter disappointment. A shallow lake or pond had been there, which the long drought and heat had dried up. I then pulled a quantity of the rushes and spread them at the foot of a large stone, which I intended for my pillow; but as I was about throwing myself down, a rattlesnake coiled, with the head erect, and the forked tongue extended in a state of frightful oscillation, caught my eye immediately under the stone. I instantly retreated a short distance, but assuming fresh courage, soon dispatched it with my stick. On examining the spot more minutely, a large cluster of them appeared under the stone, the whole of which I rooted out and destroyed. This was hardly accomplished when upwards of a dozen snakes of different descriptions, chiefly dark brown, blue, and green, made their appearance. They were much quicker in their movements than their rattle-tailed brethren; and I could only kill a few of them.

This was a peculiarly soul-trying moment. I had tasted no fruit since the morning before, and after a painful day's march under a burning sun, could not procure a drop of water to allay my feverish thirst. I was surrounded by a murderous brood of serpents, and ferocious beasts of prey, and without even the consolation of knowing when such misery might have a probable termination. I might truly say with the royal psalmist that "the snares of death compassed me round about."

Having collected a fresh supply of rushes, which I spread some distance from the spot where I massacred the reptiles, I threw myself on them, and was permitted through divine goodness to enjoy a night of undisturbed repose.

I arose on the morning of the 26th considerably refreshed; and took a northerly course, occasionally diverging a little to the east. Several times during the day, I was induced to leave the path by the appearance of the rushes, which I imagined grew in the vicinity of lakes; but on reaching them my faint hopes vanished. There was no water, and I in vain essayed to extract a little moisture from them. Prickly thorns and small sharp stones added greatly to the pain of my tortured feet, and obliged me to make farther encroachments on my nether garments for fresh bandages. The want of water now rendered me extremely weak and feverish; and I had nearly abandoned all hopes of relief, when, about half-past four or five o'clock, the old pathway turned from the prairie grounds into a thickly wooded country, in an easterly direction; through which I had not advanced half a mile when I heard a noise resembling a waterfall, to which I hastened my tottering steps, and in a few minutes was delighted at arriving on the banks of a deep and narrow rivulet, which forced its way with great rapidity over some large stones that obstructed the channel.

After offering up a short prayer of thanksgiving for this providential supply, I threw myself into the water, forgetful of the extreme state of exhaustion to which I was reduced. It had nearly proved fatal, for my weak frame could not withstand the strength of the current, which forced me down a short distance, until I caught the bough of an overhanging tree, by means of which I regained the shore.[7] Here were plenty of hips[8] and cherries, on which, with the water, I made a most delicious repast. On looking about for a place to sleep, I observed lying on the ground the hollow trunk of a large pine, which had been destroyed by lightning. I retreated into the cavity, and having covered myself completely with large pieces of loose bark, quickly fell asleep. My repose was not of long duration; for at the end of about two hours, I was awakened by the growling of a bear, which had removed part of the bark covering and was leaning over me with his snout, hesitating as to the means he should adopt to dislodge me, the narrow limits of the trunk which confined my body preventing him from making the attack with advantage. I instantly sprung up, seized my stick, and uttered a loud cry, which startled him, and caused him to recede a few steps; when he stopped, and turned about apparently doubtful whether he would commence an attack. He determined on an assault; but feeling I had not sufficient strength to meet such an unequal enemy, I thought it prudent to retreat, and accordingly scrambled up an adjoining tree. My flight gave fresh impulse to his courage, and he commenced ascending after me. I succeeded however in gaining a branch, which gave me a decided advantage over him; and from which I was enabled to annoy his muzzle and claws in such a manner with my stick as effectually to check his progress. After scraping the bark some time with rage and disappointment, he gave up the task, and retired to my late dormitory, of which he took possession. The fear of falling off, in case I was overcome by sleep, induced me to make several attempts to descend; but each attempt aroused my ursine sentinel; and after many ineffectual efforts, I was obliged to remain there during the rest of the night.

[7] Probably Crab Creek, south of Reardan, Washington.
[8] The ripened fruit of the rosebush.

I fixed myself in that part of the trunk from which the principle grand branches forked, and which prevented me from falling during my fitful slumbers.

On the morning of the 27th, a little after sunrise, the bear quitted the trunk, shook himself, "cast a longing, lingering look" towards me, and slowly disappeared in search of his morning repast. After waiting some time, apprehensive of his return, I descended and resumed my journey through the woods in a north-north-east direction. In a few hours all my anxiety of the preceding night was more than compensated by falling in with a well-beaten horse-path,[9] with fresh traces on it, both of hoofs and human feet. It lay through a clear open wood, in a north-east course, in which I observed numbers of small deer. About six in the evening, I arrived at a spot where a party must have slept the preceding night.[10] Round the remains of a large fire which was still burning were scattered several half-picked bones of grouse, partridges and ducks, all of which I collected with economical industry. After devouring the flesh I broiled the bones. The whole scarcely sufficed to give me a moderate meal, but yet afforded a most seasonable relief to my famished body. I enjoyed a comfortable sleep this night close to the fire, uninterrupted by any nocturnal visitor. On the morning of the 28th I set off with cheerful spirits, fully impressed with the hope of a speedy termination to my sufferings. My course was northerly, and lay through a thick wood. Late in the evening I arrived at a stagnant pool, from which I merely moistened my lips, and having covered myself with some birch bark, slept by its side. The bears and wolves occasionally serenaded me during the night, but I did not see any of them. I rose early on the morning of the 29th, and followed the fresh traces all day through the wood, nearly north-east by north. I observed several deer, some of which came quite close to me; and in the evening I threw a stone at a small animal resembling a hare, the leg of which I broke. It ran away limping, but my feet were too sore to permit me to follow it. I passed the night by the side of a small stream, where I got a sufficient supply of hips and cherries. A few distant growls awoke me at intervals, but no animal appeared. On the 30th the path took a more easterly turn, and the woods became thicker and more gloomy. I had now nearly consumed the remnant

9 Cox had now struck the main trail.

10 Probably the camp of a party of Indians searching for Cox and near the site of Reardan.

of my trowsers in bandages for my wretched feet, and with the exception of my shirt, was almost naked. The horse-tracks every moment appeared more fresh, and fed my hopes. Late in the evening I arrived at a spot where the path branched off in different directions: one led up rather a steep hill, the other descended into a valley, and the tracks on both were equally recent. I took the higher; but after proceeding a few hundred paces through a deep wood, which appeared more dark from a thick foliage which shut out the rays of the sun, I returned apprehensive of not procuring water for my supper, and descended the lower path. I had not advanced far when I imagined I heard the neighing of a horse. I listened with breathless attention, and became convinced it was no illusion. A few paces farther brought me in sight of several of those noble animals sporting in a handsome meadow, from which I was separated by a rapid stream.[11] With some difficulty I crossed over, and ascended the opposite bank. One of the horses approached me; I thought him "the prince of palfreys; his neigh was like the bidding of a monarch, and his countenance enforced homage."

On advancing a short distance into the meadow the cheering sight of a small column of gracefully curling smoke announced my vicinity to human beings, and in a moment after two Indian women perceived me. They instantly fled to a hut which appeared at the farther end of the meadow. This movement made me doubt whether I had arrived among friends or enemies; but my apprehensions were quickly dissipated by the approach of two men, who came running to me in the most friendly manner. On seeing the lacerated state of my feet, they carried me in their arms to a comfortable dwelling covered with deerskins. To wash and dress my torn limbs, roast some roots, and boil a small salmon, seemed but the business of a moment. After returning thanks to that great and good Being, in whose hands are the issues of life and death, and who had watched over my wandering steps, and rescued me from the many perilous dangers I encountered, I sat down to my salmon, of which it is needless to say I made a hearty supper.

The family consisted of an elderly man, and his son, with their wives and children. I collected from their signs that they were aware of my being lost, and that they, with other Indians, and white men, had been out several days scouring the woods and plains in search of me. I also understood from them that our party had arrived at

[11] The two streams mentioned were possibly present Deep Creek and Coulee Creek.

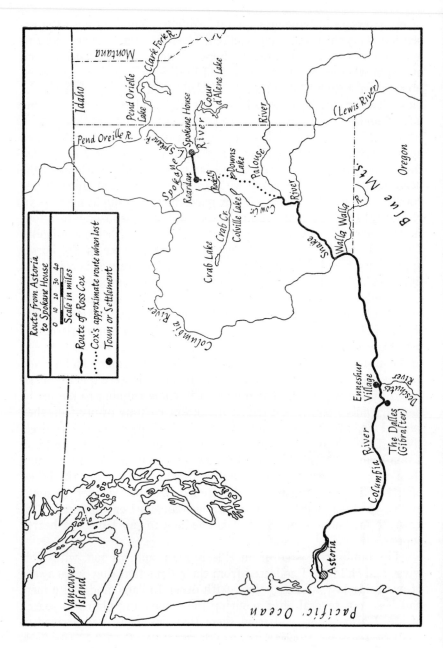

their destination, which was only a few hours' march from their habitation. They behaved to me with affectionate solicitude; and while the old woman was carefully dressing my feet, the men were endeavouring to make me comprehend their meaning. I had been fourteen days in a wilderness without holding "communion kind" with any human being; and I need not say I listened with a thousand times more real delight to the harsh and guttural voices of those poor Indians, than was ever experienced by the most enthusiastic admirer of melody from the thrilling tones of a Catalani, or the melting sweetness of a Stephens. As it was too late, after finishing my supper, to proceed farther that night, I retired to rest on a comfortable couch of buffalo and deer skins. I slept soundly; and the morning of the 31st was far advanced before I awoke. After breakfasting on the remainder of the salmon, I prepared to join my white friends. A considerable stream about ninety yards broad, called *Coeur d' Alene* River,[12] flowed close to the hut. The old man and his son accompanied me. We crossed the river in a canoe; after which they brought over three horses, and having enveloped my body in an Indian mantle of deer-skin, we mounted, and set off at a smart trot in an easterly direction. We had not proceeded more than seven miles when I felt the bad effects of having eaten so much salmon after so long a fast. I had a severe attack of indigestion, and for two hours suffered extreme agony; and, but for the great attention of the kind Indians, I think it would have proved fatal. About an hour after recommencing our journey we arrived in a clear wood, in which, with joy unutterable, I observed our Canadians at work hewing timber. I rode between the two natives. One of our men named François Gardepie, who had been on a trading excursion, joined us on horseback. My deerskin robe and sun-burnt features completely set his powers of recognition at defiance, and he addressed me as an Indian. I replied in French, by asking him how all our people were. Poor François appeared electrified, exclaimed *"Saint Vierge!"* and galloped into the wood, vociferating *"O mes amis! mes amis! il est trouvé!—Oui, oui, il est trouvé!"* *"Qui? qui?"* asked his comrades. *"Monsieur Cox! Monsieur Cox!"* replied François. *"Le voilà! le voilà!"* pointing towards me. Away went saws, hatchets, and axes, and each man rushed forward to the tents, where we had by this time arrived. It is needless to say that

12 This was the present Spokane River, about thirteen miles below the site of the fort.

our astonishment and delight at my miraculous escape were mutual. The friendly Indians were liberally rewarded; the men were allowed a holiday, and every countenance bore the smile of joy and happiness.

Chapter 9

After partaking of some refreshment we naturally reverted to the cause of my *égaremens*. It was easily explained. M'Lellan and I, as already mentioned, could only get one horse between us. On the morning of the 17th I had ridden from ten o'clock until twelve, at which hour we breakfasted. It was then M'Lennan's turn to mount. The party was divided into three divisions, and kept up rather a straggling march while in the plains. Every one had his own business to mind. Those who set off first thought I was with the second or third division; while they imagined I was with the first. In this manner they continued on for upwards of two hours, until it became my turn to ride, when M'Lennan, after galloping up and down the line of march, missed me. On communicating the intelligence to Mr. Clarke, he at once ordered the whole to stop, and sent the Indians with several men back in search of me. In the mean time I had recovered from my summer-house dream, and had crossed the track by which they returned, and by that means missed them. On comparing the places where we slept the first night, we could not have been more than three miles asunder; and although they fired shots repeatedly, I was not fortunate enough to hear any of them. The direction I took the second morning separated us farther; for they went north, and I nearly due east; and the two horsemen I saw on that evening were part of those who were scouring the country in quest of me. The arrangements made for my recovery were hastily adopted, badly carried into execution,

107

and too soon abandoned;[1] for after the third night, they imagined I had fallen a prey to the wolves, and continued on their course. On arriving at Spokan several other parties were sent out, but with what success it is needless to tell. From my youth, and consequent inexperience in the Indian country, the oldest *voyageurs* had given me up after the sixth day. A better knowledge of the productions of the soil would have enabled me to obtain other wild fruit and roots which, by contributing to my sustenance, would have greatly alleviated my sufferings; but my ignorance of such as were wholesome and nutricious prevented me from tasting any thing with which I had not been previously acquainted. On the day before my arrival, my clothes, &c., had been sold by auction; all of which were however returned by the purchasers. After a few days' rest and proper attention I became nearly renovated in health, and before the end of a fortnight every trace of my painful privations had disappeared.[2]

To such as may feel disposed to doubt the accuracy of the foregoing statement, I beg leave to say that Mr. Clarke, who then commanded the party, and who is now a member of the Hudson's Bay Company, and the other gentlemen who were with him, are still alive; and although they cannot vouch for the truth of each day's detail, they can for my absence and the extent of my sufferings, as evinced by my emaciated appearance on rejoining them. I can with truth assert that I have rather softened down than overcharged the statement, and therefore trust candid readers will acquit me of any intention to practise on their credulity. Mine, however, was not a solitary case; and the sceptical no doubt will be more surprised to learn that a few years prior to this occurrence a gentleman named Pritchard, who belonged to the North-West Company, while stationed in the neighbourhood of English River, on the east side of the mountains, lost himself, and was *thirty-five* days wandering through the woods before he was found! In some respects he was better off than I; for he was well clothed, and from his experience of the country had recourse to expedients to procure food of which I never should have thought. He supported himself for some time by setting traps for hares, a few of which he took in the Indian manner. He likewise made snares out

[1] This is a criticism of Mr. Clarke's handling of the affair, and it lends weight to Ross's explanation of how Cox came to be separated from the party.

[2] Alexander Ross says that Cox showed the effects of his ordeal for a considerable period. See *First Settlers*, 209.

of the hair of his head, with which he caught some small fish; and he also occasionally succeeded in killing a bird. These he was obliged to eat raw; and when all other resources failed, he was reduced to the necessity of eating grass, and a kind of moss, called by the Canadians *tripe de rocher*.[3] He was found by Indians close to a small stream, endeavouring to crawl on his hands and feet, in a state of utter helplessness and exhaustion; and for some days previous to his being discovered he had eaten nothing whatever. On being brought to the fort he quickly recovered his ordinary health, the possession of which, I am happy to say, he enjoys to the present moment.

The spot selected for forming our establishment was a handsome point of land, formed by the junction of the Pointed Heart and Spokan rivers,[4] thinly covered with pine and other trees, and close to a trading post of the North-West Company, under the command of a Mr. M'Millan,[5] one of their clerks, who had ten men with him. He had two other posts detached from this: one about 240 miles from it, in a north-easterly direction, among a tribe called the Flat-heads,[6] whose lands lie at the feet of the Rocky Mountains, and are well stocked with buffaloes; the other about 200 miles, nearly due north, among a tribe called the Cootonais,[7] in whose country there are plenty of beavers, deer, mountain sheep, and, at times, buffaloes. Mr. Finan M'Donald[8] of the North-West Company had charge of the post among

[3] *Tripe de roche* was "a name originally given in Canada to various edible lichens of the genera *Gyrophora* and *Umbilicaria,* which afford a slightly nutritious but bitter and purgative food." See *OED.*

[4] This post was located near the confluence of the Spokane and Little Spokane rivers.

[5] James McMillan (d. 1858) was born in Scotland and entered the service of the North West Company before 1804, at which time he was a clerk at Fort des Prairies. He was one of the pioneers of the fur trade in the interior of the Pacific Northwest. See Wallace, *Documents,* 482–83.

[6] The territory occupied by this tribe extended from the upper waters of the Columbia to the northwestern tributaries of the Missouri. See Franchère, *Narrative,* 340, n. 145.

[7] The present spelling is *Kootenai* among the Americans, *Kootenay* among the British. The North West Company built Fort Kootenay a few miles upstream on the river of that name above present Libby, Montana, and almost opposite the site of Jennings. In 1812, the Pacific Fur Company erected another post near by. See T. C. Elliott, "The Fur Trade in the Columbia Basin Prior to 1811," *Oregon Historical Quarterly,* Vol. XV, p. 245.

[8] Finan McDonald (1782–1851) was born in Scotland, entered the North West Company's service in 1804, and was with David Thompson on the Columbia River from 1807 to 1812. He married a woman of the Spokane tribe. In 1827, he retired after spending most of his life as a trader on the Columbia. See Cox's account of him in Chapter XV; Wallace, *Documents,* 463; and J. A. Myers, "Finan McDonald," *Wash-*

the Flat-heads; and a Mr. Montour[9] was stationed among the Coot-onais. Mr. Pillet was dispatched with six men to oppose the latter; and Farnham and I were destined for the Flat-heads. Owing to the length of time our men were detained at Spokan to assist in cutting down timber for the fort, we did not set out until the 17th of October. We had twelve men and fourteen loaded horses. On leaving Spokan our course for four days was north-east, and lay through a handsome open country well watered, and bounded by hills rather thickly wooded. On the evening of the 20th we encamped on the banks of a fine river, which rises in the Rocky Mountains, flows through the lands of the Flat-heads, Pointed Heart, Spokan and Chaudière[10] Indians, and falls into the Columbia about nine hundred miles from the sea. Its general course is westerly, and it is commonly called the Flat-head River.[11] The part at which we had arrived was about four hundred yards wide, with an easy current. As this was the spot for crossing to proceed to the Flat-head country, we had to construct rafts for that purpose; which being prepared on the 21st, we crossed over, and passed all our goods and horses in safety, with the exception of one of the latter, which was drowned by the awkwardness of the man who held the reins. The day after, the weather set in very cold, accompanied by snow, which continued almost incessantly for fourteen days.[12] During this period our route lay nearly due east through thick woods of lofty pine and cedar. The horses suffered dreadfully from the want of grass, the deep snow having completely covered the ground, and their only nourishment was obtained by plucking and chewing the branches of the adjoining trees. A detail of each day's proceedings would be a cold and unnecessary repetition. We rose

---

ington Historical Quarterly, Vol. XIII, pp. 196–208. Dale L. Morgan aptly characterizes him as "having somewhat the aspect of a prophet who had missed his calling," in *Jedediah Smith and the Opening of the West* (Indianapolis, Bobbs-Merrill, 1953), 122.

[9] There were two men of this name of whom this is the younger. The father was an early Indian trader who in 1784 became a partner in the North West Company, with two of the sixteen shares. He left a half-blood son, Nicolas Montour, who was a clerk at Fort des Prairies in 1804–1806, was in the Kootenay district in 1813, and was discharged by Governor Simpson in 1823 on the Saskatchewan. He is the one who fought the bloodless duel with Mr. Pillett.

[10] These were the Kettle Falls Indians, today known as the Colvilles.

[11] What Cox calls the Flathead River is today's Clarks Fork of the Columbia. The present Flathead River, which rises in the lake of the same name, is a tributary of the Clarks Fork.

[12] This would have been an extremely early snow.

each morning at day-break, loaded the horses, travelled two or three hours, when we stopped for breakfast, waited an hour for this meal, and then continued on until four or five o'clock in the evening, when we stopped for the night. The path was narrow, and the trees covered with snow, which, from the loaded horses constantly coming in collision with the branches on either side, fell down at every moment in immense masses, annoyed us considerably, and greatly impeded our progress. Where the pine predominated, the under-growth was so thick that we could not obtain sufficient space for our tent; but where the cedar prevailed, we occasionally were enabled to pitch it. This cheerless and gloomy march continued for fourteen days, during which period we seldom had a dry article of clothing on us.

On the 4th of November we cleared the woods, and arrived in a large meadow of prime grass, in which we immediately pitched our tent, and remained for three days to refresh the horses. Our principal subsistence while in the woods was horse-flesh and boiled rice; but here our hunters supplied us with some of the Rocky Mountain sheep called big-horns,[13] the flesh of which is delicious, and resembles in taste Welch mutton, but at this season is more delicate. From the time we quitted Spokan we had not seen a native. On the 7th we recommenced our journey eastward; the weather became more moderate, and the recent snows quickly vanished from the surrounding trees. For three days and a half our progress was through undulating meadows, thinly wooded, in which our hunters killed some deer. On the 10th we came to a small village of the Flat-head nation, chiefly consisting of old men, women, and children. We were quite charmed with their frank and hospitable reception, and their superiority in cleanliness over any of the tribes we had hitherto seen. Their lodges were conical, but very spacious, and were formed by a number of buffalo and moose skins thrown over long poles in such a manner as to keep them quite dry. The fire was placed in the centre, and the ground all around it was covered with mats and clean skins free from the vermin we felt so annoying at the lower parts of the Columbia. They had a quantity of dried buffalo, of which we purchased a good deal; and as they gave us to understand that the great body of their tribe were in the mountains hunting, we determined to stop here, and accordingly set about constructing a log-house. The cold now became more severe, and the snow began again to fall heavily, which induced the

[13] These animals were common in both the Cascade and Coast ranges in those years.

111

men to work hard; and before three weeks we had erected the frame of a good substantial building, which in another week was roofed in, and afforded a welcome shelter to the poor fellows whose only covering was their blankets.

While the house was being built many of the tribe arrived, from whom we purchased a number of beaver skins. Their hunt had been rather unsuccessful, and attended with disastrous results; for they informed us, that after killing buffalo sufficient for the winter, they were surprised by their old enemies the Black-feet Indians (whose lands lie on the east side of the Rocky Mountains), who killed several of their warriors, and took many prisoners. They appeared much dejected at their misfortunes; and one of the chiefs seemed to lament the loss of his wife, who had been captured with some other women by the enemy. Part of the tribe pitched their tents some distance above us at the north-west establishment.[14] They were passionately fond of tobacco, and while they remained with us never ceased smoking. Having bought all their skins, and given them credit for some articles until the spring, the greater part of them set off to make their winter's hunt, which their recent misfortunes had protracted to a very late period. When the house was finished I got a good canoe built of cedar planks in which I embarked with six men, and taking leave of Farnham, on the 18th of December descended the Flat-head River

---

[14] There is something peculiar and mysterious about this whole episode. Ross says that when he was at Spokane in the winter, from December 6 through December 9, when Cox was supposedly absent, he found that Cox was there and still showed the effects of his ordeal. See *First Settlers*, 201, 209. He also says that Farnham was sent to trade among the Flatheads, that he crossed the Rocky Mountains with them to the headwaters of the Missouri River, saw much of the country, and made a good trade. See *First Settlers*, 210–11. But he makes no mention of Cox's having been with him. Saleesh House had been established near present Thompson Falls, Montana, in 1809, by David Thompson, who had also established Kullyspell House at Sheepherder's Point on Lake Pend Oreille, near the present town of Hope, Idaho. Finan McDonald was Thompson's assistant, and, while he was in charge of both posts at different times, he was probably at Saleesh House in the winter of 1812. Cox makes no mention of the post on the lake, nor does he give any name to the fort or station that he and Farnham are supposed to have constructed. There is some evidence that there may have been an early trading post, and a large Indian village, near the site of present Noxon, Montana, which just about fits Cox's description. Cox may have made such a trip, or he may have been attempting to assume to himself an importance that he did not possess. See T. C. Elliott, "The Fur Trade in the Columbia Basin Prior to 1811," *Oregon Historical Quarterly,* Vol. XV, p. 245; and M. Catherine White, "Saleesh House, the First Trading Post Among the Flathead," *Pacific Northwest Quarterly,* Vol. XXXIII, pp. 251–63.

on my return to Spokan. Our progress was slow and full of danger, from the great number of rapids, and the force of the current. The land on each side was high, and the banks in some places so precipitous, that for three nights we could not find room enough to make our beds on shore, and were constrained to sleep in a standing position, rolled up in our cloaks and blankets, leaving the canoe in the water, fastened to poles driven some distance into the ground. On the 25th we arrived at a place where the river forked into four or five small channels, which afterwards united and formed a lake about five miles long, and two broad. We took the centre channel; but it was full of snags, which broke several of the ribs of our canoe, and we were forced to land on a marshy island, full of small willows, and without a bit of dry wood to make a fire. This was a horrible situation; and the state of our canoe prevented us from proceeding to the main land; so that we had no alternative but, seated on fallen trees and covered with our blankets, to pass the night in water up to our ancles. About midnight it commenced snowing, which continued until morning. I thought of my preceding Christmas off Cape Horn, and was puzzled to decide which was the most enviable—a tempestuous storm in the high southern latitudes, after losing a couple of men—or a half-inundated island, without fire, at the foot of the rocky mountains covered with sheets of snow. In my slumbers I imagined I was sitting at my father's table surrounded by the smiling domestic group, all anxious to partake of a smoking sirloin, and a richly dotted plumb-pudding, while the juvenile members recounted to each other with triumphant joy the amount of their Christmas boxes; but, alas!

Sorrow returned with the dawning of morn,
And the voice in my dreaming ear melted away.

The 26th opened on us with snow-clad mountains and forests. With much difficulty we succeeded in patching our battered canoe sufficiently tight to bring us to *terra firma*, where we struck up a fire of pine, spruce, and cedar, that would have roasted a solid square of oxen. We remained here all the day, and repaired the canoe, so as to enable us to proceed on the 27th. The day after, we reached the place at which we crossed on our way upwards. Here we left the canoe, set off by land on foot, and reached Spokan in time to partake of the new year's festivities. During my absence Mr. Clarke had constructed a snug and commodious dwelling-house, containing four rooms and a kitchen, together with a comfortable house for the men, and a capacious store for the furs and trading goods, the whole surrounded by paling, and flanked by two bastions with loop-holes for musketry. I passed the remainder of the winter at this place; and between hunting, fishing, reading, &c., we contrived to spend the time agreeably enough. We lived principally on deer, trout, and carp, and occasionally killed a fat horse, as a substitute for beef. Custom had now so far reconciled us to the flesh of this animal, that we often preferred it to what in Europe might be regarded as luxuries. Foals or colts are not good, although a few of our men preferred them. A horse for the table should not be under three years or above seven. The flesh of those which are tame, well-fed, and occasionally worked, is tender and firm, and the fat hard and white. It is far superior to the wild horse, the flesh of which is loose and stringy, and the fat yellow and rather oily. We generally killed the former for our own table; and I can assure my readers, that if they sat down to a fat rib, or a rump-steak off a well-fed four-year-old, without knowing the animal, they would imagine themselves regaling on a piece of prime ox beef. In February we took immense quantities of carp in Spokan River above its junction with the Pointed Heart, and in a few weeks after the trout came in great abundance.

The Spokans we found to be a quiet, honest, inoffensive tribe; and although we had fortified our establishment in the manner above mentioned, we seldom closed the gates at night. Their country did not abound in furs, and they were rather indolent in hunting. Their chief, *Illimspokanee,* or the Son of the Sun, was a harmless old man, who spent a great portion of his time between us and Mr. M'Millan. We entered into a compact with that gentleman to abstain from giving the Indians any spirituous liquors, to which both parties strictly adhered. Mr. Clarke, who was an old trader himself, had often witnessed the baneful effects of giving ardent spirits to Indians, while he was in the service of the North-West Company, at all whose establishments on the east side of the Rocky Mountains it was an almost invariable custom. When in a state of intoxication, it is quite impossible to check their savage propensities, and murder frequently is the consequence; a remarkable instance of which I subsequently witnessed in my journey across the continent. By this arrangement both parties saved themselves much trouble and expense, and kept the poor natives in a state of blissful ignorance. In other respects also we agreed very

well with our opponent, and neither party evinced any of the turbulent or lawless spirit, which gave so ferocious an aspect to the opposition of the rival companies on the east side of the mountains. The
great object of every Indian was to obtain a gun. Now a good gun
was not to be had under twenty beaver skins; a few short ones we
gave for fifteen; and some idea of the profit may be formed, when
I state that the wholesale price of a gun is about one pound seven
shillings, while the average value of twenty beaver skins is about
twenty-five pounds! Two yards of cloth, which originally cost twelve
shillings, would generally bring six or eight beavers, value eight or
ten pounds! and so on in proportion for other articles. But they were
satisfied, and we had no cause to complain. The Spokans are far
superior to the Indians of the coast in cleanliness, but by no means
equal in this respect to the Flat-heads. The women are good wives,
and most affectionate mothers: the old, cheerful and complete slaves
to their families; the young, lively and confiding; and whether married or single, free from the vice of incontinence. Their village was
situated at the point formed by the junction of the two rivers. Some
houses were oblong, others conical, and were covered with mats or
skins, according to the wealth of the proprietor. Their chief riches are
their horses, which they generally obtain in barter from the Nez
Percés, in return for the goods they obtain from us for their furs.
Each man is therefore the founder of his own fortune, and their riches
or poverty are generally proportioned to their activity or indolence.
The vice of gambling, however, is prevalent among them, and some
are such slaves to it, that they frequently lose all their horses. The
spot where

The rude forefathers of the hamlet sleep

is about midway between the village and the fort, and has rather a
picturesque effect at a distance. When a man dies, several horses are
killed, and the skins attached to the end of long poles, which are
planted in the graves; the number of horses sacrificed is proportioned
to the wealth of the individual. Besides the horse-skins, buffalo and
deer robes, leather shirts, blankets, pieces of blue, green, and scarlet
cloth, strips of calico, moccasins, provisions, warlike weapons, &c.,
are placed in and about the cemetery; all of which they imagine will
be more or less necessary for the deceased in the world of spirits. As
their lands are much infested by wolves, which destroy the foals, they

115

cannot rear horses in such numbers as the Nez Percés, from whom they are obliged to purchase them annually. They never kill any for their own use, but felt no repugnance to eat the flesh at our place. As I may hereafter have occasion to speak more of this tribe, I shall for the present revert to the continuation of our proceedings. In the beginning of May, Messrs. Farnham and Pillet returned from their wintering posts. Their success exceeded our expectations. Both Flatheads and Cootonais made excellent winter hunts, and returned in the spring loaded with beaver. Mr. Pillet fought a duel with Mr. Montour of the North-West, with pocket pistols, at six paces, both hits: one, in the collar of the coat, and the other in the leg of the trowsers. Two of their men acted as seconds, and the tailor speedily healed their wounds.

Chapter 10

Execution of an Indian for robbery—War between Great Britain and the United States—Dissolution of the Pacific Fur Company—Author joins the North-West Company, and proceeds to the Rocky Mountains—Meets a party, and returns to the sea—Robbery of goods, and successful stratagem to recover the property—Attack at night—Dog-eating—Author and three men pursued by Indians—Narrow escape

The different parties having now assembled at Spokan House, we took our departure from that establishment on the 25th of May, on our return to Astoria with the produce of our winter's trade. Mr. Pillet was left in charge of the fort with four men. We had twenty-eight loaded horses, and on the 30th of May reached the entrance of the creek off Lewis' River, where we had left our barge and canoes.

In the course of this journey we passed some of the places at which I had slept during my wanderings in the preceding August. I pointed out to my fellow-travellers several heaps of stones which I had piled together, and on which I had scratched my name.

We were detained a couple of days at the entrance of the creek, to repair the barge and canoes, in consequence of the Indians having taken a quantity of nails out of the former. Our tents were pitched close to the village, and not suspecting any dishonesty on the part of the natives, we kept no watch the first night. Our confidence, however, was misplaced, for in the morning we discovered that a daring robbery had been committed during the night. In the tent in which Mr. Clarke slept he kept a large *garde-vin*, which he had locked on retiring to rest, but the key of which he had omitted to take out. The tent was closely fastened, and while he was asleep, the strings were untied, the *garde-vin* opened, and a valuable silver goblet stolen thereout! Several loose articles were also taken, and bundles belonging to many of the men were carried away. Mr. Clarke immediately assembled

117

the principal Indians, told them of the robbery, declared if the property were returned, he would pardon the offender, but added, if it were not, and that he should find the thief, he would hang him. The chief, with several others, promised they would use their best exertions to discover the delinquent and bring back the property; but the day passed over without tidings of either. On the second night (the 31st), two sentinels were placed at each end of the camp with orders to conceal themselves and keep a sharp look-out. Shortly after midnight they observed the figure of a man creeping slowly out of one of the tents, and carrying with him a bundle of clothes, a powder horn, &c. They silently watched his progress, until they saw him in the act of jumping into a small canoe which he had in the creek, upon which they sprung forward, stopped the canoe, and seized him. We were instantly alarmed; and a general search taking place, a quantity of articles belonging to the men were missed, together with a pistol of Farnham's and a dagger of mine, all of which were stolen that night. Most of the property was found in the canoe; but he refused to give any account of the remainder. We had not the slightest suspicion of this man, who had been remarkably well treated by us; in consequence of which, and the aggravated nature of the robbery, Mr. Clarke determined to put his threat into execution. He accordingly ordered a temporary gallows to be erected, and had the arms and legs of the culprit pinioned. About eight o'clock in the morning of the 1st of June he assembled the chief and all the Indians of the village, and made a short speech, in which he told them that the prisoner had abused his confidence, violated the rights of hospitality, and committed an offence for which he ought to suffer death; that from an anxiety to keep on good terms with all their nation, he had overlooked many thefts committed while he had been there last August; which lenity, he was sorry to say, had only led to more daring acts of robbery, and that as a terror to others, and in order to show that it was not fear that prevented him for taking an earlier notice of such aggressions, he had now resolved that this robber should be hanged. The Indians acquiesced in this decision; and the chief declared that the prisoner did not belong to their tribe, but was a kind of outlaw, of whom they were all afraid. The gallows being now prepared, Mr. Clarke gave the signal, and after great resistance, during which he screamed in the most frightful manner, the wretched criminal was launched into eternity. His countrymen looked on the whole proceeding with the greatest unconcern; but the unfortunate being himself exhibited none of that wonderful self-command, or stoical indifference to death, which we observed in others, and for which Indians in general are so celebrated.[1] By the time it was supposed life was extinct, Mr. M'Lennan with three men set off with the horses on his return to Spokan, and we embarked in the canoes. The current was swift, and we arrived early the following day at the mouth of Lewis' River, a little below which we found the parties of Messrs. Mackenzie and Stuart, where we had appointed to meet them on our separation the preceding autumn. From this place we proceeded together, and arrived at Astoria on the 11th of June, 1813, without incurring any material accident. We found all our friends in good health; but a total revolution had taken place in the affairs of the Company. Messrs. John George M'Tavish[2] and Joseph La Rocque,[3] of the North-West Company, with two canoes and sixteen men, had arrived a few days before us.[4] From these gentlemen we learned for the first time, that war had been declared the year before between Great Britain and the United States,[5] and that in consequence of the strict blockade of the American ports by British cruisers, no vessel would venture to proceed to our remote establishment during the continuation of hostilities, added to which, a trading vessel which had touched at the Columbia in the early part of the spring,[6] had informed our people that the ship *Beaver* was blocked up in Canton.

[1] Alexander Ross gives a somewhat different account of this incident and of the Indian reaction to it. See *First Settlers*, 213. Mr. Farnham apparently acted as the executioner. See Stella M. Drumm, "More About Astorians," *Oregon Historical Quarterly*, Vol. XXIV, p. 344.

[2] John George McTavish (d. 1847) entered the North West Company's service in 1798. He was in the Athabaska district in 1808, and in 1813, the same year that he negotiated the purchase of Astoria, he was admitted to partnership in the company. Wallace, *Documents*, 485.

[3] Joseph Larocque (1787–1866) had entered the fur trade in 1801, and after serving on Churchill River, he had been transferred to the Columbia. See Wallace, *Documents*, 460. His knowledge of Indian languages, character, and customs made his services of especial value. He retired in 1833 with a considerable fortune, which he devoted to religious and charitable works. See Franchère, *Narrative*, 282 n.

[4] According to Franchère, McTavish and Larocque had arrived on the eleventh of April. See *Narrative*, 287.

[5] McKenzie arrived at Astoria on January 15, 1813, with the news of the outbreak of war, which he had learned at Spokane House from McTavish. Since Cox was at Spokane, why did he have to wait until he got to Astoria to hear the news?

[6] There was no trading vessel there that spring. This news was brought by Hunt when he arrived in August on board the *Albatross*.

These unlucky and unexpected circumstances, joined to the impossibility of sustaining ourselves another year in the country without fresh supplies, which, in the then posture of affairs, it would be hopeless to expect, induced our proprietory to enter into negociations with Mr. M'Tavish, who had been authorised by the North-West Company to treat with them.[7] In a few weeks an amicable arrangement was made, by which Mr. M'Tavish agreed to purchase all the furs, merchandise, provisions, &c., of our Company at a certain valuation, stipulating to provide a safe passage back to the United States, either by sea, or across the continent, for such members of it as chose to return; and at the same time offering to those who should wish to join the North-West Company and remain in the country, the same terms as if they had originally been members of that Company. Messrs. Ross, M'Lennan, and I took advantage of these liberal proposals, and some time after Mr. Duncan M'Dougall,[8] one of the directors, also joined the North-West. The Americans of course preferred returning to their own country, as did also Mr. Gabriel Franchère,[9] and a few other Canadian clerks.

The pleasure I experienced in joining an establishment, every member of which was a fellow-subject, was mingled with deep regret at parting from so many of my late associates, for some of whom I entertained a sincere regard, a regard which I feel pleasure in saying was mutual, and which the difference of country could not diminish. My friends Clapp, Halsey, and Matthews were genuine Americans of the Washingtonian school, and consequently untinctured by any of the unnatural and acrimonious hatred to the land of their forefathers

[7] According to Ross, McTavish reached Astoria the second time on October 7, and the details of the sale were finally worked out on the sixteenth, although Franchère gives the latter date as the twenty-third. The final agreement was not signed until the twelfth of November, and then only after an ultimatum from McDougall, which had been resorted to at McKenzie's suggestion. See Franchère, *Narrative*, 296; and Ross, *First Settlers*, 245–46.

[8] Since the sale was unnecessary, Duncan McDougall has been accused of betraying the interests of his employer. See Franchère, *Narrative*, 296, 405. Ross, however, defends McDougall's action. See *First Settlers*, 262. In view of all the circumstances, it is difficult to see how McDougall could have acted otherwise.

[9] From this gentleman's knowledge of the Chinook language Mr. M'Tavish made him handsome offers to join the North-West Company, which he refused. He however remained until the following spring.—R. C.

Franchère did remain until the following spring, which was only long enough to permit him to join the spring express for Montreal. In addition to Cox and Ross, Thomas McKay, Donald McLennan, Ovide de Montigny, and William Matthews, an American, joined the North West Company. McGillis, Pillett, and Wallace, in addition to Franchère, did not join.

which among a large portion of their countrymen was so prevalent at that angry period. And though the sanguine hopes they had entertained of realising in a few years an independence were destroyed by the war, I feel pleasure in being able to add, that they are now happily flourishing in their native country.

As Mr. M'Tavish expected dispatches overland from the directors at Montreal, and as it was necessary to acquaint the gentlemen inland with the change that affairs had taken at Astoria, Mr. La Rocque and I proceeded with two canoes and sixteen men well armed to the interior, with orders to leave letters at Oakinagan and Spokan, explanatory of these circumstances, and thence continue on across the Rocky Mountains to Fort William (the great central depôt at the head of Lake Superior), unless we met an express, in which case we were to return to the sea. We left Astoria on the 5th of July, and having no lading in our canoes, except provisions, we passed in safety the hostile Indians at the great rapids and falls. They were very numerous at the latter place; but seeing our men well armed, and our canoes empty, they had no idea of risking their lives, when no plunder could be obtained. As I shall have occasion hereafter to give a particular description of the country about the upper parts of the Columbia, I shall now merely mention that we passed the navigable part of it, and reached the place where one of its sources issues out of the Rocky Mountains[10] on the 2nd of September, after a tedious and laborious voyage of two months, against a strong current. We laid up our canoe, and were preparing to set out on foot, when we were agreeably surprised by the arrival of Messrs. John Stuart,[11] Alexander Stewart,[12]

[10] This was Canoe River. About a mile upstream from its confluence with the Columbia was Boat Encampment, where the traders regularly left their canoes before starting the journey overland.

[11] John Stuart (1779–1847) was born in Scotland and entered the service of the North West Company in 1799. In 1809, he accompanied Simon Fraser on the expedition in which the latter's party discovered the Fraser River and followed it to the Pacific. In this same year he was placed in charge of the New Caledonia district, and in 1813, he became a partner. In 1821, he became a chief factor in the Hudson's Bay Company. See Wallace, *Documents,* 500.

[12] Alexander Stewart (d. 1840) became an employee of the North West Company in 1796, and in 1813, when he became a partner, he was sent to the Columbia district, where he was present at the sale of Astoria. His name is often misspelled *Stuart.* It is significant that Cox makes no mention of Alexander Henry, the younger, who accompanied Stewart on his trip from Montreal to Astoria. They arrived at the latter place on November 15, 1813. See Wallace, *Documents,* 499; Franchère, *Narrative,* 298; and *Henry-Thompson Journals,* II, 747. Neither of the latter mentions such a trip to the interior by Cox, and it may be that he was merely romancing.

and Joseph M'Gillivray,[13] partners of the North-West Company, who with twenty men were on their way to Astoria, armed with full powers to join Mr. M'Tavish, in purchasing the stock of the American Company. They acquainted us that the North-West Company's ship called the *Isaac Tod* sailed from London, under the convoy of a sloop of war for the Columbia, and would arrive early in the autumn, with a large cargo for the Indian trade. These gentlemen brought several newspapers; and having heard nothing from the civilised world for two years, we devoured their contents. Mr. M'Gillivray had served the preceding campaign in the American war as a lieutenant in the Canadian chasseurs, a corps commanded by his father, the Hon. William M'Gillivray, and composed chiefly of the gentlemen and *voyageurs* of the North-West Company. He had been engaged in several smart affairs with the enemy, and was at the taking of Michilimacinac, at which and other places, he had considerably distinguished himself. He was therefore our great chronicler of recent events, and during our passage downwards our thousand and one interrogatories seldom allowed his tongue half an hour's rest. None but those who have been so long debarred from the passing scenes of the great world can form an idea of the greedy voracity with which exiles so circumstanced swallow the most trifling news. A remnant of a newspaper is invaluable; and even an auctioneer's advertisement, or a quack-doctor's puff, is read with interest.

We reached Astoria on the 11th of October, having travelled from the 5th of July upwards of two thousand three hundred miles. We remained here till the latter end of the month in the expectation of seeing the *Isaac Tod;* as that vessel did not arrive, the proprietors determined to send a strong party to the interior with a supply of such goods as the fort could furnish for the winter's trade. The necessary arrangements being completed, we set off on the 29th of October. Our party consisted of Messrs. John Stuart, Donald Mackenzie, Joseph M'Gillivray, La Rocque, M'Donald, Read, and the author, with fifty-five men. On arriving at the first rapids few Indians made their appearance; and from their peaceable demeanour, we did not think it necessary to observe our usual caution in guarding the portages.

[13] Joseph McGillivray (1790–1832) was the son of the Honorable William McGillivray. In 1813, he became a partner in the North West Company, and from that year on he was in charge of Fort Okanogan. In 1821, he became a chief trader and seven years later was transferred to New Caledonia. He retired from the fur trade in 1831. See Wallace, *Documents,* 470.

We passed the first unmolested, and had carried about one-third of the goods over the second, when we were alarmed by a loud cry, and immediately after one of the men appeared, and stated that he and another man had been attacked by a large party of the natives, who had knocked them down, and robbed them of two bales of dry goods, with which they made off into the woods, and that he feared others of the men would also be attacked. Orders were immediately dispatched to Messrs. La Rocque and M'Gillivray, who were at the foot of the portage, to advance with a few of their men, while Mr. John Stuart and I, with ten men, proceeded from the upper end. Mr. M'Donald remained in charge at one end, and Mr. Donald Mackenzie at the other.

On arriving about the middle of the portage, where the village was situated, we found the pathway guarded by fifty or sixty Indians, with their war-shirts on, and fully armed, apparently determined to dispute the passage. The moment they perceived our approach they placed their arrows in their bows, which they presented at us, at the same time jumping like kangaroos backwards and forwards, and from right to left, in such a manner as to render it almost impossible to take a steady aim at any of them. In our hurry we had not time to put on our leathern armour, and from the hostile appearance of the savages, some of our men declared they would not advance a step farther. Mr. Stuart shortly addressed them, pointing out the dangerous situation in which we were placed, between two portages; that if the enemy observed the least symptom of fear, they would become the assailants, in which case we could neither advance nor retreat, and must ultimately be cut off, adding at the same time he would do every thing in his power to avoid coming to extremities; but that, above all things, it was absolutely necessary to show them the most determined front. The men hereupon consented to fight. He then informed the Indians that he did not wish to fight—but that if the stolen goods were not returned, the white men would destroy their village and take all their property. We were imperfectly acquainted with their language, and they either did not, or affected not to understand the meaning of his address; for they still continued their kangaroo movements with their arrows presented, preserving at the same time the strictest silence. We were somewhat puzzled at this conduct; but as we were anxious to avoid bloodshed, and at the same time to recover the stolen property, Mr. Stuart judged it prudent to wait the arrival of the other party. In a few seconds Messrs. La Rocque and M'Gillivray with their men appeared at the rear of the Indians, who were thus placed between two fires; but they had the sagacity to perceive that we could not act on the offensive without endangering our own lives. About one half of them therefore quickly turned round, and by this movement presented a hostile front to each of our small parties. During this time none of their old men, women, or children, made their appearance; and as Mr. Stuart supposed they had been conveyed from the village, he requested Mr. La Rocque to advance with a few of his men into the wood on his right, and at the same time sent me with five of our party to the left, ordering each of us to seize all men, women, and children, we could find, for the purpose of detaining them as hostages until the property should be returned. Messrs. Stuart and M'Gillivray, with the remainder of the men, still kept possession of the pathway in front and rear of the village, and the enemy for some time were ignorant of the *ruse de guerre* we had adopted. I proceeded about forty yards in an oblique direction to the left, with my party, when we imagined we heard voices before us. We therefore advanced slowly and cautiously a few paces farther, until we arrived at a large rock. I sent three men round one end of it, and proceeded myself with the remaining two round the other; and, as we turned the left corner, we perceived three old men, with several women and children, sitting round a fire, some of whom were sharpening iron and flint heads for arrows, which, after being heated in the fire, were dipped into a wooden bowl containing a thick blackish liquid. On observing us they attempted to escape, when the other three men appeared. We instantly seized their armoury, and took two of the old men, three women, and some children prisoners. They were much frightened, and thought we would put them to death, but on our explaining that they would sustain no injury if our goods were returned, they appeared more tranquil, and came with us quietly until we reached Mr. Stuart, who was still in the same situation. La Rocque was equally fortunate, and had captured one old man, four women, and five children, on his side of the wood, with whom he had just appeared in sight as my party arrived.

The warriors were quite staggered at finding we had made so many prisoners, and fearing we might follow their own mode, which was either to kill them or make them slaves, they at once laid down their arms, and offered to go in search of the bales, provided we would liberate the prisoners. Mr. Stuart replied that none of them would be injured, but that they should remain in custody until the property was restored and our people safely over the portage. A guard was then stationed over the prisoners, and word was sent to M'Donald to order his men to recommence the carriage of the goods, during the progress of which we kept up a chain of sentinels *en route*. By the time we had nearly finished, three of the Indians, whose wives were captives, brought a great part of the contents of the bales, which they alleged they took by force from the thieves, who had cut open the envelopes and concealed the remainder; and they therefore hoped we would allow their relations to return home. Mr. Stuart told them he was determined not to allow one of them to stir until every article that had been stolen was brought back. The eldest of the three declared that it was very unjust of the white men to punish him and his relations for the dishonesty of others, and that when he expected a reward for his exertions in bringing back so much property, he found his wife and children were to be detained as slaves. All this appeared very plausible; but we recognized this very fellow as one of the most prominent and active of the armed band, and apparently their leader.

He made some farther remonstrances to the same effect; but finding we were inflexible, he went away with his two companions, and in about half an hour after returned, accompanied by several others, with the remainder of the stolen property. They alleged the thieves had run away, and on asking them for their chief, they said he was absent. The canoes having been now laden, Mr. Stuart told them that he should release their friends and relations for this time, but that if another attempt was ever made, the white people would punish them severely; and as a mark of his anger at their late conduct, he would not then give them the usual gratuity of tobacco. The prisoners were then released, and we pushed off. As it was rather late we could not advance more than three miles, when we encamped in a small cove on the left side, behind which was a thick wood of hazel, beech, and pine. We had a large fire at the end of the camp; and the party was divided into two watches. The forepart of the night passed off quietly; but about two o'clock in the morning we were alarmed by one of the flank sentinels being brought to the centre wounded. He stated that he and two of his comrades had approached the fire for the purpose of lighting their pipes, when several arrows were discharged at them from the wood, one of which wounded him in the left arm, upon hearing which Messrs. La Rocque and M'Donald, who commanded the watch, fired into the wood. The tents were immediately struck, and the men ordered to withdraw from the fires and concentrate themselves behind the canoes. About ten minutes afterwards a shower of arrows was discharged from the same place, followed by loud yells; but some passed over our heads, while others were intercepted by the canoes, in which they remained fast. The two watches were now ordered to fire a volley alternately, and load immediately. The first discharge caused much rustling among the leaves and branches; the second, as we supposed, completely dislodged them, and from moans heard from the retreating savages we had reason to think that some of our balls took effect. It was a cold damp morning, and what between the fatigues and dangers of the preceding day, fear, chilness, and the want of sleep, our men did not seem much disposed for fighting. Mr. Stuart therefore ordered each man a double allowance of rum, "to make his courage cheerie," and the moment daylight began to dawn the canoes were thrown into the water, and the lading immediately commenced.

The canoe-men embarked first; and we followed. The last man on shore was a celebrated half-bred hunter, named Pierre Michel,[14] and just as he was about stepping into his canoe, one of the men perceived a tall Indian emerge from the wood, and bend his bow. He had scarcely time to warn Michel of his danger ere the arrow winged its flight, and completely pierced his hat, in which it remained fixed. Michel instantly turned round, and as the savage retreated into the wood, fired, and hit him somewhere about the knee. He then sprang into the canoe. We discharged a few more shots, pushed off, and paddled quickly to the opposite side. From the greyish twilight of the morning we had only an imperfect view of the Indian; but the men who had the best opportunity of seeing him were of opinion that he was the same who had expostulated the day before about the detention of his wife, after he had brought back part of the goods. We landed about ten miles farther up on the right side, on an open point; and as the canoes wanted repairing, and the men stood in need of repose, it was deemed expedient to remain there during the day. I forgot to mention that one of our Iroquois hunters sucked the wound which the man had received from the arrow in the arm: this probably

[14] Pierre Michel was a half-blood Canadian hunter and interpreter. About all that we know of him is in Cox. See also *Henry-Thompson Journals*, II, 874.

saved the poor fellow's life, as we had reason to think that the arrow was poisoned. The day after, the arm became quite black from the wrist to the shoulder; but, by the use of caustic applications, the dangerous symptoms were dispersed, and in a few weeks he recovered his ordinary health.

From this place to the narrows and falls we saw no Indians; but at the latter we found about fifteen lodges of the Eneeshurs. As our provisions were nearly consumed, we were obliged to purchase twenty dogs from them. It was the first time I had eaten any of the flesh of this animal, and nothing but stern necessity could have induced me to partake of it. The president of our mess called it "mutton," which it somewhat resembles in taste. We generally had it roasted, but the Canadians preferred it boiled, and the majority of them seemed to think it superior to horse-flesh. In this, however, I entirely differ from them, for the latter is a cleaner animal, and in taste bears a stronger resemblance to beef than the dog does to mutton. The natives behaved themselves quietly, and did not show any disposition to pilfer.

From hence to the Wallah Wallah River we obtained no horses, and our chief support consisted of 150 dogs, which we purchased at the different villages. The Wallah Wallahs received us in their usual friendly manner, and we purchased from them about twenty good horses.

Mr. Read, accompanied by eight men (excellent hunters), left us here[15] on an experimental journey to the country of the Shoshoné or Snake Indians, on whose lands he had seen great quantities of beaver in the course of his journey across the continent with Mr. Hunt. His party took sixteen of the horses with them.

After leaving this place the weather set in very cold, accompanied by occasional showers of snow, and we became apprehensive that we should encounter much difficulty in reaching our various wintering posts. We therefore stopped at a village a short distance above Lewis' River, on the south side of the Columbia; where, with hard bargaining, and after giving an exorbitant price, we obtained six horses. With these and three men I was ordered to proceed across the country to Spokan House, for the purpose of bringing down a sufficient number of the company's horses to Oakinagan, where the canoes were to stop,

---

[15] Reed and his party had left Astoria on the fifth of July, before the sale of Astoria. Cox is mixing his chronology badly and casting doubt on the accuracy of his whole story.

the trading goods having to be conveyed from thence by land-carriage to their respective winter destinations.

Two of the horses carried our provisions and blankets; and as we learned from the Wallah Wallahs that the relations of the Indian who had been hanged by Mr. Clarke in the spring were in the plains, and had declared their determination to have satisfaction for his death, we got particular orders not to separate, or on any account to tire our horses by deer-hunting. I made the men change their muskets for short trading guns, about the size of carbines, with which, a brace of pistols, and a dagger each, we set out on our overland journey. The first two days we passed in hard galloping, without meeting any thing worth noticing; but about ten o'clock on the morning of the third day, as we were preparing to remount after breakfast, we observed three Indians about a mile distant, advancing from the direction of Lewis' River. They were mounted, and, on perceiving us, stopped a few minutes in order to ascertain our numbers. We did not like this, and made signs for them to approach, which they affected not to understand; but after reconnoitring us some time, and making themselves certain that our number did not exceed four, they wheeled about, and galloped back in the same direction. Being now of opinion that their intentions were not friendly, we increased our speed, and for upwards of three hours none of them made their appearance. Our horses being nearly exhausted, we slackened the reins for about half an hour, after putting two of the most jaded under the saddle-bags. This rest brought them to again, and probably saved us; for about two o'clock we observed large clouds of dust in a south-westerly direction, which, on clearing away, displayed to our view between thirty and forty of the savages on horseback in pursuit of us. *Sauve qui peut* was now the cry; and as the two spare horses with the saddle-bags retarded our escape, we left them behind, and galloped away for our lives. The enemy gradually gained on us; but we observed that the greater number had fallen back, or given up the pursuit, and at the end of two hours only ten were in sight. Still we did not think ourselves a match for them; but shortly after their numbers were reduced to eight, apparently well mounted and armed. Our horses began to totter, and it became quite evident could not proceed much farther at such a rate. I knew the men were made of good materials, and therefore proposed to them to dismount, take our station behind the horses, and when our pursuers came within the range of our shot, each to cover

128

his man, and fire; after which, if we had not time to reload, we could work with our pistols. They all agreed; but the moment the enemy perceived us dismount and take up our position, they at once guessed our object, and turned about for the purpose of retreating. We instantly fired, and two of their horses fell. Their riders quickly mounted behind their companions, and in a short time disappeared. We were now quite overjoyed at seeing the horse with our provisions gallop up to us; but the other, which carried our blankets was, I suppose, captured. The report of our fire-arms brought us much more important relief, by the appearance of ten young hunters belonging to the Spokan nation, with every one of whom we were well acquainted, and on whose hunting grounds we then were. On telling them of our escape, they were quite indignant, and declared that, although they were not at war with the Nez Percés Indians, they would willingly join us in pursuit of them, and chastise them for their presumption in following their white friends to their hunting grounds, adding, that they knew their chief's heart would be glad at any assistance they could render us. I thanked them for their friendly offer, which I declined, assigning as a reason, that we wished to live on good terms with all the nations, and that I had no doubt we should be able to convince the foolish people who had lately pursued us of the impolicy of their conduct towards the whites. We proceeded about ten miles farther that evening, and slept in company with the Spokans, who kept watch in turn during the night. The following day, the 21st of November, two of them accompanied us, and we arrived at the fort about four in the evening, without meeting any thing farther.

Chapter 11

Author proceeds to Oakinagan, and thence to the Flat-heads, where he passes the winter—Cruel treatment of the Black-feet prisoners by the Flat-heads—Horrible spectacle—Buffalo the cause of war between the two tribes—Women—Government—Peace and war chiefs—Wolves—Anecdote of a dog—Syrup of birch—Surgical and medical knowledge of Flat-heads—Remarkable cure of rheumatism—Their ideas of a future state; and curious tradition respecting the beavers—Name of Flat-head a misnomer—A marriage

As dispatch was necessary, owing to the lateness of the season, I remained only one night at Spokan House, and set off early in the morning of the 22d November for Oakinagan. I took two additional men with me, and fifty horses. The road was good, the distance about 150 miles, and no danger to be apprehended from Indians. Having plenty of horses to change, we went on briskly; and on the evening of the 25th arrived at the Columbia, opposite the entrance of the Oakinagan River, where the fort was built. On crossing over, I found that the northern parties had set off for their wintering quarters; and as I was appointed to take charge of those intended for the eastern posts, I slept only that night at Oakinagan, and the next morning (the 26th) had all the goods transported across the river. The following is an extract from the letter of instructions directed to me on this occasion, the whole of which is rather lengthy and uninteresting for insertion:

"On your arrival here, you will assume the immediate management of the brigade, and every thing else during the voyage;[1] and make the best of your way to Spokan House, where you will make as little

[1] This word is used generally in the Indian country for all *terraqueous* journeys; and *voyageurs* is the term applied to the Canadian canoe men.—R. C.

130

delay as possible. From thence you will proceed to join Mr. M'Millan at the Flat-heads; and if you are reduced to eat horses, either at Spokan or farther on, they ought to be the worst." The liberal writer of this economical advice[2] was in other respects a very worthy, good-natured individual, and in his own person evinced the most Spartan contempt for the good things of the table. Tobacco was his mistress; and from the moment he rose until he retired to rest, his calumet was seldom allowed to cool. I was not, however, philosopher enough to prefer the intoxicating fumes of the Virginian weed to the substantial enjoyment of fat and lean, and candidly confess, that in my choice of horses for the kettle, I wilfully departed from my instructions, by selecting those whose ribs were least visible.

We arrived safely at Spokan, at which place I slept one night, and then continued on for the Flat-heads with eight men and twelve loaded horses. We pursued the same route I had followed the preceding winter with my friend Farnham, through the thick woods along the banks of the Flat-head River, and after suffering great hardships from cold and snow, reached Mr. M'Millan on the 24th of December, with the loss of two horses, which we were obliged to leave in the woods from exhaustion. The fort[3] was about forty miles higher up in an easterly direction than the place Farnham and I had chosen for the log-house. It had a good trading store, a comfortable house for the men, and a snug box for ourselves, all situated on a point formed by the junction of a bold mountain torrent[4] with the Flat-head River, and surrounded on all sides with high and thickly wooded hills, covered with pine, spruce, larch, beech, birch, and cedar. A large band of the Flat-head warriors were encamped about the fort. They had recently returned from the buffalo country, and had revenged their defeat of the preceding year, by a signal victory over their enemies the Black-feet, several of whose warriors, with their women, they had taken prisoners. M'Millan's tobacco and stock of trading goods had been entirely expended previous to my arrival, and the Indians were much in want of ammunition, &c. My appearance, or I should rather say, the goods I brought with me, was therefore a source of great joy to both parties. The natives smoked the much-loved weed for several days successively. Our hunters killed a few mountain sheep, and I brought up a bag of flour, a bag of rice, plenty of tea and coffee, some arrow-root, and

2 Joseph McGillivray.
3 Saleesh House, near present Thompson Falls, Montana.
4 Ashley Creek.

fifteen gallons of prime rum. We spent a comparatively happy Christmas, and, by the side of a blazing fire in a warm room, forgot the sufferings we endured in our dreary progress through the woods. There was, however, in the midst of our festivities, a great drawback from the pleasure we should have otherwise enjoyed. I allude to the unfortunate Black-feet who had been captured by the Flat-heads. Having been informed that they were about putting one of their prisoners to death, I went to their camp to witness the spectacle. The man was tied to a tree, after which they heated an old barrel of a gun until it became red hot, with which they burned him on the legs, thighs, neck, cheeks, and belly. They then commenced cutting the flesh from about the nails, which they pulled out, and next separated the fingers from the hand joint by joint. During the performance of these cruelties the wretched captive never winced, and instead of suing for mercy, he added fresh stimulants to their barbarous ingenuity by the most irritating reproaches, part of which our interpreter translates as follows: "My heart it strong. —You do not hurt me. —You can't hurt me. —You are fools. —You do not know how to torture. —Try it again. —I don't feel any pain yet. —We torture your relations a great deal better, because we make them cry out loud, like little children. —You are not brave: you have small hearts, and you are always afraid to fight." Then addressing one in particular, he said, "It was by my arrow *you* lost *your* eye," upon which the Flat-head darted at him, and with a knife in a moment scooped out one of his eyes, at the same time cutting the bridge of his nose nearly in two. This did not stop him: with the remaining eye he looked sternly at another, and said, "I killed your brother, and I scalped your old fool of a father." The warrior to whom this was addressed instantly sprung at him, and separated the scalp from his head. He was then about plunging a knife in his heart, until he was told by the chief to desist. The raw skull, bloody socket, and mutilated nose, now presented a horrific appearance, but by no means changed his tone of defiance. "It was I," said he to the chief, "that made your wife a prisoner last fall; —we put out her eyes; —we tore out her tongue; we treated her like a dog. Forty of our young warriors. . . ."

The chieftain became incensed the moment his wife's name was mentioned: he seized his gun, and, before the last sentence was ended, a ball from it passed through the brave fellow's heart, and terminated his frightful sufferings. Shocking, however as this dreadful exhibition was, it was far exceeded by the atrocious cruelties practised on the female prisoners, in which I am sorry to say, the Flat-head women assisted with more savage fury than the men. I only witnessed part of what one wretched young woman suffered, a detail of which would be too revolting for publicity. We remonstrated against the exercise of such horrible cruelties. They replied by saying the Black-feet treated their relations in the same manner; that it was the course adopted by all red warriors; and that they could not think of giving up the gratification of their revenge to the foolish and womanish feelings of white men. Shortly after this we observed a young female led forth, apparently not more than fourteen or fifteen years of age, surrounded by some old women, who were conducting her to one end of the village, whither they were followed by a number of young men. Having learned the infamous intentions of her conquerors, and feeling interested for the unfortunate victim, we renewed our remonstrances, but received nearly the same answer as before. Finding them still inflexible, and wishing to adopt every means in our power consistent with safety in the cause of humanity, we ordered our interpreter to acquaint them, that, highly as we valued their friendship, and much as we esteemed their furs, we would quit their country for ever, unless they discontinued their unmanly and disgraceful cruelties to their prisoners. This had the desired effect, and the miserable captive was led back to her sorrowing group of friends. Our interference was nearly rendered ineffectual by the furious reproaches of the infernal old priestesses who had been conducting her to the sacrifice. They told the young warriors they were cowards, fools, and had not the hearts of fleas, and called upon them in the names of their mothers, sisters, and wives, to follow the steps of their forefathers, and have their revenge on the dogs of Black-feet. They began to waver; but we affected not to understand what the old women had been saying. We told them that this act of self-denial on their part was peculiarly grateful to the white men; and that by it they would secure our permanent residence among them, and in return for their furs be always furnished with guns and ammunition sufficient to repel the attacks of their old enemies, and preserve their relations from being made prisoners. This decided the doubtful; and the chief promised faithfully that no more tortures should be inflicted on the prisoners, which I believe was rigidly adhered to, at least for that winter.

The Flat-heads were formerly much more numerous than they

were at this period; but owing to the constant hostilities between them and the Black-feet Indians, their numbers had been greatly diminished. While pride, policy, ambition, self-preservation, or the love of aggrandisement, often deluges the civilised world with Christian blood; the only cause assigned by the natives of whom I write, for their perpetual warfare, is their love of buffalo.[5] There are extensive plains to the eastward of the mountains frequented in the summer and autumnal months by numerous herds of buffaloes. Hither the rival tribes repair to hunt those animals, that they may procure as much of their meat as will supply them until the succeeding season. In these excursions they often meet, and the most sanguinary conflicts follow.

The Black-feet lay claim to all that part of the country immediately at the foot of the mountains, which is most frequented by the buffalo, and allege that the Flat-heads, by resorting thither to hunt, are intruders whom they are bound to oppose on all occasions. The latter, on the contrary, assert, that their forefathers had always claimed and exercised the right of hunting on these "debateable lands," and that while one of their warriors remained alive the right should not be relinquished. The consequences of these continual wars are dreadful, particularly to the Flat-heads, who, being the weaker in numbers were generally the greater sufferers. Independently of their inferiority in this respect, their enemy had another great advantage in the use of fire-arms, which they obtained from the Company's trading posts established in the department of Forts des Prairies.[6] To these the Flat-heads had nothing to oppose but arrows and their own undaunted bravery. Every year previous to our crossing the mountains witnessed the gradual diminution of their numbers; and total annihilation would shortly have been the consequence, but for our arrival with a plentiful supply of "villanous saltpetre." They were overjoyed at having an opportunity of purchasing arms and ammunition, and quickly stocked themselves with a sufficient quantity of both.

From this moment affairs took a decided change in their favour; and in their subsequent contests the numbers of killed, wounded, and

[5] Trespassing by members of one tribe on lands claimed by another was the commonest cause of these intertribal wars.

[6] *Fort des Prairies* was a name applied to a number of forts. Cox uses it as a general term for all posts east of the Rockies. For the list see the indexes to Vorhis, *Historic Forts,* and to the *Henry-Thompson Journals.*

prisoners, were more equal. The Black-feet became enraged at this, and declared to our people at Forts des Prairies, that all white men who might happen to fall into their hands, to the westward of the mountains, would be treated by them as enemies, in consequence of their furnishing the Flat-heads with weapons, which were used with such deadly effect against their nation. This threat, as will appear hereafter, was strictly put in execution. The lands of the Flat-heads are well stocked with deer, mountain sheep, bears, wild fowl, and fish; and when we endeavoured to induce them to give up such dangerous expeditions, and confine themselves to the produce of their own country, they replied, that their fathers had always hunted on the buffalo grounds; that they were accustomed to do the same thing from their infancy; and they would not now abandon a practice which had existed for several generations among their people.

With the exception of the cruel treatment of their prisoners (which, as it is general among all savages, must not be imputed to them as a peculiar vice), the Flat-heads have fewer failings than any of the tribes I ever met with. They are honest in their dealings, brave in the field, quiet and amenable to their chiefs, fond of cleanliness, and decided enemies to falsehood of every description. The women are excellent wives and mothers, and their character for fidelity is so well established, that we never heard an instance of one of them proving unfaithful to her husband. They are also free from the vice of backbiting, so common among the lower tribes; and laziness is a stranger among them. Both sexes are comparatively very fair, and their complexions are a shade lighter than the palest new copper after being freshly rubbed. They are remarkably well made, rather slender, and never corpulent. The dress of the men consists solely of long leggings, called *mittasses* by the Canadians, which reach from the ancles to the hips, and are fastened by strings to a leathern belt round the waist, and a shirt of dressed deer-skin, with loose hanging sleeves, which falls down to their knees. The outside seams of the leggings and shirt sleeves have fringes of leather. The women are covered by a loose robe of the same material reaching from the neck to the feet, and ornamented with fringes, beads, hawk-bells, and thimbles. The dresses of both are regularly cleaned with pipe-clay, which abounds in parts of the country; and every individual has two or three changes. They have no permanent covering for the head, but in wet or stormy weather shelter it by part of a buffalo robe, which completely answers

all the purposes of a surtout. The principal chief of the tribe is hereditary; but from their constant wars, they have adopted the wise and
salutary custom of electing, as their leader in battle, that warrior in
whom the greatest portion of wisdom, strength, and bravery are combined. The election takes place every year; and it sometimes occurs
that the general in one campaign becomes a private in the next. This
"war-chief," as they term him, has no authority whatever when at
home, and is as equally amenable as any of the tribe to the hereditary
chief; but when the warriors set out on their hunting excursions to
the buffalo plains, he assumes the supreme command, which he exercises with despotic sway until their return. He carries a long whip
with a thick handle decorated with scalps and feathers, and generally
appoints two active warriors as *aides-de-camp*. On their advance towards the enemy he always takes the lead; and on their return he
brings up the rear. Great regularity is preserved during the march;
and I have been informed by Mr. M'Donald, who accompanied some
of these war parties to the field of action, that if any of the tribe fell
out of the ranks, or committed any other breach of discipline, he instantly received a flaggellation from the whip of the chieftain. He
always acted with the most perfect impartiality, and would punish one
of his subalterns for disobedience of orders with equal severity as
any other offender. Custom, however, joined to a sense of public duty,
had reconciled them to these arbitrary acts of power, which they never
complained of or attempted to resent. After the conclusion of the campaign, on their arrival on their own lands, his authority ceases, when
the peace chief calls all the tribe together, and they proceed to a new
election. There is no canvassing, caballing, or intriguing; and should
the last leader be superseded, he retires from office with apparent
indifference, and without betraying any symptoms of discontent. The
fighting chief at this period had been five times re-elected. He was
about thirty-five years of age, and had killed twenty of the Black-feet
in various battles, the scalps of whom were suspended in triumphal
pride, from a pole at the door of his lodge. His wife had been captured
by the enemy the year before, and her loss made a deep impression
on him. He was highly respected by all the warriors for his superior
wisdom and bravery; a consciousness of which, joined to the length
of time he had been accustomed to command, imparted to his manners
a degree of dignity which we never remarked in any other Indian.
He would not take a second wife; and when the recollection of the

one he had lost came across his mind, he retired into the deepest solitude of the woods to indulge his sorrow, where some of the tribe informed us they often found him calling on her spirit to appear, and invoking vengeance on her conquerors. When these bursts of grief subsided, his countenance assumed a tinge of stern melancholy, strongly indicating the mingled emotions of sorrow and unmitigated hatred of the Black-feet. We invited him sometimes to the fort, upon which occasions we sympathised with him on his loss, but at the same time acquainted him with the manner in which civilized nations made war. We told him that warriors only were made prisoners, who were never tortured or killed, and that no brave white man would ever injure a female or a defenceless man; that if such a custom had prevailed among them, he would now by the exchange of prisoners be able to recover his wife, who was by their barbarous system lost to him for ever; and if it were impossible to bring about a peace with their enemies the frightful horrors of war might at least be considerably softened by adopting the practice of Europeans. We added that he had now a glorious opportunity of commencing the career of magnanimity by sending home uninjured the captives he had made during the last campaign, that our friends on the other side of the mountains would exert their influence with the Black-feet to induce them to follow his example and that ultimately it might be the means of uniting the two rival nations in the bonds of peace. He was at first opposed to making any advances; but on farther pressing he consented to make the trial, provided the hereditary chief and the tribe started no objections. On quitting us he made use of the following words: "My white friends, you do not know the savage nature of the Black-feet; they hope to exterminate our tribe; they are a great deal more numerous than we are; and were it not for our bravery, their object would have been long ago achieved. We shall now, according to your wishes, send back the prisoners; but remember, I tell you, that they will laugh at the interference of your relations beyond the mountains, and never spare a man, woman, or child, that they can take of our nation. Your exertions to save blood show you are good people. If they fellow our example, we shall kill no more prisoners; but I tell you, they will laugh at you and call you fools."

We were much pleased at having carried our point so far; while he, true to his word, assembled the elders and warriors, to whom he represented the subject of our discourse, and after a long speech, advised them to make the trial, which would please their white friends, and show their readiness to avoid unnecessary cruelty. Such an unexpected proposition gave rise to an animated debate, which continued for some time; but being supported by a man for whom they entertained so much respect, it was finally carried; and it was determined to send home the Black-feet on the breaking up of the winter. We undertook to furnish them with horses and provisions for their journey, or to pay the Flat-heads a fair price for so doing. This was agreed to, and about the middle of March the prisoners took their departure tolerably well mounted, and with dried meat enough to bring them to their friends. Mr. M'Millan, who had passed three years in their country, and was acquainted with their language, informed them of the exertions we had used to save their lives, and prevent farther repetitions of torture and requested them particularly to mention the circumstance to their countrymen, in order that they might adopt a similar proceeding. We also wrote letters by them to the gentlemen in charge of the different establishments at Forts des Prairies, detailing our success, and impressing on them the necessity of their attempting to induce the Black-feet in their vicinity to follow the example set them by the Flat-heads. The lands of this tribe present a pleasing diversity of woods and plains, valleys and mountains, lakes and rivers. Besides the animals already mentioned, there are abundance of beavers, otters, martens, wolves, lynxes, &c.

The wolves of this district are very large and daring, and were in great numbers in the immediate vicinity of the fort, to which they often approached closely, for the purpose of carrying away the offals. We had a fine dog of mixed breed, whose sire was a native of Newfoundland, and whose dam was a wolf, which had been caught young, and domesticated by Mr. La Rocque, at Lac la Ronge, on the English River.[7] He had many rencontres with his maternal tribe, in which he was generally worsted. On observing a wolf near the fort, he darted at it with great courage. If it was a male, he fought hard; but if a female, he either allowed it to retreat harmless, or commenced fondling it. He sometimes was absent for a week or ten days; and on his return, his body and neck appeared gashed with wounds inflicted by the tusks of his male rivals in their amorous encounters in the woods. He was a noble animal, but always appeared more ready to attack a wolf than a lynx.

[7] The upper Churchill River.

Our stock of sugar and molasses having failed, we were obliged to have recourse to the extract of birch to supply the deficiency. This was obtained by perforating the trunks of the birch trees in different places. Small slips of bark were then introduced into each perforation, and underneath kettles were placed to receive the juice. This was afterwards boiled down to the consistency of molasses, and was used with our tea as a substitute for sugar. It is a bitter sweet, and answered its purpose tolerably well.

The Flat-heads are a healthy tribe, and subject to few diseases. Common fractures, caused by an occasional pitch off a horse, or a fall down a declivity in the ardour of hunting, are cured by tight bandages and pieces of wood like staves placed longitudinally around the part, to which they are secured by leathern thongs. For contusions they generally bleed, either in the temples, arms, wrists, or ancles, with pieces of sharp flint, or heads of arrows. They however preferred being bled with the lancet, and frequently brought us patients, who were much pleased with that mode of operation. Very little snow fell after Christmas; but the cold was intense, with a clear atmosphere. I experienced some acute rheumatic attacks in the shoulders and knees, from which I suffered much annoyance. An old Indian proposed to relieve me, provided I consented to follow the mode of cure practised by him in similar cases on the young warriors of the tribe. On inquiring the method he intended to pursue, he replied that it merely consisted in getting up early every morning for some weeks, and plunging into the river, and to leave the rest to him. This was a most chilling proposition, for the river was firmly frozen, and an opening to be made in the ice preparatory to each immersion. I asked him, "Would it not answer equally well to have the water brought to my bed-room?" But he shook his head, and replied, he was surprised that a young white chief, who ought to be wise, should ask so foolish a question. On reflecting, however, that rheumatism was a stranger among Indians, while numbers of our people were martyrs to it, and, above all, that I was upwards of three thousand miles from any professional assistance, I determined to adopt the disagreeable expedient, and commenced operations the following morning. The Indian first broke a hole in the ice sufficiently large to admit us both, upon which he made a signal that all was ready. Enveloped in a large buffalo robe, I proceeded to the spot, and throwing off my covering, we both jumped into the frigid orifice together. He immediately commenced rubbing my shoulders, back, and loins. My hair in the mean time became ornamented with icicles; and while the lower joints were undergoing their friction, my face, neck, and shoulders were incased in a thin covering of ice. On getting released I rolled a blanket about me, and ran back to the bedroom, in which I had previously ordered a good fire, and in a few minutes I experienced a warm glow all over my body. Chilling and disagreeable as these matinal ablutions were, yet, as I found them so beneficial, I continued them for twenty-five days, at the expiration of which my physician was pleased to say that no more were necessary, and that I had done my duty like a wise man. I was never after troubled with a rheumatic pain! One of our old Canadians, who had been labouring many years under a chronic rheumatism, asked the Indian if he could cure him in the same manner. The latter replied it was impossible, but that he would try another process. He accordingly constructed the skeleton of a hut about four and a half feet high, and three broad, in shape like a bee-hive, which he covered with deer-skins. He then heated some stones in an adjoining fire, and having placed the patient inside in a state of nudity, the hot stones were thrown in, and water poured on them; the entrance was then quickly closed, and the man kept in for some time until he begged to be released, alleging that he was nearly suffocated. On coming out he was in a state of profuse perspiration. The Indian ordered him to be immediately enveloped in blankets and conveyed to bed. This operation was repeated several times, and although it did not effect a radical cure, the violence of the pains was so far abated, as to permit the patient to follow his ordinary business, and to enjoy his sleep in comparative ease.[8]

The Flat-heads believe in the existence of a good and evil spirit, and consequently in a future state of rewards and punishments. They hold, that after death the good Indian goes to a country in which there will be perpetual summer; that he will meet his wife and children; that the rivers will abound with fish, and the plains with the much-loved buffalo; and that he will spend his time in hunting and fishing, free from the terrors of war, or the apprehensions of cold or famine. The bad man, they believe, will go to a place covered with eternal snow; that he will always be shivering with cold, and will see fires at a distance which he cannot enjoy; water which he cannot

[8] A more familiar Indian treatment was that of inducing profuse perspiration and then plunging into the icy waters of the stream.

procure to quench his thirst, and buffalo and deer which he cannot kill to appease his hunger. An impenetrable wood, full of wolves, panthers, and serpents, separates these "shrinking slaves of winter" from their fortunate brethren in the "meadows of ease." Their punishment is not however eternal, and according to the different shades of their crimes they are sooner or later emancipated, and permitted to join their friends in the Elysian fields.

Their code of morality, although short, is comprehensive. They say that honesty, bravery, love of truth, attention to parents, obedience to their chiefs, and affection for their wives and children, are the principle virtues which entitle them to the place of happiness, while the opposite vices condemn them to that of misery. They have a curious tradition with respect to beavers. They firmly believe that these animals are a fallen race of Indians, who, in consequence of their wickedness, vexed the Good Spirit, and were condemned by him to their present shape; but that in due time they will be restored to their humanity. They allege that he-beavers have the powers of speech; and that they have heard them talk with each other, and seen them sitting in council on an offending member.

The lovers of natural history are already well acquainted with the surprising sagacity of these wonderful animals, with their dexterity in cutting down trees, their skill in constructing their houses, and their foresight in collecting and storing provisions sufficient to last them during the winter months; but few are aware, I should imagine, of a remarkable custom among them, which, more than any other, confirms the Indians in believing them a fallen race. Towards the latter end of autumn a certain number, varying from twenty to thirty, assemble for the purpose of building their winter habitations. They immediately commence cutting down trees; and nothing can be more wonderful than the skill and patience which they manifest in this laborious undertaking, to see them anxiously looking up, watching the leaning of the tree when the trunk is nearly severed, and, when its creaking announces its approaching fall, to observe them scampering off in all directions to avoid being crushed.

When the tree is prostrate they quickly strip it of its branches; after which, with their dental chisels, they divide the trunk into several pieces of equal lengths, which they roll to the rivulet across which they intend to erect their house. Two or three old ones generally superintend the others; and it is no unusual sight to see them beating those who exhibit any symptoms of laziness. Should, however, any fellow be incorrigible, and persist in refusing to work, he is driven unanimously by the whole tribe to seek shelter and provisions elsewhere. These outlaws are therefore obliged to pass a miserable winter, half starved in a burrow on the banks of some stream, where they are easily trapped. The Indians call them "lazy beaver,"[9] and their fur is not half so valuable as that of the other animals, whose persevering industry and *prévoyance* secure them provisions and a comfortable shelter during the severity of winter.

I could not discover why the Black-feet[10] and Flat-heads[11] received their respective designations; for the feet of the former are no more inclined to sable than any other part of the body, while the heads of the latter possess their fair proportion of rotundity. Indeed it is only below the falls and rapids that real flat-heads appear, and at the mouth of the Columbia that they flourish most supernaturally.

Pierre Michel, the hunter, was the son of a respectable Canadian by an Indian mother. He also held the situation of interpreter, and was a most valuable servant to the Company. Michel accompanied the Flat-heads on two of their war campaigns, and by his unerring aim and undaunted bravery won the affection of the whole tribe. The war chief in particular paid great attention to his opinion, and consulted him in any difficult matter. Michel wanted a wife; and having succeeded in gaining the affections of a handsome girl about sixteen years of age, and niece to the hereditary chieftain, he made a formal proposal for her. A council was thereupon called, at which her uncle presided, to take Michel's offer into consideration. One young warrior loved her ardently, and had obtained a previous promise from her mother that she should be his. He, therefore, with all his relations, strongly opposed her union with Pierre, and urged his own claims, which had been sanctioned by her mother. The war-chief asked him if she had ever promised to become his wife; he replied in the negative. The chief then addressed the council, and particularly the lover, in favour of Michel's suit; pointing out the great services he had ren-

---

[9] A survival is the use of the present term "eager beaver."

[10] The Blackfeet received their name because of the fact that their moccasins had been discolored in the ashes of prairie fires.

[11] The application of this term to this particular tribe is unfortunate because they did not flatten the head. It is possible that the name was applied by the long-headed Blackfeet on account of the Salish's being brachycephalic, or having upright heads, and the French translated it to *Têtes Plates*. The Blackfeet term probably meant *level tops*.

142

dered the tribe by his bravery, and dwelling strongly on the policy
of uniting him more firmly to their interests by consenting to the
proposed marriage, which he said would for ever make him as one
of their brothers. His influence predominated, and the unsuccessful
rival immediately after shook hands with Michel, and told the young
woman, as he could not be her husband, he hoped she would always
regard him as a brother. This she readily promised to do, and so
ended the opposition. The happy Pierre presented a gun to her uncle,
some cloth, calico, and ornaments to her female relatives, with a
pistol and handsome dagger to his friend. He proceeded in the evening to the chief's lodge, where a number of her friends had assembled
to smoke. Here she received a lecture from the old man, her mother,
and a few other ancients, on her duty as a wife and mother. They
strongly exhorted her to be chaste, obedient, industrious, and silent,
and when absent with her husband among other tribes, always to
stay at home, and have no intercourse with strange Indians. She then
retired with the old women to an adjoining hut, where she underwent
an ablution, and bade adieu to her leathern chemise, the place of
which was supplied by one of gingham, to which was added a calico
and green cloth petticoat, and a gown of blue cloth. After this was
over, she was conducted back to her uncle's lodge, when she received
some further advice as to her future conduct. A procession was then
formed by the two chiefs, and several warriors carrying blazing flam-
beaux of cedar, to convey the bride and her husband to the fort. They
began singing war songs in praise of Michel's bravery, and of their
triumphs over the Black-feet. She was surrounded by a group of young
and old women, some of whom were rejoicing, and others crying. The
men moved on first, in a slow solemn pace, still chaunting their warlike epithalamium. The women followed at a short distance; and
when the whole party arrived in front of the fort, they formed a circle,
and commenced dancing and singing, which they kept up about twenty
minutes. After this the calumet of peace went round once more, and
when the smoke of the last whiff had disappeared, Michel shook hands
with his late rival, embraced the chiefs, and conducted his bride to
his room. While I remained in the country they lived happily together;
and as I mean to finish this chapter here, I may as well state that he
was the only person of our party to whom the Flat-heads would give
one of their women in marriage. Several of our men made applications,
but were always refused.

Chapter 12

Effect of snow on the eyes—Description of a winter at Oakinagan—News from the sea—Capture of Astoria by the Racoon *sloop of war—Offer of Chinooks to cut off the British—A party attacked; Mr. Stewart wounded; two Indians killed—Arrival of Mr. Hunt—Shipwreck of the* Lark—*Massacre of Mr. Read and eight of his men—Extraordinary escape of Dorrien's widow and children*

On the 4th of April 1814, we took leave of our Flat-head friends, on our way to Spokan House, while they proceeded to make preparations for the ensuing summer's campaign. We pursued our route partly by land, and partly by water. In some places, the snow had entirely disappeared; but in others, particularly the dense forests, it was covered with a slight incrustation.

The sun was very hot, and where its rays were reflected from the congealed, or partly dissolved masses of snow, it caused a very painful sensation in the eyes of all, and nearly blinded half the party.[1] My sight was partially injured, and my nose, lips, and cheeks so severely scorched, that I did not recover from the effects for more than a month after. We arrived safely at Spokan House on the 15th, where I found a couple of letters which had been written to me by my friend M'Gillivray from Oakinagan, at which place he had wintered, but which, from want of a conveyance, could not be forwarded to me from Spokan. Although accustomed to the style of living on the eastern side of the mountains, and well acquainted with Indians, this was his first winter on the Columbia; and, for the information of some of my readers, I shall give an extract from one of his letters; viz.

---

[1] This was snow blindness which, while a more familiar phenomenon of the Northern Plains, was not entirely unknown in the interior of the Columbia district.

Description of a Winter at Oakinagan

Oakinagan, Feb. 1814

This is a horribly dull place. Here I have been, since you parted from us, perfectly *solus*. My men, half Canadians and half Sandwich islanders. The library wretched, and no chance of my own books till next year, when the Athabasca men cross the mountains. If you, or my friends at Spokan, do not send me a few volumes, I shall absolutely die of *ennui*. The Indians here are incontestably the most indolent rascals I ever met: and I assure you it requires no small degree of authority, with the few men I have, to keep them in order. Montignier left me on the 23rd of December to proceed to Mr. M'Donald at Kamloops. On his way he was attacked by the Indians at Oakinagan Lake, and robbed of a number of horses. The natives in that quarter seem to entertain no great friendship for us, and this is not their first attempt to trespass on our good-nature. My two Canadians were out hunting at the period of the robbery; and the whole of my household troops merely consisted of *Bonaparte! Washington!!* and *Caesar!!!*[2] Great names, you will say; but I must confess, that much as I think of the two great moderns, and highly as I respect the memory of the immortal *Julius,* among these thieving scoundrels "a rose by any other name, would smell as sweet." The snow is between two and three feet deep, and my trio of Owhyee generals find a sensible difference between such hyperborean weather and the pleasing sunshine of their own tropical paradise. Poor fellows! They are not adapted for these latitudes, and I heartily wish they were at home in their own sweet islands, and sporting in the "blue summer ocean" that surrounds them.

I have not as yet made a pack of beaver. The lazy Indians won't work; and as for the emperor, president, and dictator, they know as much about trapping as the monks of *La Trappe*. I have hitherto principally subsisted on horse-flesh. I cannot say it agrees with me, for it nearly produced a dysentery. I have had plenty of pork, rice, arrow-root, flour, taro-root, tea, and coffee; no sugar. With such a variety of *bonnes choses* you will say I ought not to complain; but want of society has destroyed my relish for luxuries, and the only articles I taste above *par* are souchong and molasses. What a contrast between the manner I spent last year and this! In the first, with all the pride of a newly-created subaltern, occasionally fighting the Yankees *à la mode du pays;* and anon sporting my silver wings between some admiring *paysanne* along the frontiers. Then what a glorious winter in Montreal, with captured Jonathans, triumphant Britons, astonished Indians, gaping *habitans,* agitated beauties; balls, routs, dinners, suppers; parades, drums beating, colours flying, with all the other "pride, pomp, and circumstance of *glorious* war!"—but "Othello's occupation's gone!" and here I am, with a shivering guard of poor islanders, buried in snow, sipping molasses, smoking tobacco, and masticating horse-flesh!—But I am sick of the contrast.

[2] The individuals bearing these formidable names were merely three unsophisticated natives of the Sandwich Islands.—R. C.

On the 24th of April, Messrs. David Stuart and Clarke arrived on horseback with three men. They informed us that they had left Fort George on the 4th in company with Mr. John George M'Tavish and the gentlemen lately belonging to the Pacific Fur Company, who were British subjects, and who were on their return home to Canada. They left the main party about a day's march above Lewis' River, for the purpose of procuring provisions at Spokan, with which they were to meet the canoes at the Kettle Falls, and from thence proceed up the Columbia on their route to Canada. The intelligence brought by these gentlemen was by no means of a pleasing description. At the period of their departure from the sea the *Isaac Tod* had not arrived, nor had any accounts been received of her. That vessel sailed from London in March 1813, in company with the *Phoebe* frigate and the *Cherub* and *Racoon* sloops of war. They arrived safe at Rio Janeiro, and thence proceeded round Cape Horn to the Pacific, having previously made arrangements to meet at Juan Fernandez. The three men-of-war reached the latter island after encountering dreadful gales about the Cape. They waited here some time for the arrival of the *Isaac Tod;* but as she did not make her appearance, Commodore Hillier did not deem it prudent to remain any longer inactive. He, therefore, in company with the *Cherub,* proceeded in search of Commodore Porter, who, in the American frigate *Essex,* was clearing the South Sea of the English whalers, and inflicting other injuries of a serious nature on our commerce.[3]

At the same time he ordered Captain Black in the *Racoon* to proceed direct to the Columbia, for the purpose of destroying the American establishment at Astoria. The *Racoon* arrived at the Columbia on the 1st of December 1813. The surprise and disappointment of Captain Black and his officers were extreme on learning the arrangement that had taken place between the two companies, by which the establishment had become British property. They had calculated on obtaining a splendid prize by the capture of Astoria, the strength and importance of which had been much magnified;[4] and the con-

---

[3] He shortly after met the *Essex* at Valparaiso, and after a severe contest captured her. She is now the convict hulk at Kingstown near Dublin.—R. C.

[4] On looking at the wooden fortifications, Captain Black exclaimed, "Is this the fort about which I have heard so much? D——n me, but I'd batter it down in two hours with a four-pounder!"—R. C.

For a contrary point of view see Franchère, *Narrative,* 302; and Ross, *First Settlers,* 249–50.

tracting parties were therefore fortunate in having closed their bargain previous to the arrival of the *Racoon*.

Captain Black however took possession of Astoria in the name of his Britannic Majesty, and re-baptised it by the name of "Fort George." He also insisted on having an inventory taken of the valuable stock of furs, and all other property purchased from the American company, with a view to the adoption of ulterior proceedings in England for the recovery of the value from the North-West Company; but he subsequently relinquished this idea, and we heard no more about his claims. The Indians at the mouth of the Columbia knew well that Great Britain and America were distinct nations, and that they were then at war, but were ignorant of the arrangement made between Messrs. M'Dougall and M'Tavish, the former of whom still continued as nominal chief at the fort. On the arrival of the *Racoon*, which they quickly discovered to be one of "King George's fighting ships," they repaired armed to the fort, and requested an audience with Mr. M'Dougall. He was somewhat surprised at their numbers and warlike appearance, and demanded the object of such an unusual visit. Comcomly, the principal chief of the Chinooks, thereupon addressed him in a long speech, in the course of which he said that King George had sent a ship full of warriors, and loaded with nothing but big guns to take the Americans, and make them all slaves; and that as they (the Americans) were the first white men who settled in their country, and treated the Indians like good relations, they had resolved to defend them from King George's warriors, and were now ready to conceal themselves in the woods close to the wharf, from whence they would be able with their guns and arrows to shoot all the men that should attempt to land from the English boats; while the people in the fort could fire at them with their big guns and rifles. This proposition was uttered with an earnestness of manner that admitted no doubt of its sincerity. Two armed boats from the *Racoon* were approaching, and had the people in the fort felt disposed to accede to the wishes of the Indians, every man in them would have been destroyed by an invisible enemy. Mr. M'Dougall thanked them for their friendly offer, but added that notwithstanding the nations were at war, the people in the boats would not injure him or any of his people, and therefore requested them to throw by their war-shirts and arms, and receive the strangers as friends. They at first seemed astonished at this answer; but on assuring them in the most positive manner that

147

he was under no apprehensions, they consented to give up their weapons for a few days. They afterwards declared they were sorry for having complied with Mr. M'Dougall's wishes; for when they observed Captain Black surrounded by his officers and marines, break the bottle of port on the flag-staff, and hoist the British ensign after changing the name of the fort, they remarked that, however we might wish to conceal the fact, the Americans were undoubtedly made slaves; and they were not convinced of their mistake until the sloop of war had departed without taking any prisoners.[5]

Mr. Stuart farther informed us, that a party of seventeen men under the command of Messrs. James Keith[6] and Alexander Stewart, which had left Fort George early in January with merchandise for the interior, had been attacked by the natives between the first and second portages of the first rapids;[7] that Mr. Stewart was dangerously wounded by two arrows, one of which entered his left shoulder, and the other penetrated between his ribs close to the heart, notwithstanding which he succeeded in shooting two of the savages dead. By this time some of the men came to his assistance, and for a while succeeded in keeping back their assailants, who every moment became more daring, and evinced not merely a determination to revenge the death of their countrymen, but to seize and carry away all the merchandise in the portage. Mr. Keith having observed a large reinforcement of the savages from the opposite side approach in their war-canoes, to join those by whom Mr. Stewart was surrounded, and seeing that gentleman's wounds bleeding profusely, felt that it would have been foolish obstinacy, and would have produced an unnecessary sacrifice of lives, to remain longer in such a dangerous situation. He therefore determined to abandon the goods; and having embarked Mr. Stewart, the whole party pushed off in one canoe, leaving the other with all the property, to the mercy of the Indians. The latter were so overjoyed at becoming masters of such an unexpected quantity of plunder, that they allowed the party to effect their retreat unmolested; and on the second day the canoe reached Fort George.

<hr/>

[5] Per contra see Ross, *First Settlers*, 249.

[6] James Keith (d. 1851) was a native of Scotland who had entered the service of the North West Company about 1800 and became a partner in 1814. From 1813 to 1816 he was on the Columbia, where he seems to have been characterized by a want of energy and initiative. See Wallace, *Documents*, 459.

[7] This attack was made near Bradford's Island by members of the Yakima and Klikitat tribes, whose villages were on the north side of the river just above the falls.

Among the goods thus abandoned were upwards of fifty guns, and a considerable quantity of ammunition, which, if allowed to remain in the hands of the savages, might have been turned against us on a future occasion; and as this was the first attack which had proved successful, the proprietors at once determined not to allow it to pass with impunity. They accordingly sent Mr. Franchère to the principal friendly chiefs in the vicinity of the fort, for the purpose of acquainting them with the late occurrence, and inviting them to join our people in their intended expedition against the enemy. They readily consented, and on the following morning a brigade of six canoes, containing sixty-two men, under the command of Messrs. M'Tavish, Keith, Franchère, Matthews, &c., took their departure from Fort George.

Having no lading, they quickly reached the rapids. Everything there appeared hostile. The warriors lined the beach at different places well armed, and the old men, women, and children were invisible. A council of war was immediately held, at which two chiefs of the Clatsops (one of whom was an old female) were present. They advised the gentlemen to assume the appearance of friendship, and after entering into a parley with the natives, and inviting them to smoke, to seize one of their chiefs, and detain him as a hostage until the property should be restored. This advice was followed, and succeeded to perfection. Having by some coaxing, and repeated offers of the calumet, collected a number of the natives about them, to whom they made trifling presents of tobacco, they were at length joined by the principal chief of the place, who had for some time cautiously kept out of view. He was instantly seized, bound hand and foot, and thrown into a tent, with two men to guard him armed with drawn swords. The others were then sent away, with directions to acquaint their countrymen of their chief's captivity, and were told that if the entire of the property was not forthwith restored, he should be put to death. This had the desired effect, and shortly after all the guns, part of the kettles, and nearly one half of the other goods were brought back. They declared they could not recover any more, and asked our gentlemen, "would they not allow them any thing to place over the dead bodies of their two relations, who had been killed by Mr. Stewart?"

The most important object of the expedition having been thus attained without bloodshed, and as the aggressors had been pretty severely punished in the first instance, the party deemed it both humane and prudent to rest satisfied with what they had recovered. They also felt that an unnecessary waste of human blood might prove ultimately prejudicial to their own interests, by raising up a combined force of natives, against whom their limited numbers would find it impossible to contend. They therefore gave the chief his liberty, and presented him with a flag, telling him at the same time, that whenever that was presented to them unfurled, they would consider it as a sign of friendship; but that if any of his tribe ever approached them without displaying this emblem of peace, it would be taken as a symptom of hostility, and treated as such. The chief promised faithfully to abide by this engagement, and the parties then separated.

Mr. Hunt, late of the Pacific Fur Company, arrived at Fort George early in February this year, in a brig which he had purchased at the Sandwich Islands. When the *Beaver* had left the Columbia, this gentleman embarked in her on a trading voyage to the northward, which proved very successful. At the termination of her northern trip the season was too far advanced to permit her returning to the Columbia, in consequence of which Mr. Hunt sent her on to Canton, and embarked on board an American trading vessel on the coast.[8] Shortly after the unwelcome intelligence of the war reached him, and finding no vessel bound for the Columbia, he proceeded in the trader to the Sandwich Islands. He did not remain long here, when he re-embarked on board another trader, and after traversing an immense space of the Pacific Ocean, in the course of which he encountered many dangers, returned again to the islands. At Whoahoo he purchased a brig called the *Pedler*,[9] and was preparing to come in her to the Columbia, when he was informed by some of the natives that an American vessel had been wrecked on the island of Tahoorowa.[10] He instantly repaired thither, and found Captain Northrop, late commander of the ship *Lark*, with several of his crew, all in a state of great destitution. The

[8] Hunt had gone to Alaska in the *Beaver*, since Astor's far-flung activities included an arrangement with the Russian-American Fur Company, and he intended to return to Astoria. But because of the lateness of the season, the unseaworthiness of the ship, and his natural timidity, Captain Sowle declined to risk a crossing of the Columbia River bar again, took advantage of the discretion allowed him by Astor, and took the ship to the Hawaiian Islands. Hunt then took passage for Astoria in the *Albatross* and went on to the Marquesas Islands. He then returned to the Hawaiian Islands, where he chartered the brig *Pedlar,* and returned to Astoria.

[9] For the *Pedlar* see Kenneth W. Porter, "The Cruise of Astor's Brig *Pedlar*," *Oregon Historical Quarterly,* Vol. XXXI, pp. 223–30.

[10] The present island of Kahoolawe.

Lark had been dispatched from New York by Mr. Astor, freighted with provisions and merchandise for the establishment at the Columbia. After escaping various British cruisers, she made an excellent passage, until she arrived within about three hundred miles of the Sandwich Islands, when a sudden squall threw her on her beam ends. By this unfortunate accident the second mate and four men perished. The captain, however, and the rest of the crew, by cutting away the masts, succeeded in righting her; but she was completely waterlogged. With much difficulty they hoisted a sail on a small jury foremast. They fortunately got out of the cabin a box containing a few dozen of wine, on which, with the raw flesh of a shark they had caught, they supported nature thirteen days! At the end of this period the trade winds, which had been for some time favourable, drove the vessel on the rocky coast of Tahoorowa, where she went to pieces. The captain and his surviving crew were saved and kindly treated by the natives, who however plundered the wreck of all the property they could find.

Mr. Hunt took Captain Northrop and his men on board the brig, and sailed forthwith for the Columbia, which he reached in the beginning of February. Being ignorant of the events that had occurred during his absence, he was confounded at the intelligence he received, and censured in strong terms the precipitate manner in which the sale had been effected. It was, however, irrevocable, and he was obliged to submit.

Having no farther business at Fort George, Mr. Hunt determined on returning to the United States without loss of time. He took on board such American citizens as preferred returning home by sea to crossing the continent, and after rather a tedious voyage they all arrived safely at New York.[11]

We also learned from Messrs. Stuart and Clarke the following melancholy intelligence: On their way up, a few miles above the Wallah Wallah River, they were followed by some Indian canoes, from one of which a voice hailed them in French, and requested them to stop. They accordingly put ashore, and were joined by the Indians, among whom they were surprised to find the widow of Pierre Dorrien

[11] Mr. Hunt subsequently returned to St. Louis, at the entrance of the Missouri, in which neighbourhood he possessed extensive property, and from accounts which I have recently received, I feel pleasure in stating, has been elevated to the important office of governor of the state. A more estimable individual could not be selected for the situation.—R. C.

(a half-bred hunter, who had accompanied Mr. Read to the country of the Shoshonés the preceding autumn, as already mentioned), with her two children.[12] She told them, that shortly after Mr. Read had built his house she proceeded, with her husband and two other hunters, named Peznor and Le Clerc, between four and five days' march from the post to a part of the country well stocked with beaver, of which they succeeded in trapping a considerable quantity. One evening, about the beginning of January, while the poor fellows were thus occupied, Le Clerc staggered into her hut mortally wounded. He had merely strength sufficient to acquaint her that the savages had suddenly fallen on them while they were at their traps, and had killed her husband and Peznor.[13] He was then proceeding to give her directions as to the best means of effecting her escape; but ere he had concluded, death terminated his existence.

With that courage and self-possession of which few Indian women are devoid in times of necessity, she at once determined on flying from a spot so dangerous. With considerable difficulty she succeeded in catching two horses. On one she placed her clothes, a small quantity of dried salmon, and some beaver meat which remained in the hut. She mounted on the other with her two children, the elder of whom was only three years old, and the other did not exceed four months. Thus provided, she commenced her journey towards Mr. Read's establishment. On the third day, she observed a number of Indians on horseback, galloping in an easterly direction. She immediately dismounted with the children, and was fortunate enough to escape unnoticed. That night she slept without fire or water. Late in the evening of the fourth day, on which she expected to have arrived at Mr. Read's house, she came in sight of the spot on which it had stood, but was horror-struck at beholding there only a smoking ruin, with fresh

---

12 See also Franchère, *Narrative*, 343–44; and Ross, *First Settlers*, 265–70, which is the most accurate account. Reed had established his first post near present Vale, Oregon, but the hostility of the natives had forced him to move. Dorion and his men were killed near present Caldwell, Idaho. Reed's fort was at the mouth of the Boise River which entered the Snake River at a place different from at present.

13 This name is spelled in a variety of ways, including *Rizner, Reznor,* and *Regner.* He was a Kentuckian who had been with Andrew Henry. On his way back to St. Louis with several companions, he met the Hunt party and proceeded to join it. Along with four or five others he was left in the mountains to trap. They met Robert Stuart's party of returning Astorians and accompanied them for a short distance, but they subsequently left and returned to the Snake River country. In 1813, he and his companions joined Reed's party and were killed with them. See *Henry-Thompson Journals*, II, 885.

marks of blood scattered all around. Her fortitude, however, did not forsake her, and she determined to ascertain whether any of the party were still living.

Having concealed the children and horses in an adjoining cluster of trees, she armed herself with a tomahawk and a large knife, and after night-fall she cautiously crept towards the scene of carnage. All was silent and lonely, and at every step fresh traces of blood met her view. Anxious to ascertain if any had escaped the massacre, she repeatedly called out the various names of the party, but no voice responded. By the expiring glare of the smouldering timbers she observed a band of prairie wolves engaged in a sanguinary banquet. The sound of her voice scared them, and they fled. Fearful that they might bend their way to the spot in which she had deposited her precious charge, she hastened thither, and arrived just in time to save her children from three of those ferocious animals which were then approaching them.

From thence she proceeded the following morning towards a range of mountains not far from the upper parts of the Wallah Wallah River, where she intended to remain the rest of the winter. This place she reached on the next day in a state of great exhaustion from the want of food. Fortunately she had a buffalo robe, and two or three deer skins, with which, aided by some pine bark and cedar branches, she constructed a wigwam, that served to shelter her tolerably well from the inclemency of the weather. The spot she chose was a rocky recess close by a mountain spring. She was obliged to kill the two horses for food, the meat of which she smoke-dried, and the skins served as an additional covering to her frail habitation. In this cheerless and melancholy solitude, the wretched widow and her two poor orphans dragged on a miserable existence during a severe season. Towards the latter end of March, she had nearly consumed the last of her horse-flesh, in consequence of which she found it necessary to change her quarters. During the whole of this period she saw none of the natives, or any indication of human habitations. Having packed up as much covering and dried meat as she could carry, she placed it with her younger child on her back, and taking the elder by the hand, she bade adieu to her wintry encampment. After crossing the ridge of mountains she fell on the Wallah Wallah River, along the banks of which she continued until she arrived at its junction with the Columbia. Her reception and treatment by the tribe at that place was of the most cordial and hospitable description; and she had been living with them about a fortnight when the canoes passed, and took her up to Fort Oakinagan.

The house that had been built by Mr. Read had no paling or defence of any kind; and as the men were constantly out hunting, or procuring provisions, she supposed he had not more than one or two with him at the time they were attacked, and that the others had been cut off in the same manner as her husband and his companions. She could not assign any reason for this butchery, and up to the period I quitted the country, the cause of it was never satisfactorily ascertained. Some imagined that it was committed by the tribe to which the man belonged that had been hanged by Mr. Clarke, in revenge for his death; but this could not have been the case; for, leaving the policy or impolicy of that execution out of the question, we subsequently learned that his tribe inhabited the upper parts of Lewis' River, and never crossed the mountains beyond which Mr. Read had formed his establishment.

From the quantity of blood Dorrien's widow saw, she thinks that several of the savages must have been killed or wounded before their blood-thirsty efforts were crowned with such fatal success.

Mr. Read was a rough, warm-hearted, brave, old Irishman. Owing to some early disappointments in life he had quitted his native country while a young man, in search of wealth among regions

> *Where beasts with man divided empire claim,*
> *And the brown Indian marks with murd'rous aim;*

and after twenty-five years of toils, dangers, and privations, added another victim to the long list of those who have fallen sacrifices to Indian treachery.

Chapter 13

Arrival of the Isaac Tod—*Miss Jane Barnes, a white woman—Murder of one of our men by Indians—Trial and execution of the murderers—Death of Mr. Donald M'Tavish and five men*

We left Spokan House on the 25th of May, and reached Oakinagan on the 29th, where I found my disconsolate friend, the ex-subaltern, just recovering from the melancholy into which his hibernal solitude had thrown him. The different parties having now assembled, we all started for the sea on the 30th of May, and on the 11th of June arrived at Fort George. We were highly gratified at finding the so long expected *Isaac Tod* safe at anchor. After parting company with the men-of-war off Cape Horn, she touched at Juan Fernandez and the Gallipagos Islands, from whence she proceeded to Monterey, a Spanish settlement on the coast of California, for provisions. Here the captain was informed that a British man-of-war had put into San Francisco in distress, and was unable to leave it. This latter place is also a Spanish establishment, and is situated in lat. 38° N, about two degrees to the southward of Monterey. Captain Smith of the *Isaac Tod* immediately proceeded thither, and found the vessel alluded to was the *Racoon* sloop of war, commanded by Captain Black. This vessel, on quitting the Columbia, struck several times on the bar, and was so severely damaged in consequence, that she was obliged to make for San Francisco, which port she reached in a sinking state, with seven feet water in her hold. Finding it impossible to procure the necessary materials there to repair the damage, Captain Black and his officers had determined to abandon the vessel, and proceed overland to the Gulf of Mexico, whence they could have obtained a passage to England; but when the *Isaac Tod* arrived they succeeded, with her

155

assistance, in stopping the leaks, and putting the *Racoon* in good sailing order; after which the *Issac Tod* weighed anchor, and on the 17th of April crossed the bar of the Columbia, after a voyage of thirteen months from England.

She brought out the following passengers: viz. Donald M'Tavish[1] and John M'Donald,[2] proprietors; and Messrs. Alexander and James M'Tavish, Alexander Frazer, and Alexander Mackenzie,[3] clerks, with Doctor Swan, a medical gentleman engaged as resident physician at the fort.

The two first-named gentlemen, from their long experience of Indian living, knew well the little luxuries that would be most grateful to men so long debarred from the enjoyments of civilised life; and they accordingly brought out a few casks of bottled porter, some excellent cheese, and a quantity of prime English beef, which they had dressed and preserved in a peculiar manner in tin cases impervious to air; so that we could say we ate fresh beef which had been killed and dressed in England thirteen months before! Acceptable as were these refreshers to our memory of "lang syne," they brought out another object which more strongly recalled to our semi-barbarised ideas the thoughts of our "dear native home," than all the other *bonnes choses* contained in the vessel. This was neither more nor less than a flaxen-haired, blue-eyed daughter of Albion, who, in a temporary fit of erratic enthusiasm, had consented to become *le compagnon du voyage* of Mr. Mac——. Miss Jane Barnes had been a lively barmaid at an hotel in Portsmouth, at which Mr. Mac—— had stopped preparatory to his embarkation. This gentleman, being rather of an amorous temperament, proposed the trip to Miss Jane, who, "nothing

[1] Donald McTavish (d. 1814) was born in Scotland and probably joined the North West Company as a clerk before 1790, since he became a partner in 1799. He had served in both the English River and Athabaska districts, and in 1812, he returned to Great Britain on leave. He was in command of the expedition which sailed in the *Isaac Todd* for Astoria. See Wallace, *Documents*, 484.

[2] John McDonald of Garth (1774–?–1860). Like so many of the Northwesters, he was born in Scotland, and in 1791, he apprenticed to the North West Company as a clerk. In 1800, he became a partner. He was on the Columbia in 1811–12 and again the next year. Contrary to what Cox says, he did not arrive at Astoria on the *Isaac Todd* but rather on the *Raccoon*. He had left England in the supply ship, but at Rio de Janeiro he transferred to the sloop of war *Phoebe* and at Juan Fernández to the *Raccoon*. In 1815, he retired from the fur trade. See Wallace, *Documents*, 464.

[3] Alexander McTavish and James McTavish were both relatives of Donald McTavish. Alexander McKenzie was to lose his life in the service of Hudson's Bay Company in 1828. See Wallace, *Documents*, 475–76, 484.

156

loth," threw herself on his protection, regardless of consequences, and after encountering the perils of a long sea voyage, found herself an object of interest to the residents at the fort, and the greatest curiosity that ever gratified the wondering eyes of the blubber-loving aboriginals of the north-west coast of America. The Indians daily thronged in numbers to our fort for the mere purpose of gazing on, and admiring the fair beauty, every article of whose dress was examined with the most minute scrutiny. She had rather an extravagant wardrobe, and each day exhibited her in a new dress, which she always managed in a manner to display her figure to the best advantage. One day, her head, decorated with feathers and flowers, produced the greatest surprise; the next, her hair, braided and unconcealed by any covering, excited equal wonder and admiration. The young women felt almost afraid to approach her, and the old were highly gratified at being permitted to touch her person. Some of the chiefs having learned that her protector intended to send her home, thought to prevent such a measure by making proposals of marriage. One of them in particular, the son of Comcomly,[4] the principal chief of the Chinooks, came to the fort attired in his richest dress, his face fancifully bedaubed with red paint, and his body redolent of whale oil. He was young, and had four native wives. He told her, that if she would become his wife, he would send one hundred sea-otters to her relations; that he would never ask her to carry wood, draw water, dig for roots, or hunt for provisions; that he would make her mistress over his other wives, and permit her to sit at her ease from morning to night, and wear her own clothes;[5] that she should always have abundance of fat salmon, anchovies, and elk, and be allowed to smoke as many pipes of tobacco during the day as she thought proper; together with many other flattering inducements, the tithe of which would have shaken the constancy of a score of the chastest brown vestals that ever flourished among the lower tribes of the Columbia.

These tempting offers, however, had no charms for Jane. Her long voyage had not yet eradicated certain Anglican predilections respecting mankind, which she had contracted in the country of her birth, and among which she did not include a flat head, a half naked body, or a copper-coloured skin besmeared with whale oil.

[4] This was Cassakas, who, because of his position as heir apparent, was known, perhaps somewhat derisively, as the "Prince of Wales."

[5] Meaning that he would not insist on her wearing the light covering of the Indian females.—R. C.

Her native inamorato made several other ineffectual proposals; but finding her inflexible, he declared he would never more come near the fort while she remained there. We shortly afterwards learned that he had concerted a plan with some daring young men of his tribe to carry her off while she was walking on the beach (her general custom every evening while the gentlemen were at dinner), a practice which, after this information, she was obliged to discontinue.

Mr. Mac—— at first intended to have brought her with him across the continent to Montreal; but on learning the impracticability of her performing such an arduous journey, he abandoned that idea, and made arrangements with the captain for her return to England by way of Canton. A few words more, and I shall have done with Miss Barnes. On the arrival of the vessel at Canton she became an object of curiosity and admiration among the inhabitants of the "Celestial empire." An English gentleman of great wealth, connected with the East-India Company, offered her a splendid establishment. It was infinitely superior to any of the proposals made by the Chinook nobility, and far beyond any thing she could ever expect in England. It was therefore prudently accepted, and the last account I heard of her stated that she was then enjoying all the luxuries of eastern magnificence.[6]

About a month after the arrival of the *Isaac Tod* a circumstance occurred which, as it caused a considerable sensation for some time, I shall fully relate.

[6] Miss Barnes was fond of quotations; but she was no *Blue*. [She was not learned or pedantic.—eds.] One of the clerks was one day defending the native and half-bred women, whose characters she had violently attacked, and he recriminated in no very measured language on the conduct of the white ladies: "O Mr. Mac!" said she "I suppose you agree with *Shakespeare* that "every woman is at heart a rake?" "*Pope*, ma'am if you please." "Pope! Pope!" replied Jane. "Bless me, sir! you must be wrong; *rake* is certainly the word. I never heard of but one female Pope." Then in order to terminate the argument, she pretended to read an old newspaper which she held in her hand. He quickly discovered by her keeping the wrong end uppermost that she did not know a syllable of its contents. He quitted her abruptly; and as he was coming out I met him at the door, a wicked and malicious grin ruffling his sun-burnt features. "Well, Mac," said I, "what's the matter? You seem annoyed." "What do you think," he replied, "I have just had a conversation with that fine-looking damsel there, who looks down with such contempt on our women, and may I be d——d if the b——h understands B from a buffalo!" Her supposed education was the only excuse in his opinion to justify her usurpation of superiority; that gone, he judged her "poor indeed."—R. C.

Cox is in error here. Jane Barnes returned to England and later visited the Columbia River again, this time as the wife of Captain Robson of the ship *Columbia*. See Mary W. Avery, "An Additional Chapter on Jane Barnes," *Pacific Northwest Quarterly*, Vol. XLIV, pp. 330–32.—eds.

Fort Okanogan

Interior Trading Post

From Tacoma Edition of Irving's Astoria
(New York, G. P. Putnam's Sons, 1897)

Murder of One of Our Men by Indians

About two miles at the rear of the fort, on the Clatsop River, a place had been established for making charcoal. One of the men employed at this business was a poor half-witted American from Boston, named Judge,[7] who had crossed the continent with Mr. Hunt's party, and whose sufferings during that journey had partially deranged his intellect. He was however a capital woodsman; and few men could compete with him, as he said himself, in hewing down forests "by the acre." His comrade had been absent one day, selecting proper wood for charcoal, and on returning to the lodge in the evening he found the body of the unfortunate Judge lying stretched on the ground, with his skull completely cleft in two by the blow of an axe which was lying beside him steeped in blood. He instantly repaired to the fort, and communicated the dreadful intelligence; upon which a party was despatched for the mangled remains of poor Judge.

Mr. M'Tavish forthwith summoned all the neighbouring chiefs to attend at the fort; and on the following day there was a congress of representatives from the Chinooks, Chilts,[8] Clatsops, Killymucks,[9] and Cathlamahs. They could not assign any reason for the murder; nor indeed could any one, for Judge was the most harmless individual belonging to our establishment. They promised, however, that every exertion should be made on their part for the discovery of the perpetrators; and Mr. M'Tavish offered a large reward for their apprehension. Some time elapsed in vain inquiry; but, through the agency of the Clatsop chief, we received private information that the murderers were two of the Killymucks, and that if we sent a party well armed to his village, he would render every assistance to take them into custody. Mr. Matthews and seven men were accordingly ordered on this dangerous duty. They proceeded early in the day in a canoe up the Clatsop River, as if on a hunting excursion, and stopped late in the evening at a place previously agreed on, where they were joined by three Clatsops and a Killymuck, who was the informer. After night-fall they continued on until they arrived at the Killymuck village, where they landed. The informer having pointed out the lodges in which the murderers slept, and told their names, separated from the party. Mr. Matthews immediately proceeded to the chief's

[7] There is a strong probability that this was Archibald Pelton, mentioned earlier.
[8] Chehalis tribe.
[9] Tillamook Indians.

dwelling, and made him acquainted with the object of his visit. He appeared somewhat surprised, but stated, that having promised to assist in discovering them, he would not oppose their apprehension, provided they were allowed a fair trial, and that nothing should befall them but on the clearest testimony. This was of course agreed to; and Mr. Matthews, with his party, then cautiously approached the habitations of the two delinquents, which were adjoining each other; and having divided his men, leaving the Clatsops to mind the canoe, they entered the houses, and succeeded in seizing, binding, and hurrying the prisoners on board before the village was alarmed. The men paddled hard until they arrived at the Clatsop village, where they stopped to rest, and the following morning at day-break they reached Fort George in safety. The day subsequent to that of our arrival was fixed for the trial. It was held in the large dining-hall; and the jury was composed of the gentlemen belonging to the Company, with an equal number of Indians, consisting of chiefs and chieftain-esses, for among these tribes old women possess great authority. It appeared in the course of the investigation that revenge was the cause of the murder. About two years before this period, while houses were being built for the men, the greater number of them were lodged in tents and huts about the fort, from which the Indians were constantly in the practice of pilfering whatever they could lay their hands on, particularly at night, when the workmen were buried in sleep after the labour of the day.

Judge and three others were lodged together; and one night, when it was supposed they were fast asleep, one of them heard the noise of footsteps outside approaching the tent. Through a slit in the canvas he ascertained they were natives, and without awaking his comrades, he cautiously unsheathed his sword, and waited a few minutes in silence, watching their motions, until they at length reached the tent, the lower part of which they were in the act of raising, when, by a desperate blow of the sword, he severely cut one of their arms. The savage gave a dreadful yell, and the Canadian rushed out, when he distinctly perceived two Indians running away, and disappear in the gloom of the forest. This circumstance made some noise at the time; the parties were not discovered, and in a few weeks the event was forgotten by our people; but it was not so with the savages. They harboured the most deep and deadly revenge; and thinking that Judge was the person who had inflicted the wound, they determined to wreak their vengeance on him. For this purpose they had been for nearly two years occasionally lurking about the fort, until the fatal opportunity presented itself of gratifying their demoniacal passion. On the day of the murder, after Judge's comrade had quitted the lodge, they stole unperceived on him, and while he was engaged at the fire they felled him to the ground with a blow of his own axe, after which they split his skull, and made their escape. All these facts were brought out during the trial, which lasted the greater part of the day. Several of the witnesses underwent a strict cross-examination, particularly by the old women, who evinced much more acuteness than was displayed by the chiefs.

The prisoners made no defence, and observed a sulky taciturnity during the whole of the proceedings. They were found guilty by the unanimous verdict of the jury, and sentenced to be shot the following morning. They showed no signs of repentance or sorrow; and on being led out of the hall, the fellow whose arm had been cut held it up, and exclaimed, "Were I now free, and he alive, I would do the same thing again!"

About nine o'clock the next morning they were brought from the guard-house pinioned, and conducted to the farther end of the wharf, at which place it was arranged they were to suffer. Twenty-four men were selected by ballot to carry the dreadful sentence into execution under the command of Mr. M——, to whom the lot fell. Immense numbers of Indians belonging to the various surrounding nations were in attendance, some on shore, and others in canoes. The guns on the battery and in the bastions were loaded with grape, and attended by men with slow matches. The remainder of our people were drawn up in front of the fort, all armed with muskets and bayonets. The culprits made considerable opposition to their being tied together, and refused to kneel, or allow the caps to be drawn over their eyes. At length, between force and entreaty, these preliminaries were accomplished, and orders were given to fire. After the discharge a loud and frightful yell was sent forth from the surrounding savages; but they remained tranquil. On the smoke clearing away, it was perceived that both the unfortunate men were still alive, although several balls had taken effect. M. M—— ordered the party to reload quickly, and a second volley was discharged. One only was killed; and as the other made repeated attempts to rise, and appeared to suffer great agony, he was despatched by one of the men, who fired a ball through his head.

161

The party then gave three cheers, and retired to the fort, while the friends and relatives of the deceased took away their bodies amidst the greatest lamentations; during which not a murmur was heard, or the slightest symptom of disapprobation expressed. Shortly after a number of the chiefs and elders came up to the fort, when Mr. M'Tavish invited them into the hall, to thank them for their assistance; and having paid the promised rewards, and made various presents, they smoked the calumet of peace, and departed for their respective villages, apparently much gratified with the manner they had been treated.

Scarcely was this tragedy ended when one more fatal to the interests of the Company occurred by the melancholy and untimely death of Mr. Donald M'Tavish.[10] This gentleman had embarked in an open boat, with six *voyageurs,* to proceed to the opposite side of the Columbia. It blew a stiff gale; and about the middle of the river, owing to some mismanagement of the sail, a heavy wave struck the boat, which instantly filled and went down. With the exception of one man, they all perished; he succeeded in gaining a snag which was a few feet above the water, and on which he remained for nearly two hours, until he was rescued when in a state of great exhaustion by two Chinooks, who proceeded to his assistance in a small canoe. Thus perished the respected Mr. Donald M'Tavish, one of the oldest proprietors of the North-West Company, and for many years the principal director for managing the affairs of the interior. He had realized an independent fortune, and had, in fact, retired from the Company, when he volunteered his services to organise the new department of Columbia; after effecting which object it was his intention to have crossed the continent to Canada, and from thence to proceed to Scotland, where he had purchased an estate, on which, after a life of fatigues and hardships, he had hoped to spend an old age of ease and comfort. Mr. M'Tavish was a man of bold and decided character. His enmity was open and undisguised, his friendship warm and sincere. Sprung from a comparatively humble origin, he was the founder of his own fortune; and merit with him was sure to be appreciated without reference to a man's family or connexions.

The day after this melancholy event the body of the lamented gentleman, with those of four of the men, were found, and interred

---

[10] Alexander Henry, the younger, was also an occupant of the boat and was drowned at the same time. It is peculiar that Cox makes no mention of him.

in a handsome spot behind the north-east bastion of Fort George, where a small monument, tolerably well engraved, points to the future Indian trader the last earthly remains of the enterprising Donald M'Tavish.

Chapter 14

*Sketch of the Indians about the mouth of the Columbia—Process of flattening the head—Thievish disposition—Treatment of their slaves—Suggestions to the missionary societies—Dreadful ravages of the small-pox—Jack Ramsay—Their ideas of religion—Curious superstition—Marriage ceremonies—Anecdote—Aversion to ardent spirits—Government—War—Arms and armour—Canoes and houses—System of cooking—Utensils—Gambling—*Haiqua*—Quack doctors—Mode of burial*

1814

We remained a couple of months this summer at Fort George, making the necessary arrangements for our winter's campaign. During this period we made several excursions on pleasure or business to the villages of the various tribes, from one to three days' journey from the fort. They differ little from each other in laws, manners, or customs, and were I to make a distinction, I would say the Cathlamahs are the most tranquil, the Killymucks the most roguish, the Clatsops the most honest, and the Chinooks the most incontinent. The Chilts, a small tribe who inhabit the coast to the northward of Cape Disappointment, partake in some degree of these various qualities. The abominable custom of flattening their heads prevails among them all. Immediately after birth the infant is placed in a kind of oblong cradle formed like a trough, with moss under it. One end, on which the head reposes, is more elevated than the rest. A padding is then placed on the forehead with a piece of cedar-bark over it, and by means of cords passed through small holes on each side of the cradle, the padding is pressed against the head. It is kept in this manner upwards of a year, and is not I believe attended with much pain. The appearance of the infant, however, while in this state of compression, is frightful, and its little black eyes, forced out by the tightness of the bandages, resemble those of a mouse choked in a trap. When released from this inhuman process, the head is perfectly flattened, and the upper part of it seldom exceeds an inch in thickness. It never afterwards recovers its rotundity. They deem this an essential point of beauty, and the most devoted adherent of our first Charles never entertained a stronger aversion to a *Round-head* than these savages.[1]

They allege, as an excuse for this custom, that all their slaves have round heads; and accordingly every child of a bondsman, who is not adopted by the tribe, inherits not only his father's degradation, but his parental rotundity of cranium.

This deformity is unredeemed by any peculiar beauty either in features or person. The height of the men varies from five feet to five feet six inches; that of the women is generally six or eight inches less. The nose is rather flat, with distended nostrils; and a mouth, seldom closed, exposes to view an abominable set of short dirty irregular teeth. The limbs of the men are in general well-shaped; but the women, owing to tight ligatures which they wear on the lower part of the legs, are quite bandy, with thick ankles, and broad flat feet. They have loose hanging breasts, slit ears, and perforated noses, which, added to greasy heads, and bodies saturated with fish-oil, constitute the sum total of their personal attractions.

The good qualities of these Indians are few; their vices many. Industry, patience, sobriety, and ingenuity nearly comprise the former; while in the latter may be classed thieving, lying, incontinence, gambling, and cruelty. They are also perfect hypocrites. Each tribe accuses the other of "envy, hatred, malice, and all uncharitableness." Even the natives of the same village, while they feign an outward appearance of friendship, indulge in a certain propensity called backbiting; in this respect differing but little from the inhabitants of more civilised countries, among whom the prevalence of such ill-natured practices has, by certain envious and satirical coffee-drinkers, been unjustly attributed to the scandalising influence of tea.

[1] Doctor Swan, on examining the skulls I had taken, candidly confessed that nothing short of ocular demonstration could have convinced him of the possibility of moulding the human head into such a form.—R. C. (Dr. Swan's first name is unknown. He had come out on the *Isaac Todd* and apparently returned on it.—eds.)

Their bravery is rather doubtful; but what they want in courage they make up in effrontery. Fear alone prevents them from making any open or violent attempt at robbery; and their offences under this head, in legal parlance, may more strictly be styled petty larcenies. I have seen a fellow stopped on suspicion of stealing an axe. He denied the charge with the most barefaced impudence; and when the stolen article was pulled from under his robe, instead of expressing any regret, he burst out laughing, and alleged he was only joking. One of the men gave him a few kicks, which he endured with great *sangfroid;* and on joining his companions, they received him with smiling countenances, and bantered him on the failure of his attempt. They seldom make any resistance to these summary punishments; and if the chastisement takes place in the presence of a chief, he seems delighted at the infliction.

They purchase slaves from the neighbouring tribes for beaver, otter, beads, &c. I could never learn whether any were taken by them in war. While in good health and able to work, they are well treated; but the moment they fall sick, or become unfit for labour, the unfortunate slaves are totally neglected, and left to perish in the most miserable manner. After death their bodies are thrown without any ceremony at the trunk of a tree, or into an adjoining wood. It sometimes happens that a slave is adopted by a family; in which case he is permitted to marry one of the tribe, and his children, by undergoing the flattening process, melt down into the great mass of the community.

Chastity is an item seldom inscribed on the credit side of their account current with futurity. Indeed a strict observance of it before marriage is not an article of their moral code.

Formerly an act of post-nuptial incontinence subjected the woman to the loss of life; but in latter times infractions of conjugal rights are often connived at, or if committed *sans permission,* only slightly punished.[2]

Numbers of the women reside during certain periods of the year in small huts about the fort from which it is difficult to keep the men. They generally retire with the fall of the leaf to their respective villages, and during the winter months seldom visit Fort George. But on the arrival of the spring and autumn brigades from the interior

[2] We were told by an old man that he knew but of one instance in which a husband killed his wife for infidelity.—R. C.

they pour in from all parts, and besiege our *voyageurs* much after the manner which their frail sisters at Portsmouth adopt when attacking the crews of a newly arrived India fleet. Mothers participate with their daughters in the proceeds arising from their prostitution; and, in many instances, husbands share with their wives the wages of infamy. Disease is the natural consequence of this state of general demoralization, and numbers of the unfortunate beings suffer dreadfully from the effects of their promiscuous intercourse.

Now that the North-West and Hudson's Bay Companies have become united, and that rivalship in trade cannot be brought forward as an excuse for corrupting Indians, it would be highly desirable that the missionaries would turn their thoughts to this remote and too long neglected corner of the globe. Their pious labours have already effected wonders in the comparatively small islands of the Pacific, where idolatry, human sacrifices, and other crimes more revolting to humanity, have been abolished. I would therefore respectfully suggest to the consideration of the benevolent individuals who constitute the missionary societies, the propriety of extending the sphere of their exertions to the north-west coast of America, and from thence through the interior of that vast continent; the aboriginal inhabitants of which, with the exception of Canada and a very trifling part of the frontiers, are still buried in the deepest ignorance. During the period that France held possession of the Canadas, the Jesuits made wonderful progress in converting the Indians, and most of the natives of the two provinces are now Christians. In my journey across the continent, small wooden huts, ornamented with crucifixes and other symbols of Christianity, situated from five to seven hundred miles beyond the limits of civilization, were pointed out to me, which had formerly been inhabited by these enterprising missionaries in their progress through the wilderness. These dwellings are now deserted, but are still regarded with pious reverence by the thoughtless *voyageurs;* and even the poor Indians, who by the cessation of the Jesuit missions, have relapsed into their former habits, pay the utmost respect to the houses, which were inhabited, as they say, by "the good white fathers, who, unlike other men, never robbed or cheated them." Since the annexation of Canada to the British crown, Indian conversion has almost ceased, or has made, at most, a slow and sickly progress. Their moral amelioration is completely neglected by both English and Americans; and it is only in periods of war that we pay them any attention. The first settlers of the United States did not act so. They fought their way through the country with the Bible in one hand and the sword in the other; and it was not until the former ceased to convince that recourse was had to the latter. Objectionable, however, as this system undoubtedly was, the plan adopted by the modern Americans is more so. Their anti-republican love of aggrandizement, by the continual extension of their territorial possessions, must sooner or later destroy the unity of their confederation; and it is a subject deeply to be lamented that, in their gradual encroachments on the Indian lands, Christianity is forgotten, the word of God does not now, as in the time of their forefathers, keep in check the sanguinary sword of man; and extermination, instead of regeneration, seems to be their motto. To return to the Columbia. It is the only situation on the north-west coast, to the northward of California, free from danger; and I have no doubt that by a proper application the Hudson's Bay Company, who have now possession of Fort George, would give a passage, and afford every facility to resident missionaries. Odious as the vices are to which I have referred, the few good qualities which the Indians possess would materially assist in bringing them to a knowledge of the true religion. Independently of the beneficial results which we might naturally expect to flow from their exertions among the natives, there is another consideration which induces me to think that the Company would, for its own interest, render them every assistance in its power. I allude to the situation of a number of men in its employment whose knowledge of Christianity, owing to a long absence from their native country, has fallen into a kind of abeyance, and which would undoubtedly be revived by the cheering presence of a minister of God. Cannibalism, although unknown among the Indians of the Columbia, is practised by the savages on the coast to the northward of that river; so that by the progressive labours of the missionaries, this dreadful custom, with the others, might be gradually abolished. The settlement formed by Lord Selkirk on Red River,[3] which falls into the great Lake Winepic, and which suffered so much in its infancy from interested enemies, is at present, I am happy to hear, in a thriving condition. A missionary has been established here, whose labours have already been productive of much good. Numbers of the surrounding natives have become converts, and they are yearly increasing. The progress of civili-

[3] See Alexander Ross, *The Red River Settlement: Its Rise, Progress, and Present State* (London, Smith, Elder and Company, 1856).

zation will gradually gain ground among the western tribes; and we may indulge the pleasing hope that the day is not far distant when the missionaries, in their glorious career eastward and westward, from the St. Lawrence and the mouth of the Columbia, despite the many difficulties and dangers they must unavoidably encounter, may meet on the Rocky Mountains, and from their ice-covered summits proclaim to the benighted savages "Glory to God in the highest, and on earth peace and good-will towards men."

About thirty years before this period the small-pox had committed dreadful ravages among these Indians, the vestiges of which were still visible on the countenances of the elderly men and women. It is believed in the north-west that this disease was wilfully introduced by the American traders among the Indians of the Missouri, as a short and easy method of reducing their numbers, and thereby destroying in a great measure their hostility to the whites. The Americans throw the blame on the French; while they in turn deny the foul imputation, and broadly charge the Spaniards as the original delinquents. Be this as it may, the disease first proceeded from the banks of the Missouri, and the British are free from having had any participation in the detestable act. It travelled with destructive rapidity as far north as Athabasca and the shores of the Great Slave Lake, crossed the Rocky Mountains at the sources of the Missouri, and having fastened its deadly venom on the Snake Indians, spread its devastating course to the northward and westward, until its frightful progress was arrested by the Pacific Ocean. Some of the old *voyageurs* who were stationed at English River and Athabasca, when this scourge made its first appearance, give the most harrowing details of its ravages. The unfortunate Indians, when in the height of the fever, would plunge into a river, which generally caused instant death; and thousands of the miserable wretches by suicide anticipated its fatal termination. Whole villages were depopulated, and an old man well known in the Indian country, named Louis La Liberté, told me that one morning during its height he saw between two and three hundred bodies of men, women, and children, suspended from trees, close to an adjoining village of the Cree nation, the surviving inhabitants of which did not exceed forty persons. They believed that the "Great Master of Life had delivered them over to the Evil Spirit for their wicked courses," and for many years afterwards those who escaped, or survived the deadly contagion, strictly conformed themselves to their

169

own code of moral laws. The recollection of it, however, is now fast wearing away from their memory. Those who bore any traces of it are nearly extinct; and on the eastern side of the mountains, intoxication, and its attendant vices are becoming too prevalent. The western tribes still remember it with a superstitious dread, of which Mr. M'Dougall took advantage, when he learned that the *Tonquin* had been cut off. He assembled several of the chieftains, and showing them a small bottle, declared that it contained the small-pox; that although his force was weak in number, he was strong in medicine; and that in consequence of the treacherous cruelty of the northern Indians, he would open the bottle and send the small-pox among them. The chiefs strongly remonstrated against his doing so. They told him that they and their relations were always friendly to the white people; that they would remain so; that if the small-pox was once let out, it would run like fire among the good people as well as among the bad; and that it was inconsistent with justice to punish friends for the crimes committed by enemies. Mr. M'Dougall appeared to be convinced by these reasons, and promised, that if the white people were not attacked or robbed for the future, the fatal bottle should not be uncorked. He was greatly dreaded by the Indians, who were fully impressed with the idea that he held their fate in his hands, and they called him by way of pre-eminence, "the great small-pox chief."[4]

An Indian belonging to a small tribe on the coast, to the southward of the Clatsops, occasionally visited the fort. He was a perfect *lusus naturae,* and his history was rather curious. His skin was fair, his face partially freckled, and his hair quite red. He was about five feet ten inches high, was slender, but remarkably well made; his head had not undergone the flattening process; and he was called *Jack Ramsay,* in consequence of that name having been punctured on his left arm.[5] The Indians allege that his father was an English sailor, who had deserted from a trading vessel, and had lived many years among their tribe, one of whom he married; that when Jack was born, he insisted on preserving the child's head in its natural state, and while young had punctured the arm in the above manner. Old Ramsay had died about twenty years before this period; he had sev-

[4] This deceit, which gained wide credence among the Indians, was later at least partially responsible for the Whitman Massacre.

[5] On Jack Ramsay see also *Original Journals of Lewis and Clark Expedition, 1804–1806,* edited by Reuben Gold Thwaites (8 vols., New York, Dodd, Mead and Company, 1904–1905), III, 301.

eral more children, but Jack was the only red-headed one among them. He was the only half-bred I ever saw with red hair, as that race in general partake of the swarthy hue derived from their maternal ancestors. Poor Jack was fond of his father's countrymen, and had the decency to wear trousers whenever he came to the fort. We therefore made a collection of old clothes for his use, sufficient to last him for many years.

The ideas of these Indians on the subject of a future state do not differ much from the opinions entertained by the natives of the interior. They believe that those who have not committed murder; who have fulfilled the relative duties of son, father, and husband; who have been good fishermen, &c., will after their death go to a place of happiness, in which they will find an abundant supply of fish, fruit, &c.; while those who have followed a contrary course of life will be condemned to a cold and barren country, in which bitter fruits and salt water will form their principal means of subsistence. Mr. Franchère, who was stationed permanently at Fort George, and who obtained an accurate knowledge of their language, &c., states they have a tradition relative to the origin of mankind, of which the following is the substance: Man was at first created by a divinity named *Etalapass;* but he was originally imperfect. His mouth was not divided, his eyes were closed, and his hands and feet immoveable; in short, he was rather a statue of flesh than a living being. A second divinity, named *Ecannum,* less powerful than *Etalapass,* but more benevolent, seeing man in this imperfect state, took pity on him, and with a sharp stone opened his mouth, unclosed his eyes, and imparted motion to his hands and feet. Not satisfied with these gifts, the compassionate deity taught mankind how to make canoes, paddles, nets, and all their domestic utensils. He also overturned rocks into the rivers, which, by obstructing the progress of the fish through the waters, enabled them to take sufficient to satisfy their wants. We observed no idols among them; and although they had some small grotesque-looking figures, carved out of wood, they seemed to pay them no respect, and often offered to barter them for trifles.

Civilised countries are not exempt from superstition; it is therefore not surprising to find it exist among untutored savages. They believe that if salmon be cut crossways the fishery will be unproductive, and that a famine will follow. In the summer of 1811, they at first brought but a small quantity to the people who were then build-

171

ing the fort. As Mr. M'Dougall knew there was no scarcity, he reproached the chiefs for furnishing such a scanty supply; they admitted the charge, but assigned as a reason their fears that the white people would cut it in the unlucky way. Mr. M'Dougall promised to follow their plan, upon which they brought a tolerable good quantity, but all roasted; and which, in order to avoid displeasing them, our people were obliged to eat before sunset each day.

The negotiations preceding a marriage are short, and the ceremony itself simple. When a young man has made his choice, he commissions his parents or other relations to open the business to the girl's relations. They are to receive a certain quantity of presents; and when these are agreed on, they all repair to the house intended for the future residence of the young couple, to which nearly all the inhabitants of the village are invited. The presents, which consist of slaves, axes, beads, kettles, *haiqua*, brass and copper bracelets, &c., are now distributed by the young man, who in his turn receives an equal or perhaps greater quantity, from the girl's relations. The bride, decorated with the various ornaments common among the tribe, is then led forth by a few old women, and presented to the bridegroom. He receives her as his wife; and the elders, after wishing them plenty of fish, fruit, roots, and children, retire from the house, accompanied by all the strangers. The marriage tie is not indissoluble. A man may repudiate his wife, who is then at liberty to take another husband. Infidelity is the general cause of these separations, which however are of rare occurrence.

A man may have as many wives as his means will permit him to keep. Some have four or five. They live together in the greatest harmony; and although their lord may love one more than another, it causes no jealousy or disunion among the rest.

Many of these women, who have followed a depraved course of life before marriage, become excellent and faithful wives afterwards; an instance of which I shall here relate: In the early part of this summer, one of the clerks, who had been out on a trading excursion, happened to be present at a marriage in the Clatsop village. He was surprised at recognising in the bride an old *chere amie*, who the preceding year had spent three weeks with him in his tent, actually decorated with some of the baubles he had then given her. His eye caught hers for a moment; but his appearance excited not the least emotion, and she passed him by as one whom she had never seen.

A few days afterwards she came to the fort accompanied by her husband and the other Indians. She remained at the gate while the men were selling some fish in the trading store. Her old lover, observing her alone, attempted to renew their former acquaintance; but she betrayed no symptom of recognition, and in a cold distant manner told him to go about his business.

All the Indians on the Columbia entertain a strong aversion to ardent spirits, which they regard as poison. They allege that slaves only drink to excess; and that drunkenness is degrading to free men. On one occasion some of the gentlemen at Fort George induced a son of Comcomly the chief to drink a few glasses of rum. Intoxication quickly followed, accompanied by sickness; in which condition he returned home to his father's house, and for a couple of days remained in a state of stupor. The old chief subsequently reproached the people at the fort for having degraded his son by making him drunk, and thereby exposing him to the laughter of his slaves.

Each village is governed by its own chief. He possesses little authority, and is respected in proportion to the number of wives, slaves, &c., which he may keep. The greater number of these, the greater the chief. He is entitled, however, to considerable posthumous honour; for at his death the tribe go into mourning by cutting their hair, and for some months continue to chant a kind of funeral dirge to his memory. As each village forms a petty sovereignty, governed by independent chieftains, differences often arise between them. These differences are generally settled by giving compensation for the injury inflicted; but in the event of a serious offence, such as murder (which is very rare), or the abduction of a woman (which is not uncommon), the parties prepare for war.

The great mass of the American Indians, in their warlike encounters, fall suddenly on their enemies, and taking them unprepared, massacre or capture men, women, and children. The plan adopted by the Chinooks forms an honourable exception to this system. Having once determined on hostilities, they give notice to the enemy of the day on which they intend to make the attack; and having previously engaged as auxiliaries a number of young men whom they pay for that purpose, they embark in their canoes for the scene of action. Several of their women accompany them on these expeditions, and assist in working the canoes.

On arriving at the enemy's village they enter into a parley, and endeavour by negotiation to terminate the quarrel amicably. Sometimes a third party, who preserves a strict neutrality, undertakes the office of mediator; but should their joint efforts fail in procuring redress, they immediately prepare for action. Should the day be far advanced, the combat is deferred, by mutual consent, till the following morning; and they pass the intervening night in frightful yells, and making use of abusive and insulting language to each other. They generally fight from their canoes, which they take care to incline to one side, presenting the higher flank to the enemy; and in this position, with their bodies quite bent, the battle commences. Owing to the cover of their canoes, and their impenetrable armour, it is seldom bloody; and as soon as one or two men fall, the party to whom they belonged acknowledge themselves vanquished, and the combat ceases. If the assailants be unsuccessful, they return without redress; but if conquerors, they receive various presents from the vanquished party in addition to their original demand. The women and children are always sent away before the engagement commences.

Their warlike weapons are the bow and arrow, with a curious kind of short double-edged sword or club, two and a half feet in length by six inches in breadth. They seldom, however, fight near enough to make use of this formidable instrument.

Their armour consists of a shirt of elk-skin remarkably thick, doubled, and thrown over the shoulders, with holes for the arms. It descends to the ancles; and from the thickness of the leather is perfectly arrow-proof. The head is covered by a species of helmet made of cedar bark, bear grass, and leather, and is also impenetrable by arrows. The neck, therefore, is the only vital part of the body exposed to danger in action. In addition to the above they have another kind of armour, which they occasionally wear in place of the leathern shirt. It is a species of corset, formed of thin slips of hard wood ingeniously laced together by bear grass, and is much lighter and more pliable than the former; but it does not cover so much of the body. They have a few guns, which they seldom use. They are not good hunters; and their chief dependence for support is on the produce of the water. It is unnecessary to mention that in their warlike expeditions their faces and bodies are painted in various colours, and with the most grotesque figures.

Their canoes are of various forms and sizes. The following description of the largest kind of these vessels I take from Lewis and Clarke. It is perfectly accurate, and more technical than I could give it.

They are upwards of fifty feet long, and will carry from eight to ten thousand pounds weight, or from twenty to thirty persons. Like all the canoes we have mentioned, they are cut out of a single trunk of a tree, which is generally white cedar, though the fir is sometimes used. The sides are secured by cross bars or round sticks, two or three inches in thickness, which are inserted through holes made just below the gunwales, and made fast with cords. The upper edge of the gunwale itself is about five-eights of an inch thick, and four or five in breadth; and folds outwards so as to form a kind of rim, which prevents the water from beating into the boat. The bow and stern are about the same height, and each provided with a comb reaching to the bottom of the boat. At each end also are pedestals, formed of the same solid piece, on which are placed strange grotesque figures of men or animals rising sometimes to the height of five feet, and composed of small pieces of wood firmly united, with great ingenuity, by inlaying and mortising, without a spike of any kind. The paddle is usually from four and a half to five feet in length; the handle being thick for one-third of its length, when it widens and is hollowed and thinned on each side of the centre, which forms a sort of rib. When they embark, one Indian sits in the stern and steers with a paddle; the others kneel in pairs in the bottom of the canoe, and sitting on their heels paddle over the gunwale next to them. In this way they ride with perfect safety the highest waves, and venture without the least concern in seas where other boats or seamen could not live an instant. They sit quietly and paddle, with no other movement, except when any large wave throws the boat on her side, and to the eye of the spectator she seems lost: the man to windward then steadies her by throwing his body towards the upper side, and sinking his paddle deep into the waves, appears to catch the water, and force it under the boat, which the same stroke pushes on with great velocity.

The description of their houses, and their manner of building them, I also extract from the same authority:

The houses in this neighbourhood are all large wooden buildings, varying in length from twenty to sixty feet, and from fourteen to twenty in width.[6] They are constructed in the following manner: Two or more posts of split timber, agreeably to the number of partitions, are sunk in the ground, above which they rise to the height of fourteen or eighteen feet. They are hollowed

[6] I have seen some of their houses upwards of ninety feet long, and from thirty to forty broad.—R. C.

175

at the top so as to receive the ends of a round beam or pole, stretching from one end to the other, and forming the upper point of the roof for the whole extent of the building. On each side of this range is placed another, which forms the eaves of the house, and is about five feet high; but as the building is often sunk to the depth of four or five feet, the eaves come very near the surface of the earth. Smaller pieces of timber are now extended by pairs in the form of rafters, from the lower to the upper beam, where they are attached at both ends with cords of cedar bark. On these rafters two or three ranges of small poles are placed horizontally, and secured in the same way with strings of cedar bark. The sides are now made with a range of wide boards sunk a small distance into the ground, with the upper ends projecting above the poles at the eaves, to which they are secured by a beam passing outside, parallel with the eave poles, and tied by cords of cedar bark passing through holes made in the boards at certain distances. The gable ends and partitions are formed in the same way, being fastened by beams on the outside, parallel to the rafters. The roof is then covered with a double range of thin boards, except an aperture of two or three feet in the centre, for the smoke to pass through. The entrance is by a small hole, cut out of the boards, and just large enough to admit the body. The very largest houses only are divided by partitions; for though three or more families reside in the same room, there is quite space enough for all of them.

In the centre of each room is a space six or eight feet square, sunk to the depth of twelve inches below the rest of the floor. and enclosed by four pieces of square timber. Here they make the fire, for which purpose pine bark is generally preferred. Around this fire-place mats are spread, and serve as seats during the day, and very frequently as beds at night: there is however a more permanent bed made, by fixing in two, or sometimes three sides of the room, posts reaching from the roof down to the ground, and at the distance of four feet from the wall. From these posts to the wall itself one or two ranges of boards are placed, so as to form shelves, on which they either sleep, or stow their various articles of merchandise. The uncured fish is hung in the smoke of their fire, as is also the flesh of the elk, when they are fortunate enough to procure any, which is but rarely.

Their culinary articles consist of a large square kettle made of cedar wood, a few platters made of ash, and awkward spoons made of the same material. Their mode of cooking is however more expeditious than ours. Having put a certain quantity of water into the kettle, they throw in several hot stones, which quickly cause the water to boil; the fish or meat is then put in, and the steam is kept from evaporating by a small mat thrown over the kettle. By this system a large salmon will be boiled in less than twenty minutes, and meat

176

in a proportionately short space of time. They are not scrupulously clean in their cooking. A kettle in which salmon is boiled in the morning may have elk dressed in it the same evening, and the following day be doomed to cook a dish of sturgeon, without being washed out, or scarcely rinsed. They occasionally roast both their meat and fish on small wooden *brochettes,* similar to those used by the upper Indians.

It will no doubt be regarded as a subject of surprise, that in felling the timber for their houses, and in the laborious operation of forming their canoes, they had not, previous to our arrival, an axe. Their only instruments consisted of a chisel generally formed out of an old file, a kind of oblong stone, which they used as a hammer, and a mallet made of spruce knot, well oiled and hardened by the action of fire. With these wretched tools they cut down trees from thirty to forty feet in circumference; and with unparalleled patience and perseverance continued their tedious and laborious undertaking until their domicile was roofed or their canoe fit to encounter the turbulent waves of the Columbia.

As their chief source of subsistence depends on their fisheries, they pay great attention to their nets, in the manufacture of which they exhibit their usual ingenuity. They occasionally fish with the hook and line. They make use of the common straight net, the scooping or dipping net, and the gig. Lewis and Clarke mention that "the first is of different lengths and depths, and used in taking salmon, carr, and trout, in the deep inlets among the marshy grounds, and the mouths of deep creeks. The scooping net is used for small fish in the spring and summer season; and in both kinds the net is formed of silk grass, or the bark of white cedar. The gig is used at all seasons, and for all kinds of fish they can procure with it; so too is the hook and line; of which the line is made of the same material as the net, and the hook generally brought by the traders; though before the whites came, they made hooks out of two small pieces of bone, resembling the European hook, but with a much more acute angle, where the two pieces were joined."

Gambling is one of their most incorrigible vices; and so inveterately are they attached to it, that the unfortunate gamester often finds himself stripped of slaves, beads, *haiqua,* and even nets. Their common game is a simple kind of hazard. One man takes a small stone which he changes for some time from hand to hand, all the

177

while humming a slow monotonous air. The bet is then made; and according as his adversary succeeds in guessing the hand in which the stone is concealed, he wins or loses. They seldom cheat, and submit to their losses with the most philosophical resignation.

Haiqua, which I have so often mentioned, is a white round shell of extreme hardness, varying from one to four inches in length, and from three eights to half an inch in circumference. It is hollow, slightly curved, and tapers a little towards the ends. These shells are highly estimated, the longest being the most valuable. They are found in the neighbourhood of Nootka, and form an important article of local traffic. The Indians regulate the price of their various articles by *haiqua,* a fathom of the best description being equal in value to ten good beaver skins. The most enlightened nations are inundated with charlatans; it is therefore not surprising they should flourish among rude barbarians. Every Indian village has its quack doctor, or, as they call him, "the strong man of medicine." The moment a native is attacked with sickness, no matter of what description, the physician is sent for. He immediately commences operations by stretching his patient on his back; while a number of his friends and relations surround him, each carrying a long and a short stick, with which they beat time to a mournful air which the doctor chants, and in which they join at intervals. Sometimes a slave is dispatched to the roof of the house, which he belabours most energetically with his drum-sticks, joining at the same time with a loud voice the chorus inside. The man of medicine then kneels, and presses with all his force his two fists on the patient's stomach. The unfortunate man, tortured with the pain produced by this violent operation, utters the most piercing cries; but his voice is drowned by the doctor and the by-standers, who chant loud and louder still the mighty "song of medicine."

At the end of each stanza the operator seizes the patient's hands, which he joins together and blows on. He thus continues alternately pressing and blowing until a small white stone, which he had previously placed in the patient's mouth, is forced out. This he exhibits with a triumphant air to the man's relations; and with all the confidence and pomposity of modern quackery, assures them the disease is destroyed, and that the patient must undoubtedly recover. Mr. Franchère states he has seen some of them carefully envelop the small stone, which they call the source of evil, in a piece of cedar bark, and throw it into the fire.

It frequently happens that a man, who might have been cured by a simple dose of medicine, is by this abominable system destroyed; but whether recovery or death be the consequence, the quack is equally recompensed. Some of the more intelligent undoubtedly perceive the imposition which these fellows practise; but the great faith which the ignorant and superstitious multitude have in their skill, deters any man from exposing their knavery. Latterly, however, numbers of their sick have applied for relief and assistance at Fort George; and as our prescriptions have been generally attended with success, their belief in the infallibility of those jugglers has been considerably weakened.

From the doctor to death, the charlatan to the coffin, the transition is not unnatural. When a Chinook dies, it matters not whether from natural causes or the effects of quackery, his remains are deposited in a small canoe, the body being previously enveloped in skins or mats. His bow, arrows, and other articles are laid by his side. The canoe is then placed on a high platform near the river's side, or on rocks out of the reach of the tide, and other mats tied over it. If the relations of the deceased can afford it, they place a larger canoe reversed over the one containing his body, and both are firmly tied together. His wives, relatives, and slaves go into mourning by cutting their hair; and for some time after his death repair twice a-day, at the rising and setting of the sun, to an adjoining wood to chant his funeral dirge.

Chapter 15

Voyage to the interior—Party attacked, and one man killed—Arrive at Spokan House—Joy of the Indians at our return—The chief's speech— Sketch of Mr. M'Donald—Duel between him and a chief—Kettle Indians, their surprise at seeing white men—Curious account of an hermaphrodite chief—Death of Jacques Hoole

On the 5th of August, 1814, we left Fort George. Our party, including proprietors and clerks, consisted of sixty men in nine heavily loaded canoes. We arrived early the third day at the foot of the rapids. It was here our men had been robbed the preceding autumn; and here also Mr. Stewart's party had been attacked, and himself wounded the following winter. We therefore took more than usual precautions, and formed a strong guard to protect the carriers. The natives were numerous, but evinced no disposition to be troublesome. As the chief did not appear with the flag, a party proceeded to the village and inquired for him. They were told he was absent from home. The Indian whom we suspected of having fired at Michel was also invisible. Their non-appearance looked rather suspicious, and induced us to be doubly cautious. By hard labour we finished the portage in one day, and encamped at the upper end. We arranged the goods and canoes in such a manner as to prevent a surprise, and the whole party was divided into two watches. At intervals during the night we heard footsteps among the rocks, and in the woods; but it passed over quietly, and at day-break we commenced reloading. A few of the natives came to us unarmed, and brought with them some fish and roots, which we purchased, and having distributed some tobacco among them, pushed off. The day after we reached the narrows and falls in safety.

When the last portage had been nearly finished numbers of the

180

Eneeshurs collected about us, and became very troublesome. They made several attempts to pilfer, and we were constrained to use some violence to keep them in check. We asked repeatedly for the chief, but were answered that he was in the plains hunting. This we did not believe, and finding that they still persevered in seizing every loose article they could pick up, we were obliged to order corporal punishment to be inflicted on three of the ringleaders. They went away followed by a numerous party of their friends. Their looks betokened revenge; and the few who remained told us to be on our guard, as they heard the others talking in a threatening manner. We therefore reloaded quickly, and crossed over to the opposite side. It was high and rocky, and possessed many points from which an enemy could attack us with effect. The day-light was fast receding; every one lent a hand to work the canoes, and still no place presented itself at which we could land with safety. With much difficulty and labour we at length reached the long rocky island already mentioned; and as it was then quite dark, we had no alternative but to land in a small sandy bay surrounded by high craggy rocks, of which the island was chiefly composed. We could not procure any wood, and were obliged to dine and sup on some cold boiled rice which had been left from morning. It was judged adviseable not to pitch the tents; and we slept on the beach behind the bales and cases of merchandise in rather an irregular manner. The first watch, to which I belonged, passed over tranquilly; and we retired to sleep at midnight, on being relieved by the second.

Our repose was not of long continuance. About half an hour before day-break the cry of *Les sauvages nous fléchent! Les sauvages nous fléchent!*[1] rung in our ears, followed by the report of several shots. Every man instantly seized his arms, and we discharged a volley at a rocky eminence which commanded the little bay, and from which the enemy had fired down on our sentinels. This dislodged the savages; but owing to the darkness of the morning, and our ignorance of the interior of the island, we did not think it prudent to pursue them.

It was impossible to ascertain whether any of our balls had taken effect on the enemy; and apprehensive of another attack in a spot so badly calculated for defence, and in which we were completely exposed, orders were given to load the canoes. In the hurry attendant upon this operation we did not at first miss one of our men, named

[1] The savages are shooting at us with arrows.—R. C.

Baptiste L'Amoureux,[2] whom we found lying wounded at the farther end of the bay, at which he had been posted as a sentinel. His moans conducted us to the spot. A ball had passed through his left breast, and came out near the shoulder. Every assistance was rendered him, but in vain; he never uttered a word; and ere the morning dawned he had ceased to breathe. We did not before imagine these savages had any fire-arms among them; but we had been mistaken.

No other fatality occurred, although several of the party had wonderful escapes. An arrow passed through the collar of one man's coat, and the nightcap of another was pierced through. Mr. La Rocque and I slept together, and an arrow penetrated six inches into the ground between our necks. Our safety may in a great degree be attributed to a number of the arrows having been intercepted by the bales and cases of trading goods.

The canoes were quickly loaded, and at daybreak we pushed off from this dangerous spot. As we paddled up the south side of the river some arrows were discharged at us from the island. We fired a few shots in return; but from the manner the assailants were covered, we conjectured our balls fell harmless.

On nearing the upper end of the island, we caught a passing view of forty or fifty of the savages not more than two hundred yards distant. Orders were immediately given to those who had their guns ready to fire; but before a trigger was pulled they had vanished. We landed at the spot; and a few of us, who ascended the rocks, observed them at a considerable distance running like hunted deer. We discharged a few random shots after them, upon which we re-embarked and proceeded on our voyage. At half-past eight we put ashore at a low sandy point covered with willows and cotton wood, for the purpose of breakfasting, and interring the body of L'Amoureux. The men were immediately set to work to dig a grave, into which were lowered the remains of the unfortunate Canadian. A few short prayers were said in French; and after the earth was thrown in, to a level with the surface, it was covered over with dry sand in such a manner as to keep the natives in ignorance of the occurrence.

We remained here a few hours to refit, at the end of which we resumed our journey. We saw no Indians during the remainder of the day, and encamped late on a low stony island, above a rapid, on which we found plenty of drift wood. The following day we passed

[2] He had come out with David Thompson.

182

a few villages of the friendly tribes, from whom we purchased some horses for the kettle. From hence to the Wallah Wallahs, with whom we stopped one day, nothing particular occurred. They received us in their usual friendly manner; and on inquiring from them to what tribe the Indians belonged who had given my small party such a chase the preceding autumn, they replied that they were relatives of the man who had been hanged by Mr. Clarke on Lewis' River, and were part of the Upper Nez Percés, that they were very bad people, much addicted to thieving, and that we should be very cautious how we fell in their way, as they had vowed to kill a white man as a satisfaction for the death of their relation.

We met a few of the Nez Percés at the mouth of Lewis' River; they appeared friendly, and sold us some horses. From this place nothing particular occurred until the 23d of August, on which day we arrived at Oakinagan. The news of the attack had preceded us, accompanied by the usual exaggerations of Indians. Mr. Ross, who was in charge of that establishment, informed us that the first intelligence he received stated that ten white men and twenty Indians had been killed. By other accounts our loss was varied from fifteen to twenty, and one statement destroyed half the party, and sent the remainder back to the sea, with the loss of all the goods.

From this place Mr. Keith proceeded with dispatches to the other side of the mountains; and the various parties separated for their summer destinations. Mine was Spokan House, in company with Messrs. Stewart, M'Millan, and M'Donald. We left Oakinagan on the 27th, and reached Spokan on the 31st of August. The trading goods had been exhausted long before, and the Indians had been upwards of two months without ammunition. Our arrival therefore was hailed with great joy.

The whole tribe assembled round the fort, and viewed with delight the kegs of powder and the bales of tobacco as they were unloaded from the horses. A large circle was formed in the court-yard, into the centre of which we entered, and having lit the friendly calumet, smoked a few rounds to celebrate the meeting. A quantity of tobacco was then presented to each of the men, and the chief delivered a long oration; part of which, addressing us, ran as follows:

"My heart is glad to see you: my heart is glad to see you. We were a long time very hungry for tobacco; and some of our young men said you would never come back. They were angry, and said to me, 'The white men made us love tobacco almost as much as we love our children, and now we are starving for it. They brought us their wonderful guns, which we traded from them; we threw by our arrows as useless, because we knew they were not so strong to kill the deer as the guns; and now we are idle, with our guns, as the white men have no fire-powder, or balls, to give us, and we have broken our arrows, and almost forgotten how to use them: the white men are very bad, and have deceived us.' But I spoke to them, and I said, You are fools; you have no patience. The white mens' big canoes are a long time coming over the Stinking Lake[3] that divides their country from ours. They told me on going away that they would come back, and I know they would not tell lies." Then turning to his countrymen, he continued, "Did I not tell you that the white men would not tell lies? You are fools, great fools, and have no patience. Let us now show our joy at meeting our friends; and to-morrow let all our hunters go into the plains, and up the hills, and kill birds and deer for the good white men." They then commenced dancing, jumping, and crying out in a most discordant manner,

> *The good white men, the good white men,*
> *Our hearts are glad for the good white men,*
> *The good white men, the good white men,*
> *Dance and sing for the good white men.*

Then giving three cheers, something like the "Hip, hip, hurra!" of our domestic bacchanalians, they retired to the village.

The next morning the hunters procured a fresh stock of ammunition, and, for some weeks following, our table was plentifully supplied with excellent grouse, wild geese, and ducks in prime order. We had planted the year before some turnips, potatoes, cabbage, and other esculents, which yielded a pretty good crop. The quantity was increased the following spring; and this autumn we had an abundance of these vegetables. We had brought up a cock, three hens, three goats, and three hogs. The Indians were quite astonished at beholding them. They called the fowl "the white men's grouse"; the goats were denominated "the white men's deer," and the swine, "the white men's bears." They inquired if animals of the above description were all tame in our country; and on being answered in the affirmative, they asked, if they caught some of those to which they compared them,

[3] The sea. So called from its saline qualities.—R. C.

184

could we tame them in a similar manner? We told them to catch a few young ones, and we would make the attempt. A young bear was shortly secured; he was tied in the stye with the pigs, and fed daily by one of our Canadians, of whom he became very fond, and who in a short time taught him to dance, beg, and play many tricks, which delighted the Indians exceedingly.

While we were here a curious incident occured between Mr. M'Donald and an Indian, which I shall preface by a short account of the former. He belonged to a highly respectable family which emigrated from Inverness-shire to Canada while he was a lad. His first accents were lisped in Gaelic; but in the capital of the Highlands, so celebrated for its pure English, he made considerable progress in our language. On arriving in Canada he was obliged to learn French, in which he had made some proficiency, when he joined the North-West Company as an apprentice-clerk. At the period I speak of he had been ten years absent from Canada, and had travelled over an immense extent of Indian country. He seldom remained more than one winter at any particular place, and had a greater facility of acquiring than of retaining the language of the various tribes with whom he came in contact. He was subject to temporary fits of abstraction, during which the country of his auditory was forgotten, and their lingual knowledge set at defiance by the most strange and ludicrous *mélange* of Gaelic, English, French, and half a dozen Indian dialects. Whenever any thing occurred to ruffle his temper, it was highly amusing to hear him give vent to his passion in *Diaouls, God d——s, Sacres,* and invocations of the "evil spirit" in Indian. He was however a good-natured, inoffensive companion, easily irritated, and as easily appeased. His appearance was very striking: in height he was six feet four inches, with broad shoulders, large bushy whiskers, and red hair, which for some years had not felt the scissors, and which sometimes falling over his face and shoulders, gave to his countenance a wild and uncouth appearance. He had taken a Spokan wife, by whom he had two children. A great portion of his leisure time was spent in the company of her relations, by whom, and indeed by the Indians in general, he was highly beloved. Their affection however was chastened by a moderate degree of fear, with which his gigantic body and indomitable bravery inspired them.

One day as we were sitting down to dinner, one of our men, followed by a native, rushed into the dining-room, and requested we would instantly repair to the village to prevent bloodshed, as Mr. M'Donald was about to fight a duel with one of the chiefs. We ran to the scene of action, and found our friend surrounded by a number of Indians, all of whom he kept at a respectful distance. He had his fowling-piece, which he changed from one hand to the other, and appeared violently chafed. The chief stood about twenty yards from him, and the following colloquy took place between them, which for the information of my *unlearned* readers, I shall translate.

M'D.—"Come on, now, you rascal! you toad! you dog! Will you fight?"

Indian.—"I will:—but you're a foolish man. A chief should not be passionate. I always thought the white chiefs were wise men."

M'D.—"I want none of your jaw: I say you cheated me. You're a dog! *Will* you fight?"

Indian.—"You are not wise. You get angry like a woman; but I will fight. Let us go to the wood. Are you ready?"

M'D.—"Why, you d——d rascal, what do you mean? I'll fight you here. Take your distance like a brave man, face to face, and we'll draw lots for the first shot, or fire together, whichever you please."

Indian.—"You are a greater fool than I thought you were. Who ever heard of a wise warrior standing before his enemy's gun to be shot at like a dog? No one but a fool of a white man would do so."

M'D.—"What do you mean? What *way* do you want to fight?"

Indian.—"The way that all red warriors fight. Let us take our guns, and retire to yonder wood; place yourself behind one tree, and I will take my stand behind another, and then we shall see who will shoot the other first!"

M'D.—"You are afraid, and you're a coward."

Indian.—"I am not afraid; and you're a fool."

M'D.—"Come then, d——n my eyes if I care. Here's at you your own way." And he was about proceeding to the wood, when we interfered, had the combatants disarmed, and after much entreaty induced our brave Gael to return to the fort.

The quarrel originated in a gambling transaction, in which M'Donald imagined he had been cheated, and under that impression struck the chief and called him a rogue. The latter told him he took advantage of his size and strength, and that he would not meet him on equal terms with his gun. The imputation roused all his ire. He instantly darted into the field with his fowling-piece, followed by the

186

chief, when by our arrival we prevented an encounter which, in all probability, would have proved fatal to our friend.

The gigantic figure, long red flowing locks, foaming mouth, and violent gesticulation of M'Donald, presented a striking and characteristic contrast to the calm and immutable features of the chieftain. His inflexible countenance was for a moment disturbed by something like a smile, when he told his opponent that no one but a fool would stand before a gun to be shot at like a dog. In fact, M'Donald's proposition appeared to him so much at variance with his received notions of wisdom, that he could not comprehend how any man in his senses could make such an offer. On explaining to him afterwards the *civilised* mode of deciding gentlemanly quarrels, he manifested the utmost incredulity, and declared that he could not conceive how people so wise in other respects, should be guilty of such foolishness. But when we assured him in the most positive manner that we were stating facts, he shook his head, and said, "I see plainly there are fools every where."

M'Donald was a most extraordinary and original character. To the gentleness of a lamb he united the courage of a lion. He was particularly affectionate to men of small size, whether equals or inferiors, and would stand their bantering with the utmost good-humour; but if any man approaching his own altitude presumed to encroach too far on his good nature, a lowering look and distended nostrils warned the intruder of an approaching eruption.

One of our Canadian *voyageurs,* named Bazil Lucie, a remarkably strong man, about six feet three inches high, with a muscular frame, and buffalo neck, once said something which he thought bordered on disrespect. Any man under five feet ten might have made use of the same language with impunity, but from such a man as Lucie, who was a kind of bully over his comrades, it could not be borne; he accordingly told him to hold his tongue, and threatened to chastise him if he said another word. This was said before several of the men, and Lucie replied by saying that he might thank the situation he held for his safety, or he should have satisfaction *sur le champ.* M'Donald instantly fired, and asked him if he would fight with musket, sword, or pistols; but Lucie declared he had no notion of fighting in that manner, adding that his only weapons were his fists. The pugnacious Celt resolving not to leave him any chance of escape, stripped off his coat, called him *un enfant de chienne,* and challenged him to fight *comme un polisson.* Lucie immediately obeyed the call, and to work

187

they fell. I was not present at the combat; but some of the men told me that in less than ten minutes Bazil was completely disabled, and was unfit to work for some weeks after.

M'Donald frequently, for the mere love of fighting, accompanied the Flat-heads in their war excursions against the Black-feet. His eminent bravery endeared him to the whole tribe, and in all matters relating to warfare his word was a law. The following anecdote, which was related to me by several Indians, will at once show his steady courage and recklessness of danger. In the summer of 1812, at the buffalo plains they fell in with a strong party of the Black-feet, and a severe contest ensued. M'Donald was to be seen in every direction, in the hottest of the fire, cheering and animating his friends; and they at length succeeded in driving the Black-feet to take shelter in a thick cluster of trees, from whence they kept up a constant and galling fire on the Flat-heads, by which a few were killed, and several wounded. In vain he exerted all his influence to induce his friends to storm the trees, and drive the enemy from their cover.

Their mode of attack was extremely foolish, and productive of no benefit; for each warrior advanced opposite to the spot from whence the Black-feet fired, and after discharging a random shot into the group of trees, instantly galloped away. M'Donald, vexed at this puerile method of fighting, offered to take the lead himself to dislodge the enemy; but, with the exception of the war-chief, they all refused to join him. He therefore resolved to try the effect of example, and putting his horse into a smart trot, rode opposite to the place from whence the chief fire of the Black-feet proceeded; he then dismounted, took a deliberate aim at the head of a fellow which had just popped from behind a tree, and let fly. The bullet entered the Blackfoot's mouth, and he fell. A shower of balls instantly whizzed about M'Donald and his horse; but he, undismayed, re-loaded, while his friends cried out and besought him to retire. He covered another in the same manner, who also fell, after which he calmly remounted, and galloped to his party uninjured. A prisoner, who was subsequently taken, declared that the only two killed of those who had taken refuge among the trees, were both shot in the head by the "big white chief," as they termed our friend. His friends at Forts des Prairies repeatedly wrote to him that the Black-feet complained greatly of his having joined the Flat-heads, who had, by his assistance and that of Michel, become powerful, and that they vowed vengeance against them if ever they fell in their way; but M'Donald paid no attention either to their warning or our entreaties. War was his glory, and "piping peace" his aversion. Up to the period I quitted the Columbia he escaped harmless; but I regret to state that a few years afterwards, one of the enemy's balls brought him to the ground. Half a dozen savages instantly rushed on him, and commenced hacking his skull with their tomahawks. The scalping-knife was in the act of beginning its dreadful operation, and in a moment all would have been over, had not the war-chief, accompanied by a few friends, dashed to his assistance, killed three of the Black-feet, and rescued their benefactor from impending death. He subsequently recovered; but I understand the wounds he then received have left evident traces of their violence on his bold and manly front.

About seven hundred miles from Fort George, and ninety from Spokan House, there is an immense fall in the Columbia, between sixty and seventy feet perpendicular, at low water, and about forty-five in the spring and early part of the summer, when the melting snow contributes to swell the mighty torrent. The basin at the foot of the cascade resembles a boiling cauldron, in consequence of which the fall is called *La Chaudière*.[4] A small tribe, called *Les Chaudières*, reside at this place: their village is situated on the north side, just below the fall, where they remain the greater part of the year. They take little beaver; but their lands are well stocked with game and fish; there is also abundance of wild fruit, such as choke-cherries, currants, small strawberries, with black and blue berries. They take vast quantities of salmon, which they dry and preserve for use during the winter and spring months. Cleanliness cannot be ranked amongst their virtues. Their habitations are filthy in the extreme, and the surrounding atmosphere is impregnated with the most noxious effluvia, produced by the piscatory offals which lie scattered about their dwellings. I visited their village in September, in company with my friend M'Donald, his wife, some of her relations, and two of our own men. They received us in a friendly manner, and treated us to abundance of roast and boiled salmon. A small branch of this tribe reside in the interior, about a day and a half's march to the northward. A family of them, consisting of a father, mother, and several children, arrived at the falls the day before us. They had never seen white men, and their astonishment was extreme at the great contrast exhibited between the

4 Kettle Falls.

189

tall, raw-boned figure, and flowing red hair of my friend, compared to the cropped head, John-Bullish face, low and somewhat corpulent person of the author. The old woman requested to see my arms uncovered; and having gratified her, she begged to see my breast. I accordingly opened my shirt, and she at length became satisfied that the skin was all white, of which she appeared previously to entertain some doubts. Her curiosity was next directed to what she looked upon as the supernatural colour of M'Donald's hair, and expressed a wish to have a close examination of it. He complied, and having sat down, she commenced an inquisitorial search about its radical terminations, after certain animalculi which shall be nameless. She appeared much disappointed at not finding a solitary "ferlie," the absence of which she attributed to the extraordinary colour of his hair, which she said frightened them away. Then turning to me, and observing mine was of a darker hue, she asked if I would allow her to take a "look." I immediately consented; but her eyes and digits having for some time toiled in vain, she appeared annoyed at her want of success, and rose up quite vexed, declaring we were altogether "too clean."

We visited a small tribe, consisting of not more than fifteen families, who occupied a few hunting lodges about midway between Spokan House and the Chaudière Falls. Their language is a dialect of that spoken by the natives of the above places, but approaching more nearly to the Spokan. Their immediate lands consist of beautiful open prairies, bounded by clear woods, and interspersed with small rivulets and lakes. The latter are visited in the autumnal months by numbers of wild-geese and ducks, and their hills are well stocked with grouse. They are are an inoffensive race, and received us with every demonstration of friendship. We remained a week among them, during which period we had excellent sport. The aquatic birds were large and fat; and the grouse much beyond ours in size; and so tame, that they seldom took wing until we approached within a few yards of them.

The chief of this tribe is an extraordinary being.[5] The Indians allege that he belongs to the epicene gender. He wears a woman's dress, overloaded with a profusion of beads, thimbles, and small shells; add

---

[5] This whole incident is open to question, since it seems to be foreign to the culture of the tribes of the area. Professor Erna Gunther of the Department of Anthropology in the University of Washington is of the opinion that this person *might have been* a medicine man.

Courtesy Public Archives of Canada

Jasper House, Canadian Rocky Mountains
from Paul Kane's Wanderings of an Artist

Portage
from a water color by Peter Rindisbacher

Courtesy Public Archives of Canada

Fort Chipewyan

from a water color by Sir George Back, R.N.

Fort William in 1805

to which, the upper part of the face and the manner of wearing the hair are quite feminine; but these appearances are more than counterbalanced by a rough beard, and a masculine tone of voice, which would seem to set his virility beyond dispute. He never gambles, or associates with either sex, and he is regarded with a certain portion of fear and awe by both men and women, who look upon him as something more than human. He has a calm and rather stern countenance, and I never observed any tendency towards a relaxation of his risible muscles. He is usually attended by two or three children, to whom he pays great attention. Their chief occupation is to catch his horses, collect provisions, make fires, and cook his meals. When they attain a proper age, he gives them a portion, gets them married, and dismisses them; after which he selects from the largest and poorest families a fresh set of juvenile domestics. Their parents make no opposition, and are glad to get them so well provided for.

This chief possesses a large number of horses, some of which are the finest in the country. We purchased a few, and found him liberal in his dealings. He is free from the canting hypocrisy so common among Indians; and if he finds any of his young attendants tell a lie, or prevaricate in the least, the offender is punished by a flogging and sent home, after which no consideration whatever would induce him to take back the delinquent.

He seldom visited our fort; but whenever we called on him we were received with a degree of courteous hospitality which I never experienced elsewhere. He was communicative, and inquisitive, and ridiculed the follies of the Indians in the most philosophical manner. Of these he inveighed principally against gambling, and their improvident thoughtlessness in neglecting to provide during the summer and autumnal months a sufficient quantity of dried salmon for the spring, which is the season of scarcity; by which neglect they have been frequently reduced to starvation. He had heard of M'Donald's quarrel with the Indian, which he adduced as one of the bad effects resulting from gambling, and added, "had the Spokan been mad enough to follow the foolish custom of your countrymen, it is probable one of you would have been killed about a foolish dispute arising out of a bad practice, which every wise man should avoid."

He inquired particularly about our form of government, laws, customs, marriages, our ideas of a future life, &c. Our answers proved generally satisfactory; but the only two things he could not reconcile to wisdom, was the law of primogeniture and the custom of duelling. The first, he said, was gross injustice; and he thought no one but a man bereft of his senses could be guilty of the latter. Our knowledge of his language was necessarily imperfect, owing to which the attempts I made to explain to him some of the abstruse doctrines of our religion were rather bungling; but he appeared much pleased whenever he ascertained that he comprehended what I wished to convey; and, at the conclusion of our discourse, said he would be glad to converse with some of the wise men we call priests on these matters, and more particularly on the subject of a future state.

He is fond of tobacco; and the Indians say they often see him sitting late at night, enjoying his calumet at the door of his tent, and observing the various revolutions in the firmament. On all subjects therefore connected with the changes of weather his opinion is deemed oracular, and I understand he is seldom or never mistaken in his prognostications.

Although clothed in the garments of a female, I have hitherto classed this uncommon being among the masculine portion of the human race; and from his muscular frame, bushy beard, and strong decided tone of voice, I conceive myself justified in so doing. I never saw him angry but once, and that was occasioned by observing some private whispering and tittering going on in his presence, which he suspected had some allusion to his doubtful gender. His countenance instantly assumed a savage fierceness; but he quickly regained his composure on finding that the supposed offenders had changed their conduct.

His dwelling was covered with large deer-skins, and was completely water-proof. The interior was remarkably clean, and spread over with mats. In one corner he had a stock of dried provisions, stored in leather and mat bags, which in periods of scarcity he shared liberally among the tribe; in fact he wanted nothing that could add to his happiness or comfort, and possessed a degree of calm contentment uncommon among savages, and which would put to the blush much of the philosophical wisdom of civilised man.

While preparing for an autumnal journey to the sea, we learned that one of our free hunters, named Jacques Hoole, had been murdered by the Black-feet. His too was a character *hors du commun*. He was a native of France, and had been a soldier. He began his military career in Scotland in 1745, was slightly wounded and made prisoner at Culloden.[6] After being exchanged he was sent to Canada, and was actively engaged in the old American war. He was present in the battle on Abraham's Plains,[7] when the gallant Wolfe lost his life, and was one of the men who assisted in carrying the Marquis de Montcalm into Quebec, after he had received his death-wound.

The conquest of Canada induced him to quit the army. He married and became a farmer. On the revolutionary war breaking out, the gallant veteran bade adieu to the plough, became a sergeant of militia, and for the second time stood the siege of Quebec; in a sortie from which he received a wound in the knee, which caused a slight lameness during the remainder of his life.

On the termination of the war, misfortunes came crowding on him. The republicans had destroyed his farm; his wife proved faithless, and his children disobedient. He therefore determined to proceed with some traders to the interior of the Indian country. He would not engage in the service of the Company, but preferred trapping beaver on his own account, which he afterwards disposed of at the nearest trading post. This extraordinary old man was ninety-two years of age at the period of his death. I saw him the year before, and he then possessed much of the lightness and elasticity of youth, with all the volatility of a Frenchman. His only luxury was tobacco, of which he consumed an incredible quantity. From his great age he was called "Père Hoole." The Canadians treated him with much respect, and their common salutation of *"Bon jour, père,"* was answered by *"Merci, Merci, mon fils."* His body was found by the Flat-heads, close to a beaver dam; a ball had penetrated his temples, and the few white hairs that remained on his aged head did not prevent his inhuman butchers from stripping it of the scalp. His clothes remained on him; but his horses, traps, and arms had been taken by the murderers.

[6] The Battle of Culloden in 1746 saw the quelling of the last Jacobite uprising and the final defeat of the attempt of Bonnie Prince Charlie to gain the throne of England.
[7] In American history, the Battle of Quebec.

Chapter 16

The party attacked by the natives at the Wallah Wallah River—Two killed —Encamp on an island for safety—Indians demand two white men as a sacrifice—Arrival of a chieftain—His speech, and peace restored

On the 24th of October we proceeded overland with the produce of the summer's trade to Oakinagan, where, being joined by the people of that district, we embarked for Fort George, at which place we arrived on the 8th of November.

There were few natives at the falls or rapids, and they conducted themselves quietly. We examined the spot in which we had interred poor L'Amoureux, and found it untouched. The low state of the water at this advanced season caused us to make a few *décharges,* which would not have been necessary in the summer. It however enabled us to shoot down the great narrows below the fall without taking out a pack. We remained only a few days at Fort George, from which place we took our departure for the interior on the 18th of November.

We had eight canoes, and our party consisted of Messrs. Keith, Stewart, La Rocque, M'Tavish, M'Donald, M'Millan, M'Kay, Mackenzie, Montour, and myself. We had fifty-four canoe-men, including six Sandwich Islanders. We passed in safety the places where hostility was apprehended; and the day after we had passed the falls, we threw by our leathern armour as no longer necessary, and the men stowed their muskets into long cases, which were placed under the trading goods in the bottom of the canoes.

On arriving a few miles above the entrance of the Wallah Wallah River, at a place about equidistant between that and Lewis' River, a number of canoes filled with natives paddled down on our brigade, apparently without any hostile design. We were on the south side, and advancing slowly with the poles. Mr. Keith was in the first canoe, Mr. Stewart in the second, Messrs. La Rocque and M'Millan in the third, Messrs. M'Donald and M'Kay in the fourth, M'Tavish and I in the fifth, Montour in the sixth, Mackenzie in the seventh, and Pierre Michel, the interpreter, in the eighth.

The Indians at first asked a little tobacco from Mr. Keith, which he gave them; they then proceeded to Mr. Stewart, who also gave them a small quantity; after which they dropped down on Messrs. La Rocque and M'Millan, from whose canoe they attempted to take some goods by force, but were repulsed by the men, who struck their hands with the paddles. They next came to M'Donald, and seized a bale of tobacco which was in the forepart of his canoe, which they attempted to take out. At the same time my canoe was stopped, as well as those in the rear, and a determined resolution was evinced to plunder us by force.

We were awkwardly circumstanced: the only arms were those in the possession of the officers; and, with the exception of the paddles, the men had no weapons ready. Anxious to avoid coming to extremities, as long as possible, without compromising our character, we endeavoured to keep them in check with the paddles; but our efforts were unavailing, and some hard blows were given and received. Still we refrained from the *dernier resort,* and Mr. Keith gave orders not to fire while there was a possibility of saving the property. The fellow who had seized the bale in M'Donald's canoe, was a tall athletic man; he resisted all their entreaties to let it go, and had taken it partly out of the canoe, when M'Kay gave him a severe blow with the butt end of his gun, which obliged him to drop the prize. He instantly placed an arrow in his bow, which he presented at M'Donald; but the latter coolly stretched forth his brawny arm, seized the arrow, which he broke, and threw into the fellow's face. The savage, enraged at being thus foiled, ordered his canoe to push off, and was just in the act of letting fly another arrow, when M'Kay fired and hit him in the forehead. He instantly fell; upon which two of his companions bent their bows; but before their arrows had time to wing their flight M'Donald's double-barrelled gun stopped them. He shot one between the eyes, and the ball from the second barrel lodged in the shoulder of the survivor. The moment they fell, a shower of arrows was discharged at us; but owing to the undulating motion of their canoes, as well as ours, we escaped uninjured. Orders were now issued to such as had

195

their arms ready, to fire; but in a moment our assailants became invisible. After they had discharged their arrows, they had thrown themselves prostrate in their canoes, which, drifting rapidly down the current, were quickly carried beyond the reach of our shot.

We lost no time in putting ashore for the purpose of arming the men, and distributing ammunition. The few Indians who were on our side of the river fled on seeing us land, and those who had gained the opposite bank fired several shots at us; but, owing to the great distance, their balls fell short. The Columbia at this place was nearly a mile wide; night was fast approaching, and it was necessary to select a proper place for an encampment, at which we might remain, until measures should be adopted for bringing about a reconciliation with the natives. A short distance higher up in the centre of the river lay a narrow island, about two miles in length, quite low, void of timber, and covered with small stones and sand. It was deemed the safest place to withstand an attack, or prevent a surprise; and orders were therefore given to collect as much drift-wood as possible on the main shore for the purpose of cooking. This was speedily effected, after which we pushed off, but had not proceeded more than one hundred yards when several arrows were discharged at us from the side we had just left, although at the time we embarked no Indian was visible for miles around. One man was slightly wounded in the neck, and another rather severely in the shoulder; a few of the arrows struck the canoes; but the greater part did not reach us. We however gained the island without further injury, and forthwith proceeded to intrench ourselves behind a line of sand-banks, by which we were effectually covered from the range of the enemy's shot from either side.

The brigade was divided into three watches. The night was dark, cold, and stormy, with occasional showers of rain. It was judged prudent to extinguish the camp fires, lest their light might serve as a beacon to the Indians in attacking us. This precaution, although by no means relished by the men, probably saved the party; for, about an hour before day-break, several of the savages were discovered close to the camp, which they were silently approaching on their hands and feet; but on being fired at by our sentinels they quickly retreated, apprehensive of injuring each other in the dark; and shortly after we heard the sound of their paddles quitting the island.

Our meditations this night were far from pleasing; and when we reflected on the hopelessness of our situation, in the centre of a great river, the natives on each side of which were brave, powerful, and hostile; our numbers comparatively few, and the majority men in whose courage we could not confide; added to which, the impossibility of procuring the least assistance, we almost despaired of being able to join our friends in the interior. We therefore made up our minds for the worst, interchanged short notes directed to such of our friends as we felt anxious should know our fate, and resolved to sell our lives dearly.

Shortly after day-break a council of war was held; and after some discussion, we determined to quit the island, demand a parley, and offer a certain quantity of goods to appease the relations of the deceased.

The only dissentient to a compromise was our Highland friend M'Donald, whose spirit could not brook the idea of purchasing safety from Indians.

It blew a strong gale during the day, which prevented us from embarking, and constrained us to pass another melancholy night on the island, without wood sufficient to make a solitary fire.

Towards midnight the storm subsided; the sky was dark, and not a star twinkled through the gloomy atmosphere. Mr. Keith commanded the second watch, and I was sitting with him at the extremity of the camp, when we observed a large fire on a hill in a north-west direction. It was immediately answered by one in the opposite point, which was followed by others to the eastward and westward; while the indistinct sounds of paddles from canoes crossing and recrossing, afforded strong proofs that our enemies, by vigilant watching, and constant communication, had determined that we should not escape them in the dark.

Shortly after these threatening indications, a flight of ravens passed quietly over our heads, the fluttering of whose wings was scarcely audible. Some of the Canadians were near us, and one of them, named Landreville, in rather a dejected tone, said to his comrades, "My friends, it is useless to hope. Our doom is fixed: tomorrow we shall die." "*Cher frère,* what do you mean?" eagerly inquired half a dozen voices. "Behold yon ravens," he replied; "their appearance by night in times of danger betokens approaching death. I cannot be mistaken. They know our fate, and will hover about us until the arrows of the savages give them a banquet on our blood."

Landreville in other respects was a steady sensible man, but, like his countrymen, deeply imbued with superstitious ideas. Mr. Keith saw the bad impression which these ominous forebodings were likely to produce on the men, and at once determined to counteract it. This he knew it would have been useless to attempt by reasoning with people whose minds such absurd notions would have closed against conviction, and therefore thought it better to combat their prejudices with their own weapons. "I have no doubt, my friends," said he, "that the appearance of ravens at night portends either death or some great disaster. We believe the same thing in Scotland; the opinion prevails throughout all Europe, and you have inherited it from your French ancestors; but at the same time I must tell you, that no fatality is ever apprehended, except their appearance is accompanied by croaking; *then* indeed the most direful consequences are likely to follow; but when their flight is calm and tranquil, as we have just witnessed, they are always the harbingers of good news." This well-timed reply completely dissipated their fears, and the poor fellows exclaimed, "You are right, sir, you are right. We believe you, sir; you speak reason. Courage, friends; there's no danger."

The morning of the 1st of December rose cold and bright over the plains of the Columbia, as we prepared to quit our cheerless encampment. The *voyageurs* were all assembled by Mr. Keith, who told them that every exertion consistent with reason should be adopted towards effecting an amicable arrangement; but that it was absolutely necessary to show the savages a bold front, and that while we tendered them the hand of peace, we should make them feel that we were not influenced by the dread of war. He reminded them of the many glorious deeds performed in Canada by their gallant French ancestors, a few hundreds of whom often defeated as many thousand Indians, and concluded by expressing a hope that they would not degenerate from the bravery of their forefathers. They replied by three cheers, and declared themselves ready to obey all his orders.

He next addressed the Sandwich Islanders, and asked them, would they fight the bad people, who had attempted to rob us, in case it was necessary? Their answer was laconic: "Missi Keit, we kill every man you bid us." So far all was satisfactory; and after having examined their muskets, and given each man an additional glass of rum, we embarked, and in a few minutes reached the northern shore, where we landed. Two men were left in each canoe; and the remainder of the party, amounting to forty-eight, including all the known shades

198

of humanity, ascended the bank. None of the natives were visible, and we remained about half an hour undecided as to what course we should adopt, when a few mounted Indians made their appearance at some distance. Michel, the interpreter, was sent forward alone, carrying a long pole, to which was attached a white handkerchief, and hailed them several times without obtaining an answer.

They appeared to understand the import of our white flag; and after a little hesitation two of them approached, and demanded to know what we had to say? Michel replied that the white chiefs were anxious to see their chiefs and elders, and to have a "talk" with them on the late disagreeable affair. One of them replied that he would inform his friends, and let us know the result; upon which he and his companion galloped off. They returned in a short time, and stated that the neighbouring chiefs, with the friends and relatives of the men who had been killed, would join us immediately.

In less than half an hour a number of mounted Indians appeared, preceded by about 150 warriors on foot, all well armed with guns, spears, tomahawks, bows, and well furnished quivers. They stopped within about fifty yards of our party. Among them we recognized several of the Wallah Wallahs; but in vain looked for our old friend Tamtappam,[1] their chief: he was absent.

A group of between thirty and forty equally well armed now approached from the interior. Their hair was cut short as a sign of mourning; their bodies were nearly naked, and besmeared with red paint. This party consisted of the immediate relatives of the deceased; and as they advanced they chanted a death-song, part of which ran as follows:

"Rest, brothers, rest! You will be avenged. The tears of your widows shall cease to flow, when they behold the blood of your murderers; and your young children shall leap and sing with joy, on seeing their scalps. Rest, brothers, in peace; we shall have blood."

They took up their position in the centre; and the whole party then formed themselves into an extended crescent. Among them were natives of Chimnapum, Yackaman, Sokulk, and Wallah Wallah tribes. Their language is nearly the same; but they are under separate chiefs, and in time of war always unite against the Shoshoné or Snake Indians, a powerful nation, who inhabit the plains to the southward.

From Chili to Athabasca, and from Nootka to the Labrador, there

[1] Ross gives the name as *Tummeatapam*. See *First Settlers,* 240.

is an indescribable coldness about an American savage that checks
familiarity. He is a stranger to our hopes, our fears, our joys, or our
sorrows; his eyes are seldom moistened by a tear, or his features relaxed by a smile; and whether he basks beneath a vertical sun on the
burning plains of Amazonia, or freezes in eternal winter on the icebound shores of the Arctic Ocean, the same piercing black eyes, and
stern immobility of countenance, equally set at nought the skill of the
physiognomist.

On the present occasion, their painted skin, cut hair, and naked
bodies, imparted to their appearance a degree of ferocity from which
we boded no good result. They remained stationary for some time,
and preserved a profound silence.

Messrs. Keith, Stewart, La Rocque, and the interpreter, at length
advanced about mid-way between both parties unarmed, and demanded to speak with them; upon which two chiefs, accompanied
by six of the mourners, proceeded to join them. Mr. Keith offered
them the calumet of peace, which they refused to accept, in a manner
at once cold and repulsive.

Michel was thereupon ordered to tell them that, as we had always
been on good terms with them, we regretted much that the late unfortunate circumstance had occurred to disturb our friendly intercourse; but that as we were anxious to restore harmony, and to
forget what had passed, we were now willing to compensate the relations of the deceased for the loss they had sustained.

They inquired what kind of compensation was intended; and on
being informed that it consisted of two suits of chiefs' clothes, with
blankets, tobacco, and ornaments for the women, &c., it was indig-
nantly refused; and their spokesman stated that no discussion could
be entered into until two white men (one of whom should be the big
red-headed chief) were delivered to them to be sacrificed, according
to their law, to the spirits of the departed warriors.

Every eye turned on M'Donald, who, on hearing the demand,
"grinned horribly a ghastly smile," and who, but for our interposi-
tion, would on the spot have chastised the insolence of the speaker.
The men were horrified, and "fear and trembling" became visible in
their countenances, until Mr. Keith, who had observed these symptoms of terror, promptly restored their confidence, by telling them
that such an ignominious demand should never be complied with.

He then addressed the Indians in a calm, firm voice, and told them that no consideration whatever should induce him to deliver a white man to their vengeance; that they had been the original aggressors, and in their unjustifiable attempt to seize by force our property, the deceased had lost their lives; that he was willing to believe the attack was unpremeditated, and under that impression he had made the offer of compensation. He assured them that he preferred their friendship to their enmity; but that, if unfortunately they were not actuated by the same feelings, the white men would not, however deeply they might lament it, shrink from the contest. At the same time he reminded them of our superiority in arms and ammunition; and that for every man belonging to our party who might fall, ten of their friends at least would suffer, and concluded by requesting them calmly to weigh and consider all these matters, and to bear in recollection, that upon the result of their deliberation would in a great measure depend whether white men would remain in their country, or quit it for ever.

The interpreter having repeated the above, a violent debate took place among the principal natives. One party advised the demand for the two white men to be withdrawn, and to ask in their place a greater quantity of goods and ammunition; while the other, which was by far the most numerous, and to which all the relatives of the deceased belonged, opposed all compromise, unaccompanied by the delivery of the victims.

The arguments and threats of the latter gradually thinned the ranks of the more moderate; and Michel told Mr. Keith that he was afraid an accommodation was impossible. Orders were thereupon issued to prepare for action, and the men were told, when they received from Mr. Keith the signal, to be certain that each shot should tell.

In the mean time a number of the natives had withdrawn some distance from the scene of deliberation, and from their fierce and threatening looks, joined to occasional whispers, we momentarily expected they would commence an attack.

A few of their speakers still lingered, anxious for peace; but their feeble efforts were unavailing when opposed to the more powerful influence of the hostile party, who repeatedly called on them to retire, and allow the white men to proceed on their journey as well as they

201

could. All but two chiefs and an elderly man, who had taken an active part in the debate, obeyed the call, and they remained for some time apparently undecided what course to adopt.

From this group our eyes glanced to an extended line of the enemy who were forming behind them; and from their motions it became evident that their intention was to outflank us. We therefore changed our position, and formed our men into single files, each man about three feet from his comrade. The friendly natives began to fall back slowly towards their companions, most of whom had already concealed themselves behind large stones, tufts of wormwood, and furze bushes, from which they could have taken a more deadly aim; and Messrs. Keith and Stewart, who had now abandoned all hope for an amicable termination, called for their arms.

An awful pause ensued, when our attention was arrested by the loud tramping of horses, and immediately after twelve mounted warriors dashed into the space between the two parties, where they halted, and dismounted. They were headed by a young chief, of fine figure, who instantly ran up to Mr. Keith, to whom he presented his hand in the most friendly manner, which example was followed by his companions. He then commanded our enemies to quit their places of concealment and to appear before him. His orders were promptly obeyed; and having made himself acquainted with the circumstances that led to the deaths of the two Indians, and our efforts towards effecting a reconciliation, he addressed them in a speech of considerable length, of which the following is a brief sketch:

"Friends and relations![2] Three snows have only passed over our heads since we were a poor miserable people. Our enemies the Shoshonés, during the summer, stole our horses, by which we were prevented from hunting, and drove us from the banks of the river, so that we could not get fish. In winter, they burned our lodges by night; they killed our relations; they treated our wives and daughters like dogs, and left us either to die from cold or starvation, or become their slaves.

"They were numerous and powerful; we were few, and weak. Our hearts were as the hearts of little children: we could not fight like warriors, and were driven like deer about the plains. When the thunders rolled, and the rains poured, we had no spot in which we could

[2] Cox, in common with most of the other writers of his generation, never fails to have his Indians speak in the classical rhetoric of the day.

seek a shelter; no place, save the rocks, whereon we could lay our heads. Is such the case today? No, my relations! it is not. We have driven the Shoshonés from our hunting grounds, on which they dare not now appear, and have regained possession of the lands of our fathers, in which they and their fathers' fathers lie buried. We have horses and provisions in abundance, and can sleep unmolested with our wives and our children without dreading the midnight attacks of our enemies. Our hearts are great within us, and we are *now a nation!*

"Who then, my friends, have produced this change? The white men. In exchange for our horses and for our furs, they gave us guns and ammunition; then we became strong; we killed many of our enemies, and forced them to fly from our lands. And are we to treat those who have been the cause of this happy change with ingratitude? Never! Never! The white people have never robbed us; and, I ask, why should we attempt to rob them? It was bad, very bad!—and they were right in killing the robbers." Here symptoms of impatience and dissatisfaction became manifest among a group consisting chiefly of the relations of the deceased; on observing which, he continued in a louder tone: "Yes! I say they acted right in killing the robbers; and who among you will *dare* to contradict *me?*

"You know well my father was killed by the enemy, when you all deserted him like cowards; and, while the Great Master of Life spares me, no hostile foot shall again be set on our lands. I know you all; and I know that those who are afraid of their bodies in battle are thieves when they are out of it; but the warrior of the strong arm and the great heart will never rob a friend." After a short pause, he resumed: "My friends, the white men are brave, and belong to a great nation. They are many moons crossing the great lake in coming from their own country to serve us. If you were foolish enough to attack them, they would kill a great many of you; but suppose you should succeed in destroying all that are now present, what would be the consequence? A great number would come next year to revenge the death of their relations, and they would annihilate our tribe; or should not that happen, their friends at home, on hearing of their deaths, would say we were a bad and a wicked people, and white men would never more come among us. We should then be reduced to our former state of misery and persecution; our ammunition would be quickly expended; our guns would become useless, and we should again be driven from our lands, and the lands of our fathers, to wander like deer and wolves in the midst of the woods and plains. I therefore say the white men *must* not be injured! They have offered you compensation for the loss of your friends; take it; but, if you should refuse, I tell you to your faces that I will join them with my own band of warriors; and should one white man fall by the arrow of an Indian, *that* Indian, if he were my brother, with all his family, shall become victims to my vengeance." Then, raising his voice, he called out, "Let the Wallah Wallahs, and all who love me, and are fond of the white men, come forth and smoke the pipe of peace!" Upwards of one hundred of our late adversaries obeyed the call, and separated themselves from their allies. The harangue of the youthful chieftain silenced all opposition. The above is but a faint outline of the arguments he made use of, for he spoke upwards of two hours; and Michel confessed himself unable to translate a great portion of his language, particularly when he soared into the wild flights of metaphor, so common among Indians. His delivery was impassioned; and his action, although sometimes violent, was generally bold, graceful, and energetic. Our admiration at the time knew no bounds; and the orators of Greece or Rome, when compared with him, dwindled in our estimation into insignificance.

Through this chief's mediation, the various claimants were in a short time fully satisfied, without the flaming scalp of our Highland hero; after which a circle was formed by our people and the Indians indiscriminately. The white and the red chiefs occupied the centre, and our return to friendship was ratified by each individual in rotation taking an amicable whiff from the peace-cementing calumet.

The chieftain whose timely arrival had rescued us from impending destruction was called "Morning Star." His age did not exceed twenty-five years. His father had been a chief of great bravery and influence, and had been killed in battle by the Shoshonés a few years before. He was succeeded by Morning Star, who, notwithstanding his youth, had performed prodigies of valour. Nineteen scalps decorated the neck of his war horse, the owners of which had been all killed in battle by himself to appease the spirit of his deceased father. He wished to increase the number of his victims to twenty; but the terror inspired by his name, joined to the superiority which his tribe derived from the use of fire-arms, prevented him from making up the desired complement, by banishing the enemy from the banks of the Columbia.[3]

[3] The Indians consider the attainment of twenty scalps as the summit of a warrior's glory.—R. C.

His handsome features, eagle glance, noble bearing, and majestic person, stamped him one of Nature's own aristocracy; while his bravery in the field, joined to his wisdom in their councils, commanded alike the involuntary homage of the young, and the respect of the old.

We gave the man who had been wounded in the shoulder a chief's coat; and to the relations of the men who were killed we gave two coats, two blankets, two fathoms of cloth, two spears, forty bullets and powder, with a quantity of trinkets, and two small kettles for their widows. We also distributed nearly half a bale of tobacco among all present, and our youthful deliverer was presented by Mr. Keith with a handsome fowling-piece, and some other valuable articles.

Four men were then ordered to each canoe, and they proceeded on with the poles; while the remainder, with the passengers, followed by land. We were mixed pell-mell with the natives for several miles. The ground was covered with large stones, small willows, and prickly pears; and had they been inclined to break the solemn compact into which they had entered, they could have destroyed us with the utmost facility.

At dusk we bade farewell to the friendly chieftain and his companions, and crossed to the south side, where we encamped, a few miles above Lewis' River, and spent the night in tranquillity.

It may be imagined by some, that the part we acted in the foregoing transaction betrayed too great an anxiety for self-preservation; but when it is recollected that we were several hundred miles from any assistance, with a deep and rapid river to ascend by the tedious and laborious process of poling, and that the desultory Cossack mode of fighting in use among the Indians, particularly the horsemen, would have cut us off in piece-meal ere we had advanced three days, it will be seen that, under the circumstances, we could not have acted in any other manner.

We reached Oakinagan without further interruption on the 12th of December, at which place we remained a few days, to recruit the men, and prepare for the land journey with the horses.

205

Chapter 17

Author and party lost in a snow-storm—Curious instance of mental abstraction—Poor Ponto—Arrive at Spokan House—A marriage—Great ravine—Agates—Hot-springs—Kitchen-garden—Indian manner of hunting the deer—Method adopted by the wolves for the same purpose—Horse-racing—Great heat

On the 13th of December the Spokan brigade to which I was attached took its departure from Oakinagan. The party consisted, besides, of Messrs. Stewart, M'Tavish, M'Millan, and Montour; with twenty-one Canadians, and four Sandwich Islanders. We had twenty-six loaded horses; and in addition to our ordinary stock of provisions, we purchased forty dogs from the natives at Oakinagan, which were killed, after we had crossed the river, and formed part of the loading.

The cold was intense, and the ground covered with ten to twelve inches of snow. This necessarily impeded our progress, and prevented us from advancing more than twelve miles a day.

On the 16th, which was the fourth day of our journey, it snowed incessantly. The line of march was long and straggling, and those in front were several miles in advance of the rear division, of which I had charge with M'Tavish. We had eight loaded horses, with four Canadians, and two Sandwich Islanders.

Towards evening a heavy storm arose from the north-east, which added to the desolation by which we were surrounded; while the chilling monotony of the wide and extended plains was partially varied by immense masses of drifting snow, which, like the fitful vapour that so often enshrouds our northern mountains, occasionally concealed from our view the cheerless extent of the wintry horizon. On the approach of darkness the violence of the storm subsided; but

206

it was followed by one of those calm, clear, freezing nights so common in the interior of America, and from the death-benumbing influence of which it is nearly impossible to avoid that sleep from which many an unfortunate wanderer never awakens. We were now completely bewildered; all traces of the path had been destroyed by the drift; the cold became every instant more painfully intense, and

Horsemen and horse confessed the bitter pang.

Three of the poor animals having at length given up, we were reluctantly obliged to stop and unload them; and after searching, in vain, for wood to make a fire, we were compelled to make a large excavation in the snow, in which we resolved to pass the night.[1]

The horses which carried our provisions and blankets were ahead, and we fired several shots in the hope of obtaining relief, but without success. M'Tavish and I, however, fortunately obtained a blanket from one of the men, with which, and some of the saddle-cloths, we contrived to guard against the effects of the piercing cold during the night.

We arose with the first dawn of morning, and prepared to renew our march; but on mustering the horses, we found one of them dead, and the two Sandwich Islanders dreadfully frost-bitten. To add to our distress, M'Tavish and I had omitted the wise precaution of placing our moccasins under our bodies (the warmth of which would have preserved them from being congealed), in consequence of which we found them, on awakening, frozen as hard as clogs. All our endeavours to soften them by puffing, rubbing, &c., were unavailing, and we were ultimately obliged to have recourse to an extraordinary process, which produced the desired effect. After reloading, we resumed our march; which, owing to the depth and hardness of the snow, was painfully tedious. We had not advanced more than three miles when I missed my fowling-piece; and imagining that I had left it at the place where we had passed the night, I returned to look for it; but on arriving at the spot, I was much annoyed to find the object of my search lying across my arms! To account for this instance of mental abstraction, it is necessary to remember the disagreeable situation in which I was placed: in charge of a party who had lost itself in a trackless wilderness of snow, and unable to discover any vestiges of its companions;

[1] Compare this with a somewhat similar account given in Ross, *First Settlers,* 201–204.

two of the number disabled from walking, and both men and horses almost exhausted from cold and want of nourishment; in addition to which, I had been accustomed for some days previously to carry my fowling-piece over the left shoulder, from which I suddenly missed the weight, and, without mentioning the circumstance to any of the men, turned back on my fool's errand.

Shortly after rejoining the party we came in view of a cluster of small trees, from the centre of which arose large volumes of friendly vapour. Here we found Messrs. Stewart and M'Millan with the remainder of the brigade, comfortably seated round a cheering fire, partaking of a plentiful breakfast. We hastened to join them, and quickly dispatched part of a hind-quarter and a few ribs of roasted dog.

Mr. Stewart had a beautiful English water-spaniel, called Ponto. After breakfast he asked M'Tavish how he liked his fare; to which the latter replied that he thought it was excellent. "And pray, my dear Alick," said Stewart, "do you know what you have just been eating?" "Not exactly," replied he; "I liked the meat so well that I never thought of asking its name; but I suppose it is one of the wild sheep that I hear you have in these parts." "No indeed," said Stewart; "finding ourselves short of provisions, we were obliged to kill Ponto, on part of which you have made so hearty a breakfast." "Poor Ponto!" ejaculated the philosophical Highlander; "I am sorry for him; but it cannot now be helped." Ponto was a fine animal, full of vivacity, and had become a general favourite. I could not account for his death, seeing there was no necessity to justify the murder of a *civilised* dog, while several of those which had been purchased at Oakinagan still remained untouched. On inquiring the reason, I was told that in consequence of his being in excellent condition, he was deemed a fit dish *pour la table d'un bourgeois*.[2] This was by no means satisfactory, as I observed at the men's messes several prime pieces of the native dogs, which I thought ought to have satisfied people more fastidious than we had a right to be on such an occasion; besides, I would have preferred picking the bones of the most *maigre* of the Indian breed, to the plumpest of our own faithful companions. Their keen eyes, sharp noses, and pointed upright ear, proclaim their wolfish origin, and fail to enlist our sympathies in their behalf; in consequence of which our repugnance to partake of them in periods of necessity is considerably diminished.

[2] The Canadians call every proprietor *un bourgeois*.—R. C.

208

We rested at this encampment the remainder of the day to refresh the horses, and in the evening I was highly delighted at again seeing the animated figure of poor Ponto as lively and playful as ever. He had not been injured, and the melancholy story of his death, &c., was nothing but the pure invention of the "old one's" to work on our juvenile sympathies.[3]

From hence to Spokan we had a tedious and miserable march of seven days in deep snow, in the course of which we lost five horses; and of those which survived the journey, several perished during the winter.

I remained at Spokan in company with Messrs. Stewart and M'Tavish, and passed rather an agreeable winter. The deer were not so numerous as in former seasons, and we chiefly subsisted on horses. Towards the latter end of January carp became plentiful in Spokan River, and about a month later the trout-fishing commenced. We took large quantities of both, which afforded us excellent amusement; and from that period until late in the spring, we generally breakfasted on fish and dined on horse.

In the course of the winter an incident occurred which threatened at the time to interrupt the harmony that had previously existed between our people and the Spokan Indians. One of our younger clerks, having become tired of celibacy, resolved to take a wife; and as none of the Columbian half-breeds had attained a sufficiently mature age, he was necessitated to make his selection from the Spokan tribe. He therefore requested the interpreter to make an inquiry in the village, and ascertain whether any unappropriated comely young woman was willing to become the partner of a juvenile chief. A pretty-looking damsel, about seventeen years of age, immediately became a candidate for the prize. As her father had died some years before, she was under the guardianship of her mother, who, with her brother, settled the terms of the negotiation. Blankets and kettles were presented to her principal relations; while beads, hawk-bells, &c., were distributed among the remaining kindred. About nine o'clock at night the bride was conducted to the fort-gate by her mother, and, after an apathetic parting, she was consigned to the care of one of the men's wives, called "the scourer," conversant in such affairs, who had her head and body thoroughly cleansed from all the Indian paint and grease with which

[3] That Cox was subjected to "hazing" is evidence that he was still considered a newcomer or "tenderfoot."

they had been saturated. After this purification she was handed over to the dressmaker, who instantly discharged her leathern chemise, and supplied its place by more appropriate clothing; and the following morning, when she appeared in her new habiliments, we thought her one of the most engaging females that we had previously seen of the Spokan nation.

Matters rolled on pleasantly enough for a few days, and the youthful couple appeared mutually enamoured of each other; but a "little week" had scarcely passed over their heads, when one day about two o'clock, a number of young warriors well mounted galloped into the court-yard of the fort armed at all points. Their appearance was so unusual, and unlike the general manner of the Spokan nation, that we were at a loss to account for it, and vague suspicions of treachery began to flit across our imaginations; but the mystery was shortly cleared up. The bride, on perceiving the foremost horseman of the band enter the court, instantly fled into an adjoining store, in which she concealed herself; while he and his associates dismounted, and demanded to speak with the principal white chief, at the same time requesting the other chiefs would also appear. His wishes having been complied with, he addressed us in substance to the following effect: "Three snows have passed away since the white men came from their own country to live among the Spokans. When the Evil Spirit thought proper to distress the white people by covering the waters of the rivers with ice, so that they could not catch any fish, and sent snow all over the mountains and the plains, by means whereof their horses were nearly destroyed by the wolves,—when their own hunters in fact could not find an animal, did the Spokans take advantage of their afflictions? Did they rob them of their horses like Sinapoil dogs? Did they say, The white men are now poor and starving; they are a great distance from their own country and from any assistance, and we can easily take all their goods from them, and send them away naked and hungry? No! we never spoke or even thought of such bad things. The white men came amongst us with confidence, and our hearts were glad to see them; they paid us for our fish, for our meat, and for our furs. We thought they were all good people, and in particular their chiefs; but I find we were wrong in so thinking." Here he paused for a short period; after which he thus recommenced: "My relations and myself left our village some days ago for the purpose of hunting. We returned home this morning. Their wives and their children leaped

210

with joy to meet them, and all their hearts were glad but mine. I went to my hut, and called on my wife to come forth; but she did not appear. I was sorrowful and hungry, and went into my brother's hut, where I was told that she had gone away, and had become the wife of a white chief. She is now in your house. I come, therefore, white men, to demand justice. I first require that my wife be delivered up to me. She has acted like a dog, and I shall live no more with her; but I shall punish her as she deserves. And in the next place, I expect, as you have been the cause of my losing her, that you will give me ample compensation for her loss." Our interpreter immediately explained to the Indian that the girl's relatives were the cause of the trick that had been played on him, and added, that had our friend been aware of her having been a married woman, he never would have thought of making her his wife. That he was willing to give him reasonable compensation for her loss; but that she should not be delivered to him except he undertook not to injure her. He refused to make any promise, and still insisted on her restitution; but as we had reason to fear that her life would have been sacrificed, we refused to comply. The old chief next addressed him for some time; the result of which was, that he agreed to accept of a gun, one hundred rounds of ammunition, three blankets, two kettles, a spear, a dagger, ten fathoms of tobacco, with a quantity of smaller articles, and to leave his frail helpmate in quiet possession of her pale-faced spouse, promising never more to think of her, or do her any harm. Exorbitant as these terms were, it was judged advisable to accede to them rather than disturb the good feeling that had hitherto subsisted between us. After we had delivered the above articles to him, we all smoked the calumet; on perceiving which, the fugitive, knowing that it was the ratification of peace, emerged from her place of concealment, and boldly walked past her. late lord. She caught his eye for a moment; but no sign of recognition appeared; and neither anger nor regret seemed to disturb the natural serenity of his cold and swarthy countenance.

Shortly after the arrival of the parties from the Cootonais and Flat-heads, we took our departure for the sea, and having joined the gentlemen at Oakinagan, proceeded together, and arrived without accident on the 3rd of April at Fort George. Here we found a handsome brig belonging to the Company, which had arrived some time before, well loaded with articles necessary both for the interior and coasting trade.

We remained only a fortnight at the fort, which we again left on the 16th of April for the interior. We saw few Indians on the Columbia until we reached the Wallah Wallah River, at which we stopped half a day to purchase horses. We recognised several of the party who had attacked us the preceding autumn, particularly the relatives of the Indians who had been killed, and who were easily distinguished by their short-cropped hair. They came however among us unarmed, and all recollection of that unpleasant affair seemed to have vanished from their memories.

About forty miles above Lewis' River, Messrs. Stewart, M'Millan, and I, with three men, quitted the canoes to proceed overland to Spokan House. During this journey, which occupied five or six days, we did not meet a single native; and with the exception of a few stunted red cedar trees, and some juniper birch and willow, the country was divested of wood. Early on the morning of the second day we entered a remarkable ravine,[4] with high, bold, and rocky sides, through which we rode upwards of twenty miles, when we were obliged to leave it in order to follow our direct course. The soil in this ravine is a fine whitish-coloured clay, firm and hard. There is but little vegetation, except on the sides, where clusters of willow and choke-cherry are occasionally met with. While we rode through it we passed several small lakes, round the shores of which I picked up some very fine pebbles of the agate species, extremely hard, and possessing great delicacy and variety of shading. The banks of the Columbia, from the falls up to Lewis' River, abound with pebbles of the same description; some of which I brought home, and had cut. They take a beautiful polish, and in the opinion of lapidaries far exceed the cornelian in value.

It is a curious circumstance that we observed no rattlesnakes in this valley; and we subsequently learned from the Indians that they never saw any; although those reptiles are very numerous in the plains on each side. The natives were unable to assign any cause for this; and, except it be in the peculiarity of the soil, we were equally at a loss to account for it.

The following day we passed two warm springs, one of which was so hot, that in a short time water in a saucepan might be easily boiled

---

[4] This was Drumheller Canyon which lies to the east of the Saddle Mountains and the Frenchman Hills and contains several small lakes and potholes of the type mentioned by Cox.

over it. They were both highly sulphuric; but we had not time, nor indeed were we prepared to analyse their properties. The soil in their immediate vicinity was firm white clay, and the grass quite brown.

On leaving the canoes we expected to have reached Spokan on the third day; but in consequence of having no guide, joined to the difficulty of finding water, we took double the time on which we had calculated. Our provisions had failed; and we were about killing one of our jaded horses, when we came in sight of a few lean deer, two of which we shot. This supply brought us to Spokan House, which place we reached on the 12th of May. The party with the trading goods arrived a few days after from Oakinagan.

I passed the summer at Spokan with the gentlemen already mentioned, in addition to Messrs. Mackenzie and Montour, in as agreeable a manner as men possibly could in such a country. Our kitchen-garden now began to assume a thriving appearance, and, in addition to a fine crop of potatoes, we reared a quantity of other excellent esculents. The soil was deep and rich; and a few melons and cucumbers, which we had put down, throve admirably. The Indians, who at first would not touch any thing which we planted, began at length to have such a relish for the produce of the garden, that we were obliged to have sentinels on the watch to prevent their continual trespasses. We offered some of them potatoes to plant, and pointed out the good effects that would result from their cultivation; but they were too thoughtless and improvident to follow our advice. We strongly impressed on their minds that if the system was generally adopted it would prevent the recurrence of famine; to which they were subject; but to this they replied, that it would interfere with their hunting and fishing, and prevent their women from collecting their own country fruits and roots in the autumn, and thereby render them lazy. All our arguments were unavailing, and we were obliged to allow them to continue in their own course.

During the summer we made several excursions of from one to three weeks' duration to the neighbouring friendly tribes, for the purpose of obtaining a more accurate knowledge of their respective lands. Of the information thus obtained I shall have to speak hereafter. In some of these journeys we had to cross the great ravine already mentioned. It is computed to be about eighty miles in length, and presents all along the same rocky and precipitous sides. The pathways are so steep and dangerous, that even Indians in passing them are obliged to dismount, and loaded horses must be partly lightened. Some of the horses by missing their footing have been killed, and many severely injured, in descending these precipices. The bottom throughout consists of the same firm white soil, interspersed with small lakes. Several bold insulated rocks are scattered here and there throughout the ravine, some of which exceed a quarter of a mile in circumference, and are partially clothed with choke-cherry and other inferior kinds of vegetation.

From small horizontal channels worn on the sides of the rocks, and which seemed to indicate the action of water, we were led to imagine that this valley was formerly one of the channels of the Columbia, the course of which we supposed must have been changed by one of those extraordinary convulsions in the natural world, the causes of which are beyond human knowledge.

In the great plains between Oakinagan and Spokan there are at particular seasons numbers of small deer. The editor of Lewis and Clarke classes them as antelopes; but how much soever they may resemble those animals in swiftness and shape, their horns, as described by naturalists, are totally different. Their flesh is sweet and delicate, and they generally go in small herds. Towards the latter end of the summer they are in prime condition, and at that season we had some excellent sport in hunting them. The Indians, however, are not satisfied with our method of taking them in detail. On ascertaining the direction the deer have chosen, part of their hunters take a circuit in order to arrive in front of the herd, while those behind set fire to the long grass, the flames of which spread with great rapidity. In their flight from the devouring element they are intercepted by the hunters, and, while they hesitate between these dangers, great numbers fall by the arrows of the Indians.

The wolves almost rival the Indians in their manner of attacking the deer. When impelled by hunger, they proceed in a band to the plains in quest of food. Having traced the direction which a herd have taken, they form themselves into a horseshoe line, the extreme points of which they keep open on the grand ravine. After some cautious manoeuvring they succeed in turning the progress of the deer in that direction. This object effected, they begin to concentrate their ranks, and ultimately hem in their victims in such a manner, as to leave them no choice but that of being dashed to pieces down the steep and rocky sides of the ravine, or falling a prey to the fangs of their merciless pursuers.

During this summer we had also some good horse-racing in the plains between the Pointed Heart and Spokan lands. In addition to the horses belonging to those tribes, we had a few from the Flat-heads, and several from the Chaudière Indians. There were some capital heats, and betting ran high. The horses were ridden by their respective owners, and I have sometimes seen upwards of thirty running a five-mile heat. The course was a perfect plain, with a light gravelly bottom, and some of the rearward jockeys were occasionally severely peppered in the face from the small pebbles thrown up by the hoofs of the racers in front.

Thus passed the summer of 1815, decidedly the most pleasant and agreeable season I enjoyed in the Indian country. Hunting, fishing, fowling, horse-racing, and fruit gathering, occupied the day; while reading, music, backgammon, &c., formed the evening pleasures of our small but friendly mess. The heat was intense during this summer. The thermometer averaged from 84° to 96°, and on one occasion, the 5th of July, on which day we had a horse-race, it rose to 111° in the shade. The heat was however generally moderated by cooling breezes; otherwise it would have been quite insupportable.

Towards the latter end of August, and during the month of September, about noon, the thermometer generally stood at 86°, while in the mornings and evenings it fell to 35°, or 30°.

Chapter 18

Letter from Mr. Stuart—His account of New Caledonia—Navigation of the Columbia obstructed by ice—Miserable situation of the party during the winter—Author frost-bitten—Amusements—Departure of Mr. Keith—His letters—Author and party quit their winter encampment—Rapid change of seasons—Arrive at Fort George

Mr. Alexander Stewart with his family left us early in September, to take charge of Lesser Slave Lake,[1] an important department on the east side of the mountains, at which place it had been arranged he was to pass the winter. He expected to have met Mr. Keith at the portage of the Rocky Mountains, on his way to the Columbia with dispatches from Fort William; but a month elapsed before the arrival of that gentleman, and during which period himself and family suffered great privations from want of food, &c.

The distracted state of the interior, owing to the disputes between the North-West and Hudson's Bay companies, added to other unexpected circumstances, impeded the progress of Mr. Keith, who did not reach the portage until the 15th of October. He parted from Mr. Stewart on the following day, and reached the Chaudière Falls on the 22nd, where he left his canoes, and arrived at Spokan House on the 24th, having previously ordered the men to drop down to the mouth of the Spokan River, at which place we were to join them. Among others, I received a letter by him from my friend Mr. John Stuart, dated New Caledonia,[2] 25th April, 1815, from which the following is an extract:

[1] Alexander Stewart was sent to Lesser Slave Lake in 1815. See Wallace, *Documents,* 499.

[2] This district is very extensive, and lies on the west side of the Rocky Mountains. It communicates with Athabasca department by Peace River, and extends from lat. 52° to 55° North.—R. C.

216

Letter from Mr. Stuart

I find that the affairs of the Columbia appear to be getting from bad to worse; and that the many difficulties and hardships, added to the dangers peculiar to that unfortunate department, are hard to bear, and will keep me particularly anxious until I hear the result of the expedition of this spring to and from Fort George. Although the various encounters you have had with the natives should have taught them to respect the whites, and convince them that nothing is to be gained by force; yet, as the attack of last autumn[3] was both daring and premeditated, I am afraid it is but the forerunner of greater aggression. You will, however, have one great advantage in the spring, which is, that if the natives be at that season numerous along the communication, it must be with a hostile design, and perhaps by beginning the assault yourselves, you will be enabled to counteract its effects. Plausible, however, as this may appear in theory, it might probably have a different effect in practice. I shall therefore leave off my advice, lest you might say to me what Hannibal did to the pedant. Although I deeply regret my absence from my friends on the Columbia, I have no cause to complain of my lot; for here, if not perfectly quiet, we are at least *hors de danger*. Messrs. M'Dougal and Harman[4] are with me in the department. They are not only excellent traders, but (what is a greater novelty in this country) real Christians, and I sincerely wish that their steady and pious example was followed by others. We are at separate posts; but as we feel great delight in each other's company, we visit as often as the situation of the country and our business will permit; and in their conversation, which is already rational and instructive, I enjoy some of the most agreeable moments of my life.

The salmon failed with us last season. This generally occurs every second year, and completely so every fourth year, at which periods the natives starve in every direction.

They are of a lazy, indolent disposition, and as a livelihood is rather easily procured, seldom give themselves much trouble in hunting the beaver or any animal of the fur kind.

We have no buffalo or deer, except the *cariboux* (rein-deer); and not many even of those; so that, properly speaking, we may say that water alone supplies the people of New Caledonia with food.

The natives are numerous, and live stationary in villages of the same description as those on the lower part of the Columbia. In their looks and

[3] Alluding to the attack at the Wallah Wallah River, the particulars of which are already detailed.—R. C.

[4] Daniel Williams Harmon (1778–1845) was a Vermonter who was sent in 1810 to New Caledonia in the service of the North West Company. He remained there for over eight years. His journals were published under the title *Journal of Voyages and Travels in the Interior of North America* (Andover, Mass., Flagg and Gould, 1820). They were edited by the Reverend Daniel Haskel. See Wallace, *Documents*, 455.

manner they bear a great affinity to the Chinooks. The meaning of their national name is "Carriers,"[5] but the people of each village have a separate denomination. In a north-eastern direction, their country nearly borders the Columbia; but no white man knows how far it extends towards the north-west. Their language little varies from that spoken on the sea-coast. The Carriers are naturally of an open and hospitable disposition; but very violent, and subject to sudden gusts of passion, in which much blood is often shed. However, those quarrels are soon made up, and as soon forgotten.

They seldom, even in the most favourable seasons, kill many beaver in winter, the depth of the snow being, as they allege, too great. The utmost we can therefore do is to collect the produce of their summer hunt; which, as we have to go in different and distant directions, is a work of much labour, and takes up a great portion of our men's time. We have no cause to complain of last year's trade; and to finish my letter like a true North-Wester, I have great pleasure in acquainting you that our returns are about 95 packs,[6] which is sufficient proof that the country is worth being attended to, and that it is susceptible of great improvement.

We left Spokan House on the 26th of October, and, having joined the canoes, proceeded to Fort George, at which place we arrived on the 8th of November.

Owing to the advanced season of the year, we hastened our departure for the interior, and accordingly succeeded in quitting the fort on the 19th of November. Our party upwards consisted of Messrs. Keith, Montour, Mackenzie,[7] and myself, with fifty *voyageurs,* and Rivet,[8] the interpreter. Not being accustomed to travel at such a late period, we found the weather rather cool for the first few days. Owing to the absence of the Indians, few of whom were on the banks of the Columbia, we were deprived of our ordinary supply of horses and dogs for the kettle, and were forced to have recourse to our winter stock of flour, pork, and rice.

After passing the second falls the cold became more severe; and

[5] This tribe received its name as the result of its pculiar funeral customs, which are described by Cox in his appendix. See also *George Simpson's Journal,* 37 n.

[6] Each pack weighs ninety pounds, and contains on an average from fifty to sixty beaver-skins.—R. C.

[7] This was Alexander McKenzie who is not to be confused with the more famous Sir Alexander Mackenzie.

[8] This was probably François Rivet, who had been with Lewis and Clark as far as Fort Mandan. He probably was with the party of Americans who came west of the Rocky Mountains in 1807 and was involved in the Jeremy Pinch affair. See J. Neilson Barry, *Oregon Historical Quarterly,* Vol. XXXVIII, p. 430.

occasional pieces of ice drifting down the current made us fear that our progress would be considerably obstructed in proportion as we advanced. Our apprehensions were unfortunately realised. As far as the entrance of Lewis' River the navigation was tolerably free; but from thence the masses of floating ice became so large and numerous, that our frail little barks were in momentary danger of being stove to pieces, and it required all the skill and labour of our men to avoid them, and prevent the fatal consequences that would have inevitably followed such collisions. When it is recollected that we had to stem a strong current in vessels built some of thin cedar plank, and others of the bark of the birch-tree, and all heavily laden, it may naturally be supposed that our fears were not groundless.

For three days our advance was slow through this dangerous navigation; but early on the fourth a scene presented itself which seemed likely to put a final stop to our progress. Some large masses of ice in their descent got entangled among the numerous rocks of a long and crooked rapid;[9] these were quickly followed by others, until the whole presented at the time of our arrival a line about a quarter of a mile in extent, of high, sharp, and fantastically-shaped glaciers. Our men immediately commenced the portage with the greatest good-humour, and finished it late in the evening, when we were obliged to encamp in the dark, with scarcely wood sufficient to cook our cheerless supper. The current on the following day was partially free from ice, and we began to hope that we had passed the worst, until we arrived at a particular bend of the river, at which there was another rapid,[10] choked up with a similar chain of glaciers, but of greater magnitude. The men, who had endured excessive hardships, still did not grumble, and began the portage in high spirits. We had not advanced more than half over it when the approach of darkness, joined to an unexpected supply of driftwood, induced us to stop for the night, which we passed in tolerable comfort. We finished the portage the following morning before breakfast; and the remainder of the day was hard labour between rapids and drifting ice. We encamped late at the foot of a long rapid. The men were greatly fatigued, and some of them knocked up.[11] Early the next morning, after each man got a

9 Priest Rapids received its name because in 1811 a party of *voyageurs* saw a number of natives there, one of whom was performing certain rites which seemed to be an imitation of Catholic worship. See Franchère, *Narrative*, 344–45.

10 Pacquin Rapid, now known as Cabinet Rapids.

11 This expression to the English merely means all tired out.

refreshing glass of rum, they commenced their work, and finished the portage at noon. About two miles above this we were again obliged to unload, and carry the goods and canoes upwards of nine hundred yards.

The exhaustion of the men this evening was extreme, and it became quite apparent that they could not much longer endure a continuance of such dreadful hardship.

We had previously ascertained that the river was frozen a considerable distance, and during a walk of three miles, which I took with Mr. Keith, it was one firm thick body of ice.

We breakfasted on the following morning at our encampment; shortly after which a body of the men approached the tent, and sent in word that they wished to speak to Mr. Keith. He came out, when their spokesman, Basil Lucie, one of the best and most obedient men in the brigade, begged leave in a respectful manner to address a few words to him on their present situation. He stated that he and his comrades were reduced to the lowest degree of weakness from the excessive and unexpected labour they had undergone; that while there was the least possibility of reaching their destination they did not repine; but from the continued mass of ice and chains of rapids before them, that object was at present unattainable. He hoped Mr. Keith would not consider their conduct in a mutinous point of view. They were ready and willing to attempt all that men could achieve, with even the slightest prospect of success; but worn down as they were, they felt themselves quite inadequate to make any further efforts towards extricating us from our disagreeable situation.

Mr. Keith glanced at the group, in whose features he read a coincidence of sentiment with their speaker, joined to a determination of manner which, though humble and respectful, still evidently showed that their resolution was definitely fixed, and was the result of previous deliberation.

The principles of passive obedience and nonresistance in which the Canadian *voyageurs* are brought up, appeared to be endangered by this combination; and the idea that his men were the first that ever dared, in the Indian country, even to remonstrate, gave a temporary shock to his pride; it was, however, transient. Justice and reason triumphed, and dissipated in a moment the slight symptoms of wounded dignity that at first ruffled his countenance.

Mr. Keith told them that he had no wish to force them to any labour incompatible with their strength; that his only object was if possible to get to their destinations, which at present he admitted could not be done; that he did not find fault with them for the expression of their sentiments, and regretted that they had not all a more comfortable wintering ground.

Lucie, after a short consultation with the men, replied that they all felt particularly grateful for the kind and considerate manner he had received their appeal, and promised that no exertions on their part should be wanting to contribute to the comfort of himself and the other gentlemen.

There was fortunately about the encampment plenty of driftwood, of which in a short time they collected an immense quantity. The trading goods were piled up in a safe situation; and with the assistance of the canoes, tarpaulins, and sails, the men constructed tolerably good cots for themselves.

We had a large tarpaulin porch erected in front of our tent, to which it was joined. In this porch we sat to enjoy the fire, the sparks from which we feared would have injured the canvass of our cold habitation. Our situation was disagreeably novel. About three hundred miles from our nearest post, with no means of approaching it, and no provisions save the scanty supply we had brought for consumption on our journey, and the usual quantities of rice and flour for our winter holidays. We had seen no Indians for several days, and our hopes of succour from them were consequently very weak. Our hunters were also unsuccessful, and reported that the surrounding country was devoid of any animals that could be made subservient to our support. Neither did they in their different trips see any vestiges of the natives; and most of the poor fellows returned from their cold and hungry journeys with frost-bitten fingers and toes.

About ten miles from our encampment, in the midst of the extensive plains on the north side, there is a high and conically shaped hill, which has been honoured with the name of Mount Nelson,[12] to which Mr. Keith and I determined to proceed, for the purpose of surveying the surrounding country. The ground was covered with congealed snow, and after an arduous walk we reached the summit of the solitary mountain. We had a widely-extended prospect of the great plains in their wintry clothing. Their undulations reminded us of the ocean, when the troubled waves begin to subside after a storm; while

12 This has not been identified.

221

the occasional appearance of leafless trees in the distance, partially diversifying the chilling scene, resembled the shattered masts of vessels that had suffered in the conflict of waters.

In vain did we strain our eyes to catch a glimpse of any thing in human or animal shape. Neither man, nor fowl, nor cattle, nor beast, nor creeping thing, met our longing and expectant gaze. Animated nature seemed to have abandoned the dreary solitude, and silent desolation reigned all around.

We reached the encampment late in the evening, shortly after which I felt an unusual pain under the ball of one of my great toes. On examination, I ascertained that during our late walk a hole had been worn in the sole of the moccasin, which caused the toe to be frost-bitten. By the advice of our experienced Canadians I had it immediately rubbed with snow, keeping it, at the same time, some distance from the fire. The operation was painful; but it preserved the joint. After a few days' rubbing, the skin became white, and ultimately peeled off like that of a whitlow when it begins to heal. This was succeeded by a new covering, which in a short time became as strong as formerly.

A few years before, one of the clerks, named Campbell,[13] while out with a hunting party, met with a similar accident. He was a novice in the country, and contrary to the advice of his men, kept the frozen part at the fire, and refused to rub it with snow. The consequence was a mortification, which in a few days proved fatal; for at the place where the circumstance occurred he was between two and three thousand miles from medical assistance.

This was the only time, during my residence in America, that I got nipped by the frost; indeed the inhabitants of our islands in general bear cold better than the Canadians, several of whom belonging to our party, although they were more warmly clothed, suffered severely in their extremities.

Were it not for the plentiful supply of fuel, our situation would have been insupportably miserable in this wretched encampment. As it was, our time passed heavily enough. Our travelling library was on too small a scale to afford much intellectual enjoyment. It only consisted of one book of hymns, two song-books, the latest edition of

[13] The Reverend J. Neilson Barry of Portland, Oregon, one of the outstanding authorities on the history of the Northwest, says that there is no record of a clerk by this name west of the Rocky Mountains.

Joe Miller,[14] and Darwin's[15] *Botanic Garden.* The Canadians could not join us in the hymns, and we endeavoured in vain to tune our pipes for profane harmony. "Yankey Doodle," the "Frog's Courtship," and the "Poker," were the only three that came within the scope of our vocal abilities. In fine weather our friend Mackenzie attempted with tolerable success the simple ditty of

> *The devil flow away with the little tailor,*
> *And the broad-cloth under his arm.*

Our constant perusal of "Old Joe" made us so intimately acquainted with all his super-excellent good things, that we unconsciously became punsters, and were noted for many a day thereafter as the greatest men in the country for choice hits and *double-entendres.*

As for Darwin, we were almost tempted to commit him to the flames; for to read of the loves of the plants, when we knew they were all buried in their cold, cold grave, and waiting like ourselves for the renovating influence of spring, only gave additional torment to our situation.

In the intervals between harmony, joking, and botany, as we sat striving to warm ourselves under the tarpaulin porch, half blinded by the puffs of smoke sent in by cold easterly gusts, we endeavoured to amuse each other by a detail of each schoolboy adventure, each juvenile anecdote, and each

> *Moving accident by flood or field,*

that had ever befallen us. But on the arrival of dear delightful Christmas—that happy season of festivity, when the poor man's table displays the accumulated savings of an economical advent, and the rich man's groans under more than its accustomed profusion; when emancipation from the birch expands the youthful heart into joy and gladness, and the partially forgotten friendships of the old are renewed with greater fervency; when all denominations of Christians combine social pleasure with innocent amusement, and join in praise and thanksgiving to Him who came to save us—our thoughts wandered towards home, and the happy faces surrounding the quiet and domestic hearth. The contrast was too strong for our philosophy, and we were almost tempted to call down inverted benedictions on the

---

[14] Joe Miller of the famous *Jest-book* which was published in at least eight editions.

[15] Erasmus Darwin was the grandfather of Charles Darwin.

unfortunate beaver, and those who first invented beaver hats, beaver bonnets, and beaver cloaks! From that moment I began to balance between the comparatively pleasing uncertainties of civilised life, and the sad realities to which the life of an Indian trader is exposed. On the one side I placed—exile, starvation, Indian treachery, piercing colds, or burning heats, with the damp earth too often for a bed; no society for a great portion of the year, except stupid Canadian *voyageurs*, or selfish suspicious natives; ideas semi-barbarised by a long estrangement from the civilised world; and should I even survive these accumulated evils, and amass a few thousands, to find, on returning to my native country, the friends of my youth dead, and myself forgotten; with a broken-down and debilitated constitution; an Indian wife, and a numerous offspring, whose maternal tint, among the proud and the unthinking, too often subjects them to impertinent insult and unmerited obloquy.

To a British reader it would be useless to enumerate the opposing items, or to mention on which side the scale preponderated; it is enough to say that I determined on the earliest opportunity to exchange dog for mutton, and horse for beef; icy winters and burning summers for our own more temperate climate; and copper beauties for fair ones.

1816

A few men who had been dispatched on foot to Oakinagan succeeded in reaching that place, and returned early in January with sixteen horses, so wretchedly lean, that they were quite unfit for the kettle, and almost unserviceable for any purpose. However, after a few days' rest, Mr. Keith selected eight of the strongest, which he loaded; and with which, accompanied by Mr. Montour and a party of the men, he set off for Oakinagan. They took the greater portion of the portable *vivres* with them.

Mr. Keith's departure was a sensible loss to our little society. Gifted by nature with faculties of no ordinary description, he had the advantages of an early and excellent education, which he subsequently improved by an extensive course of reading. He also possessed a sound, vigorous understanding, with a strong memory; and had not fortune cast him among the wilds of savage America, I have no doubt he would have attained eminence in any profession he might have chosen in his native country.

Mackenzie and I passed six more melancholy weeks in this spot, during which period we did not see an Indian. Our time would have passed heavily enough, only that we fortunately agreed on no single subject. Episcopacy and Presbyterianism, with all of their off-shoots, formed a prolific source of polemical recreation; and when we became tired of the Mitre and the Kirk, we travelled back to Ossian and the Culdees. We argued on the immutability of the Magellanic clouds. We discussed the respective merits of every writer to whom the author-ship of Junius has been attributed. We differed on the best mode of cooking a leg of mutton, and could not agree as to the superiority of a haggis over a harico, or of Ferintosh over Inishowen. Plum-pudding and rice had each its champion; and when he rose in all its strength and thought to destroy me with the plentiful variety of a Scotch break-fast, I at once floored him with the solid substantiality of an English dinner. Thus with empty stomachs and half-famished bodies we argued on luxuries while we anticipated starvation; and we often awoke from the pleasing dream of a fat "sirloin," to attack the mel-ancholy ribs of a fleshless horse.[16]

Mr. Keith reached Oakinagan on the 28th January, and on the following day addressed me a letter, an extract from which may not be uninteresting to the reader.

The loaded horses performed the journey hither in about the time we had anticipated, having arrived here without any material accident (except drowning *Guenillon*) yesterday. As for myself, having left them on the 26th, accompanied by Francois, with the intention of reaching the fort that day, I accomplished my object at the expense of your *Poil de Souris* and my *Blond*. The latter gave up about three miles from the end of his journey; and yours brought me on slowly. Having once got ahead, I had no alternative but to push on *bon gré mal gré*, or encamp without blanket or supper; which circumstance I hope you will receive as a sufficient excuse for the rough treatment I gave your horse. *Grosses pattes* had the honour of carrying my saddle-bags for two days and a half, both as a punishment for his laziness, and as a relief to hard-working horses. Our business here

---

[16] Poor Mackenzie! In 1828 I received a letter from the Columbia, announcing the melancholy intelligence that he and four of his men had the preceding year been sur-prised by the savages on Fraser's River, who barbarously murdered the entire party. —R. C.

McKenzie was killed by Clallam Indians on Lummi Island. See Hubert Howe Ban-croft, *History of the Northwest Coast* (2 vols., San Francisco, A. L. Bancroft and Com-pany, 1884), II, 483.

has been considerably retarded in consequence of our having given a *régal* to the men in lieu of the New-Year's festivities, which you know were *douloureusement triste*. The party for Thompson's River took their departure the day before yesterday; and owing to some delay about procuring Indian canoes, the Spokan people only crossed the river to-day. I have settled with Mr. Ross to send you four additional horses for consumption, in charge of two men, who will leave this on the 1st proximo. The weather here has been latterly very mild, which, coupled with other circumstances, induces me to think that you have been enabled to quit your encampment.

Mr. Keith was, however, mistaken as to his hopes of a favourable change in the navigation. Another letter, dated "Spokan House, February 10th," says:

After a very unpleasant and irksome journey, occasioned by bad roads and the low and exhausted state of our horses, I arrived here on the 8th, and the loaded horses yesterday. We left several of the poor animals on the way. *Le Gris le Galeux* I left in charge of a middle-aged Indian, with a note addressed to you. I was obliged to give six others in charge to the bearer, whom you will please to reward. They were quite exhausted. Their names are, *La Gueule de travers, La Tête Plate, La Courte Oreille, La Crème de la petite Chienne, La Poil de Souris,* and *Gardepie.* As you will probably be reduced to avail yourself of the same shifts, I should hope those horses will be tolerably well recruited by the time of your arrival. *Mon Petit Gris, La Queue Coupée, De la Vallée,* with *La Crème de la Corne fendue,* and *La petite Rouge (nez blanc),* belonging to the Company, have been left in charge of the bearer's brother. Upwards of three hundred beavers have been picked up since our departure for the sea; but starvation is staring us in the face, unless we eat the melancholy remnant of our lean horses. The natives are abundantly supplied with *chevreuil;* but they cannot be prevailed on to risk killing their emaciated and worn-down horses by bringing any meat to the fort. I am daily flattering myself by anticipation with the pleasure of seeing you pop in. However, as this is leap-year, we must make some extra allowance. Were all leap-years invariably attended with the same combination of difficulties and obstacles which we have encountered this winter, I would cheerfully give up one day *quadrennially* of my life, at the expense of shortening my existence, provided such a sacrifice could preserve things in their natural channel.

About the middle of February the snow and ice began to show strong symptoms of solar influence. The former disappeared with wonderful rapidity, and the loud cracking of the latter gave notice of its continual disruption. I sent a few men a day's march ahead, who brought back word that the ice was so far broken up, that we might try our fortune once more on water. We therefore prepared for embarkation; and having killed our two last horses, we bade adieu on the 16th of February to our hibernal encampment, without experiencing one feeling of regret at the separation. For a few days our progress was slow and exposed to much danger from the immense quantity of floating ice, to avoid which required all the strength and ingenuity of our *voyageurs*.

After many narrow escapes we reached Oakinagan on the 28th of February, with empty stomachs and exhausted bodies.

To a person accustomed to the gradual revolutions of the seasons in Europe, an American winter changes with surprising rapidity. In less than a week from the first appearance of warmth,

> ———— *subdued,*
> *The frost resolves into a trickling thaw,*
> *Spotted the mountains shine; loose sleet descends,*
> *And floods the country round. The rivers swell,*
> *Of bonds impatient. Sudden from the hills,*
> *O'er rocks and woods in broad brown cataracts,*
> *A thousand snow-fed torrents shoot at once!*

The disappearance of the snow was followed by the most delightful and refreshing verdure, and the early symptoms of vegetation gave us assurance that

> *Gentle spring in ethereal mildness*

was once more about to gladden the heart of man; while the light-hearted Canadians under its genial influence again chanted forth their wild and pleasing *chansons à l'aviron*.

We remained a few days at Oakinagan to recruit the men; after which I proceeded with my party to Spokan House, at which place we arrived on the 9th of March.

Mr. Keith had been for some time under great anxiety as to our fate, and had dispatched several Indians towards the Columbia with letters to me, some of which I received *en route*.

The Flat-head and Cootonais parties had arrived a few days previously; but owing to their want of a sufficient supply of goods, occasioned by our stoppage on the ice, they made an indifferent winter's trade. We had scarcely time to recount to each other the various *uncos* we had experienced during the winter, when we were obliged to prepare for our spring voyage to the sea. We left Spokan House on 20th of March, and having joined the other parties at Oakinagan, proceeded with them downwards. The Columbia was one continued torrent, owing to the thousand little rivulets which the thaw had forced into it, and the beds of which in the summer season are quite dry or hardly visible. Our passage was consequently rapid, and we arrived at the sea on the 3rd of April. Our friends at Fort George were all in prime health, and had weathered out the winter in a much more comfortable manner than we had. Mr. M'Tavish had made a trip in the Company's schooner to the southward, and touched at the Spanish settlements of Monterey and San Francisco, at which places, in exchange for the produce of England, he obtained a plentiful supply of an article which is in great request among the Chinese, and for which the unsophisticated traders of Canton will barter their finest commodities; I mean *bonâ-fide* silver made into the shape of Spanish dollars, half-dollars, or pistareens.

As fresh supply of trading goods was required in the interior, our stay at Fort George was necessarily short. It was, however, a complete carnival among proprietors, clerks, interpreters, guides, and canoe-men. Each *voyageur* received a liberal extra allowance of rum, sugar, flour, &c., and a fortnight of continual dissipation obliterated all recollection of the frozen and lenten severity of the by-gone winter.

Chapter 19

*Author placed in charge of Oakinagan—Erects new buildings there—Mus-
quitoes—Sagacity of the horses—Rattlesnakes good food—Sarsaparilla—
Black snakes—Climate—Whirlwinds—Handsome situation—Character of
the tribe—Manner of trading—Extraordinary cures of consumption*

On the 16th of April we took our departure for the interior. Our party
consisted of sixty-eight men, including officers. Few Indians were on
the banks of the river, and they conducted themselves peaceably. We
arrived at Oakinagan on the 30th, from whence Mr. John George
M'Tavish, accompanied by Messrs. La Rocque, Henry, and a party
of Canadians, set off for the purpose of proceeding across the mountains to Fort William, the grand central depot of the interior on the
east side.

Mr. Ross, who had been for the last two years in charge of Oakinagan, was by a new arrangement detained this year at Fort George
as one of the staff clerks; and I was selected as commandant of the
former place. Messrs. M'Millan and Montour were sent to Spokan,
and my friend M'Donald proceeded to Kamloops, his old quarters.
A sufficient number of men were left with me for all purposes of hunting, trading, and defence; but, for the first time since I entered the
country, I found myself without a colleague or a companion.

I had a long summer before me: it is the most idle season of the
year; and as it was intended to rebuild and fortify Oakinagan during
the vacation, I lost no time in setting the men to work.

The immediate vicinity is poorly furnished with timber, and our
wood-cutters were obliged to proceed some distance up the river in
search of that necessary article, which was floated down in rafts. We
also derived considerable assistance from the immense quantities of

229

drift-wood which was intercepted in its descent down the Columbia by the great bend which that river takes above Oakinagan. "Many hands make light work"; and our men used such dispatch, that before the month of September we had erected a new dwelling house for the person in charge, containing four excellent rooms and a large dining-hall, two good houses for the men, and a spacious store for the furs and merchandise, to which was attached a shop for trading with the natives. The whole was surrounded by strong palisades fifteen feet high, and flanked by two bastions. Each bastion had, in its lower story, a light brass four-pounder; and in the upper, loop-holes were left for the use of musketry.

Our living consisted of salmon, horse, wild-fowl, grouse, and small deer, with tea and coffee, but without the usual adjuncts of milk, bread or butter. However, we looked upon those articles as excellent fare, and in point of living therefore had no cause of complaint throughout the summer.

I brought from Fort George a few bottles of essence of spruce, and by following the printed directions made excellent beer,[1] which in the warm weather I found a delightful and healthy beverage.

Owing to the intense heat the men were obliged to leave off work every day at eleven, and did not resume until between two and three in the afternoon, by which period the burning influence of the sun began to decline. In the interval they generally slept.

The musquitoes seldom annoyed us at midday; but when we wished to enjoy the refreshing coolness of a morning or evening's walk, they fastened on us with their infernal stings, against which we had no defence except leather. By smoking, we might indeed keep them at a civil distance from our noses and the parts thereunto adjacent; but this was a preventive which, if constantly practised, would have in a short time reduced our tobacco to a small quantity.

The annoyance during our meals was worse. We were obliged to have an iron pot at each end of the table, filled with saw-dust or rotten wood; which substance, when ignited, produced a quantity of thick smoke without flame. It effectually drove them away; but it was a desperate remedy; for during the process of mastication we were nearly suffocated from the dense clouds of vapour by which we were

---

[1] A recipe for spruce beer can be found in Anders Sparman, *A Voyage Round the World with Captain James Cook in H. M. S. Resolution,* translated by Huldine Beamish and Averill MacKenzie Grieve (London, Robert Hale, Ltd., 1953), 26, 190.

enveloped. In the mean time our tormentors hovered about the doors and windows, watching the gradual dispersion of the smoke; and the moment the atmosphere became sufficiently clear they charged in from all directions on our heads, necks, ears, face, and hands, from whence it was impossible to dislodge them, until a fresh supply of saw-dust, thrown over the dying embers, put them once more to flight.

The horses also suffered severely from these insects and the horse-flies. We caused several fires of rotten wood to be made in the prairie in which they were grazing, and round which they instinctively congregated to avail themselves of the protection afforded by the smoke. Those which had short tails and cropped manes suffered more than the other; for with these weapons of nature (of which, in America, at all events, it is cruel to deprive them) they could whisk off great numbers of the enemy; while the cropped horses, having no such defence, often had their hoofs and legs severely burned by standing in the fires to avoid the stings of their assailants. I have often observed the poor animals, when the smoke began to evaporate, gallop up to the fort, and neigh in the most significant manner for a fresh supply of damp fuel; and on perceiving the men appointed for that purpose proceed to the different fires, they followed them, and waited with the most sagacious patience until the smoke began to ascend and disperse their tormentors.

The point of land upon which the fort is built is formed by the junction of the Oakinagan River with the Columbia.

The point is about three miles in length and two in breadth. At the upper end is a chain of hills, round the base of which runs a rocky pathway leading to the upper part of the river. Rattlesnakes abound beyond these hills, and on the opposite sides of the Oakinagan and Columbia rivers. They are also found on both sides of the Columbia, below its junction with the former stream; but it is a curious fact, that on the point itself, that is, from the rocks to the confluence of the two rivers, a rattlesnake has never yet been seen. The Indians are unable to account for this peculiarity; and as we never read of St. Patrick having visited that part of the world, we were equally at a loss to divine the cause. The soil is dry, and rather sandy, and does not materially differ from that of the surrounding country.

Immense quantities of sarsaparilla grow on Oakinagan Point, which at times proved very beneficial to some of our valetudinarians.[2]

[2] Some of our men were salivated by taking a strong decoction of this root.—R. C.

There are also scattered over it a profusion of wild flowers, some of beautiful hues, but scarcely any odour. Among them the sun-flower, for height and luxuriance, is conspicuous. This is the favourite plant of the delightful little humming-bird (called by the Canadians *oiseau des dames*), in the flowers of which it banquets nearly the livelong day.

Numbers of black snakes are found on the point; but they are perfectly harmless. We caught some of them in the rooms; and a few have been found at times quietly coiled up in the men's beds. The rattlesnakes were very numerous about the place where the men were cutting the timber. I have seen some of our Canadians eat them repeatedly! The flesh is very white, and, they assured me, had a delicious taste.[3] Their manner of dressing them is simple. They at first skin the snake in the same manner as we do eels, after which they run through the body a small stick, one end of which is planted in the ground, leaning towards the fire; by turning this *brochet* occasionally, the snake is shortly roasted. Great caution however is required in killing a snake for eating; for if the first blow fails, or only

[3] The meat of the rattlesnake is very similar in taste and appearance to the white meat of chicken.

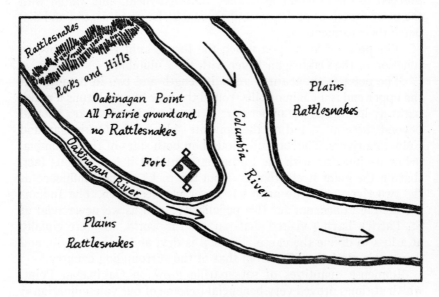

Location of Oakinagan Point

partially stuns him, he instantly bites himself in different parts of the body, which thereby becomes poisoned, and would prove fatal to any person who should partake of it. The best method is to wait until he begins to uncoil and stretches out the body, preparatory to a spring; when, if a steady aim be taken with a stick about six feet long, it seldom fails to kill with the first blow.

The climate of Oakinagan is highly salubrious. We have for weeks together observed the blue expanse of heaven unobscured by a single cloud. Rain, too, is very uncommon; but heavy dews fall during the night.

Several dreadful whirlwinds occurred during the summer, which in their effects more resembled the sirocco than anything I had ever experienced in America. When the men observed these sudden and dangerous squalls rising, they threw themselves prostrate on the ground, to avoid the clouds of sand and dust, which otherwise would have blinded them. They were generally most violent on the hottest days; and on some occasions they forced the planks which were piled at the saw-pit several feet into the air.

The situation of Oakinagan is admirably adapted for a trading town.[4] With a fertile soil, a healthy climate, horses in abundance for land carriage, an opening to the sea by the Columbia, and a communication to the interior by it and the Oakinagan; the rivers well stocked with fish; and the natives quiet and friendly; it will in my opinion be selected as a spot pre-eminently calculated for the site of a town, when civilisation (which is at present so rapidly migrating westward) crosses the Rocky Mountains and reaches the Columbia.

The natives of Oakinagan are an honest, quiet tribe. They do not muster more than two hundred warriors; but as they are on terms of friendship with the Kamloops,[5] Sinapoils,[6] and other small tribes in their rear, and as the Columbia in front forms an impassable barrier against any surprise from their old enemies the Nez Percés, they have in a great degree forgotten the practice of "glorious war," and are now settled down into a peaceful and rather a slothful tribe. Their

[4] Okanogan was one of the most successful of the fur posts of the period and for all three companies that occupied it.

[5] The Kamloops tribe lived farther north and on the Canadian side of the present boundary. Fort Kamloops was on the Thompson River, a tributary of the Fraser, and almost due north of Fort Okanogan.

[6] The Sanpoils were a small and rather poor tribe living in the vicinity of the Sanpoil River.

principal occupations consist in catching and curing salmon, and occasionally hunting for deer and beaver, neither of which abounds on their lands. Acts of dishonesty are of rare occurrence among either men or women; and breaches of chastity among the latter are equally infrequent.

The chief is an old man, who apparently possesses but little power. However, from their settled habits of living, and long abstinence from war, I should imagine there is very little necessity for the exercise of his authority.

Their principal amusement is gambling, at which they are not so quarrelsome as the Spokans and other tribes; but when any doubtful case occurs, it is referred for arbitration to one of their elders, by whose decision the parties strictly abide.

Mr. M'Gillivray passed the winter of 1813–14 here, and had only four or five men with him, two of whom were generally absent hunting. The buildings at that period were very poorly defended; and were the natives actuated by feelings of hostility, they could have easily robbed the fort and destroyed his little party. This circumstance will show in the strongest point of view their friendly feelings towards us.

Their manner of trading resembles that of most other tribes. A party arrive at the fort loaded with the produce of their hunt, which they throw down, and round which they squat themselves in a circle. The trader lights the calumet of peace, and directing his face first to the east, and so to the other cardinal points, gives at each a solemn puff. These are followed by a few short quick whiffs, and he then hands the calumet to the chief of the party, who repeats the same ceremony. The chief passes it to the man on his right, who only gives a few whiffs, and so on through the whole party until the pipe is smoked out. The trader then presents them with a quantity of tobacco to smoke *ad libitum*, which they generally finish before commencing their barter, being, as they say themselves, "A long time very hungry for a smoke."

When the smoking terminates, each man divides his skins into different lots. For one, he wants a gun; for another, ammunition; for a third, a copper kettle, an axe, a blanket, a tomahawk, a knife, ornaments for his wife, &c., according to the quantity of skins he has to barter.

The trading business being over, another general smoking match takes place; after which they retire to their village or encampment.

They are shrewd, hard dealers, and not a whit inferior to any native of Yorkshire, Scotland, or Connaught, in driving a bargain.

The Oakinagan mode of curing some of our diseases would probably startle many of the faculty. The following case in particular passed under my own observation:

One of the proprietors had in the year 1814 taken as a wife a young and beautiful girl, whose father had been one of the early partners, and whose mother was a half-breed (her grandmother having been a native of the Cree tribe); so that, although not a pure white, she was fairer than many who are so called in Europe. He proceeded with her to Fort George; but the change of climate, from the dry and healthy plains of Forts des Prairies to the gloomy forests and incessant rains on the north-west coast, was too much for her delicate frame, and she fell into a deep consumption. As a last resource her husband determined to send her to Oakinagan to try the change of air, and requested me to procure her accommodation at that place for the summer. This I easily managed. She was accompanied by a younger sister, and an old female attendant.

For some days after her arrival we were in hourly expectation of her death. Her legs and feet were much swoln, and so hard, that the greatest pressure created no sensation; her hair had fallen off in such quantities as nearly to cause baldness; a sable shade surrounded her deeply sunk eyes. She was in fact little more than a skeleton, with scarcely any symptoms of vitality, and her whole appearance betokened approaching dissolution. Such was the state of the unfortunate patient, when an old Indian, who had for some days observed her sitting in the porch-door, where she was brought supported on pillows to enjoy the fresh air, called me aside, and told me he had no doubt of being able to cure her provided I should agree to his plan, but added, that he would not give any explanation of the means he intended to use, for fear we might laugh at him, unless we consented to adopt them. We accordingly held a consultation; the result of which was, that the Indian should be allowed to follow his own method. It could not make her worse, and there was a possibility of success.

Having acquainted him with her acquiescence he immediately commenced operations by seizing an ill-looking, snarling, cur dog, which he half strangled; after which he deliberately cut its throat. He then ripped open the belly, and placed the legs and feet of the patient inside, surrounded by the warm intestines, in which position

235

he kept them until the carcase became cold. He then took them out, and bandaged them with warm flannel, which he said was "very good." The following day another dog lost its life, and a similar operation was performed. This was continued for some time, until every ill-disposed cur in the village had disappeared by the throat-cutting knife of our dog-destroying doctor, and we were obliged to purchase some of a superior breed. While she was undergoing this process she took in addition a small quantity of bark daily in a glass of port wine. In the mean time the swelling gradually decreased, the fingers lost their corpse-like nakedness, the hectic flushes became rarer, and "that most pure spirit of sense," the eye, gave evident tokens of returning animation. When her strength permitted, she was placed on the carriage of a brass field piece, supported by bolsters, and drawn occasionally a mile or two about the prairie. The Indian continued at intervals to repeat this strange application, until the swelling had entirely disappeared, and enabled her once more to make use of her limbs.

Two-and-thirty dogs lost their lives in bringing about this extraordinary recovery, and among them might truly be numbered

> *Mongrel, puppy, whelp, and hound,*
> *And curs of low degree.*

She gradually regained possession of her appetite; and when her husband arrived in the autumn from Fort George, for the purpose of crossing the mountains, she was strong enough to accompany him. The following summer, on my journey across the continent, I met them at Lac la Pluie. She was in the full enjoyment of health, and "in the way which ladies wish to be who love their lords."

Before I quit this subject I may be permitted to mention another remarkable cure by means nearly similar, which occurred at Fort George. One of the proprietors, who had been stationed there for two years, had, like his countryman Burns, an unconquerable *"penchant à l'adorable moitié du genre humain."* And among the flat-headed beauties of the coast, where chastity is not classed as the first of virtues, he had unfortunately too many opportunities of indulging his passion. His excesses greatly impaired his health, and obliged him to have recourse to the most powerful medicine of the *materia medica*. His constitution was naturally weak, and the last attack was of so serious a nature, as to deprive him for some days of the powers of articulation. The contents of the medicine chest were tried in vain, and all hopes of his recovery had been abandoned, when a Clatsop Indian undertook to cure him. Mr. M.—— consented, and a poor horse, having been selected as a sacrifice, was shot. The Indian then made an opening in the paunch sufficiently wide merely to admit the attenuated body of the patient, who was plunged in a state of nudity into the foaming mass of entrails up to the chin. The orifice was tucked in tightly about his neck, to prevent the escape of steam, and he was kept in that situation until the body of the animal had lost its warmth. He was then conveyed to bed, and enveloped in well-heated blankets.

The following day he felt considerably better; and in a few days afterwards another horse suffered. He underwent a second operation, which was attended by similar results. From thence he slowly regained his strength; and by adhering to a strict regimen, was finally restored to his ordinary health. Horses are scarce at Fort George, were it not for which circumstance, Mr. M.—— assured me he would have killed two or three more from the beneficial effects they produced on his constitution. His late illness, however, was so dangerous, and his recovery so unexpected, that it checked for the future his amatory propensities.

Chapter 20

Author nearly blinded by hawks—Foxes—Great number of wolves—Their method of attacking horses—Lynxes—Bears—Anecdote of a kidnapping bruin—Ingenious plan of getting off bear-skins—Account of the horses on the Columbia—Great feat performed by one

In the great plains on the east side of the Columbia, between Oakinagan and the Spokan lands, there are, during the autumnal months, plenty of deer, grouse, wild ducks, and geese.

I spent a great portion of this period with a few of my men and some Indians on shooting excursions, and had excellent sport.

We stopped one very sultry day about noon to rest our horses, and enjoy the cooling shade afforded by a clump of sycamore-trees with a refreshing draught from an adjoining spring. Several large hawks were flying about the spot, two of which we brought down. From their great size, immense claws, and large hooked beaks, they could have easily carried off a common-sized duck or goose. Close to our resting-place was a small hill, round the top of which I observed the hawks assemble, and judging that a nest was there, without communicating my intention to any of the party, I determined to find it out.

I therefore cautiously ascended the eminence, on the summit of which I perceived a nest larger than a common-sized market basket, formed of branches of trees, one laid regularly over the other, and the least of which was an inch in circumference. Around it were scattered bones, skeletons, and half-mangled bodies of pigeons, sparrows, humming-birds, &c. Next to a rattlesnake and a shark, my greatest aversion is a hawk; and on this occasion it was not diminished by observing the remains of the feathered tribe, which had, from time to time, fallen a prey to their voracious appetite. I therefore determined to destroy the nest, and disperse its inhabitants; but I had scarcely commenced the work of demolition with my dagger, when old and young flew out and attacked me in every direction, but particularly about my face and eyes; the latter of which, as a punishment for my temerity, they seemed determined to separate from their sockets.

In the mean time I roared out lustily for assistance, and laid about me with the dagger. Three men promptly ran up the hill, and called out to me to shut my eyes, and throw myself on the ground, otherwise I should be shortly blinded, promising in the mean time to assist me. I obeyed their directions; and just as I began to kiss the earth, a bullet from one of their rifles brought down a large hawk, apparently the father of the gang. He fell close to my neck, and in his expiring agonies made a desperate bite at my left ear, which I escaped, and in return gave him the *coup de grace,* by thrusting about four inches of my dagger down his throat. The death of their chieftain was followed by that of two others, which completely dispersed them; and we retired after breaking up their den.

Red foxes and wolves are also in great numbers about the plains; but their skins are not now purchased by the Company, as the price given for them would not defray the expense of their carriage.

The prairie wolves are much smaller than those which inhabit the woods. They generally travel together in numbers, and a solitary one is seldom met with. Two or three of us have often pursued from fifty to one hundred, driving them before us as quickly as our horses could charge.

Their skins are of no value, and we do not therefore waste much powder and ball in shooting them. The Indians, who are obliged to pay dear for their ammunition, are equally careful not to throw it away on objects that bring no remunerating value. The natural consequence is, that the wolves are allowed to multiply; and some parts of the country are completely overrun by them. The Indians catch numbers of them in traps, which they set in the vicinity of those places where their tame horses are sent to graze. The traps are merely excavations covered over with slight switches and hay, and baited with meat, &c., into which the wolves fall, and being unable to extricate themselves, they perish by famine, or the knife of the Indian. These destructive animals annually destroy numbers of horses, particularly during the winter season, when the latter get entangled in the snow; in which situation they become an easy prey to their light-footed pursuers, ten or fifteen of which will often fasten on one animal, and with their long fangs in a few minutes separate the head from the body. If however the horses are not prevented from using their legs, they sometimes punish the enemy severely; as an instance of this, I saw one morning the bodies of two of our horses which had been killed the night before, and around were lying eight dead and maimed wolves, some with their brains scattered about, and others with their limbs and ribs broken by the hoofs of the furious animals in their vain attempts to escape from their sanguinary assailants.

While I was at Spokan I went occasionally to the horse prairie, which is nearly surrounded by partially-wooded hills, for the purpose of watching the manoeuvres of the wolves in their combined attacks. The first announcement of their approach was a few shrill currish barks at intervals, like the outpost firing of skirmishing parties. These were answered by similar barking from an opposite direction, until the sounds gradually approximated, and at length ceased on the junction of the different parties. We prepared our guns, and concealed ourselves behind a thick cover. In the mean time, the horses, sensible of the approaching danger, began to paw the ground, snort, toss up their heads, look wildly about them, and exhibit all the symptoms of fear. One or two stallions took the lead, and appeared to wait with a degree of comparative composure for the appearance of the enemy.

The allies at length entered the field in a semi-circular form, with their flanks extended for the evident purpose of surrounding their prey. They were between two and three hundred strong. The horses, on observing their movement knew from experience its object, and dreading to encounter so numerous a force, instantly turned round, and galloped off in a contrary direction. Their flight was the signal for the wolves to advance; and immediately uttering a simultaneous yell, they charged after the fugitives, still preserving their crescent form. Two or three of the horses, which were not in the best condition, were quickly overtaken by the advanced guard of the enemy. The former, finding themselves unable to keep up with the band, commenced kicking at their pursuers, several of which received some severe blows; but these being reinforced by others, they would have shortly dispatched the horses, had we not, just in time, emerged from our place of concealment, and discharged a volley at the enemy's centre, by which a few were brought down. The whole battalion instantly wheeled about, and fled towards the hills in the utmost disorder; while the horses, on hearing the fire, changed their course and galloped up to us. Our appearance saved several of them from the fangs of their foes; and by their neighing they seemed to express their joy and gratitude at our timely interference.

Although the wolves of North America are the most daring of all the beasts of prey on that continent, they are by no means so courageous or ferocious as those of Europe, particularly in Spain or the South of France, in which countries they commit dreadful ravages both on man and beast;[1] whereas an American wolf, except forced by desperation, will seldom or ever attack a human being, a remarkable instance of which is mentioned in the detail of my wanderings in the eighth chapter. The lynxes are by no means so numerous as the wolves, but they are equally destructive, and individually more daring. They generally travel alone, or in couples, and seldom fly as the wolves do on the first approach of man. The largest American lynx does not exceed in size an English mastiff.

Bears are scarce about the plains, but they are found in considerable numbers in the vicinity of the woods and lakes. Their flesh is excellent, particularly in the summer and autumnal months, when roots and wild fruit are had in abundance. They are most dangerous animals to encounter, especially if they are slightly wounded, or that any of their cubs are in danger, in which case they will rush on a man, though he were armed at all points; and woe to him if Bruin should once enfold him in his dreadful grasp.

I have seen several of our hunters, as well as many Indians, who had been dreadfully lacerated in their encounters with bears: some have been deprived of their ears, others had their noses nearly torn off, and a few have been completely blinded. From the scarcity of food in the spring months they are then more savage than at any other season; and during that period it is a highly dangerous experiment to approach them.

[1] During the late Peninsular war, the Duke of Wellington had occasion to send dispatches by a mounted dragoon, to a general of division not quite a day's march distant from headquarters. The answer not having arrived at the period it was expected, His Grace dispatched three others to ascertain the cause. They found the mangled remains of their unfortunate comrade lying beside those of his horse, and the greater portion of the flesh eaten off their bodies. His sword was firmly grasped in his mutilated hand, and the dead carcases of seven or eight wolves which lay about him exhibited strong marks of the sabre, and of the desperation with which he fought before he was overpowered by numbers.—R. C.

The following anecdote will prove this; and, were not the fact confirmed by the concurrent testimony of ten more, I would not have given it a place among my *memorabilia*.

In the spring of this year (1816) Mr. M'Millan had dispatched ten Canadians in a canoe down the Flat-head River on a trading excursion. The third evening after quitting the fort, while they were quietly sitting round a blazing fire eating a hearty dinner of deer, a large half-famished bear[2] cautiously approached the group from behind an adjacent tree; and before they were aware of his presence, he sprang across the fire, seized one of the men (who had a well-furnished bone in his hand) round his waist, with the two fore paws, and ran about fifty yards with him on his hind legs before he stopped. His comrades were so thunder-struck at the unexpected appearance of such a visitor, and his sudden retreat with *pauvre Louisson,* that they for some time lost all presence of mind, and, in a state of fear and confusion, were running to and fro, each expecting in his turn to be kidnapped in a similar manner; when at length Baptiste Le Blanc, a half-breed hunter, seized his gun, and was in the act of firing at the bear, but was stopped by some of the others, who told him he would inevitably kill their friend in the position in which he was then placed. During this parley Bruin relaxed his grip of the captive, whom he kept securely under him, and very leisurely began picking the bone which the latter had dropped. Once or twice Louisson attempted to escape, which only caused the bear to watch him more closely; but on his making another attempt, he again seized Louisson round the waist, and commenced giving him one of those infernal embraces which generally end in death. The poor fellow was now in great agony, and vented the most frightful screams; and observing Baptiste with his gun ready, anxiously watching a safe opportunity to fire, he cried out, *Tire! tire! mon cher frère, si tu m'aimes. Tire, pour l'amour du bon Dieu! A la tête à la tête!* This was enough for Le Blanc, who instantly let fly, and hit the bear over the right temple. He fell, and at the same moment dropped Louisson; but he gave him an ugly scratch with his claws across the face, which for some time afterwards spoiled his beauty. After the shot, Le Blanc darted to his comrade's assistance, and with his *couteau de chasse* quickly finished the sufferings of the man stealer, and rescued his friend from impending death;

2 This was probably a grizzly, which will attack a man, often without provocation of any sort. For a very similar story see Parker, *Journal of an Exploring Tour,* 197.

for with the exception of the above-mentioned scratch, he escaped uninjured. They commenced the work of dissection with right good-will; but on skinning the bear, they found scarcely any meat on his bones; in fact, the animal had been famishing, and in a fit of hungry desperation made one of the boldest attempts at kidnapping ever heard of in the legends of ursine courage.

The skins of these animals are not at present held in the same estimation that they were formerly, particularly the brown or grizzly kind, few of which are now purchased. Good rich black ones and cubs still bring a fair price at the trading posts nearest to Canada and Hudson's Bay.

About twenty-five years ago the Company had a great number of bear-skins lying in their stores, for which there was no demand. One of the directors, a gentleman well known for the fertility of his expedients as an Indian trader, hit upon a plan for getting off the stock, which succeeded beyond his most sanguine expectation. He selected a few of the finest and largest skins in the store, which he had made into a hammercloth, splendidly ornamented in silver with the royal arms. A deputation of the directors then waited upon a late Royal Duke with the hammercloth, and respectfully requested that he would be graciously pleased to accept it as a slight testimony of their respect. His Royal Highness returned a polite answer, and condescendingly consented to receive the present. A few days afterwards the King held a levee, and his illustrious son proceeded to court in his state-coach with its splendid hammercloth. It attracted universal attention; and to every inquiry as to where the skins were obtained, the answer was, "from the North-West Company." In three weeks afterwards there was not a black, or even a brown bear-skin in the Company's warehouse; and the unfortunate peer, who could not sport a hammercloth of bear, was voted a bore by his more lucky brethren.

The skin of the red fox is not now accounted valuable; and scarcely any are purchased. The Indians therefore seldom trouble themselves in hunting these animals, and in some districts they are consequently greatly on the increase. There are no black foxes on the Columbia; but next to them in beauty and value are the silver grey, which bring a high price, and several of which are purchased at Oakinagan and Spokan. The mandarins of China hold them in great estimation, and those which we sent to Canton were eagerly purchased for their use.

The number of horses among the various tribes on the Columbia and its tributary streams differs with the circumstances of the country. Among the Flat-heads, Cootonais, Spokans, &c., whose lands are rather thickly wooded, there are not more than sufficient for their actual use, and every colt, on arriving at the proper age, is broken in for the saddle. But in the countries inhabited by the Wallah Wallahs, Nez Percés, and Shoshonés, which chiefly consist of open plains, well watered and thinly wooded, they are far more numerous, and thousands are allowed to go wild. Their general height is about fifteen hands, which they seldom exceed; and ponies are very scarce. Those reared in the plains are excellent hunters, and the swiftest racers; but are not capable of enduring the same hardships as those bred in the vicinity of the high and woody districts. We have seen from seven hundred to a thousand wild horses in a band; and some of the party who crossed the continent by the Missouri route, told me that in parts of the country belonging to the Snake Indians, bands varying from three to four thousand were frequently seen; and further to the southward they are far more numerous.[3] The Indian horses are never shod; and, as we were equally with them deprived of smith, farrier, and iron, we were unable to introduce that valuable practice into the country. Owing to this circumstance, their hoofs, particularly of such as are in constant work, are nearly worn away before they are ten or eleven years old, after which they are unfit for any labour except carrying children. They are easily managed, and are seldom vicious. An Indian horse is never taught to trot. The natives dislike this pace, and prefer to it the canter or light gallop. They are hard taskmasters; and the hair-rope bridles, with the padded deerskin saddles which they use, lacerate the mouths and backs of the unfortunate animals in such a manner as to render them at times objects of commiseration to men of harder hearts than the late worthy member for Galway. In summer they have no shelter from the heat, in winter no retreat from the cold; and their only provender throughout the year is the wild loose grass of the prairies, which in the latter season is generally covered with snow, and in the former is brown and arid, from the intense heat of the sun.

I have already given some details of the hardships to which the

[3] The Spaniards at San Francisco informed our traders that in the year 1812, they were obliged to kill upwards of thirty thousand horses in California in order to preserve sufficient grass for the buffalo, the fat of which forms an article for exportation.—R. C.

horses in this country are subject, and shall merely add one anecdote more. In the spring of 1813, before the dissolution of the Pacific Fur Company, while I was stationed at Spokan House with Mr. Clarke, he received a letter from Mr. Farnham, who had the charge of the party sent to the Flat-heads, stating that he had arrived at the Flat-head portage, a distance of seventy-two miles from Spokan House, where he should be obliged to remain a few days to recruit his horses; that his trading goods were exhausted, and he was entirely out of tobacco; that a large party of Flat-heads were following them with a quantity of valuable skins; that his rival, Mr. M'Donald, was also unsupplied with tobacco; that whichever of them got the first supply of that article would, by treating the Indians to a grand smoking-match, succeed in getting the produce of their hunt; and that in order to attain that object, it was absolutely necessary the tobacco required should be with him that night, otherwise the natives would all go over in a body to Mr. M'Donald, with whom they had been longer acquainted than with him.

It was eleven o'clock in the forenoon when this letter reached us, and Mr. Clarke thought it impossible for any horse to go a distance of seventy-two miles during the remainder of that day. At all events, he knew that none of the Company's horses were fit for such a task, and was about giving up the idea as hopeless, when I offered to undertake it, with a celebrated horse of his own, called *Le Bleu*. The case was important; a blow was necessary to be struck; and although he prized the horse above all his chattels in the Indian country, he at once determined to sacrifice his private feelings to the interests of the Company. Two men were selected to accompany me, and orders were given to catch *Le Bleu*. He was a noble animal, between fifteen and sixteen hands high, seven years of age, admirably built, and derived his name from his colour, which was a dappled white and sky-blue. He was also a prime racer, and had beaten all competitors on the turf.

Owing to the delay occasioned by catching the horses we did not start till twelve o'clock. I remained in company with the men for the first two hours at a slight canter, after which I took the lead in a hard gallop, and quickly lost sight of them. I followed an excellent well-beaten pathway for upwards of sixty miles through the Pointed Heart Plains; but late in the evening it brought me to a thick wood, through which it runs for a distance of ten miles, when it terminates at the portage.

245

Shortly after entering the wood, night overtook me; and I several times lost the pathway, which, owing to darkness, and a quantity of fallen trees and brushwood, became extremely intricate. The sagacity of my horse, however, extricated me from these *égaremens,* and a little after eight o'clock I emerged from the forest, and was delighted at the cheering appearance of a range of fires along the banks of the river. The *Bleu,* which had been for some time drooping, on seeing the light, knew his task was at an end, and galloped up in fine style to Farnham's tent, when he was immediately let loose to regale himself in the prairie.

I had brought a few fathoms of thick twist-tobacco with me; on learning which the Indians crowded about us, and in a few seconds each man's head was enveloped in clouds of smoke. They promised that we should have all their skins; but in order to make assurance doubly sure, we requested them to bring their respective packages to the tent, and deposit them therein until morning. This was at once complied with, after which the smoking recommenced. About two hours after, two of our rivals arrived with a quantity of tobacco. They had started from Spokan shortly after me, but were never able to overtake the gallant *Bleu.* They were much better acquainted with the intricacies of the pathway through the wood than I was; and if their horses had been equal to mine, it is very probable the result would have been different. They were much chagrined at our success; and on taxing the Indians with having deserted them for strangers, they replied, that being the first to satisfy their hungry cravings for tobacco, they could do no less than give us the preference, but added that they would punctually pay them any debts which they had contracted with Mr. M'Donald, which promise they faithfully kept.

About midnight the two men, whom I had left behind me, reached the encampment. They also were for some time lost in the wood, and like myself were obliged to depend on the sagacity of their horses to set them right.

We returned to Spokan House by easy stages; but I did not ride the *Bleu.* In less than a week after he was perfectly recovered from the fatigue of his journey, and in the summer of the same year beat the fleetest horses of both Companies, on the race-course.

Chapter 21

Letter from the proprietors—Author winters at Oakinagan—Letter from Mr. Mackenzie—A number of horses stolen—Successful plan to recover them—Description of soil, climate, productions, &c., of the lower part of the Columbia

The summer of 1816 did not tend to diminish my growing aversion to the Indian country. Horse-racing, deer-hunting, and grouse-shooting were pleasant pastimes enough, but the want of companionable society rendered every amusement "stale, flat, and unprofitable." Zimmerman[1] in vain displayed the charms of solitude: he never vegetated among savages. Bad French and worse Indian began to usurp the place of English, and I found my conversation gradually becoming a barbarous compound of various dialects. The cherished object too of a young man's ambition was still at an immeasurable distance, and I felt that an old age of affluence could only be purchased by the sacrifice in youth of all the comforts of social life. In the midst of these and similar reflections the monotony of my life was, for a moment, relieved by the arrival of Mr. Donald Mackenzie with two canoes and twenty men from Fort William. This gentleman had been one of the proprietors of the Pacific Fur Company, from which, after its dissolution, he changed to the North-West. He was now on his way to Fort George with dispatches, and took charge of the autumn brigade to that place. By Mr. Mackenzie I received letters from home, which at once determined me to apply for leave to quit the country; and having written to the proprietors to that effect, I received the following answer; viz.

[1] Johann Georg van Zimmermann (1728–95) was a Swiss philosopher. His *Üder die Einsamkeit* was published in 1755, with a revised edition in 1784–85.

247

Fort George, September 30th, 1816

Dear Sir,

In acceding to your most earnest request of being discharged from our service ensuing spring, we give way to the voice of nature and of humanity, which cannot, will not for a moment allow us to hesitate, when the object is to re-animate and cheer up the drooping spirits of your venerable and aged parents. At the same time rest assured that on no other consideration could we ever be induced to part with your most useful services, more particularly at a period when we are on the eve of being put to such shifts to fill up the different requisitions.

As to your character, as far as prudence, integrity, and perseverance, joined to an unceasing desire to please and render yourself useful, can command regard, you certainly are deservingly entitled to ours, and no encomium on our part could add to our high opinion of your merit.

In expectation of seeing you next spring at this place, prior to your taking your final departure, we remain, with sincere regard,

Dear Sir,
Your most obedient servants,
James Keith,
Angus Bethune,
Donald Mackenzie,
For North-West Company.

Mr. Mackenzie was himself the bearer of this letter. He strongly urged me to change my resolution, and declared if I consented to remain in the country my promotion should take place in a short time after the expiration of my engagement; but as my mind was made up to return home, I refused acceding to his friendly wishes.

It was arranged I should pass the winter in my present post (Oakinagan), in which, on account of my popularity with the natives, I had succeeded in obtaining more furs than most of my predecessors. Mr. Mackenzie went to Spokan with Messrs. M'Donald and Montour for the outposts, Mr. Ross proceeded to Kamloops, and Mr. M'Millan to his old post at the Flat-heads.

Mr. Mackenzie had made arrangements with the chiefs of the various tribes for the transmission of an express from Oakinagan to Fort George, promising to each a handsome present, provided it reached its destination, and that an answer was brought back. In pursuance of this plan, he forwarded dispatches to the sea, to which he received an answer, as will be seen from the following letter:

Letter from Mr. Mackenzie

Spokan House, February 12th, 1817

Dear Cox,

It was but yesterday, on my return from the *Nez-Percés*, that I had the pleasure of perusing your much esteemed letter of the 29th of December. My despatches reached Fort George in thirty-six days, and were answered on the 12th of December; so that in sixteen days from the fort they reached your place. The safety of this conveyance will, I hope, do away with the necessity of the usual Fall voyage to the sea. On arriving here I found I had ninety souls to provide with the necessaries of life, and therefore determined on an excursion to Lewis River. Your friend, Mr. M'Donald, accompanied me, and, besides the Canadians, I took ten Sandwich Islanders, whom I armed and accoutred quite *en militaire*. The *Nez-Percés* did not half relish the swarthy aspect of these invincibles, and fancied I intended to resent former grudges. However, we did not see them all.

My trip has simply answered the purpose of obtaining provisions for the passing day, which, at this post, I assure you has been no contemptible attainment. The horses I purchased are already nearly consumed; you will therefore, I trust, excuse my sending two of my people in your direction. I have ordered them to encamp in your environs; and the Nipising, who is chasseur, is to supply your board with game. It will prove a seasonable variety to your dried salmon.

I regret the frost prevents me sending you potatoes: they would be of no service. I have received accounts from Mr. M'Millan. He informs me he was nearly surrounded by the Piegans (the Black-feet); but they were prevented by hunger from advancing near enough to the fort. He has had a lucky escape. Should you be induced to alter your mind about quitting the Company, I shall feel very happy by your remaining with us. You may rely on all I have told you. You need feel no scruples on that head. I passed an agreeable time with our friend Finan. He is certainly a most worthy mortal, and desires to be remembered to you.

Yours, &c.
Donald Mackenzie[2]

Mr. Mackenzie, as already mentioned, had crossed the continent with Mr. Hunt. In the course of that journey he passed through the lands of the Snake Indians, in which he observed great numbers of beavers; and his chief motive in coming to the Columbia was to form a trading establishment in that dangerous district, no attempt at which had been made since the massacre of Mr. Read and his party. Mr. Mackenzie was peculiarly qualified for this hazardous undertaking. He was an experienced trader, and possessed an accurate knowl-

[2] This gentleman is now governor of the colony established at Red River.—R. C.

edge of the localities of the country. He could, with his rifle, drive a dozen balls consecutively at one hundred paces through a Spanish dollar, which accomplishment alone was enough to secure him the respect of the Indians. To the most cautious prudence he united the most dauntless intrepidity; in fact, no hardships could fatigue, no dangers intimidate him. As we had many reasons to suspect that the Pierced-noses, through whose lands a party proceeding to the country of the Snakes must pass, were actuated by feelings of hostility, Mr. Mackenzie undertook the winter's trip to Lewis' River, not so much for the purpose of purchasing horses (for that Mr. M'Donald could have done), as to form a judgment from personal observation of their disposition. Although his reception was not the most friendly, he was satisfied there was little danger to be apprehended, and he therefore determined to make the attempt early in the summer.

I passed five weary winter months at Oakinagan without a friend to converse with; and the severity of the season debarred me from the exercise of field sports, which, during the summer, partially relieved the unsocial tedium of my existence. Tea and tobacco were my only luxuries; and my pipe was my pot-companion. Dried salmon was our principal article of food, with a bit of lean deer, with which the natives occasionally supplied us, like

Angels' visits, few and far between.

Our horses were too few and too poor for the kettle; and scarcely a week elapsed that one did not fall a victim to the villanous wolves which infested the snow-covered plains.

One morning in the beginning of February, the men whom I had sent out to collect the horses found ten missing, and the fresh traces of human feet in the snow convinced them they must have been stolen. I immediately sent for the Oakinagan chief, and told him I should require his assistance in recovering the horses. This he readily granted, and forthwith ordered five of his young men to catch their horses and join him at the fort. I selected three Canadians and two Sandwich Islanders to accompany me, and in less than an hour all our warlike arrangements were completed. We proceeded in the first instance to the prairie; and the chief having made his observations, declared at once they must have been stolen by the Sinapoils. It had snowed hard the preceding night; which circumstance, without the assistance of the Indians, would have puzzled our men to find out the traces of the robbers. The chief however quickly discovered their route, and we followed his guidance until late in the evening, when we were obliged to stop to rest the horses, and take a little refreshment. He told me we were within a few hours' march of the robbers, and advised us to continue on during the night, by which means we were certain of catching them unprepared, when we could kill them all, and recover our horses. Having no relish for raising scalps, I declined his sanguinary proposal; at which he did not appear too well pleased. We resumed our journey before day-break the following morning; and after riding about two hours, the chief desired us to dismount, and lead our horses. We complied. In less than half an hour our path opened into a small glen, in the bottom of which were half a dozen mat-covered lodges, and around them we perceived about fifteen horses scraping the snow. The stolen ones were among them. We instantly mounted; and before the robbers were aware of our approach we had surrounded their miserable encampment. On hearing the warwhoop of our Oakinagan allies, they rushed out, partly armed; but seeing our numbers, they held down their bows, and quietly submitted. I never saw such a group of meagre wretches. They were quite naked; and

Sharp misery had worn them to the bones.

Their wives and children crouched under mats, and kept up a howling cry, while the Oakinagan chief thus addressed them:

"Sinapoils! you are dogs; you are robbers. You stole the horses from our good friends the white men; and as a punishment we shall now take away your horses." One of them replied: "We are dogs; we are robbers; we did steal the good white men's horses; but we are poor, and cold, and hungry. The wolves destroyed all our own horses but five; and as our dried salmon was all gone, and our wives and children starving, sooner than see them die, we took the horses from the white men, because we knew they were good people, and could easily purchase others. We are sorry for what we have done; but if you take our five remaining horses, we shall all die of hunger."

This appeal made no impression on the flinty-hearted chief, who counselled us to take the five horses as a punishment to the robbers. I refused however to adopt his advice; for, independently of the inhumanity of such a course, I did not deem it prudent to resort to measures of severity against a tribe who might have many oppor-

251

tunities of retaliating on our hunters in the plains. I therefore told them that in consequence of their starving condition, we would abstain from punishing them on that occasion, but any future trespass should not escape with impunity. As they all appeared to want something to eat, I ordered one of their horses to be shot, and leaving the body for their own use, we returned to the fort, which we reached late that evening. Our forbearance produced no expression of gratitude from the Sinapoils; and the chief reproached us for having acted in such a mild manner. I made him and his young men a suitable present, and so ended this pursuit of the "black-mail" drovers.

As this was the last winter I spent in the Indian country, I shall, before commencing the journal of my voyage across the continent, give some brief remarks on the soil and productions of the various districts on the Columbia, the manners and customs of the different tribes, their distinctive peculiarities, &c.

The climate about the entrance of the river, and thence to the first rapids, is mild. The mercury seldom falls below the freezing point; and never rises above 80. Westerly winds prevail during the spring and summer months, and are succeeded by north-westers, which blow pretty freshly during the autumn. October ushers in the south wind and rain, both of which continue without intermission until January, when the wind begins to veer to the westward; but the rain seldom ceases until the termination of April. The gentlemen who have wintered at Fort George tell me the torrents which pour down during this period are dreadful. For weeks together the sun is invisible; and the only protection for those whose duty compels them to be in the open air is a shirt made from the intestines of the sea-lion, the parts of which are ingeniously sewed together with fine threads of *nerf*. A kind of *capuchon*, or hood, is attached to the collar; and when this *garde-pluie* is on, the wearer may bid defiance to the heaviest rain. These shirts are made by the natives in the vicinity of the Russian settlements to the northward of the Columbia, and some of them are neatly ornamented.

Nature has been peculiarly bountiful to the natives of this district; and nothing but the grossest neglect of her gifts can reduce them to want. The spring months supply them with immense quantities of small fish resembling pilchard, which by Lewis and Clarke are called anchovies. These are smoke-dried, and form an important article of barter with the upper Indians for roots.

From June to the latter end of August they have an abundance of deliciously-flavoured salmon, which, from its richness, at first produced a general dysentery among our people.

We found the wild raspberries an excellent remedy for this disorder, which was effectually checked by their astringent qualities.[3]

The months of August and September furnish a plentiful supply of prime sturgeon. This fish attains a great size. Some of those we took were eleven feet in length, and, with the entrails out, weighed from three to four hundred pounds.

This period also produces a variety of wild fruit: in June, small white strawberries of sweet flavour; these are followed by red and amber raspberries of the ordinary size, but somewhat sour. They are found in moist shady grounds, and grow on bushes from ten to fifteen feet high.

During the months of July, August, and September, the following kinds of fruit are obtained in considerable quantities; viz. blue-berries, black-berries, wild cherries, gooseberries, wild pears, and a species of bitter crab-apple, which cannot be used unless coddled or boiled.

There is an evergreen about the size of a common gooseberry bush, and with small thick leaves resembling laurel. In the month of August it produces abundance of fruit of a small oblong form, which grow in thick clusters. This fruit has an insipid taste but is looked on as healthy, and great quantities of it may be eaten without injury. It is much esteemed by the natives, who preserve it for their winter use, by making it into small cakes, which are gradually dried before a slow fire.

The country also abounds in various nutritive roots, of which the Indians are extremely fond, and some of which are excellent anti-scorbutics. They collect large quantities of a kind resembling young onions,[4] which, in the first instance, they dry on hot stones. They are then pulverised, and, being worked into a paste, are formed into loaves from five to six pounds weight, which they lay by for seasons of scarcity. This bread has a taste resembling liquorice. An inferior description of fish resembling salmon is taken in the months of October and November. It is poor, dry, and has an insipid taste. The

[3] The subject matter of this chapter is paralleled in Franchère, *Narrative,* Chap. XVIII.

[4] The root of the edible thistle. See Franchère, *Narrative,* 322.

flesh is white, the teeth long, the snout bent like the beak of a parrot, and it contains very little substance.[5]

The principal quadrupeds are the elk, red deer, black-tailed deer; the black, brown, and grizzly bear, the last of which is extremely ferocious; the wolf, panther, tiger-cat, wild-cat, marmot, beaver, land-otter, musk-rat, wood-rat, and, the most valuable of all the fur tribe, the sea-otter. White bears[6] are occasionally killed on the coast to the northward of the Columbia; but they are scarce.

The most remarkable of the feathered tribe are the black, brown, and nun eagle; the hawk, pelican, and cormorant; the swan, heron, crane, bustard, grey and white goose, and various species of wild ducks, &c.

The soil in the valleys consists of a bed of rich black mould, about six inches in depth, which covers a stratum of grey earth extremely cold. The latter lies on a layer of large gravelly sand; and under all is a bed of hard flinty stones. On the high grounds, under a thin covering of black mould, are found good quarry stones well adapted for building. There is a bank of white earth resembling chalk to the southward of Point Adams; and further on, in the same direction, the Indians find red, green, and yellow earths, and a species of heavy shining clay, resembling lead-mine. No limestone is found in the neighbourhood.

Few of the various vegetable seeds which were planted came to perfection. The turnips indeed attained a prodigious size. One weighed fifteen pounds and a half, and was thirty-three inches in circumference; they were in flower at the end of December, and were left in the ground; but the seeds were destroyed by the mice which infested the garden. The radishes throve tolerably well; but owing to the coldness of the earth, the potatoes failed the second year.

The trees most common in the neighbourhood of Fort George are the cedar, spruce, pine, alder, &c. The cedars are from twenty to thirty feet in circumference, and proportionably high. The alders are also extremely large, some of them measuring from twelve to twenty inches in diameter. A few leagues above the fort, ash and oak are found; the former is of tolerable size; but the latter, compared with its noble brother in England, is a mere dwarf.

[5] The dog salmon.

[6] Cox probably had reference to the polar bear, although in the early days the grizzly was sometimes referred to as a white bear.

In the fourteenth chapter, I have referred to the peculiarities, moral qualities, and mechanical ingenuity of the natives who reside about the mouth of the Columbia. Little therefore remains to be said on these subjects. The same kind of houses and canoes, the same flattening of the heads, an equal love of thieving and lying on the part of the men, shameless profligacy among the women, the same mode of living, and a similarity in their manner of burial, are observable among the various tribes, from the rapids to the ocean. They all, too, speak the same language, which is decidedly the most unpronounceable compound of gutturals ever formed for the communication of human thoughts, or the expression of human wants. The following are a few of their words:[7]

Icht, one	*Stouktekane,* eight
Makust, two	*Quaiust,* nine
Thlown, three	*Itallilum,* ten
Lakut, four	*Ekoun icht,* eleven
Quannum, five	*Ekoun makust,* twelve
Takut, six	*Makust thlalt,* twenty
Sinebakust, seven	*Moolak,* a deer
Equannet, salmon	*Mittaight o kok,* sit down
Kaienoult, tobacco	there
Passischqua, a blanket	*Tane tse koolama,* show me
Tillikum, men	your pipe
Kamoox, a dog	*Patlach nain maika?* will you
Sakquallal, a gun	give it to me?

Mr. Franchère, who attained a more thorough knowledge of their language than any one in the Company's service, states that the letters *F, V,* and others, are not articulated in any of their words. The letter *R* is also wanting; but some words, pronounced with a thick guttural lisp, such as *chreluit,* approach its sound. The combinations *thl, tl,* and *lt,* are frequent, and are also very common in the language spoken by the Mexicans.

In proportion as we approach the rapids from the sea, female impurity becomes less perceptible; beyond this point it entirely ceases. I think it necessary to mention this fact, in consequence of the sweeping censure passed by Lewis and Clarke on all the women between

[7] The vocabulary as given in the appendix to Ross, *First Settlers,* differs slightly from that given here.

the Rocky Mountains and the sea. The reader must not suppose that I wish to cast any doubt on the general accuracy of those intelligent travellers; indeed, circumstanced as they were, the immense fund of correct and valuable information in their journal is surprising; but in this instance they have wandered from the fact.

Having ascended the Columbia nine times, and descended it eight, I had better opportunities of judging the manners of the natives than those who merely passed up and down; and during those various journeys I never saw the slightest approximation to levity of manners among the women above the rapids.

The two most important rivers which fall into the Columbia below the rapids are the Wallamat,[8] or Multnomah, and the Coweliskee.[9] The entrance of the former is about one hundred miles from the sea, and its general course is a little to the eastward of south. I was merely a few miles above its junction with the Columbia; but Messrs. Clapp, Franchère, and Halsey, who ascended it a considerable distance, state that it runs through a low well-wooded country for upwards of sixty miles, when the navigation is interrupted by a considerable fall,[10] above which the channel contracts, and the banks become higher and less woody. The climate in the Wallamat is remarkably mild, and not so moist as that on the coast. It possesses a rich and luxuriant soil, which yields an abundance of fruits and roots.[11] The Indians are tranquil; there are no noxious reptiles; beaver, deer, and elk are plentiful; and when, in the course of time, the improvements of scientific cultivation extend to the Columbia, the country about the Wallamat will be rendered one of the most delightful districts to the westward of the Rocky Mountains. We know little of the Coweliskee. It enters the Columbia about half a day's march below the Wallamat from the northward; its banks are high, and thickly wooded, and the current much interrupted by rapids. Our traders, owing to the difficulty of the navigation, did not ascend it more than thirty miles. The tribe who inhabit its banks are called the Skilloots. They are friendly, and differ little from the lower Indians.

[8] The present Willamette River.
[9] The Cowlitz River.
[10] Near present Oregon City, Oregon.
[11] A few years since the tobacco plant was discovered in the Wallamat. The samples sent home are, I understand, of an excellent description.—R. C.

Chapter 22

Description of climate, soil, &c., above the rapids—Sketch of various tribes — The Chohoptins — Yackamans — Oakinagans — Sinapoils — Spokans — Anecdote—Pointed Hearts—Cause of war—Cootonais—Kettle Indians— Kamloops, &c.

I have already alluded so often to the natives about the first rapids, and the great falls, that I may here pass them over with a few words explanatory of the causes that induced them to commit so many acts of hostility. In their various contests with the tribes below the former, and above the latter, they were generally the greatest sufferers, owing to the fire-arms which those opposed to them obtained from us in exchange for their furs, horses, &c.

There are no animals of the fur kind in the neighbourhood of the falls, and scarcely any about the rapids.[1] There is therefore nothing to induce us to establish a trading post at either place; and as the natives are aware of this, and of their consequent inability to procure fire-arms, &c., they, like the Black-feet, identify us with their old enemies, and allow no opportunity to escape of attacking and robbing us. A small party, unencumbered by merchandise, may pass in safety; otherwise, as has been already seen, it is a hazardous experiment.

From the falls to the lands of the Spokans, the climate is remarkably healthy: in summer, excessively hot; in winter, intensely cold; but subject during these seasons to little variation. A cloud is seldom seen; and during the various journeys I have made up and down the Columbia, I did not witness in the above space ten rainy days.

The soil is unproductive, and is chiefly a light yellowish sandy clay.

[1] The animals which Lewis and Clarke saw at this place, and which they called sea-otters, are seals. We have killed them as high up as the Dalles below the falls.—R. C.

257

The plains are covered with a short kind of grass, mixed with prickly pears, wormwood, and tufts of long coarse grass from three to four feet high. Patches of clover are here and there visible, and in their vicinity the chappallel, and the camas or quamash roots, mentioned by Lewis and Clarke, are found. Wild onions grow in considerable quantities along the banks of the river above the falls. They are small, and from March to May their flavour is excellent; but after the latter month they lose their relish, and become dry and hard.

Cotton-wood, small willow, sumac, furze, and sarsaparilla, are also found occasionally on the sides of the Columbia; but from the falls, until we approach Spokan River, none of the larger trees are visible. Throughout this distance (about five hundred miles) our only fuel was derived from the timber drifted down by the spring freshes from the upper parts of the Columbia, and which in some particular bends of the river accumulates in great quantities. In other places, however, it is very scarce; and when we could not purchase drift-wood from Indians, we were often obliged to encamp without any fire.

The principal animals are horses, small deer, prairie wolves, red foxes, badgers, polecats, hares, and dogs. Otters are sometimes seen; but the great staple animal, the beaver, is a stranger to this district. The Indians allege that buffaloes were formerly numerous about the plains,[2] and assert that the remains of these animals are still found. Between Lewis' River and Spokan House we saw many bleached antlers of elk, together with the large curved horns of the sheep which are now found in the vicinity of the Rocky Mountains. These animals have long since fled from the plains. None of the present race of Indians have seen any of them, and are unable to account for their disappearance. We were equally at a loss to divine the cause; and whether the annual burning of the grass by the natives in hunting the deer had any influence in driving them away, I shall leave to the curious in animal emigration to determine.

No rattlesnakes are seen below the falls. A short distance above them these reptiles make their first appearance, and are numerous so far as the Chaudière Falls, a couple of days' march above which they totally disappear. There is in some places a small black snake,[3] the bite of which causes death much quicker than that of the rattlesnake.

[2] The regions referred to here are those of the Big Bend and the Palouse.

[3] This snake cannot be identified except that Cox may have had reference to a small variety of rattlesnake that strikes without warning and is known locally as a "stem-winder."

An old Indian near Oakinagan told me that a child of his, a girl about five years old, one day looking for blue-berries with other children, was bitten by a very small black snake, and died in about an hour afterwards. There are numbers of dark-brown, green, and garter snakes, but they are perfectly innocuous.

I have already spoken of the Wallah Wallahs, and of their friendly disposition. With the exception of the attack in the autumn of 1814, they never manifested any hostility to our people; and we had reason to know the part they took in that transaction was compulsory. The entrance of their river is in lat. 46° 4'. There is scarcely any beaver on their lands; but deer, wild fowl, and roots, are obtained in plenty, and, with the salmon, constitute their principal food. They are a well-formed race, cleanly in their persons, good hunters, and excellent horsemen. The Chohoptins,[4] or Nez Percés, differ little from them in their language, customs, or mode of living. The productions of their lands are nearly similar; and they have immense bands of wild and tame horses. They reside principally on the banks of Lewis' River, and are a numerous and powerful tribe. They and the Wallah Wallahs are constantly at war with the Shoshonés, or Snake Indians, who inhabit the great plains to the southward. The only cause assigned by the Wallah Wallahs for this war is, that the Snakes interdict them from hunting the black-tailed deer, which are numerous on their lands, and in retaliation they oppose the latter in their endeavours to catch salmon in the Columbia. They allege that this opposition would cease if the Shoshonés abandoned their claim to the exclusive right of hunting the black-tailed deer. As this is a privilege, however, which the latter are not willing to concede, their warfare may be interminable.

The Yackamans[5] are a numerous tribe, who inhabit the lands on the northern banks of the Columbia, from its junction above Lewis' River until some distance above a river which flows from the northward, and is called after the name of the tribe. They are on friendly terms with the Chohoptins and Wallah Wallahs, and make common cause with them against the Shoshonés.

From the falls to this place, there is little variation in the dress of the natives. The men wear leathern shirts and gaiters, and the women are covered with shifts of the same material; but a short distance above the Yackaman River, and from thence to Oakinagan, we

[4] The Shahaptians were the Nez Percés.
[5] The Yakima Indians.

259

met during the fishing season some straggling bands, wretchedly poor, and nearly naked. The men are without any garments. The women wear a leathern belt round the waist, from which a narrow slip passes from the front, and is secured behind, something in the manner of the *maro* worn by the male natives of the Sandwich Islands. The rest of their persons is quite naked; and their appearance, particularly that of their old women, is extremely disgusting. They have few horses; and other animals are scarce on their lands.

Continuing our course upwards, we arrive among the Oakinagans, where decency in covering again appears. Of this tribe I have already spoken sufficiently, and shall therefore merely remark, that although far from cleanly in their lodges, they keep their persons always well covered. The latitude of Oakinagan is 48° 6' north, and the longitude about 117° west.

The next tribe we meet are the Sinapoils, who occupy a district on the northern banks of the Columbia, between the Spokan and Oakinagan rivers. They subsist principally on salmon and cammas, and sometimes small deer. Beaver is scarce; and they are consequently poorer than the neighbouring tribes, on whose lands that valuable animal abounds. They are dirty and slothful, and, from their habits of dishonesty, are regarded by the other natives with the utmost contempt. From the poverty of their territory no trading post has been hitherto established amongst them. This circumstance has indisposed them towards the white men, and they seized every opportunity of committing depredations on our people. They are however poor in arms, and poorer in spirit; and their aggressions were chiefly confined to petty pilfering and horse-stealing.

The Sinapoils are much addicted to gambling, and its concomitant vice, quarrelling. We could never rightly ascertain whether they had a chief; but from their insubordination, local feuds, and love of thieving, we were inclined to doubt the existence of any controlling authority. They never committed any open act of hostility on us; but this we had good reason to know was occasioned by the manner in which they were kept in check by the friendly tribes of Spokan, Oakinagan, and Kamloops; any of whom would not only willingly take our part, but would punish the assailants with greater severity than we might be inclined to use if left to our own discretion.

In justice however to this unfortunate race, it must be borne in mind that they are tantalised by seeing in the possession of their neighbours, the Oakinagans and Spokans, various articles which they obtain in exchange for the productions of their more favoured lands; and the Sinapoils therefore cannot resist the temptation, when opportunity offers, to steal from the traders what the poverty of their country prevents them from obtaining honestly.

About forty-five miles above the Sinapoil village, Spokan River joins the Columbia from the eastward. At Oakinagan the plains begin to disappear; and from thence to the Sinapoil lands high naked bluffs predominate. A short distance above the latter place some straggling pines become visible, which increase thence upwards in size and quantity. The Spokans have a small village at the entrance of their river, but their chief and permanent place of residence is about forty miles higher up, where we built our fort, and where the Pointed Heart River joins the Spokan from the south-east. Their lands present a pleasing variety of well-wooded hills, open prairies, and rich flat bottoms, which produce abundance of nutritive roots and wild fruit. Beaver, deer, and various kinds of wild fowl, &c., are occasionally plentiful, while their river supplies them with excellent salmon, trout, and carp. Yet, notwithstanding these advantages, such is their improvidence, that they are often reduced to starvation. In times of scarcity they collect a quantity of pine moss, which they boil, and form into a kind of black cake about half an inch thick. It is a horrible preparation, and has a bitter saponaceous taste.

The Spokans are an honest friendly tribe. They are good hunters, but somewhat indolent, fond of gambling, despotic husbands, and indulgent fathers. Their women are great slaves, and most submissive to marital authority. They did not exhibit the same indifference to the superior comforts of a white man's wife as that displayed by the Flathead women, and some of them consequently became partners of the *voyageurs*. They made excellent wives, and in general conducted themselves with propriety. Although the Spokan men are extremely jealous, and punish with severity any infidelity on the part of their wives, they are themselves not over-scrupulous in their own conduct. We learned from the wives of the *voyageurs*, that female violation is by no means uncommon among them. The frequent journeys which the women in the execution of their laborious duties are obliged to make alone into the woods in search of fuel, roots, &c., afford great facility to the commission of this offence; and the ravisher depends on impunity from the well-known fear of the woman to tell her husband, who might either abandon her, or, by taking the offender's life, embroil their respective families in a sanguinary contest.

Slavish and submissive as the Spokan women are, they do not all tamely submit to the occasional lapses of their husbands; an instance of which occurred in the summer of 1815, while I was at Spokan House. One of the tribe named *Singhelsasscoghaght* (or the horse), from his great swiftness, and dexterity in riding, was a tall and rather handsome Indian. He was remarkable for his gallantries, and it was also whispered among the females that he never spared a woman whom he caught unprotected in the woods. His wife had for some time suspected him of carrying on an intrigue, and, being constantly on the watch, she soon discovered that her suspicions were not groundless. The very night of the discovery, while he was in a profound sleep, she inflicted on him a dreadful injury, of which he died before morning. On the intelligence becoming public, a crowd of his relations assembled round the lodge, to whom she openly avowed herself as the author of his death, stating at the same time her reasons for committing the dreadful act; but she had scarcely finished, when an arrow from her husband's brother quivered in her heart. Her relations instantly collected. Guns, arrows, and tomahawks were in immediate requisition, and before we could arrive to check the bloody conflict, two men and two women had fallen victims. Our presence restored tranquillity; and, as the sufferers on each side were equally divided, we experienced no great difficulty in bringing about a reconciliation, and each party rested satisfied with its respective loss.

The Pointed Hearts, or, as the Canadians call them, *les Coeurs d' Alênes*[6] (Hearts of Awls), are a small tribe inhabiting the shores of a lake about fifty miles to the eastward of Spokan House. Their country is tolerably well stocked with beaver, deer, wild-fowl, &c.; and its vegetable productions are similar to those of Spokan. Some of this tribe occasionally visited our fort at the latter place with furs to barter, and we made a few excursions to their lands. We found them uniformly honest in their traffic; but they did not evince the same warmth of friendship for us as the Spokans, and expressed no desire for the establishment of a trading post among them. They are in many respects more savage than their neighbours, and I have seen some of them often eat deer, and other meat, raw. They are also more unfeeling husbands, and frequently beat their wives cruelly.

[6] Probably because of a reputation for stinginess in their dealings with other Indians.

About twenty years before our arrival, the Spokans and Pointed Hearts were at war, caused by a kind of Trojan origin. A party of the former had been on a hunting visit to the lands of the latter, and were hospitably received. One day a young Spokan discovered the wife of a Pointed Heart alone, some distance from the village, and violated her. Although she might have borne this in silence from one of her own tribe, she was not equally forbearing with regard to a stranger, and immediately informed her husband of the outrage. He lost no time in seeking revenge, and shot the Spokan as he entered the village. The others fled to their own lands, and prepared for war. A succession of sanguinary conflicts followed, in the course of which the greatest warriors of both sides were nearly destroyed. At the end of a year, however, hostilities ceased; since which period they have been at peace. The two nations now intermarry, and appear to be on the best terms of friendship.

Leaving the Pointed Hearts, we cross the Flat-head River, and come to the Cootonais, who inhabit a small and beautiful district near the foot of the Rocky Mountains, and about sixty miles to the north-east of the Flat-head lands. It is nearly surrounded by a chain of lofty and thickly wooded mountains, and is consequently very difficult of access. Beaver is plentiful in this country, and of a superior description. Otters, martens, and bears, are also found, with excellent deer and mountain sheep.[7]

The Cootonais are the remnant of a once brave and powerful tribe, who, like the Flat-heads, were perpetually engaged in war with the Black-feet for the right of hunting on the buffalo grounds. Previous to our arrival among them they entertained the most deadly hatred against white men, to whom they attributed all their misfortunes, owing to the assistance which their enemies received in arms and ammunition from the North-West Company's people to the eastward of the mountains.

They appeared to be perfectly aware that beaver was the only object that induced us to visit their country; and they accordingly exerted themselves to procure it, not, as some of them candidly declared, for our interest, but for the purpose of obtaining fire-arms, spears, &c., to enable them to meet their old enemies the Black-feet on more equal terms.

[7] The tobacco plant has lately been discovered in this district.—R. C.

They are a very peculiar tribe. Their language bears no affinity whatever to that of any of the western nations.[8] It is infinitely softer and more free from those unpronounceable gutturals so common among the lower tribes. As with the Flat-heads, buffalo is the cause of all their misfortunes; for although, as I have before mentioned, their lands abound in plenty of other animals, their hereditary attachment to the buffalo is so unconquerable, that it drives them every year to the plains, where they come in contact with the Black-feet. In these contests they are generally victors, but they always return with diminished numbers. They have latterly entered into a kind of alliance, offensive and defensive, with the Flat-heads, by which they have agreed that neither party shall make peace with the Black-feet until the latter shall permit them to hunt without molestation on the buffalo plains. As this is a concession not likely to be granted, it is probable that the war will terminate only with the extermination of one or other of the parties.

The Cootonais are by no means so warm-hearted towards the whites as their neighbours the Flat-heads; but Mr. Montour, who spent some years among them, states, that they are strictly honest in all their dealings, and remarkable for their adherence to truth; a virtue, by the bye, of which few Indians can boast. Polygamy is unknown among them; and he never knew an instance wherein any of their women admitted overtures of an improper nature. They appear to be jealous of white men, and studiously conceal their females whenever any of the traders approach their lodges.

A Cootonais seldom smiles. He thinks that sooner or later he is doomed to fall in the field of battle; and this certainty of death, joined to the number of relatives annually killed in their constant warfare, imparts to his features a settled melancholy.

The greatest cleanliness and neatness are observable about their persons and lodges. They are rather handsome, above the middle size, and, compared with other tribes, remarkably fair. On the whole, we may say of this interesting people, that, in their intercourse with white men, they are rather haughty and reserved; in conversation, candid; in trade, honest; brave in battle; and devotedly attached to each other and their country. The trading post established among the Cootonais is situated in about 49° 30′ north latitude, and 115° west longitude.

[8] The Kootenais were of the Kitunahan linguistic family.

The Chaudières or Kettle Indians,[9] and the small band under the hermaphrodite chief, are mentioned in earlier chapters, together with the productions of their respective lands. The Chaudière Fall is situated in 48° 37′ north latitude, and the longitude, by chronometer, is about 116° west.

A small tribe exists on the upper lakes of the Columbia, which wanders about in straggling parties of three, four, or five each. They appear to be timid in approaching white people, but are not unfriendly. They have no horses, are poor hunters, go nearly naked, and subsist principally on fish.

About 150 miles to the north-west of Oakinagan, in the direction of Thompson's River, the Company has a post established among a tribe called the Kamloops, to which there is a communication by land, or by means of the Oakinagan River and Lake. Beaver is rather plentiful in this quarter, and, with salmon, constitutes their chief riches. They have few horses, and deer are scarce on their lands. Messrs. La Rocque and M'Donald, who wintered among them, state that the Kamloops are less friendly than any tribe among whom we had posts established. They are addicted to thieving and quarreling, wear little covering, and are extremely dirty in their persons. Like other tribes, they are subject to occasional famine, owing to their neglecting to provide in the fishing season sufficiency of salmon for the periods of scarcity.

Beyond Kamloops to the northward, the department of New Caledonia commences, inhabited by a tribe called the Carriers, of whom I have given a sketch in a letter from Mr. John Stuart. A more comprehensive description of their country, its productions, &c., will be found in the Appendix.

From the upper parts of the Columbia and its subordinate streams, to the lower falls, the natives inter their dead in a similar manner to that which I have described among the Spokans. From the falls to the lower rapids the bodies of the deceased are enveloped in mats and skins, and placed in cemeteries in a retired situation; one of which is described in the early part of this volume. Thence to the mouth of the river the dead are placed in canoes in a manner mentioned in my sketch of the Chinooks.

They all believe in a future state of rewards and punishments. Their moral code differs but little from that of the Flat-heads. The

[9] The present Colville tribe.

265

articles of food, clothing, &c., most in use amongst them while living, they hope also to enjoy in the abodes of future happiness; while, in their place of punishment, cold, hunger, and thirst, await the bad people.

There is one item in the Oakinagan creed relative to future torments, which is, I imagine, peculiar to that tribe. An evil spirit, with face, arms, and legs like a man, and a long tail and ears like a horse, jumps about from tree to tree with a stick in his hand, with which he unmercifully belabours all the condemned, who are prevented by the agility of his movements from touching him. This is an additional punishment to what all other tribes believe their wicked will have to suffer.

We never brought ardent spirits amongst them for the purposes of barter, and therefore cannot say how far an abundance of it would have seduced them to its intemperate use; but the few whom we knew to have tasted any did not seem to relish it, except on one occasion that we gave a few glasses to old Illimspokanee, the chief of the Spokans. He staggered home in a state of intoxication, and in a couple of days returned and begged for a little more of the "strong water" (rum), but as we did not wish to encourage its consumption by the Indians, and were apprehensive of the evil effects which his example might produce, we refused to give him any more, alleging that our stock was exhausted.

The treatment of the women differs materially among the various tribes. Where food is principally obtained by the exertions of the men (as among the Cootonais, Flat-heads, Spokans, &c.), the women are condemned to great drudgery. When a hunter kills a deer, he merely cuts out the tongue, or takes enough for a meal, and on returning to his lodge dispatches his wife for the body. She is guided to the spot by notches which he has made in the trees. She also collects firewood, carries water, cooks, makes and cleans his shirts, prepares the meat and fish for curing, &c. They possess little or no influence, and, notwithstanding their laborious duties, seem perfectly contented. Among the lower tribes, however, where their exertions in collecting the Wappitoo roots contribute to the general support, they assume an air of liberty and independence quite unknown among the upper natives; and in all cases of importance the elderly women equally with the men are consulted.

From the foregoing brief sketch it will be seen that those qualities which may be ranked among the virtues are more conspicuous among the warlike tribes of the Cootonais and Flat-heads than among those lower down. With the exception of slips of red cloth, or a few feathers adorning their heads, they enter the field of battle perfectly naked,

Pride in their port, defiance in their eye.

Their bravery is pre-eminent; a love of truth they think necessary to a warrior's character. They are too proud to be dishonest, too candid to be cunning. Their many avocations leave them no leisure for gambling; and their strict subordination, joined to the necessity of exerting all their energies against the common enemy, prevents them from quarrelling.

Here I may close my account of the occurrences, &c., which came under my observation during my residence on the Columbia and its tributary streams. A few characteristic sketches of the Canadians, half-breeds, Iroquois, &c., will appear in the Appendix; together with an interesting description of New Caledonia, and a statement of various circumstances which occurred subsequent to my quitting the Indian country, and the insertion of which here would, I imagined, have broken in on the chronological order of my narrative.

Towards the latter end of March, 1817, the other wintering parties joined us at Oakinagan, from whence we all proceeded to Fort George, which we reached on the 3rd of April.

Chapter 23

Ascent of the Columbia—Its lakes—Dangerous navigation—High water—
Arrive at the mountains—Melancholy detail of the death of six of the party

WEDNESDAY, APRIL 16TH, 1817. At one P. M. on this day we took our departure from Fort George under a salute of seven guns. Our party consisted of eighty-six souls, and was perhaps the largest and most mixed that ever ascended the Columbia. In it were five Scotsmen, two English, and one Irish; thirty-six Canadians, twenty Iroquois Indians, two Nipisings, one Cree, and three half-breeds; nine natives of the Sandwich Islands; with one boy, a servant, two women, and two children. The whole embarked in two barges and nine canoes (two of which were of bark), each containing on an average twenty-two packages, each weighing ninety pounds.

Owing to a strong head-breeze, we were unable to double Tongue Point, on the west side of which we were obliged to encamp in view of the fort. We remained here on the 17th and 18th, during which days it blew a perfect hurricane from the eastward, accompanied by heavy showers. Our tents were repeatedly blown down and we might have suffered heavily from the incessant rain, had not the governor of Fort George considerately dispatched to us an additional quantity of port and rum, with which we succeeded in neutralizing the overpowering humidity of the atmosphere.

The wind having moderated on the morning of the 19th, we resumed our voyage after breakfast. We had occasional showers during the day, and passed some scattered lodges of natives, from whom we purchased a quantity of excellent sturgeon. Encamped a little after five o'clock on Oak Point.[1]

[1] Oak Point is a well-known point on the Columbia River, named by Lieutenant

We embarked at day-break on the 20th, with calm weather; purchased a quantity of sturgeon. Towards evening a smart breeze sprung up in our favour, which enabled us to hoist sail, and we continued on in fine style until five, when we encamped at the village of Kyeassino, a friendly chief, a short distance below the mouth of the Multnomah or Wallamat. We had a few slight showers during the day.

On the 21st we arose with the dawn, and embarked. Some of the canoes having struck on sunken trees, we were obliged to put ashore for a couple of hours to repair the damage and dry the goods. We encamped at dusk about five miles above *La Prairie du Thé*[2] so called by the Canadians from a species of mint which grows in it, and which they are fond of using as a substitute for tea. Passed a few lodges of Indians, but did not stop. Weather same as yesterday.

The morning of the 22nd was cloudy and chilly, with a slight head-breeze, which lasted nearly the entire day. We however made good way; and at three P. M. arrived at the foot of the rapids. Made two discharges, and passed them *sans accident*. Encamped at sun-set at the west end of the portage. As this was the scene of several attacks, we formed a strong barricade of canoes and goods about the encampment, and divided the party into three watches. Several of the natives visited us. The men were unarmed and well-behaved; and the females appeared solicitous to bestow their favours on some of our people. They appeared somewhat surprised and offended to find that love had no influence in our camp, and left us late in the evening, evidently chagrined at their reception.

The night passed over quietly; and we commenced the portage at day-break, on the morning of the 23rd, with cool calm weather. The Indians behaved very friendly, and offered their services to assist in carrying the goods. We did not think it prudent to refuse them, and at half-past ten the portage was cleared. We breakfasted at the upper end, and purchased a few salmon from the natives, to whom we gave the usual present of tobacco; after which we proceeded on. The weather during the day was extremely warm for the season. Put ashore once to repair the canoes, and encamped late in the evening at the point of the Mangy Dog.[3]

Broughton in 1792 from the fact that he saw oaks at this place. It is on the south bank near present Mayger, Oregon. See Franchère, *Narrative,* 261, n. 74.

[2] La Prairie du Thé is about twenty-eight miles above Fort Vancouver and near present Washougal, Washington.

[3] Uncertain. In the early days Hood River was known as Dog River, and it was in that vicinity.

The weather continuing calm, we embarked at half-past one on the morning of the 24th; but owing to the darkness, several of our canoes struck on sunken rocks and trees, which compelled us to put ashore at day-light to repair the damage. At nine we proceeded on, and doubled Cape Horn[4] in calm weather, a circumstance of very rare occurrence in voyages on the Columbia.

At three P. M. arrived at the *Dalles* (narrows) and immediately began the portage, but were only enabled to get half through it, when we encamped. The young chief, and the old chieftainess, accompanied by several Indians, paid us a visit. They were unarmed, and conducted themselves peaceably.

We finished the portage at ten o'clock on the morning of the 25th, and breakfasted before embarking; after which we continued on, with a strong breeze in our favour. Passed several dangerous points; and with much difficulty, owing to the low state of the water, we succeeded in making our way without unloading, through the narrow channel to the right of the small *Dalles*. At four P. M. we encamped at the foot of the Great Falls on the south side.[5] A few Indians crossed over to our encampment; but the weather being wet and stormy, they shortly after returned.

26TH. It blew a strong gale the greater part of last night, but moderated at day-break, when we crossed to the north side, and commenced the portage, which we finished in two pauses. We purchased twenty dogs for the kettle. None of the natives who came to us were armed, and we never observed them so tranquil. Our number, however, was sufficient to insure us a respectful reception among any single tribe of the Columbia. Mr. Mackenzie wrote a letter here to Fort George, which he intrusted to one of the chiefs, who promised to have it safely conveyed to its destination. On quitting this place we distributed a quantity of leaf-tobacco among the Indians, who crowded round the canoes, eagerly expecting this last act of our friendship. It was past eleven when we embarked. We had a strong breeze in our favour all day, and passed several bad rapids. Encamped late, a short distance above John Day's River, so called from its having been the place at which that hunter was attacked.

We had a strong aft breeze during the greater part of the 27th, which enabled us to go *à la voile*. Purchased seven horses, moderately

4 Cox's Cape Horn was probably present Mitchell Point.
5 Celilo Falls.

cheap, from a party of Shyatogoes and Wallah Wallahs, who followed us the greater part of the day, and encamped with us at night.

28TH. Embarked at the usual hour with a slight aft wind; about noon it increased to a double-reefed-topsail gale, which again fell away at four to a gentle breeze. Saw very few Indians, and encamped at six P. M. a little below the Grand Rapid,[6] on the south side. The weather on the 29th was clear, and the wind favourable. We passed the Grand Rapid at two P. M. without injuring a canoe, and had a fine breeze all the afternoon. Shortly after sun-set we made our beds a little above the Wallah Wallah River. Tamtappam the chief, and several of his tribe, visited us, and promised to trade some horses.

We slept until nine on the morning of the 30th, and began re-dividing and re-distributing the men and baggage for Mr. Mackenzie's tour to the Shoshoné Indians. We purchased nine horses from Tam-tappam, and gave for each goods to the value of seven beaver skins, by the north-west tariff. The weather during the day was rather warm and boisterous.

THURSDAY, 1ST OF MAY. Left the Wallah Wallahs after breakfast, with a slight breeze. Between twelve and one we put ashore at the mouth of Lewis' River, where we took an early dinner; after which Mr. Mackenzie, with twenty-two men and three canoes, left us under a salute of three cheers. We continued on, up the Columbia, and en-camped after sun-set two miles above the Yackaman River.[7] Passed a few Indians, from whom we traded one horse. It blew pretty fresh during the day.

Nothing particular occurred on the 2nd. The weather was warm, and we encamped near the beginning of the marl-banks, called by the Canadians, from their colour, *les Terres Jaunes*.[8]

The 3rd was equally devoid of interest. The weather was rather windy; and we encamped at the foot of the Priest's Rapid.[9] We saw none of the natives for the last two days.

After breakfast on the morning of the 4th, the party who were to cross the Rocky Mountains bid adieu to the loaded canoes, and the gentlemen of the Columbia. It consisted of Messrs. Bethune, M'Dougall, Joseph M'Gillivray, Alexander M'Tavish, and myself,

[6] The Grand Rapid was above the mouth of the Umatilla River and about eighteen miles below Fort Walla Walla.

[7] The Yakima River.

[8] White Bluffs.

[9] Priest Rapid is ten miles long, in the course of which the river drops seventy feet.

with sixteen men, Holmes the tailor, and the boy Perrault, in two canoes. Encamped about three leagues below Pacquin's Rapid. Fine weather all day.

5TH. Breakfasted at the above rapid; at which we were constrained to unload part of the lading, and about noon arrived at the portage of the Rocky Island Rapid.[10]

While Gingras and Landreville were getting one of the canoes up the rapid, the latter made a false stroke of his pole, by which it missed bottom, and the canoe was upset in the middle of the waves. Gingras held fast by the bars until it was drawn into an eddy, when he found bottom, and got ashore. In the mean time eight men leaped into the other canoe, and instantly pushed off to the assistance of Landreville, who was for a couple of minutes invisible; when at length, appearing above the surface of the water, they seized him by the hair, and drew him on board nearly lifeless. All our luggage was subsequently picked up; and we remained here the remainder of the day to dry it, and repair the canoes. A few poor Indians visited us. They had no provisions to trade, and appeared to be more in want of food and clothing than any I had ever seen. One old woman in particular was completely naked, and presented a most disgusting appearance.

Nothing of consequence occurred on the 6th or 7th; and about sun-set on the 8th, we reached Oakinagan Fort, where we passed the night.

At four P. M. we bid adieu to Oakinagan, having previously killed two horses, the flesh of which we took with us. Encamped a short distance above the road leading to Spokan House. The weather, for the last few days, was remarkably mild. It changed, however, on the 10th; on which day we had incessant rain. We encamped three leagues above *la rapide d'ignace*.[11]

On Sunday the 11th we embarked at day-break. The late rain gave the country a most refreshing appearance; and along the banks of the river we pulled a quantity of small wild onions, which grew in great abundance, both among the rocks, and in the low bottoms. Encamped five miles below the entrance of Sinapoil River, a small stream which falls into the Columbia from the north. Weather rather sultry.

[10] Rock Island, just below Wenatchee, Washington.

[11] The present Box Canyon, so called because Ignace, an Iroquois Indian who was with David Thompson in 1811, had been thrown out of the canoe but rescued in passing these rapids. See "Journal of David Thompson," edited by T. C. Elliott, *Oregon Historical Quarterly,* Vol. XV, pp. 48–49.

The men had hard work on the 12th. Owing to the sudden rise of the water, caused by the late rain and melting of the snows, we were obliged to disembark several times during the day, to allow the canoes to be dragged up with lines. Encamped opposite the entrance to Spokan River. The country from Oakinagan to this place is quite devoid of wood, but the banks of the river are bold, and in many places rocky. This naturally contracts the river into a more narrow compass, and makes the current much more difficult to stem.

We began, the morning of the 13th, by making a portage above our encampment; after which we breakfasted, and pursued our route. We had a strong smooth current all day, and encamped on the south side a few leagues below the Grand Rapid. From Spokan River, upwards, the banks of the Columbia are rather thickly wooded, and present a very picturesque appearance. There are also several rich bottoms of red and white clover, and some aromatic herbs,

Wasting their sweetness on the desert air.

Met a couple of families of poor beggarly Indians. Very sultry weather all day.

14TH. On arriving at the Grand Rapid[12] we were forced to carry the canoes, as well as the baggage, to the upper end. This occupied the greater portion of the day, and we did not finish it before three P. M. At four we arrived at the Great Kettle Falls, the portage of which we completed at sun-set. Encamped at the upper end of the falls; shortly after which an Indian arrived from Spokane House with letters from Mr. M'Donald, which contained no intelligence of interest.

Embarked at the usual hour, on the 15th, and made pretty good way until one P. M., when we arrived at a particular part of the river, called the First Dalles, or narrows, above the Kettle Falls,[13] where the channel is confined between a range of high and dangerous rocks, nearly a mile in extent; the whole of which distance the men were obliged to carry the canoes and baggage. Encamped at *la Rivière de Beliers*,[14] so called from some mountain sheep having been killed near the spot by our hunters some years before. The Indians assert

[12] Just below Kettle Falls and opposite the northern boundary of the Colville Indian Reservation.

[13] The Little Dalles, just below the town of Northport, Washington, and probably the narrowest place in the Columbia River for more than one thousand miles. Here the river literally turns itself sideways.

[14] The Kettle River.

273

that no rattlesnakes are to be found on either bank of the Columbia above this river; and all our men, who had been previously in the employment of the Company, hunting in that part, fully corroborated this statement. The Rivière de Beliers comes from the north-west.

About seven o'clock on the morning of the 16th we passed the mouth of the Flat-head River,[15] which falls into the Columbia over a foaming cascade, caused by a large collection of immense rocks, which choke up the entrance. During the day we passed a number of small rivers, which, owing to the melting of the snow, caused by the excessive heat, had been swollen into torrents. The force of the current rushing out from these rivers repeatedly drove the canoes back with great violence, and it required all the skill and strength of our men to pass them. Encamped late, near M'Gillivray's River,[16] a fine bold stream, which takes its rise in the Rocky Mountains, and running in nearly a north-east direction, through the Cootonais lands, here joins the Columbia. A refreshing breeze from the north sprung up in the evening. The country on each side, from the Kettle Falls to this place, is thickly wooded, principally with pine, spruce, and small birch. The northern shore is rather low; but the south side presents a bold rocky appearance. About an hour before we encamped we observed a large black bear in the act of swimming across the river, which Mr. M'Gillivray wounded. The enraged animal instantly changed its course downwards, and came in contact with our canoe, into which it attempted to get, by seizing the gunwale with its fore paws. This nearly upset us; but the foreman aimed a well-directed blow at his head with his pole, which completely stunned it, and we succeeded in hauling it on board. It was in rather good condition, and proved a welcome and unexpected treat.

17TH. Set off a little before sun-rise; and about an hour afterwards entered the first lake formed by the Columbia.[17] It is between eleven and twelve leagues long, and about one and a half in breadth, the current smooth and steady, and pretty free from snags or sunken trees. The shores are bold and well wooded with a variety of timber of fine size; and in the distance we first caught a view of the most western chain of the Rocky Mountains covered with snow. A headwind, during the greater part of the day, considerably retarded our

15 The present Pend Oreille River.
16 The Kootenai River.
17 Lower Arrow Lake.

progress; and we encamped late, near the upper end of the lake, where a few Indians visited us. They appeared to be very poor, and brought about a dozen beaver skins to trade, which we told them we could not purchase, as we were obliged to cross the mountains, but that our party, going downwards in the autumn, would stop a few days with them, and trade all the skins they had. They were rather disappointed; but a little tobacco, and some trifling presents, sent them away in good humour.

Shortly after, embarking on the morning of the 18th, we left the lake, and entered that part of the river called the Straits, which separates the Upper from the Lower Lake. It is only a few miles in length, and quickly brought us to the Upper Lake,[18] which is not so long as the first. The high hills in its immediate vicinity were covered with snow, the chilling influence of which we sensibly experienced by the cold blasts from shore. Encamped at sun-set at the upper end of the lake, on a fine sandy beach. During the day we struck on two sand-banks, and were slightly injured by a sunken tree. Saw no Indians.

19TH. About two miles above our encampment of last night the Columbia becomes very narrow, with steep and thickly wooded banks, covered with immense quantities of fallen trees. The current is very strong, and owing to the great height of the water, the men at intervals had scarcely any beach on which to walk in dragging up the canoes. Our progress was consequently slow; and we put ashore for the night about fifteen miles above the lake.

At nine o'clock on the morning of the 20th we reached the Second Dalles,[19] or narrows, which are formed by a contraction of the channel of the river into a very small compass. There are high and slippery rocks on each side, which makes it a work of great danger and difficulty to pass them. The baggage was all carried by the men, and the canoes were towed up with strong lines, after being in great danger of filling from the frightful whirlpools close along the shore. The weather became much cooler from the proximity of the mountains. Several patches of snow were observable on the beach during the day, and towards evening some rain fell.

From dawn of day until noon on the 21st we did not make three miles, owing to the impetuosity of the current, the shelving banks, and

18 Upper Arrow Lake.
19 A short distance above Revelstoke, British Columbia.

275

the extreme weakness of our men, several of whom were knocked up. We were detained at one place upwards of four hours to repair our shattered canoes, and encamped about six o'clock on a low gravelly point. We had several smart showers during the afternoon.

22ND. About two P. M. arrived at a place called the Upper Dalles,[20] where the river is again confined for a considerable distance between a line of high slippery rocks. Got about half-way through this channel, and stopped for the night in a small nook formed by the rocks, on which we lay scattered and exposed to severe rain during the night.

We rose wet and unrefreshed on the morning of the 23rd, and in five hours passed the Dalles, the upper part of which consists of a chain of whirlpools, which compelled us to carry both canoes and baggage some distance over the rocks; in the execution of which duty some of the men narrowly escaped with their lives. Those who carried our canoe, from mere exhaustion fell several times, by which it was much damaged; and we were detained until 3 P. M. to get it repaired. Encamped at dusk on a sandy beach, for which we had been some time on the look-out. The rain continued during the evening and the night to pour down in torrents.

Our progress on the 24th was equally slow. The various tributary streams which we passed on this and the last two days, and which take their rise from the surrounding mountains, had by the recent rains been swollen into torrents, the waters of which, as they rushed with head-long force into the Columbia, repeatedly drove us back with irresistible strength, and at times we were in danger of filling. On two occasions, where the opposite shore of the Columbia consisted of perpendicular rocks, we were obliged, after various fruitless attempts to pass the minor streams, to unload and carry the canoes and baggage some distance along their banks until we reached a smooth space of current, when we crossed, and by that means surmounted the difficulties of their respective embouchures. It rained on us all the afternoon.

25TH. Nothing of importance occurred on this day to vary the disagreeable tedium of our journey. The foreman, steersman, and four of the middlemen of our canoe were quite knocked up, while

---

[20] These were also known as Les Dalles des Morts and are some forty miles above Revelstoke. See "Edward Ermatinger's York Factory Express Journal, Being a Record of Journeys Made Between Fort Vancouver and Hudson Bay in the Years 1827–1828," *Transactions of the Royal Society of Canada*, Vol. VI (1912), Section II, 77, n. 7.

those in the other canoe were comparatively strong and healthy; indeed the distribution of the men was grossly partial, and was productive in the sequel of the most deplorable consequences. It rained hard all day; and on retiring to rest we had not a dry article of covering about us.

On the 26th we only made three miles, in the course of which our canoe filled in a dangerous rapid,[21] and we were near perishing. We succeeded however in gaining a low stony island, on which there was no wood to light a fire: our pemmican was completely damaged by the late accident; and, as a climax to our misery, it rained incessantly the whole day.

The river here opened out to a considerable breadth, and in some places was very shallow. The Rocky Mountain portage at which we were to leave our canoes appeared in sight, and was not more than three miles distant. As we threw our jaded bodies on our stony couch this evening, we most truly experienced that

> *Weariness can snore upon the flint,*
> *When restive sloth makes the down-pillow hard.*

We rose at the usual hour on the 27th, and at nine A. M. arrived at the entrance of Canoe River,[22] where the portage commences,[23] and with indescribable pleasure we bade a final adieu to our crazy battered canoe. Messrs. M'Dougall and Bethune[24] had reached it the day before, and had almost despaired of seeing us. Finding so many of our men invalids, those gentlemen deemed it imprudent to bring them across the mountains, the fatigues of which they would not be able to encounter. Six Canadians, and Holmes the English tailor,

21 There are several rapids above Les Dalles des Morts, the ascent of which is difficult and dangerous.

22 Canoe River is the most northerly tributary of the Columbia, where the latter, after coming from the south, makes a big bend and commences to flow south. In 1811, David Thompson had wintered here, and the stream got its name from the fact that here he had built the canoes which were to carry him down the Columbia.

23 The Canoe River is navigable for only a short distance upstream. Here, where the portage began, and where the boats were cached, was what was known as Boat Encampment, and was the site of Thompson's camp.

24 Angus Bethune (1783–1858) was born near Lake Ontario. He took service with the North West Company before 1806, at which time he was a clerk at Lake Winnipeg. In 1813, he was transferred to the Columbia and became a partner the next year. In 1821, he and Dr. John McLoughlin were delegates to negotiate with the Hudson's Bay Company. After the merger he became a chief factor but seems to have retired from the fur trade before 1825. See Wallace, *Documents*, 426.

were therefore sent back in the best canoe to Spokan House. Out of the seven men, two only were able to work; but, as the current was in their favour, it was hoped they would arrive in three days at the Kettle Falls, from whence they could easily reach Spokan. As our stock of provisions was very scanty, we could only spare them enough for the above period. On separating from their comrades, some of them appeared dejected and melancholy, and foreboded that they would never see Canada again. Their prophecy, alas! was but too true.[25]

[25] I did not hear the fate of this unfortunate party until three years afterwards. The following is the melancholy detail. On leaving the Rocky Mountains, they drove rapidly down the current until they arrived at the Upper Dalles, or narrows, where they were obliged to disembark. A cod-line was made fast to the stern of the canoe, while two men preceded it along the banks with poles to keep it from striking against the rocks. It had not descended more than half the distance, when it was caught in a strong whirlpool, and the line snapped. The canoe for a moment disappeared in the vortex; on emerging from which, it was carried, by the irresistible force of the current to the opposite side, and dashed to pieces against the rocks. They had not the prudence to take out either their blankets or small quantity of provisions, which were of course all lost. Here then the poor fellows found themselves deprived of all the necessaries of life, and at a period in the year in which it was impossible to procure any wild fruit or roots. To return to the mountains was impossible, and their only chance of preservation was to proceed downwards, and to keep as near the banks of the river as circumstances would permit. The continual rising of the water had completely inundated the beach, in consequence of which they were compelled to force their way through an almost impervious forest, the ground of which was covered with a strong growth of prickly underwood. Their only nourishment was water; owing to which, and their weakness from fatigue and ill health, their progress was necessarily slow. On the third day poor Maçon died, and his surviving comrades, though unconscious how soon they might be called on to follow him, determined to keep off the fatal moment as long as possible. They therefore divided his remains in equal parts between them, on which they subsisted for some days. From the swollen state of their feet their daily progress did not exceed two or three miles. Holmes, the tailor, shortly followed Maçon, and they continued for some time longer to sustain life on his emaciated body. It would be a painful repetition to detail the individual death of each man. Suffice it to say that in a little time, of the seven men, two only, named La Pierre and Dubois, remained alive. La Pierre was subsequently found on the borders of the upper lake of the Columbia by two Indians who were coasting it in a canoe. They took him on board, and brought him to the Kettle Falls, from whence he was conducted to Spokan House.

He stated that, after the death of the fifth man of the party, Dubois and he continued for some days at the spot where he had ended his sufferings, and on quitting it they loaded themselves with as much of his flesh as they could carry; that with this they succeeded in reaching the upper lake, round the shores of which they wandered for some time in vain in search of Indians; that their horrid food at length became exhausted, and they were again reduced to the prospect of starvation; that on the second night after their last meal, he (La Pierre) observed something suspicious in the conduct of Dubois, which induced him to be on his guard; and that shortly after they had lain down for the night, and while he feigned sleep, he observed Dubois cautiously opening his clasp knife, with which he sprung on him, and inflicted on his hand the

278

blow that was evidently intended for his neck. A silent and desperate conflict followed, in which, after severe struggling, La Pierre succeeded in wrestling the knife from his antagonist, and having no other resource left, he was obliged in self-defence to cut Dubois' throat; and that a few days afterwards he was discovered by the Indians as before mentioned. Thus far nothing at first appeared to impugn the veracity of his statement; but some other natives subsequently found the remains of two of the party near those of Dubois, mangled in such a manner as to induce them to think that they had been murdered; and as La Pierre's story was by no means consistent in many of its details, the proprietors judged it advisable to transmit him to Canada for trial. Only one Indian attended; but as the testimony against him was merely circumstantial, and unsupported by corroborating evidence, he was acquitted.—R. C.

Chapter 24

Our baggage and provisions were divided between the nine remaining men, who, in consequence of the number we had sent back, were obliged to carry about ninety pounds weight each,[1] besides their own kits, which in such cases are never taken into consideration.

Canoe River, which here joins the Columbia, is one of its principal sources, and is situated in lat. 52° 7' 9" N. In the dry season, it is broad but very shallow, and near its entrance spreads over several sandy shoals.

On the morning of the 28th of May at ten o'clock we set off on foot along the banks of Canoe River, which winds its way through a wide and cheerless valley. We had not proceeded far when we found it impossible, from the great rise of the water, to pass the ordinary fords. It appeared like a lake, and completely set at nought the topographical knowledge of our guide. This obliged us to strike into the woods, our progress through which was extremely fatiguing, and at three P. M. we bivouacked about two miles beyond a long woody point, which stretches some distance across the valley. The weather was cloudy all day, with slight showers, which, during the night, increased to heavy rain, from which we had no shelter.

We rose early on the morning of the 29th of May, in no very

---

[1] In 1814, the party which included Gabriel Franchère had had only fifty pounds for each man. See *Narrative,* 351. In the interior, however, the usual load at the portages was two ninety-pound packages.

enviable situation. A thick mist still enveloped us, and rendered the awful solitude of this gloomy valley peculiarly impressive. It appeared never to have been trodden by the foot of man, until the enterprising spirit of British commerce, after having forced its way over the everlasting snows of the Rocky Mountains, penetrated into this anti-social glen, and from thence entered the mighty waters of the Columbia. As the mists gradually ascended into the higher regions, we obtained a more distinct view of the surrounding scenery. On the northern side tiers of mountains, thickly covered with large pine and cedar, towered to an immeasurable height; while the southern presented dark perpendicular rocks of immense altitude, partially covered with moss, stunted pine, &c., over which at intervals cascades of seven or eight hundred feet high forced a passage to swell the torrent below. The sun, except in the intervals between the rocks, was invisible; and, with the exception of our own party, no trace of animated nature could be distinguished in this magnificent solitude.

About eleven A. M. we passed a second woody point, which runs into the valley from the north side, and at two P. M. stopped for the remainder of the day. The men were much fatigued from their heavy loads, and some of them were hardly able to proceed.

We set off at day-break on the 30th, sometimes skirting, and at others fording the river. At seven A. M. we arrived at a particular part, called the *grande traverse*,[2] owing to its great depth and breadth. To cross this was a measure of much danger. We all advanced in line, the tallest and strongest mixed alternately with the lowest, each holding the other firmly by the hand. This arrangement was peculiarly necessary; for during our progress several of the smaller men were swept off their legs by the force of the current, and would inevitably have perished, but for the support they derived from their stronger brethren. We effected the passage between eight and nine, when we were obliged to stop to dry our clothes, and breakfast. After this, which did not occupy much time, we proceeded on, and about noon encamped within a short distance of the *grand côte*,[3] or principal hill which we have to ascend in passing from the Columbia. Weather charming all day.

Shortly after dawn on the morning of the 31st we commenced the

[2] The party was ascending present Wood River, a tributary of Canoe River.

[3] This was a steep ascent of more than three thousand feet in the course of seven or eight miles. See "Edward Ermatinger's York Factory Express Journal," 79, n. 4.

steep ascent of the first great hill. At its base were cedar and pine trees of enormous magnitude; but, in proportion as we ascended, they decreased in size, and at the summit of the hill their appearance was quite dwarfish. We completed the ascent in about four hours and a half, and did not find it so difficult as we had anticipated. This however may be attributed to our having commenced the task early in the morning.

A short time before we reached the summit, and from thence to the level of the table land, our progress lay through a wilderness of deep snow, which we had to beat down to form a pathway for the loaded men. This work, owing to the holes into which several of the party occasionally fell, was both fatiguing and dangerous.

At one P. M. we arrived at two small lakes, between which we encamped. They are only a few hundred feet each in circumference, and the distance between them does not exceed twnty-five or thirty feet.[4] They lie on the most level part of the height of land, and are situated between an immense cut of the Rocky Mountains. From them two rivers take their rise, which pursue different courses, and fall into separate oceans: the first winds into the valley we had lately left, and, after joining the upper part of the Columbia, empties itself into the North Pacific; while the other,[5] called the Rocky Mountain River,[6] a branch of the Athabasca, follows first an eastern and then a northern course, until it forms a junction with the *Unjiga,* or Peace River. This falls into Great Slave Lake, the waters of which are ultimately carried by Mackenzie's River to the Arctic Ocean.

The country round our encampment presented the wildest and most terrific appearance of desolation that can be well imagined. The sun shining on a range of stupendous glaciers, threw a chilling brightness over the chaotic mass of rocks, ice, and snow, by which we were surrounded. Close to our encampment one gigantic mountain of a conical form towered majestically into the clouds far above the others,[7] while at intervals the interest of the scene was heightened

[4] Franchère, *Narrative,* 353, says they were not more than two hundred feet apart.

[5] These, which are a pair of tarns or mountain pools, are known as the "Committee's Punch Bowl," a name which was bestowed by Governor George Simpson in 1824. See *George Simpson's Journal,* 34.

[6] The Whirlpool River.

[7] This is called M'Gillivray's Rock, in honour of the late Mr. Wm. M'Gillivray, a principal director of the Company.—R. C. (This was probably the present McGillivray Ridge. It is not over 8,779 feet in height. In this connection Professor Merk comments

by the rumbling noise of a descending *avalanche;* which, after being detached from its bed of centuries, increased in bulk in its headlong career downwards, until it burst with a frightful crash, more resembling the explosion of a magazine than the dispersion of a mass of snow.

One of our rough-spun unsophisticated Canadians, after gazing upwards for some time in silent wonder, exclaimed with much vehemence, "I'll take my oath, my dear friends, that God Almighty never made such a place!"

SUNDAY, JUNE 1. Set off about an hour before day-break in deep snow; and at nine o'clock, having arrived at its termination, we stopped for breakfast. For the last few miles this lofty valley widens considerably, and permits the sun to act with greater effect, in consequence of which the snow quickly disappears beneath its all-dissolving influence. At eleven A. M. we reached a charming spot of rich meadow ground called by our hunters *l'encampement du fusil,* in which we found five of the Company's horses quietly grazing. Their harness was placed in a conspicuous situation adjoining a large fire, the remains of which were burning at the period of our arrival. These horses had been sent to meet us from our establishment at the east end of the mountains, and, from the fresh traces about the fire, we judged that the persons to whose care they had been intrusted had only left that morning. They proved an acceptable relief to our poor men, who quickly transferred to them their loads; after which we resumed our journey with great spirits, and encamped at four P. M. on the banks of the mountain stream, which for the last few leagues begins to assume the appearance of an important river.

Took advantage of the refreshing coolness of the morning of the 2nd, and advanced some miles before sun-rise. Stopped twice during the day to refresh the horses, and at two P. M., after passing through a thick wood of small pine a few miles in length, we arrived on the banks of the Rocky Mountain River, at a particular spot called the *Traverse du Trou,*[8] where it was necessary for our party to cross. All hands immediately set about preparing a raft, which was quickly constructed. The river at the crossing-place was between three and

that there was something about Athabaska Pass which led the early fur traders to exaggerate the height of its mountain peaks. See *George Simpson's Journal*, 35 n.—eds.)

[8] The difficulty in crossing was because of high water. Franchère, in 1814, had experienced no difficulty. See *Narrative*, 355.

four hundred yards wide, with a gentle current running smoothly about a quarter of a mile in length, when it is broken by a broad and rather shallow rapid. The horses were first sent over, and gained the opposite bank in safety. Four men then embarked on the raft with part of the baggage; but owing to their having lost bottom too soon with their poles, the raft was carried in a few minutes into the rapid, where it became entangled among the rocks. The place was fortunately shallow, and they succeeded after some difficulty in gaining the shore. The raft was lost, and we were therefore obliged to construct another. I embarked on it in company with Messrs. M'Gillivray and M'Dougall, Gingras the guide, Louis, an Iroquois Indian, and a half-breed lad named Perrault. We took with us the remainder of the baggage. After pushing off, we poled away with might and main, and had crossed two thirds of the river, when, on the point of entering an eddy, which would have brought us out of all danger, we lost bottom with our poles, and were carried almost instantaneously into the rapid, through which we were driven a short distance, when we were brought up by the rocks, on which one end of the raft became fast. Gingras instantly jumped over, and quickly gained the shore. One of the men, who had crossed over first, immediately came off to us with a line for the purpose of trying to secure the raft until the baggage could be transported ashore. Having fastened one end, he returned, accompanied by Perrault, each carrying heavy bundles. This, however, lightened the raft so much, that it instantly swung round; the line, one end of which was held by the Canadian, snapped in two, and before we had time to look about us, we found ourselves again descending the rapid. All hands immediately jumped overboard, and seized the raft, in the hope of stopping its progress; but the overpowering strength of the current baffled all our puny efforts. We might as well have attempted to arrest the flight of an eagle, or stop a cannon ball in its career. M'Gillivray, Louis, and I, after receiving some severe contusions, succeeded in regaining the raft; but M'Dougall parted company, and having clambered up the sides of a craggy rock, which was a few feet above the surface of the water, remained perched on its summit for some hours, in a most pitiable condition, from which he was not extricated until late in the evening.

Only three of us now remained, and we had neither pole nor paddle, by which we could guide our course. We quickly cleared the rapid; but had scarcely time to breathe an aspiration of thanksgiving, when we were hurried into another, from which we again escaped harmless. On emerging from this we were forced with inconceivable rapidity through a succession of cascades and rapids, two miles in extent; in the course of which, owing to our repeatedly striking on the rocks, the timbers began to separate. A brief space of smooth water at length appeared, and we once more indulged a faint hope of escape, when a loud and roaring noise announced the immediate vicinity of a cataract. The current became swifter. I looked in vain for relief to my two companions. But neither the active mind of my friend M'Gillivray, ever fertile in resources, nor the long experience of the Iroquois, accustomed from his infancy to similar scenes, could suggest any chance of escape. The thunders of the cataract now dinned in our ears; the spray from the boiling abyss began to envelope us; and every succeeding moment diminished the slight hopes which had hitherto occasionally shot across our bewildered senses. An attempt to describe my feelings would be vain. The frightful rapidity of the current, joined to the apprehension of instant annihilation, banished even the recollection of "kindred home," which, for a moment, obtruded itself on my imagination. With hope fled despair, and in silent resignation we awaited our fate; but at the moment when it appeared inevitable, the sharp eye of M'Gillivray observed that the raft was caught by a counter current immediately above the fall. He had a small stick, with which he sounded, and found the depth did not exceed three feet. He instantly jumped overboard, followed by Louis and myself; and with a little exertion we succeeded in dragging the raft into an eddy, free from the influence of the great body of water, from whence we easily brought it to shore without the loss of a single article! Our companions on shore, after we had been carried out of their sight, had abandoned all hopes of ever seeing us again, and were therefore agreeably surprised at finding us once more safe on *terra firma*.

Messrs. Alexander M'Tavish, Bethune, and four men, still remained on the western side, and in consequence of the narrow escape which our two first parties had, they determined not to attempt crossing in such a dangerous spot. Having loaded our horses, we proceeded about five miles below the traverse, when we encamped. M'Tavish's party passed the night on the opposite bank in a miserable situation, being totally deprived of either food or covering, and without means even to make a fire.

Started early on the morning of the 3rd, and after travelling about four miles we arrived opposite the spot where our friends had passed the night. They had no means of joining us but by a raft. The river was smooth; which circumstance, strengthened by the irrepressible gnawings of hunger, conquered their dislike to that mode of crossing. Having neither axe nor line, they collected as many pieces of driftwood as they could find on the beach, which they bound together by withes, after which they embarked. The raft however had scarcely left the shore when it began to give way, and Messrs. Bethune, M'Tavish, and two men immediately jumped off, and regained the land at the expense of a good ducking. The other two men however succeeded in crossing the river on separate pieces, and joined us in safety.

François, a Creole, now volunteered to swim over on horseback, and bring with him an axe and some line for the purpose of making a raft lower down. This proposition was gladly accepted, and having taken the strongest of our five horses, he plunged in and gained the opposite bank.

As Mr. Bethune did not like to venture a second time at this place, we appointed to meet him at the junction of the Rocky Mountain with the Athabasca River, where we hoped he would be able to join us. We then continued our progress, and at nine A. M. arrived at the mouth of the river, where it joins the Athabasca; and, to our great surprise, observed Mr. Bethune's party proceeding at a great distance down the western bank of the river. We hailed them, and fired several shots; but as they paid no attention to our signals, we imagined they were acquainted with a better place to cross the river than that which we had pointed out.

We therefore set all hands to work to construct rafts for our party. The Athabasca River at this place was about four hundred yards wide, the current strong, but free from rapids, and with the exception of two rocks in the centre of the river, there was no apparent danger to be apprehended. We remained until one o'clock, making two rafts, with poles and paddles necessary for working them. The horses were first sent across, followed by two men, after which we embarked five on each raft, and pushed off. I took care not to separate from my friend M'Gillivray and the Iroquois. After poling for a few minutes we lost bottom, and were obliged to have recourse to the paddles, with which we worked on tolerably well until we reached the centre of the stream, where we found the current much more rapid than we

Thomas Douglas, Fifth Earl of Selkirk (1771–1820)

"Old Stone House" at Sault Ste Marie. The house was completed when Lord Selkirk passed through Sault Ste Marie in 1815.

had anticipated. Owing to this circumstance, and the difficulty of steering the raft, we found ourselves carried along with great velocity towards one of the rocks already mentioned. The danger was imminent; for, had we come broadside against it, we should undoubtedly have gone to pieces and perished. We therefore exerted ourselves to the utmost to prevent the collision, and were so far fortunate as to escape, with merely a slight shock from the corner of the raft touching a projecting point of the rock. After this we went on smoothly, and reached the eastern side in safety, having drifted about a mile down the river from the place of embarkation.

The horses were quickly loaded, and we proceeded along the banks about nine miles, when, ascending a hill, which commanded an extensive prospect, we observed a volume of smoke some distance ahead. Supposing it had been made by our lost companions, two active men were sent to ascertain the fact. They shortly returned, and stated they had seen a fire on the opposite bank of the main river, but no appearance of any human being about it. We therefore conjectured the fire had been made by Bethune's party, and that they had continued on.

We accordingly increased our pace, in the hope of overtaking them, and arrived late in the evening at an uninhabited house, heartily tired. This place is called the "Old Fort,"[9] and was built several years before as a hunting-lodge for trappers, but owing to the scarcity of provisions was subsequently abandoned. Its lat. is 52° 53′ 10″ N.

From the junction of the two rivers to the Old Fort, the country on each side presents a pleasing variety of prairies, open woods, and gently rising eminences; and one spot in particular, called *La prairie de la Vache*[10] (in consequence of buffalo having been formerly killed in it), forms a landscape, that for rural beauty cannot be excelled in any country. Some slight showers during the day.

JUNE 4TH. Early this morning we dispatched two parties in quest of Messrs. M'Tavish, Bethune, and the men who remained with them, and at nine o'clock they returned, bringing them all back in safety, but in a state of great exhaustion from want of food, and exposure

[9] This was Henry's House, located where the Miette River enters the Athabaska River, near the present resort town of Jasper, Alberta. See *George Simpson's Journal*, 31, 32 n.

[10] Buffalo Prairie. Ermatinger located it about half way between the junction of the Whirlpool and Athabaska rivers and the mouth of the Miette River. See "Edward Ermatinger's York Factory Express Journal," 81.

without covering to the night air. They had advanced within four miles of our encampment, when they perceived our men; and the river being smooth, they constructed a raft and crossed over in safety. Remained here a couple of hours to refresh the party, after which the horses were loaded, and we proceeded for about three miles through a handsomely diversified country, when our progress was arrested by a bold mountain torrent, which fell into the Athabasca. It was too deep to ford, and we were again obliged to have recourse to our old expedient of rafts in order to cross it.

The navigation of the main river from this place to Rocky Mountain House being free from obstructions, Mr. M'Dougall determined to proceed thither by water; and taking four of the men with him, they embarked on one of the rafts, and we quickly lost sight of them. We continued on through a handsome country with a tolerable pathway until sun-set, when we encamped on the border of a small rivulet which runs into the Athabasca.

We loaded our horses at three in the morning of the 5th, and for a couple of hours were quite shrouded in oceans of mist; but as it began to dissipate, we had an extensive view of the surrounding scenery.

The genial influence of a June sun relieved the wintry perspective of snow-clad mountains, and as it rose above the lofty summits, imparted a golden tinge to the green savannahs, the open woods, and the innumerable rivulets which contributed their waters to swell the Athabasca. It was indeed a landscape of contrarieties, scarcely to be met with but in the Alpine regions of the Rocky Mountains.

At eight A. M. we arrived at a hunting-lodge belonging to the Company. No person was in it; but we found what was much more acceptable, the body of a buffalo, which had been recently killed, and left for us by the hunters. It was none of the fattest; but to such half-famished devils it was an unexpected luxury. Having eaten, or rather devoured our breakfast, and reserved sufficient for supper, we resumed progress with renovated spirits. At eleven we came to a considerable stream, which it was necessary to cross. It had recently however spread over a flat bottom, and, forming a shallow lake of some acres in extent, completely covered the pathway; in consequence of which our guide experienced much difficulty in conducting us through it.

About a mile beyond this river we arrived at the foot of a stupendous rock, called *Le Rocher de Miette*,[11] over which we had to pass.

We commenced our task a little after eleven; and at half-past two arrived at its base on the northern side, where we remained an hour to refresh the horses. The road over this rock is tolerably good, but extremely steep. The horses surmounted it with great labour; and the knees of the majority of our party were put to a severe test in the ascent. From the summit we had an extensive view of the country, the general features of which do not differ materially from the scenery through which we passed the preceding day. A little above the southern point of the rock we observed that the Athabasca River opened into a lake of about three miles in length, and two in breadth, and a few miles below its northern extremity the river formed another lake of nearly similar dimensions. Independently of these, the continual accession of waters which the Athabasca received from its tributary streams caused it to burst its natural boundaries, and in many places we had to wade from one to two miles through the flood. Encamped at sun-set, at the head of the lower lake, and, maugre our fatigue from travelling "o'er mountain and through flood," succeeded in dispatching with wonderful celerity the remains of our buffalo.

At eight A. M. on the morning of the 6th we came opposite Rocky Mountain House,[12] which is built on the western shore of the second lake. A canoe was immediately dispatched for us, and we crossed the river. This building was a miserable concern of rough logs, with only three apartments, but scrupulously clean inside. An old clerk, Mr. Jasper Hawes, was in charge, and had under his command two Canadians, two Iroquois, and three hunters. Its lat. is 53° 18' 40" N. Mr. M'Dougall had arrived the day before us, after leaving his raft at the upper end of the lower lake, from whence he and his party walked to the house.

We expected to have found a supply of provisions here, that would enable us to reach English River; but, to our extreme disappointment, none was to be had. Mr. Hawes informed us that the hunters were not able to kill more animals than were barely sufficient to support his party, but added, that there was every probability of our obtaining a supply from Lesser Slave Lake, where Mr. Alexander Stewart had wintered, and whose party we expected to join in our route to

---

[11] This is a great cubical rock opposite Jasper House. Franchère's party had been able to go around it. See "Edward Ermatinger's York Factory Express Journal," 108, n. 3; and Franchère, *Narrative*, 356–57.

[12] Jasper House.

Fort William. Remained here all day getting our canoes into order, preparatory to our bidding farewell to the Rocky Mountains. The distance from the Columbia to this place, which we travelled on foot, is by computation about eighty-five or ninety miles. This took nearly ten days to accomplish. Some of our men were greatly exhausted; but when we take into consideration the fatigues which they endured in ascending the Columbia, the burdens they carried in crossing the mountain, joined to the difficulties of the road, it must be acknowledged that few could surpass them in strength, patience, or perseverance. The house is situated near a stream called *La Rivière à la Boucane*,[13] in consequence of some of the hunters who first visited this place having alleged that they saw a volcano near its source, which emitted great quantities of smoke. On making inquiry from our people, I could not learn that they had ever seen an actual eruption; but they assert that in the autumnal months the ground is quite hot, and that smoke issues from it in various places; during which period, they add, a strong sulphuric smell pervades the atmosphere.

We saw nothing from which we could judge whether the mountains contained any metallic ores or metals, and I could not find on the banks of the various streams any of those fine agates which I found on the Columbia. We, however, had no time, nor were we qualified to enter into scientific researches; and it will not be until civilisation has approached a few hundred leagues nearer those great mountains that their various productions will be known. At present, however, I am of opinion that they contain nothing sufficient to repay a party in visiting them merely for scientific purposes. The animals found in the various passes of the mountains are the buffaloes, ibex, big-horns, or mountain sheep, bears, and sometimes a few wolves. These are too well known to require any description here. Some of the Upper Crees, a tribe who inhabit the country in the vicinity of the Athabasca River, have a curious tradition with respect to animals which they state formerly frequented the mountains. They allege that these animals were of frightful magnitude, being from two to three hundred feet in length, and high in proportion; that they formerly lived in the plains, a great distance to the eastward; from which they were gradually driven by the Indians to the Rocky Mountains; that they destroyed all smaller animals; and if their agility was equal to their size, would have also destroyed all the natives, &c. One man has as-

13 Franchère called this the Smoky River.

serted that his grandfather told him he saw one of those animals in a mountain pass, where he was hunting, and that on hearing its roar, which he compared to loud thunder, the sight almost left his eyes, and his heart became as small as an infant's.

Whether such an animal ever existed I shall leave to the curious in natural history to determine; but if the Indian tradition have any foundation in truth, it may have been the mammoth, some of whose remains have been found at various times in the United States.

The height of the Rocky Mountains varies considerably. The table land which we crossed I should take to be about eleven thousand feet above the level of the sea. From the immense number of rapids we had to pass in ascending the Columbia, and its precipitous bed above the lakes, I consider that at their base the mountains cannot be much under eight thousand feet[14] above the level of the Pacific, and from the valley of Canoe River to the level part of the heights of land cannot be less than three thousand feet, but the actual altitude of their highest summits must be much greater. They are covered with eternal ice and snow, and will probably be for ever inaccessible to man.

JUNE 7TH. We were detained a considerable portion of this day getting the canoes finished, and at half-past one P. M. we took leave of the melancholy hermitage of Mr. Jasper Hawes. We had two good bark canoes and six men in each. The lake extended about half a mile below the house, when we entered the river, the current of which is very strong, with here and there a few rapids, at none of which we were obliged to unload.

Encamped at dusk on a small low island. Had several smart showers during the day.

JUNE 8TH. It rained the greater part of the night. Embarked at day-break in a thick fog, which continued upwards of two hours. At eight damaged our canoes in a rapid, at the foot of which we stopped to breakfast and repair. At noon passed a small river from the east called M'Leod's Fork. Late in the evening passed two lodges of Indians, and encamped a short distance below them. They paid us a visit, and proved to be Crees of the Forts des Prairies department. They brought with them a few bags of dried meat and fruit, which

---

[14] Boat Encampment was at an altitude of two thousand feet, according to Ermatinger, while Athabaska Pass was over six thousand feet. See "Edward Ermatinger's York Factory Express Journal," 80; but compare with Franchère, *Narrative*, 359. See also *George Simpson's Journal*, 30 n.

they wished to barter for rum; but as we had none of that cheering beverage to give them, we tendered them our bills on the Company, for which they would have obtained value from any proprietor or clerk of the establishment; at the same time explaining to them, that we stood in great need of provisions. Mr. Bethune knew that they were attached to the interests of our rivals the Hudson's Bay Company, and therefore offered them higher prices than he would have done to those of a friendly tribe; but it was all unavailing. They would hear of nothing—speak of nothing—until rum was produced; and on finding that none could be obtained, those splendid specimens of savage hospitality carried away their extra provisions, although they were informed that we had not enough to subsist on for a couple of days!

From Rocky Mountain House to this place the country on each side of the river is low, and tolerably well wooded, but a strong and marked difference is observable in the size of the trees on the eastern side of the mountains. Here all is dwarfish and stunted;[15] while on the Columbia the vegetable world is seen in its richest and most magnificent forms—including all the varieties from a luxuriant growth of black-berry or wild-cherry, to the stately pine, and majestic cedar. It is difficult to account for this difference; but if I might hazard an opinion, I would attribute it to the great humidity of the climate on the Columbia. There, westerly and south-westerly winds prevail eight months out of the twelve, and carry with them immense masses of clouds from the North Pacific. A great portion of these break over the high lands on the coast; and such as escape are arrested in their flight eastward by the Rocky Mountains, and burst over their western base. So that at the very source of the Columbia the pine and cedar are as gigantic as at its entrance into the ocean.

[15] It was this situation that was responsible for the region's being known as the "Land of Little Sticks."

Chapter 25

*Descent of the Athabasca River—Party disappointed in receiving provisions
—Elk River and Lake—Join the brigade from Lesser Slave Lake—Arrive
at Ile à la Crosse—Dreadful effects of the opposition between the North-
West and Hudson's Bay companies—Sketch of Mr. Peter Ogden*

MONDAY, JUNE 9TH. At eleven A.M. passed a small river from the eastward,[1] called the Pembina, from a profusion of berries of that name
which grow on its banks. At two P. M. stopped at a hunting-lodge
of free Iroquois. The head of the family had a letter addressed "To
the gentlemen from the Columbia." It was eagerly broken open, and
we found it was written by Mr. Alexander Stewart, and dated from
Lesser Slave Lake,[2] from which place he was on the point of setting
off with his winter's trade of furs for Fort William. In it he regretted
his inability to assist us with any provisions, alleging as a reason, that
he had a bare sufficiency for the support of his own people outwards,
but recommending that a portion of our party should be sent to Slave
Lake, where they would find fish enough during the summer, and be
able to set off the ensuing spring without any fear of starvation.

This intelligence was dreadful, the more so from its being unexpected; for the spring party from the Columbia had hitherto, after
crossing the mountains, invariably obtained from the people at Lesser
Slave Lake a fresh stock of dried meat or other food sufficient to support them to English River, or Cumberland House. We of course expected the usual supply, all hopes of which were now banished by Mr.
Stewart's letter. A council was immediately held to consider what

[1] The Pembina River comes in from the east but is the largest southern tributary
of the Athabaska.

[2] Lesser Slave Lake was to the west and north of where the party was then
traveling.

plan we should adopt in this emergency, when it was suggested that M'Tavish and I should proceed forthwith with six men to Slave Lake, and remain there until the spring for our passage to Canada. To me, another year in the Indian country would be an age. The idea was horrible; and I at once refused to accede to such an arrangement. M'Tavish was equally unbending, and declared his fixed determination to proceed. It was urged that we had not provisions for three days, and that with such a scanty allowance, and no certainty of procuring a supply, inevitable starvation awaited us. Finding that this gloomy picture made no impression on us, recourse was had to threats, and it was pretty broadly insinuated that force would be adopted to compel obedience. Matters now became desperate; we loaded our guns, trimmed our flints, the hilt of the dirk became more conspicuous, and menace was answered by defiance. The canoe-men looked on in silent amazement, but did not attempt to interfere; indeed had they been so inclined, we felt certain that those belonging to our own canoe would not have deserted us. Our opponents at length thought it prudent to yield to our wishes, and a sort of sulky reconciliation took place, after which we embarked. We had previously ascertained from the Iroquois, that Mr. Stewart's brigade was not more than four days ahead; and as they were heavily laden with furs, while our canoes were quite light, we determined to strain every nerve to overtake them. The river was broad, with a swift current, and free from rapids; and we therefore continued on all night, a disagreeable head-wind occasionally annoying us.

JUNE 10TH. The Athabasca is here a noble river, flowing through a rich pasture country thinly wooded. Saw several tracks of buffalo; but while we had the current in our favour, we did not think it prudent to stop. The stream carried us down in fine style, until six P. M., when we arrived at the entrance of *La Rivière de la Biche* (Elk River),[3] where we left the Athabasca, which, pursuing the course I have already mentioned, ultimately discharges its waters into the Arctic Ocean. For the last 150 miles its navigation was uninterrupted by rapids, with a smooth steady current, and the soil on each bank of the richest description.

We now shaped our course easterly, and ascended *Rivière de la Biche* about three miles, when we encamped. The water was very low, and we were dreadfully tormented with musquitoes; but our hunters

3 Franchère called this the "Little Red Elk River." See *Narrative,* 365.

having discovered some fresh tracks of buffalo, cheered our drooping spirits a little.

June 11th. Rose at day-break, but could scarcely see twenty yards ahead, from a thick fog. Owing to the shallowness of the river, the passengers preferred walking, in order to lighten the canoes. Made half a breakfast of our dried pemmican, of which we had not now enough for dinner. At ten A. M. the river became wider and deeper, which enabled us to embark and resume the paddles. At eleven passed a small stream called Auger's River, and about two P. M. came up to a recent encampment of the Slave Lake brigade, the fires of which were still burning. Here we also found some pieces of buffalo meat, which those gentry did not think fat enough to carry, but which proved very grateful to our poor fellows. At eight passed the river Pinette, and encamped at dusk. The land on each side was very low, and thinly wooded with small pine and poplar. In some parts we observed patches of prairie ground of two or three miles in extent. Saw one buffalo, about three in the evening, but missed him.

June 12th. We had good deep water for paddling, from day-break until six A. M., when the river for about four miles spread over a stony bottom, which obliged us to land, while the men worked up with the lines and poles. It then became narrower and deeper, and continued so far several miles, until eleven A. M., when it entered Lac de la Biche, which we crossed in three hours with calm weather. As we approached the eastern shore, we observed smoke issuing from a small cove, and immediately after the white canvass of a tent met our delighted eyes. A few minutes more brought us to land, when we had the inexpressible pleasure of meeting Mr. Alexander Stewart, and the Slave Lake brigade, consisting of eight canoes, and about forty-five men. This was a fortunate circumstance. We had not eaten a mouthful that day, up to two o'clock, with starvation staring us in the face, no natives on our route, and our chance of killing animals more than doubtful. We now, however, recompensed ourselves for all these uncertainties and apprehensions, by a plentiful repast of roast buffalo and white-fish.

This lake, from the time we took to traverse it, I should suppose to be about thirty miles in circumference. It is nearly circular, and abounds in white-fish. The surrounding country is extremely low, without any rising ground in sight, and on the western side the land is quite marshy. The shores are tolerably wooded, principally with pine, birch, and poplar.

During the night a number of the men were employed on the lake catching fish by torch-light, and were rather successful.

JUNE 13TH. About three miles to the eastward of our encampment lies a small lake, called by the Canadians *Le Petit Lac de Biche*.[4] The country between the two lakes forms the height of land which divides the waters that fall into the Arctic Ocean from the eastward, from those which fall into Hudson's Bay from the westward. Mr. Stewart's men had commenced this portage[5] yesterday, and it took us the greater part of this day to finish it; which will not appear extraordinary, when it is considered that ten large canoes, and between two and three hundred packs of beaver, each weighing upwards of ninety pounds, had to be carried three miles through a swampy marsh, full of underwood, during the greater part of which time it rained heavily. Encamped at four P. M. on the shore of a little lake which we had previously crossed, and which was not more than half a mile in breadth.

JUNE 14TH. It continued raining the greater part of the night. Commenced another portage this morning, of 250 paces in length, which brought us to a small stream called Little Beaver River, into which we threw the canoes. There was not sufficient water to float them when loaded, in consequence of which we had to construct dams at intervals of 400 or 500 paces. This was both a tedious and laborious work; and we encamped at six P. M., having advanced only five miles since morning. Some of the men were sent ahead, to make more dams. The passengers walked during the day, and our hunters killed one fat moose deer. The country is thinly wooded and marshy, and full of wild onions and a species of plant which served as an excellent substitute for cabbage.

JUNE 15TH. It rained hard all night, and the greater part of this forenoon, owing to which we did not start until twelve o'clock, and, being obliged to continue the damming system all day, our progress was of course extremely tedious. Passed several handsome prairies, and observed in many places along the banks of the little river marks of beaver cuttings. Birch, pine, and poplar, form the principal timber here. Made a small portage, and encamped at seven P. M. Our hunters killed another prime moose.

---

[4] This is Beaver Lake.

[5] This portage between the waters of the Athabaska and Beaver rivers was known as the "Portage la Biche." See *George Simpson's Journal,* 21 n.

JUNE 16TH. Set off at three A. M., still in the dams. At seven made a short portage, at the end of which we stopped to breakfast and repair the canoes, which had been greatly shattered by their ditch navigation. About one P. M. we had a sufficient body of water to admit of our embarking, and we proceeded with a tolerably smooth current until half-past four, when we encamped, having overtaken our hunters, who had killed a fat bull-buffalo, and two beavers, on which we made an excellent dinner. The country was not so well wooded as yesterday. We had cloudy, and occasionally rainy weather, which for the season was also rather chilly.

JUNE 17TH. Embarked at half-past three A. M. Made several portages on account of rapids and shoals. Our progress was therefore slow. Killed a buck-moose in good condition. On shore the greater part of the day. It consisted principally of rich meadow land, with clusters of birch and poplar scattered here and there along the banks of the river. Encamped at six P. M.

JUNE 18TH. Set off at four, and had a pretty smooth steady current all day. The country now assumes a more picturesque appearance, rather thickly wooded, and the banks of the river more bold and hilly. The rapidity of our progress brought us considerably in advance of the hunters, and at three P. M. we put ashore to wait for them. The place at which we stopped was called *La Jolie Butte,* by way of pre-eminence, from the varied and handsome landscape by which it was surrounded. The hunters joined us at six, after which we continued on, and encamped at eight P. M. in sight of Moose Portage.[6] Only three beavers were killed this day.

JUNE 19TH. Sent the hunters off ahead at day-break, and at half-past five commenced Moose Portage, which we passed in less than two hours. Here we found, fixed on poles in a conspicuous part of the portage, some letters from the gentlemen stationed at Forts des Prairies, containing satisfactory news. From their date we conjectured that the messengers who brought them must have been very recently at the portage. At nine A. M. joined the hunters, who had just returned from a long chase to the northward, in the course of which they only killed one bull and one moose; and as we stood in great need of a

[6] Moose Portage led from the Beaver River southward to the Saskatchewan River by way of Moose Creek. Cox did not traverse it, and he probably had reference to passing a rapid, or some similar obstruction in the Beaver River, at the north end of the portage.

supply, we were obliged to stop here the remainder of the day, to give the meat-men time to bring in the bodies of those animals. The hunters, however, started off ahead.

JUNE 20TH. The meat-men did not return until nine this morning, when we embarked; but at eleven the hunters' signal drew us to shore, and the meat-men were dispatched. They remained away six hours, and returned at five P. M. loaded with the carcases of an immensely sized bull, and a huge grizzly bear. Encamped at eight, at the Portage de Lac Froid, a small lake, the water of which some of our people imagine is colder than that of Beaver River,[7] and, in order to account for this extra frigidity, it is supposed that it is fed from the bottom by springs of a peculiar nature. I tasted it; but whether it was owing to the heat of the weather, or to a vitiated palate, I must candidly confess, that I could not discover any perceptible difference in its temperature.

The country through which we passed for the last few days is highly diversified with hill and dale, meadow-ground and timber, and has many charming spots for building.

JUNE 21ST. Set off at four A. M., and drove down the current in fine style until two P. M., when we came up with our hunters. They had just returned after a long and fatiguing pursuit of a herd of buffaloes, three of which they killed, besides five they wounded, but which made their escape. Encamped here, and sent off a party for the meat. A ridge of pretty high hills thickly wooded runs parallel with the course of the river from Lac Froid to this place. M'Tavish and I took a stroll inland in the track of the hunters, and had not proceeded more than a mile when we observed several buffaloes grazing. I instantly fired, and hit one under the left shoulder. The remainder fled; but the wounded animal, bellowing in a frightful manner, with rage and fury flashing from his rolling eyes, charged on us. We retreated behind the cover of a tree, from whence M'Tavish took a steady aim, and lodged a ball in his head directly over the right eye. He instantly fell, and we cautiously approached him, but took care to plant a

[7] Cox was following the route which was later used by the Lesser Slave Lake Brigade and by the Columbia Express. This ran from the Athabaska River to Cumberland House via the Beaver and English rivers and Frog Portage. The difficulty with it was that the Beaver River was a troublesome piece of navigation that made necessary the use of the uneconomical northern canoe, which was only about four feet wide and twenty-five long, and not especially suitable for freighting purposes. And this canoe had to be used for the entire distance. See *George Simpson's Journal*, 27 n.

couple more bullets about his head before we came within arm's length.

JUNE 22D. The meat-men did not return until half-past ten this morning, when we set off, but were obliged to stop from twelve to three for another buffalo which our hunters had killed. Encamped at eight P. M. in a handsome prairie on the north side. Observed recent marks of buffalo and moose, and numerous beaver cuttings.

JUNE 23D. Embarked at half-past three A. M. Stopped about an hour for a moose which was killed about half a mile inland. The river for the last two days had no rapid of any consequence, and the weather was very warm. A little after eight P. M. observed a small leather hut on the north side, in which we found three free trappers, who had been formerly *engagés* of the North-West Company; but who, after the expiration of their engagement, preferred the wild and wandering life of a trapper, to remaining in the Company's service, or returning to Canada. We encamped a little below their hut, and they visited us after supper. Their news was by no means of an agreeable nature. They informed us, that they had learned from some natives that a party of the Cree Indians[8] from Forts des Prairies, urged by large promises of reward from the Hudson's Bay Company, had gone on a war expedition to destroy our establishment at *Ile à la Crosse* and all its inmates, adding, that whether successful or not, it was more than probable we might meet this party *en route.*

As this intelligence was quite unexpected, and as we were badly prepared to encounter a war party of savages, Mr. Stewart, who had now the command, ordered the hunters not to advance more than a mile ahead, and, in case they observed any appearance of natives, to return immediately to the main brigade. In the mean time our fire-arms were put in order, and the men, the greater part of whom had no weapons save their knives, were ordered to furnish themselves with clubs. We then retired to rest, leaving five sentinels and an officer on guard to be relieved every two hours.

JUNE 24TH. Set off at half-past three A. M. At half-past two P. M. passed Lac Vert,[9] a small lake so called from the greenish tinge of its water. Encamped at half-past seven at the entrance of a small river

[8] The Crees were an important Algonquian tribe, closely related to the Chipewyans. Like all the tribes of the plains, they were rovers, and while their usual habitat was the Saskatchewan and Assiniboine river valleys, they often ranged as far north as the Athabaska River. See *George Simpson's Journal,* 159 n.

[9] Although there is a Green Lake, it is a little to the south of the route, and this may be one of the small lakes along the course of La Poule d'Eau, or Waterhen, River.

called La Poule d'Eau. The country these two days is thinly wooded, and very flat. In many places the river had overflowed its banks. Saw no animals.

JUNE 25TH. Embarked at half-past three. Stopped from eleven to two, to repair the canoes, and dry some of the beaver which had been slightly damaged from leaks. The country through which we passed this day was quite flat and marshy, occasioned by the inundations in times of high water. Encamped at dusk, at the entrance of a small river called La Plonge.

JUNE 26TH. Beaver River at this place branches into several channels. We took the principal one, and at eleven A. M. arrived at its termination where it enters the lake of *Ile à la Crosse*,[10] nearly opposite the fort. Stopped here for half an hour *pour se faire la barbe*, and make other little arrangements connected with the toilet. These being completed, we embarked, but having the fear of the Crees before our eyes, our progress was slow and cautious across the lake, until our avant-couriers announced to us that the flag of the North-West floated from the bastions, and that all was safe. The *Chanson a l'aviron* was instantly struck up, and at one P. M. we reached the wharf, where we were met by Messrs. M'Murray[11] and Ogden,[12] who were in charge of the fort. Those gentlemen had also heard the rumoured intention of the Crees to attack the establishment, but they were of opinion that the attempt would not be made. They had only eight men under their command; but the place was surrounded by strong palisades, and flanked by two bastions, which although not very beautiful specimens of fortification, would have puzzled a battalion of Indians to take. The Hudson's Bay Company had a fort on

10 Lake Île-à-la-Crosse was an important point in the history of the fur trade. Both companies had forts there, and after 1821, it became an important supply depot for the Hudson's Bay Company.

11 Thomas McMurray (1779?–1849) was the son of a trader by the same name. He was first in the service of the XY Company, and after its merger with the North West Company, he was sent as a clerk to Rainy Lake. In 1816, he became a partner and in 1821 a chief trader. See Wallace, *Documents*, 483.

12 Peter Skene Ogden (1794–1854) is one of the most famous names in the history of the fur trade. He was born in Quebec and in 1811 joined the North West Company. From then until 1818 he was at Île-à-la-Crosse. In 1818, he was transferred to the Columbia and in 1820 became a partner. In 1821, he was passed over in the merger, but he carried his appeal to London so successfully that in 1823 he was made a chief trader and in 1835 a chief factor. The greater part of his career was spent on the Pacific coast, where his greatest claim to fame was his rescue of the captives after the Whitman Massacre. See Wallace, *Documents*, 489.

a point of land running into the lake, which was not more than a quarter of a mile distant from our establishment. It had been taken the preceding winter by the North-West Company, and at the period of our arrival there were about 20 (men) prisoners in it, and upwards of 120 women and children, besides dogs innumerable. They were miserably supplied with provisions, and all seemed dejected and emaciated. Their principal reliance for food was on the lake; and when the fish failed, their chief support was *tripe de rocher*. I conversed with some of the men. They were from the Orkneys,[13] and wished they were safe home again. They spoke in no flattering terms of the treatment they received from their captors, but admitted that such of the North-Westers as had been made prisoners by their party fared no better.

It will undoubtedly sound odd in the ears of British readers, to hear of forts attacked and prisoners taken by commercial companies, natives of the same country, and subjects of the same king. To account for this it will be necessary to take a short retrospect, in order to explain the causes that led to a state of things which was ultimately productive of so many disastrous and melancholy consequences.

The opposition between the Hudson's Bay and the North-West companies was for many years carried on without any violent breach of the peace on either side. As I have observed in the introduction, the indolent habits of the persons belonging to the former, unstimulated by any hope of extra reward or prospective promotion, gave to the North-West Company powerful advantages, of which they did not fail to avail themselves; and while their enterprising agents explored the most remote parts of the continent for the extension of their trade, their chartered opponents, with a Dutch-like kind of apathy, quietly confined themselves to their ancient territory.

Both parties were thus situated, when the late Earl of Selkirk conceived the idea of establishing a colony of Scotch and Irish on the Red River,[14] which falls into Lake Winepic. The soil was fertile, the climate temperate, and, were it not for its great distance from civilisation, was admirably calculated for a new settlement. It was, however, the great depot of the North-West Company for making

[13] The Orkney men are said to have been favored by the Hudson's Bay Company because of their proficiency as fishermen, but their usefulness was not as great in the interior as it was on salt water.

[14] The Red River of the North, which rises in the United States and flows northward. It constitutes the boundary between the states of North Dakota and Minnesota.

301

pemmican, the principal article of food used by their canoe-men in voyaging. If the colony succeeded, it would gradually cut off the buffalo, from which the pemmican is made, and ultimately oblige the Company to import from Canada, at an enormous expense, a great portion of the provisions necessary for their travelling parties. It may therefore be supposed, that the settlers were not regarded with the most friendly feelings; and every obstacle short of actual violence was thrown in the way of their location. Their first year was one of incredible hardships, arising from their ignorance of the country and its productions, and the total failure of their provisions; which, joined to the various modes of annoyance practised by the North-West Company, induced the greater part to avail themselves of an offer made by members of that concern to transport them gratuitously to Canada in their canoes.

The want of success in his first attempt at colonisation being, in a great degree, caused by the opposition of the North-West Company, Lord Selkirk determined to adopt retaliatory measures; and for this purpose purchased a number of shares in the Hudson's Bay Company, of which he became an active director. His Lordship was well aware that several clerks, who had been many years in the service of the rival Company, were discontented at not having been sooner promoted to the proprietory, and that the claims of the old and faithful were too often passed over, while young favourites of comparatively little experience were placed above them. It was therefore an important object with him to induce as many as possible of those so dissatisfied to join his party by the offer of large salaries, which several, at the expiration of their various engagements with the North-West Company, accepted.

The most active of these gentlemen was Mr. Colin Robertson,[15] an enterprising trader who had often ventured his life, both among Indians and white men, to advance the interests of his establishment. Having a perfect knowledge of the business of the interior, Lord Selkirk entrusted him with its chief management; and as he knew from experience the great superiority of the Canadian voyageurs over the

[15] Colin Robertson (1779–1842) had become a Northwester in 1804, but he was dismissed from the service in 1809 by John McDonald of Garth, a very unfortunate dismissal, as time was to prove. In 1812, he entered the service of Lord Selkirk. Later he was arrested by the North West Company, but he escaped and went to England, where he was present during the merger negotiations between the two companies. He then became a chief factor in the Hudson's Bay Company. See Wallace, *Documents,* 494.

Orkney men, in the management of canoes, &c., he engaged a number of them at Montreal at a much higher rate of wages than had been previously paid by the North-West Company.

The opposition between the rival parties now assumed a new and more marked character, and the invigorating spirit which had been infused into the hitherto cautious councils of the Hudson's Bay, by the daring policy of Mr. Robertson, soon became manifest. He knew the strong holds and the weak points of his opponents, and being of opinion that much depended on the first impression made on the Indians, he at once determined to push for Athabasca, the great northern department of the North-West, and the most productive in beaver. No rival trader had ever before ventured to encroach on Athabasca, and this unexpected invasion was deemed the *ne plus ultra* of audacity, the seizure of the bull by the horns.

Mr. Robertson was successful in his first expedition. The high prices he offered for their furs seduced the natives from their allegiance to their old masters, and hundreds came crowding to his standard. In other parts of the interior the struggle was more obstinate, and the North-Westers, to secure the wavering loyalty of the Indians, were compelled to keep pace with the advanced prices of their opponents.

A reinforcement of settlers having in the mean time arrived at Hudson's Bay, they were dispatched to the Red River, where they built a strong fort, and began to re-establish the colony. Several of the natives joined them, and the influence of the North-West became sensibly diminished in that quarter.

Thus far Lord Selkirk's plan of operations for the year 1814–15 succeeded beyond his expectations; and great preparations were made by him for opening the ensuing campaign on a much more extended scale. The exertions of the North-Westers were equally vigorous. Double the usual quantity of trading goods was sent to the interior, the men's wages were raised, and several clerks were elected proprietors. The orders to both parties were, to secure as much provisions and furs as they could collect, *coute qui coute.*

Mr. Clarke,[16] lately of the Pacific Fur Company, on his arrival in Canada from the Columbia, was engaged by Lord Selkirk, and proceeded with a strong force to Athabasca, in which department he

[16] This was the same John Clarke under whom Cox had served at Fort Spokane. For an evaluation of him see *George Simpson's Journal,* 10–11 n.

had spent many years while in the service of the North-West, during which period he was a great favourite with the Chepewyans.

It is not my intention however to give a detail of the various quarrels, the prisoners made, the forts surprised, or the lists of killed and wounded, on each side; but from the following extracts of letters, which I received before quitting the Columbia, it will be seen that the Hudson's Bay people were the greatest sufferers.

Fort William, 28th July, 1816

You already know the strong opposition that came into the country, the greatest part of which went to Athabasca, and Slave Lake. You must also have heard of their success at the former place, having been obliged from starvation to give themselves up to the North-West; although your old friend[17] swore he would rather die than come under any obligations to our people. He lost seventeen men by famine. At Slave Lake they were more successful; but at the different establishments they had in other parts of the country, they lost thirteen more by starvation. Last June they received a mortal blow from the Cossacks[18] of Red River; of which affair, as I was on the spot a few days after, I shall give you a detail. You of course know that two of our forts were taken, and all the property; and that Captain Cameron[19] was made prisoner. The forts were subsequently burned.

Mr. A. M'Donell,[20] who was stationed at *Qu'appelle* river,[21] held his fort in defiance of them. He was threatened with destruction if he made any attempt to pass downward. His opponent however started with his men, and returns of furs and provisions; of the latter he had about three hundred *taureaux* (pemmigans) well guarded, as they thought, but those *blackguard Brulés* (I know not from what cause) fell in with them, took them all prisoners, and carried the property to Mr. M'Donell. No blood was shed on this occasion. Some time after Mr. M'Donell being anxious for the arrival of

17 Mr. Clarke.—R. C.

18 A *nom de guerre* given by the writer to the sons of white men by Indian wives. They are also called *Bois Brûlés,* but why, it is difficult to determine.—R. C. (This name, which literally translates as "Burnt Wood," was given them on account of their complexion. They were also known as "charcoal faces." These were the famous "metis" whose story has been very fascinatingly told in Joseph Kinsey Howard, *Strange Empire, a Narrative of the Northwest* [New York, Morrow, 1952].—eds.)

19 This gentleman was a proprietor of the North-West Company.—R. C.

20 Alexander MacDonell (d. 1835) was a clerk on Red River. In 1814, he had been made a partner and placed in charge of that department. He played a prominent part in the Selkirk troubles, but following the merger he retired from the fur trade. See Wallace, *Documents,* 464–65.

21 The Qu'Appelle River in southern Saskatchewan, a tributary of the Assiniboine. The name that translates as "Who Calls" was given because the area was supposed to be haunted.

the gentlemen from the northward, sent a party of five Canadians with two carts, loaded with provisions for us, by land; and the above *blackguards* took upon themselves to accompany them, to the number of fifty. On passing by the colony, at the distance of two miles, they were stopped by the governor and twenty-six men well armed. The *Brulés* were at that time but thirteen, including the Canadians. A few words arose between the governor and one of our men. The former ordered his men to fire, when two only, with much reluctance, obeyed. The fire was immediately returned by the *Brulés,* when seven instantly fell. A retreat was begun by the Hudson's-Bay people; but out of twenty-six, only four escaped. Officers killed, Governor Semple, Messrs. M'Lean, Rogers, Holt, Wilkinson, and Doctor White. A Mr. Burke, who commanded their artillery, was wounded and is now a prisoner here with three others. The *Brulés* had only one man killed, and one wounded. They took the fort, with a great quantity of arms and ammunition, and have sworn vengeance against every description of Hudson's-Bay men. Even the Indians attached to the interests of the latter, were obliged to come under the banners of the *Brulés.* They were commanded by six officers, some of whom you know.[22] This happened on the 19th of June, and we arrived on the 23rd.

Lord Selkirk is coming up in person with a strong force, expecting, no doubt, to carry every thing before him. His body-guard was taken from him before leaving Montreal, as the regiment was disbanded. He has however hired some of them on his own account. We expect him daily. His friend Miles M'Donell with two canoes went in almost to *Bas de la Rivière;*[23] but on learning from the Indians the above intelligence, he thought proper to change his course, and immediately returned to wait his Lordship's orders. Five of the canoes are stuck fast near this place, one further on, and three have returned to the *Sault* in a state of mutiny. By this you may see what his Lordship's prospects may be.

Fort William, 30th July, 1826

My Dear Cox,

Times have much altered since I have been on this side of the mountains. The habits of indolence which I acquired on the banks of the Columbia, render every thing on this busy bustling scene rather disagreeable; and, to add to my vexation, notwithstanding my long services, and my exertions to

[22] The leader of this party, Mr. Alexander Fraser, is the same individual who lost his life at the commencement of the year 1829 in Paris, in a quarrel with a Mr. Warren, who was subsequently tried for the offence, and sentenced to eighteen months imprisonment. Mr. Fraser was wholly blameless in the unfortunate affair, which ended in his death.—R. C.

[23] This was the name given to the mouth of the Winnipeg River. *George Simpson's Journal,* 164.

avoid it, I have been appointed to winter in a most villanous starving post, with a strong force of Hudson's Bay to oppose me.

Mr. Clarke was remarkably unfortunate in his Athabasca expedition. He lost numbers of his people from starvation; and in order to save the remainder he was forced to capitulate, surrender his fort, and the whole of his property.

At Red River, during the winter, the Hudson's Bay drove all before them. They took several of our forts, and made a prisoner of one of our proprietors (Mr. Cameron) whom they sent to the Bay, to be from thence transmitted for trial to England. They met however with a severe blow in the spring. They attacked a party of half-breeds, and were defeated with the loss of twenty-five men, including three officers. Their forts and provisions fell into our hands, their men were made prisoners, and the whole of their Colonists and traders were driven out of the Red River.

We are daily expecting Lord Selkirk with a force of two hundred men from Montreal, but he will be undoubtedly forced to retreat from want of provisions. He is yet ignorant of the disasters that have befallen his favourite Colony. What the result will be, time must determine.

The writers of those letters were two of the most moderate men in our Company; but from the apathy they evince in speaking of the ruthless massacre of the unfortunate settlers, the *esprit de corps* which animated the fighting members may be conjectured. In fact, the infernal spirit of rivalry had attained such a height, that the mildest and bravest of both parties became in turn the most reckless desperadoes. Force was the only tribunal to which they appealed, and arms their only arguments.

The peace with the United States had thrown idle in Canada a number of soldiers whose regiments had been disbanded. Among those was de Meuron's regiment, upwards of two hundred of which were engaged by Lord Selkirk, as a *corps d'observation,* to awe the North-Westers. On hearing however of the fate of the Colonists at Red River, he did not think it prudent to venture beyond Fort William, and immediately returned to the seat of government in Canada. A number of the most influential members of the rival Companies had been the year before appointed magistrates for the Indian territory; and owing to the representations of his Lordship, as to the manner in which his Majesty's subjects were murdering each other with impunity, the Governor-General issued a proclamation, commanding the immediate arrest of all persons concerned in the recent outrages, and threatening with the severest punishment all future breaches of the peace.[24] His Excellency also appointed Messrs. Coltman[25] and Fletcher,[26] two gentlemen of the highest respectability, and unconnected with either Company, as commissioners to proceed forthwith to the Indian country, for the purpose of investigating into the origin of the outrages, and to order the arrest of all persons implicated, with a view to their being transmitted to Canada for trial. It was however rather late in the season to proceed to the interior, and their departure was therefore delayed until the spring of 1817.

In the mean time, the war was carried on with unabated vigour during the winter of 1816–17. One partner, one clerk, and a few men belonging to the North-Westers, were captured by the Hudson's Bay people; but the latter were generally defeated. Several of their officers and numbers of their men were made prisoners; and some of their forts were obliged to capitulate on unconditional terms.

The spirit of ruinous competition had at this period gained such a height, that the prices given to the Indians for their furs, after deducting the expenses of carriage and other contingent charges, far exceeded their value to the Company. Their profits became sensibly diminished, and the persons who derived the greatest benefits from the opposition were the clerks and other *employés*.

Such was the situation of affairs when we arrived at Ile à la Crosse. As I have already mentioned, the Hudson's Bay establishment at this place had been captured the preceding winter by the North-West, and the officer in charge sent forward to join some more of his companions in captivity.

We remained a couple of days at the fort to refresh the men, and were hospitably entertained by our hosts on excellent white-fish, and tea without sugar. One of those gentlemen, Mr. Peter Ogden, was nearly related to a high judicial functionary, and in early life was destined for the same profession. The study of provincial jurispru-

---

[24] This document was forwarded by express to the interior, and treated with sovereign contempt by the majority of those to whom it was addressed.—R. C.

[25] William Batchelor Coltman was a merchant of Quebec who in 1812 was appointed a member of the Executive Council of Lower Canada. In 1816, he was sent as a commissioner to investigate the disturbances in the Indian countries, and in 1817, he visited Red River. His report is in Vol. IV of the *Collections of the State Historical Society of North Dakota*. See Wallace, *Documents*, 433.

[26] John Fletcher was born in England and became a member of the English bar. In 1810, he was appointed one of the commissioners to investigate the Selkirk disturbances, but he did not go farther west than Lake Superior. See Wallace, *Documents*, 442.

dence, and the seignorial subdivisions of Canadian property, had no charms for the mercurial temperament of Mr. Ogden; and, contrary to the wishes of his friends, he preferred the wild and untrammelled life of an Indian trader, to the "law's delay," and the wholesome restraints which are provided for the correction of overexuberant spirits in civilised society. His accounts of his various rencontres with Orkney men and Indians would have filled a moderate-sized octavo, and if reduced to writing would undoubtedly stagger the credulity of any person unacquainted with the Indian country; and although some of his statements were slightly tinctured with the prevalent failing of *La Guienne,* there was *vraisemblance* enough throughout to command our belief in their general accuracy. In a country, however, in which there is no legal tribunal to appeal to, and into which the "King's writ does not run," many acts must be committed that would not stand a strict investigation in *Banco Regis.* "My legal primer," said Ogden, "says that necessity has no law; and in this place, where the custom of the country, or as lawyers say, the *Les non scripta* is our only guide, we must, in our acts of summary legislation, sometimes perform the parts of judge, jury, sheriff, hangman, gallows and all!"

Chapter 26

English River—Pass numerous lakes and rapids—Arrive at Cumberland House—Saskachawane River—Lake Winepic—Aurora Borealis—River Winepic—Meet various parties—Rainy Lake and Fort—Death of an Indian

SUNDAY, JUNE 29TH. At half-past eleven A. M. this day we bid adieu to the humorous, honest, eccentric, law-defying Peter Ogden, the terror of Indians, and the delight of all gay fellows.

It blew pretty fresh during the day, which obliged us to keep our square-sail closely reefed. We generally kept from two to six miles from shore, and occasionally shipped a good deal of water. Encamped at eight P. M. at the extremity of the lake. It is computed to be eighteen leagues in length, and from three to five in breadth, and is indented by a number of deep bays, the shores of which were at times scarcely visible with the naked eye. A few islands are scattered over it, on which we observed immense numbers of pelicans.

JUNE 30TH. Embarked at three A. M. At five, passed the Portage Sonnant,[1] which was followed by several bad rapids, through which we ran without unloading. At six, passed Cariboeuf River, celebrated for its excellent fish, and at eight passed the Portage de la Puisse, where we stopped to breakfast and repair the canoes. At half-past two, passed the Portage des Anglais; and at six crossed Knee Lake, a pretty large body of water. Encamped at eight at La Rivière Croche: charming weather all day.

JULY 1ST, 1817. Embarked at three A. M. and at four overtook

---

[1] Cox has now entered the English River (the upper part of the Churchill River), which has many lakes, rapids, and obstructions along its course, thus making necessary much portaging.

309

the loaded canoes, which we passed. Crossed Lac du Sable with a stiff breeze, and shot down Les Rapides des Serpens, without unloading. This brought us into Lac des Serpens, which we crossed with a fair wind at half-past ten, and immediately after entered Lac des Souris; at the end of which we breakfasted. Continued on at noon with a fine breeze across Lac des Epingles, and at half past-two passed the portage at its termination. At three passed the Portage des Bouleaux, at which we only took out half the loading; and at four passed another portage called Le Canot Cassé. Shortly after crossed Le Lac d'Huile d'Ours with a fair wind, and encamped at six, a little below *Le Rapide qui ne parle point*. Four lodges of the Chepewyan Indians were near our encampment, from whom we purchased a small quantity of meat. We also caught nine excellent pike. It rained occasionally during the evening. Saw three moose and five bears, but could not get a shot at them.

JULY 2ND. On examining our nets this morning we found only six pike, a miserable supply for so many people. Set off at three A. M. with a fair wind, and had tolerably good navigation until eight, when we arrived at the Portage des Halliers, at the southern end of which we breakfasted. At one passed the Portage de Traite; at two, that of the Petit Rocher, and at three, a demi-portage called Les Ecors, where the lading only was carried. Encamped at five, at La Rivière des Côtes, where we expected to make a good haul with our nets. We caught ten pike during the day at the different portages. Saw two large bears, but could not hit them. Weather very warm.

JULY 3RD. Our nets this morning produced thirty white-fish, pike, pickerel and carp. Embarked at three A. M. and crossed Le Lac du Diable with a fair breeze. At six finished the Portage du Diable on the left side. The road is long, crooked, and narrow; which accounts, I should suppose, for the name given by the Canadians to the portage. A small lake next followed, which brought us to a chain of short ugly rapids called Les Petits Diables, down which we shot without unloading, but damaged the canoes considerably. At the end of the last "Little Devil," we were obliged to unload the trading packages, &c. At this place the water forces its way through three small straits into a lake about five miles long, which is terminated by Le Rapide de l'Outre, at the end of which we breakfasted. At ten renewed our progress, and entered Le Lac de l'Outre, which brought us to a portage called Le Petit Rocher de la Montagne, which we finished at half-past twelve. At two made the Portage de la Montagne. The distance between the two portages does not exceed half a mile, and they derive their name from high rocky eminences in the vicinity. Encamped at five, at the south end of Le Lac de la Queue Dépouillée; where we set our nets. Passed some fine rising grounds during the day, well stocked with spruce, poplar, birch, cypress, and willow. Near the water's edge, we observed quantities of wild gooseberry, currant, strawberry, blue-berry, &c.

JULY 4TH. Caught only twenty carp, pike, and white-fish. Started at three. At five arrived at the entrance of Rivière au Rapide, where there are a couple of small houses for the rendezvous of the people belonging to Lac la Ronge,[2] a trading establishment situated about six leagues from this place. As this was esteemed a capital fishing spot, we sent on the loaded canoes, and remained ourselves here the remainder of the day, to recruit our stock of provisions. Weather very sultry all day.

JULY 5TH. Caught only thirty fish, seventeen of which were speared. Embarked at three, and in half an hour afterwards made the portage of La Rivière au Rapide, which is very short. This brought us into a handsome lake, and at six made the Portage de l'Ile, over a small island, by which a circuitous passage by the river is considerably shortened. After re-embarking we passed through another lake interspersed with islands, which brought us to a narrow rapid channel, through which we passed until we arrived at Portage de Barril at eight o'clock, where we overtook the loaded canoes. They had only caught fish enough for breakfast. After quitting this place we entered another lake a few miles in extent, in the centre of which was a very bad rapid. At nine arrived at another portage called Le Grande Rapide du Fort de Traite. It is the longest carrying place on English River. Here we breakfasted and repaired the canoes. Caught also eight good pike. Proceeded on at eleven, and crossed Le Lac du Fort de Traite in three hours and a half, with rather a head-wind the greater part of the way.

At three passed the Portage du Fort de Traite,[3] which is rather long. Here took leave of the English River, which, taking the name of Churchill, turns down to Hudson's Bay. During the six days that

---

[2] Lac la Ronge is a few miles south of the English River and is connected with the latter by a small stream, then called the Rapid River, but now known as the Montreal River.

[3] This is Frog Portage.

we were sailing down this river, we crossed sixteen lakes, and passed upwards of thirty rapids, at sixteen of which we were obliged to make portages.

A little after three P. M. entered a small river[4] with an imperceptible current, in which we had not proceeded more than half a mile, when it widened considerably, and presented to our view an extensive prospect of fine flat country, bounded at a great distance by well-wooded hills. A little further on, the channel again became quite contracted, and more difficult to navigate, owing to several small islands interrupting the course of the current. At one *détroit,* we were obliged to unload and carry the goods some distance. This brought us to a lake which we crossed at half-past four, and on the shores of which we encamped, for the purpose of trying to procure a supper of fish. Killed two hares, a pair of ducks, and a brace of partridges during the day, which we boiled with *tripe de rocher,* a species of nutritive moss growing on the rocks, and which made excellent soup.

JULY 6TH. Embarked at three. Our nets only produced four fish this morning. Entered Lac du Bois at half-past three, and crossed it in five hours. It is a fine body of water, surrounded by a champaign country, tolerably well wooded. At the end of the lake made three small portages close to each other, and about two miles lower down made half a portage, called Le Décharge au Lac du Bois, all which we completed at half-past ten A. M. Mr. Stewart's canoe and mine remained here the rest of the day to fish; one only of the loaded canoes joined us. Dined and supped chiefly on *tripe de rocher.*

JULY 7TH. We caught during the night, with the net, lines, and spears, fifty well-assorted fish, which gave a tolerable meal to our half-starved hard-working men. Set off at the usual hour. At seven crossed Pelican Lake, at which we stopped to breakfast. Here also we caught a few carp.

Proceeded on at nine, and shortly after arrived at the head of Lac Miron, where we remained till noon wind-bound. The weather having moderated a little, we embarked about a quarter-past twelve, but had not reached more than the centre of the lake when we were overtaken by a storm of thunder, and heavy rain, accompanied by dreadful squalls from every quarter of the compass. To return was impossible, and we continued occasionally shipping large quantities of water, and

[4] The small stream is the headwaters of the present Sturgeon-Weir River. Cox has now crossed into the watershed of the Saskatchewan River.

momentarily expecting to be upset by the violence of the storm. We crossed, however, in safety; and at four, encamped at the Portage d'Epinettes, for the purpose of drying ourselves, and spreading the nets. The weather continued rainy and squally during the night.

JULY 8TH. This morning only produced five pike for the two canoes. Started at half-past three. At four, made the short Portage de l'Ile; and at half-past seven passed the Portage des Bouleaux dans la Rivière Creuse. It was long and slippery, owing to the recent rains. Shortly below it, ran down a dangerous rapid, called la Carpe, without unloading, and were near perishing from the intricacy of the channel. At nine, made the Portage de la Carpe, at the end of which we breakfasted, repaired the canoes, and caught twenty white-fish with a kind of hook formed by one of the men out of the handle of the cooking-kettle. Proceeded on at noon, through a clear channel, until three P. M. when we arrived at the Rapide des Ecors, which we shot down without unloading. At five, made the Portage de la Pente, after which a steady uninterrupted current brought us, at half-past six, to Lac Castor.[5] Here Mr. Stewart's canoe took the lead, and we continued on in a heavy gale and thunderstorm until night overtook us in the centre of the lake. We were for some time in a very critical situation, owing to the darkness, which was only relieved by an occasional flash of lightning. We at length approached the shore, and observed a long, high, and rocky point, which it would be madness to attempt to double. Orders were therefore given to land at the most practicable part; and, after beating about for some time in search of a beach, we succeeded about eleven o'clock in running the canoes into a small cove at the southern end of the point. It rained on us the whole night, and we had not a mouthful of provisions.

JULY 9TH. The gale continued without intermission, accompanied by heavy rain all the forenoon; and owing to our tent being in Mr. Stewart's canoe, we were deprived of any shelter. About five P. M. the weather moderated, and enabled us to push off. We doubled the point in safety, after which we hoisted sail, and in half an hour afterwards joined Mr. Stewart, who had encamped at the head of La Rivière Maligne, where he waited our arrival. Stopped here the remainder of the day, being anxious to ascertain how the loaded canoes had weathered out the gale. The unsettled state of the wind prevented us from catching any fish, and we were obliged to retire again on this night to our stony couch supperless.

[5] Beaver Lake.

JULY 10TH. Embarked at three A. M. and entered La Rivière Maligne.[6] We had not proceeded far, when, in running down La Rapide Croche, our canoe came in contact with the rocks, by which eight ribs were broken, and it was otherwise badly damaged. This delayed us some time to repair. After launching again we had not proceeded through more than two or three miles of smooth water, when we got into a chain of shallow, crooked, and rocky rapids, in every one of which we sustained more or less injury. At eight A. M. passed the mouth of Rat River,[7] a small stream; and within a quarter of nine, arrived at the termination of La Rivière Maligne, where it discharges its waters into Cumberland House Lake. This river is most appropriately named by the Canadians; for I believe, for its length, it is the most dangerous, cross-grained piece of navigation in the Indian country.

Owing to a head-wind, we were unable to proceed until half-past four P. M., when it veered about in our favour. We instantly hoisted sail, and made the Grande Traverse in three hours. Encamped at nine on a low muddy beach. Caught three small fish, which were boiled with some *tripe de rocher*, and afforded a spoonful of soup to each of the poor famished men.

JULY 11TH. Started at two A. M., and a short distance above our encampment passed the lodge of a fisherman belonging to Cumberland House, from whom we obtained a most welcome and seasonable supply of three prime sturgeon. At four, made the Traverse de l'Ile with a strong side breeze, when we landed to allow time to our hungry *voyageurs* to regale themselves on the fisherman's supply. A roaring fire quickly crackled on the beach, and in less than an hour the sturgeon entirely disappeared. Proceeded on at six, and at seven arrived at Cumberland House,[8] of which we found a gentleman named Fairis[9]

[6] The stream to which this name is given flows from Beaver Lake into Namen Lake and is about twenty-five miles long.

[7] The Goose River. Rat Portage is just above the junction of the two streams.

[8] In 1774, Samuel Hearne of the Hudson's Bay Company built a post at the eastern end of the lake which was given the name in honor of Prince Rupert, Duke of Cumberland, first governor of the Hudson's Bay Company. It was considered a very strategic spot. In 1780, the North West Company erected a post which it also named Cumberland House and located it about one hundred yards from its rival station. It was at the north end of the lake and on a river called the Little English or Tearing River. This post was also known as Fort Sturgeon Lake. See Vorhis, *Historic Forts,* 57.

[9] Hugh Faries or Farris (1779–1852) was born in Montreal and joined the North West Company at some time before 1804, when he was a clerk at Rainy Lake. He was

in charge, who treated us to an excellent breakfast of tea, fish, and steaks. Remained here during the day to recruit the men.

At this period the rival Companies had large forts here, which were well fortified; but no breach of the peace had occurred during the winter between the respective traders. Friendly intercourse was out of the question, and a suspicious kind of armed neutrality was preserved on each side.

The country round Cumberland House is low, with a rich soil and thinly wooded. Land animals are scarce; but the lake furnishes an abundance of white-fish, pike, and sturgeon. A few horses are employed about the forts chiefly for domestic purposes. The Indians who occasionally visit it, are a friendly well-disposed tribe, rather addicted to the use of ardent spirits.

JULY 12TH. Sent off the loaded canoes at one P. M.; but did not start ourselves till five, when we took our leave of Mr. Fairis, and shortly afterwards encamped on an island not far from the fort.

JULY 13TH. At three A. M. embarked, and entered the Saskachawane River,[10] a noble broad stream with a strong steady current, uninterrupted by rapids. According to Canadian computation, we made forty-nine leagues before night set in. I doubt the accuracy of this calculation, although we certainly made wonderful progress. The country on each side of the river is extremely low, and totally devoid of timber, but is dreadfully prolific in mosquitoes. Those insects swarmed about us in such myriads, that we in vain attempted to effect a landing, and to preserve the small quantity of blood still remaining in our veins, were constrained to pass the entire night on the water, driving quietly and calmly down the current. Numerous parties however of the enemy occasionally swarmed about our heads, which we partially protected by constant smoking.

Early on the morning of the 14th we entered Lac Vasé, and made the first traverse in Lac Bourbon[11] with a fair wind, but in the midst of the most dangerous swells.

one of the first officers of that company to cross the Rocky Mountains, being at Fort George in New Caledonia in 1807. From 1812 to 1817 he was at Cumberland House. In 1821, he became a chief trader and in 1838 a chief factor. See Wallace, *Documents,* 439.

10 The Saskatchewan River.

11 Cedar Lake is about thirty miles long and in reality only an expansion of the river. See "Edward Ermatinger's York Factory Express Journal," 90, n. 4. Lac Vasé is a small overflow at the discharge of the river into Lake Bourbon. It is now known as Muddy Lake. See Franchère, *Narrative,* 377.

The wind having increased to a heavy gale, we were obliged to put ashore at eight o'clock on Martel's Island, where we were detained until four P. M., when we were enabled to proceed. Passed the Grande Traverse of Bourbon Lake in moderate weather, and encamped at ten P. M. on a low stony island, which we selected in consequence of its being free from musquitoes. Here we found several hundred gull's eggs, on which we made an excellent supper. The weather for the last few days was extremely sultry, with thunder and lightning at intervals. This night we found it rather cool.

JULY 15TH. Embarked at three A. M. Hard rain during the morning. On quitting Bourbon Lake we entered a long strait full of dangerous rapids, which brought us to Lac de Travers[12] about five miles in breadth. On leaving this we entered another chain of dangerous rapids, which finally brought us, at seven A. M., to the great rapid[13] of Lac Winepic. This exceeded by far, in body of water and general magnitude, any rapid I had seen to the eastward of the Rocky Mountains. The canoes were let down for a distance of three miles with double lines; and in some places, where large rocks projected into the river, the lading was taken out, and carried to the other side of the point. Reached the foot of the rapid without any accident, at a quarter before nine, where we stopped to breakfast. Four Canadian free trappers, named Montreuil, Raçette, Martin, and son, were encamped at this place with their squaws. As it blew too hard to attempt entering Lake Winepic, we pitched our tents and partook of an excellent breakfast with old Martin, consisting of cherry-tree tea, with boiled and fried sturgeon. Late in the evening we were agreeably surprised by the arrival of a party bound to the interior, consisting of Messrs. John D. Campbell,[14] Alexander M'Donell, Samuel Black,[15] and my old

12 Cross Lake. The greatest extent of this lake was north and south so that it was crossed rather than traversed. See Franchère, *Narrative*, 377.

13 The Grand Rapids of the Saskatchewan are just above its outlet into Lake Winnipeg.

14 John Duncan Campbell (1773–1835) was born in New York, the son of a United Empire Loyalist who migrated to Canada. He entered the North West Company before 1799 and spent a part of this time of service in the English River district. In 1803, he became a partner. He was involved in the Selkirk troubles and on the merger of the two companies retired from the fur trade. See Wallace, *Documents,* 431.

15 Samuel Black (d. 1841) was a native of Aberdeen, Scotland, and was born about 1785. In 1802, he became a clerk with the XY Company and two years later joined the North West Company. He was very active in the struggle against the Hudson's Bay Company and in 1821, along with Peter Skene Ogden, was excluded from the merger. But in 1823, he was admitted as a chief trader, and in 1837, he became a chief factor.

Columbian companion, M'Kay, with sixteen men and two canoes. They pitched their tents alongside ours; and as their garde-vins were tolerably well stocked, we sat up the entire night swallowing the news which they brought from the civilised world.

JULY 16TH. Embarked at three A. M., having previously purchased from Martin six sturgeon for each canoe. The morning was calm and cloudy as our little flotilla entered the great waters of Lake Winepic. About eight o'clock a smart breeze sprung up, which enabled us to hoist sail. At ten it increased to a close-reefer, and we scudded along for a couple of hours in glorious style; at times two or three miles from the shore. About noon, however, the gale became so violent that we were compelled to make the best of our way to a landing-place, where we pitched our tents for the day.

JULY 17TH. It blew a perfect hurricane the entire day, which prevented us from attempting to embark.

JULY 18TH. Shortly after midnight the gale moderated, and at half-past one this morning we set off in calm weather. About sun-rise a favourable breeze sprang up, which wafted us on till twelve, when its increasing violence again obliged us to seek the shore, a few miles above La Pointe Maligne;[16] a long rocky neck of land so called, which stretches some distance into the lake, and which in stormy weather is difficult to double. Remained here until six P. M., when the gale having moderated, we again embarked and continued on all night, alternately with the sail and the paddle.

JULY 19TH. Light fair breezes wafted us on gently during the greater part of the day. They rather impeded than accelerated our progress; for by the custom of voyaging, the paddles are laid aside while the sail is hoisted, and the men very naturally keep it up while the smallest breath ruffles the water. At four passed l'Ile de St. Martin; and at eight, encamped at a point called La Tête de Picheu. Weather dark and calm during the night.

JULY 20TH. Embarked at two A. M., with a stiff breeze, which brought us past La Tête de Brochet in fine style. The wind having increased to a hard gale, we put ashore at half-past eleven, at the south side of the Traverse des Iles d'Ecorce, which it would be dangerous to attempt passing in stormy weather. About five it moderated,

In 1841, he was murdered near the mouth of the Columbia River. See Wallace, *Documents*, 426.

[16] Probably the long point, or the Grand Detour.

and we continued on with a fair wind all evening. The navigation here being rather dangerous, and the weather extremely dark, it was judged prudent to encamp at ten P. M., in a snug little cove on the northern shore, about half-way between La Tête de Chien and Le Détroit du Duc. The country all round was in a state of conflagration, the smoke from which was quite suffocating. The scene was magnificent, and there was imparted to it a terrible degree of interest by the howling of wolves and other beasts of prey, which the extending flames forced from their long-frequented haunts.

The Aurora Borealis too appeared in all its splendid kaleidoscope variety of forms. At times a vertical battalion of strange figures seemed to rush in fierce encounter on an horizontal phalanx; the whole mass became mingled, and in an instant flew off into new and more fantastic shapes. A loud and crackling noise occasionally struck on our ears, and it was difficult to determine whether it proceeded from the evanescent meteors above, or the falling timbers of the burning forest below.

JULY 21ST. Left our encampment at half-past two A. M. And at five passed through a small strait called Le Détroit du Duc,[17] where the two shores approach to within a quarter of a mile of each other. Beyond this, however, the lake again widens to five leagues.

At ten a smart breeze sprung up. Met two Indians (Sauteus)[18] in a small canoe close to a rocky point called Le Tête de Bœuf, from whom we purchased a small quantity of dried meat. At noon a hard gale came on, accompanied by thunder, heavy rain, and dangerous squalls. We, however, continued on for some time; but having shipped a good deal of water, we were forced to put ashore a few miles below another strait, named Le Détroit de la Tête be Bœuf, at which place we stopped for the remainder of the day.

JULY 22ND. Embarked at four A. M., with a steady breeze, which continued the greater part of the day. At noon doubled La Point de Metasse in a hard gale, which nearly filled the canoes. Here we breakfasted, and at two P. M. arrived at Fort Alexander,[19] situated at the end of Lake Winepic, and at the entrance of Winepic River. Messrs.

[17] The Narrows.

[18] The Soteux, Saulteus, or Saulteaux Indians were members of the great Chipewyan family that inhabited the region around Lake Huron and Lake Superior.

[19] Fort Alexander was built in 1792 about three miles from the mouth of the Winnipeg River, and was also known as Fort Bas-de-la-Rivière. See Vorhis, *Historic Forts*, 30, 38.

Montreal in 1803
from a painting by Richard Dillon

Bytown (Ottawa) in 1830

The Trapper's Bride

from a water color by A. J. Miller

Heron[20] and Crebassâ[21] were in charge, with three men and a dozen women.

JULY 23RD. Remained at Fort Alexander until three P. M. when we bid adieu to our friend Mr. Alexander Stewart, who was not to proceed beyond this place. We previously sent off the loaded canoes at an early hour in the morning.

Winepic River is greatly obstructed by rapids; at numbers of which portages must be made, or part of the goods unloaded. In the last case they are only called *Décharges*. It would be tiresome and useless to give the various names by which the Canadians distinguish those places. We passed six in the afternoon, and encamped at dusk at the head of Portage des Chênes.

JULY 24TH. Set off at day-break, and encamped at seven P. M., after having made five portages during the day. In passing through Lac de Bonnet, we met Mr. Hughes,[22] a proprietor, who with six men in a canoe was proceeding to Forts des Prairies, of which department he had charge. Weather extremely sultry.

JULY 25TH. Commenced our morning's work by making seven portages "all in a row," at the upper end of which we stopped to breakfast and repair the canoes. Here we were overtaken by Mr. Crebassâ in a light canoe with twelve men, on his way to Fort William with dispatches. Encamped late at the end of Portage Brûlé.

JULY 26TH. We had much thunder and torrents of rain the greater part of last night, by which our goods and covering were quite wet. Remained a few hours at the encampment to dry our clothes, &c. At eight A. M. Mr. Leith,[23] one of the proprietors, accompanied by Lieu-

---

[20] James Heron (fl. 1812–1832) was a native of county Donegal, Ireland. He entered the employ of the Hudson's Bay Company in 1812 but deserted three years later because "of bad treatment." In 1817, he was with the North West Company at Fort Alexander. In 1832, he was discharged from the service and retired to Canada. See Wallace, *Documents,* 458.

[21] John Crebassa was a former XY Company clerk who had been in the district since about 1801. See Franchère, *Narrative,* 369 n.

[22] James Hughes (1772–1853) had entered the service of the North West Company about 1791 and had served from 1798 to 1817 in the Fort des Prairies department, during which time he had become a partner. In 1821, he retired but ran through his savings, and in 1830, at the age of sixty, he entered the employ of the Hudson's Bay Company as a clerk. See Wallace, *Documents,* 458–59.

[23] James Leith (1777–1838) was born in Scotland and had been with the XY Company before joining the North West Company in 1804. He had served at several different posts. In 1816, he was at Rainy Lake and the next year was sent to Red River to arrest some of Selkirk's men. He retired in 1830. See Wallace, *Documents,* 461.

tenant Austin of the 37th Foot, with thirteen of his regiment, and twelve well-armed Iroquois, arrived at our encampment. They were on their way to Red River, for the purpose of arresting all the delinquents they could catch, who had been concerned in the recent outrages. We stopped to breakfast with them. While it was preparing, I asked one of the soldiers (an Irishman), how he liked the mode of travelling in that country? "By J——, Sir," he replied, "it's awkward enough. Here we are cramped up in a bit of a canoe, put like chayney gods, with our muskets and knapsacks, striving to keep our clothes and coutrements clane. We haven't seen a sign of Christianity these two or three months; nor even a horse, or a cow, or a sheep; nothing during the entire day; just rocks, rivers, lakes, portages, waterfalls, and large forests; bears roaring a tattoo every night, and wolves howling a *réveille* every morning. O! to the devil I bob it!—Give me India or Spain, with all their hard fighting, before such an infernal, outlandish, unchristian country."

Parted from those gentlemen a little after nine o'clock, and shortly after overtook the brigade of loaded canoes. Passed two lodges of Sauteus, and encamped late a few miles above Portage de l'Ile. Weather during the day excessively sultry.

July 27th. Embarked at day-break. About five A. M. Colonel Dickson, and a gentleman named Gale, passed us on their route to Red River. Their journey also was connected with the investigation ordered by the Governor-General. About an hour afterwards we met Messrs. Simon M'Gillivray, jun., and Roderick M'Leod,[24] with two canoes, bound for Athabasca; we remained to breakfast with them and stopped a couple of hours. A smacking breeze during the greater part of the day gave the men considerable relief from paddling.

Encamped at seven P. M. a few miles below the Portage des Rats.

July 28th. Passed Rat Portage early.[25] A few lodges of natives were encamped at it, from whom we could purchase nothing. On quitting this portage we entered Lac du Bois,[26] with tolerably calm weather. We employed the paddle and sail alternately, until one P. M., when we arrived at a long and narrow peninsula, which stretches a

[24] Alexander Roderick McLeod (d. 1840) became an employee of the North West Company in 1802 and two years later was at Rocky Mountain House. In 1821, he was at the Grand Portage and by the merger became a chief trader. In 1825, he was at Fort Vancouver. In 1839, he returned to Canada and died the next year. See Wallace, *Documents,* 480.

[25] Rat Portage was where the river flows from the Lake of the Woods.

[26] The Lake of the Woods.

considerable distance into the lake. A portage was made across this point in a short time, by which the tedious and circuitous passage round its extremity was avoided. We observed great quantities of wild rice growing here, which the Canadians called *la folle avoine*. Had a fair wind all the afternoon, and encamped at half-past seven, within three leagues of the Grande Traverse.

JULY 29TH. Observed some faint appearances of the Aurora Borealis during the night. Set off at day-break, and at ten A. M. passed the Grande Traverse with a light breeze. This brought us to Lac la Pluie River,[27] at the entrance of which we passed a few natives. During the evening passed a Mr. Grant, with a few men, who were returning in a canoe to the fort at Lac la Pluie,[28] from a provision voyage. Encamped at seven P. M.

JULY 30TH. Set off at the usual hour. At two P. M. met Mr. M'Pherson,[29] with a brigade of eleven loaded canoes, bound for Athabasca. Not a *voyageur* in the whole party, at the period we met them, could be accused of sobriety. Encamped at dusk.

JULY 31ST. At nine A. M. arrived at the fort of Lac la Pluie,[30] in which we found a number of gentlemen, guides, interpreters, and *engagés*, some outward-bound, and others belonging to various departments destined for the interior. Among them was my old esteemed friend, Mr. La Rocque, whose name frequently occurs in the eventful scenes of the Columbia, to which place he was now about returning with a reinforcement of forty men, principally Iroquois Indians, from Canada.

We remained seven days at Lac la Pluie, waiting the arrival of goods from Fort William, and making the necessary distribution of men, &c., for the different trading posts. This place is a considerable depot of provisions; so that during our stay we fared sumptuously

27 The Rainy River.
28 Rainy Lake.
29 Murdock McPherson (1796?–1863) was born in Scotland and became associated with the North West Company in 1816. In 1817, when Cox met him, he was en route to the Athabaska. In 1834, he became a chief trader with the merged company and in 1847 a chief factor. He retired in 1851. Wallace, *Documents,* 483.
30 The North West Company had built a post at the outlet of Rainy Lake, a short distance down the river. It was captured by Lord Selkirk's men in October, 1816, but the following September the North West Company reacquired possession. Later, a Hudson's Bay Company post was established in the vicinity. See Vorhis, *Historic Forts,* 157–58; and Sir George Simpson, *Journal of Occurrences in the Athabasca Department,* edited by E. E. Rich (Toronto, The Champlain Society, 1938), 418.

on cakes, pemmican, tea, coffee, wild-fowl, fish, and deer; with a moderate modicum of rum and shrub. We had two excellent fiddlers; and as several of the gentlemen had wives, we got up three or four balls, in which the exhilarating amusement of the "light fantastic toe" was kept up to a late hour in the morning. We walked through no lazy minuets; we had no simpering quadrilles; no languishing half-dying waltzes; no, ours was the exercise of health; the light lively reel, or the rattling good old-fashioned country dance, in which the graceful though untutored movements of the North-West females would have put to the blush many of the more refined votaries of Terpsichore.

Several lodges of Sotoes, or as the Canadians spell the word *Sauteus,* were encamped near the fort. They were formerly a very powerful tribe; but the small-pox, war, and rum, have considerably diminished their numbers. They are greatly addicted to the use of ardent spirits, and make a point never to commence a barter of their furs until a suitable quantity of rum be given to them gratuitously. When they recover from the intoxication produced by this preliminary debauch, they proceed to business. A certain portion of their furs is set apart for a gun, another for ammunition, a third for blankets, a fourth for tomahawks or knives, a fifth for tobacco, a sixth for the wants of the wife and children, and then a portion for rum.

I visited the encampment of this party after they had finished their trade. The men were gambling and drinking to excess. While joy sparkled in the eyes of some, others, whose losses had been great, looked like demons. A dispute arose between two fine young men respecting a knife. One gave his antagonist a blow across the face, upon which the other darted to his lodge, seized his gun, and taking a deadly aim shot the aggressor through the body. He was in the act of drinking rum out of a pint measure, when he received the fatal bullet. He did not start, no feature changed, and he walked on, singing a war-song, carrying the rum in his hand, until he raised his foot to pass over the threshold of his lodge, when he fell dead at the door.

A scene of indescribable confusion followed. Each warrior ran for his gun, dagger, or tomahawk, while the women and children flew towards the fort for protection. Fearful that an indiscriminate massacre would be the consequence, a number of gentlemen rushed among them and with much persuasion, joined to some force, succeeded in disarming the more violent, and restoring tranquillity. Compensation was ultimately made to the relatives of the deceased; and so terminated this drunken homicide.

Chapter 27

Leave Rainy Lake—Messrs. M'Gillivray and La Rocque—Sketch of Messrs. Wentzel and M'Neill—Great falls of the mountain—Description of Fort William, its inhabitants, &c.

THURSDAY, AUGUST 7TH. At two P. M. took our departure from Lac la Pluie for Fort William, in two light canoes, containing nine *voyageurs* each. Messrs. Robert Henry[1] and Alexander M'Tavish were in one; and Messrs. Ferdinand Wentzel,[2] Hector M'Neill, and myself, were in the other. Mr. La Rocque and party set off at the same time for the Columbia; and Messrs. Joseph M'Gillivray and William Henry[3] for Athabasca and Lesser Slave Lake.

By the new distribution, I was deprived of the pleasure of my friend M'Tavish's company, which I much regretted; however, as we were to proceed together in the same brigade to Canada, the separation was infinitely less painful than that which I experienced in parting from my old friends M'Gillivray and La Rocque.

We had spent many happy days together on the banks of the dis-

[1]Robert Henry (1778–1859) was an adopted nephew of Alexander Henry, the elder, and had joined the North West Company as a clerk. In 1810, he became a partner. From 1811 to 1815 he was in the Athabaska department and retired two years later. See Wallace, *Documents,* 457.

[2] William Ferdinand Wentzel (fl. 1799–1832) was of Norwegian ancestry, his father being a merchant in Montreal. In 1799, he became a member of the North West Company and was for many years a clerk in the Athabaska district. He joined the Hudson's Bay Company at the time of the merger but retired from the fur trade in 1825. See Wallace, *Documents,* 505.

[3] William Henry (1783?–1864?) was the eldest son of Alexander Henry, the elder, who had joined the North West Company in 1801 and served as a clerk in several districts including the Athabaska and Red River. From 1812 to 1816 he was on the Columbia and in 1817 was at Fort William. He apparently retired in 1823. See Wallace, *Documents,* 457.

tant Columbia. Our studies and amusements were the same. We had suffered in common many privations incident to that dangerous district; and whether in a canoe, or on horseback; over a hit of backgammon, or on the midnight watch, there was a community of feeling that peculiarly endeared us to each other. I was about re-entering the busy scenes of civilised life, while they were returning to encounter all the dangers and hardships attendant on a trader's occupation; and the pressure therefore of the parting grasp was rendered doubly painful by the reflection, that in all human probability we should never meet again.

Those only who knew them as I did, and were acquainted with their many excellent, social qualities, "their scorn for wrong, their zeal for truth," can appreciate the justice of this poor tribute to the manliness of their character, and the steady sincerity of their friendship.

About an hour after quitting the fort, we made one portage; and shortly after passed a small trading post of Lord Selkirk's.

Encamped about six P. M. on an island in the lake.

AUGUST 8TH. Embarked at half-past one A. M. Had a steady breeze all the morning. Made several portages. Messrs. H. Mackenzie[4] and M'Lean, of the North-West Company, passed us on their way to Winepic River, and shortly after we met six canoes belonging to the Hudson's Bay Company, twenty-five days from Point Meuron, bound to the interior. Passed several Indian encampments, at which we procured a quantity of wild rice. This we boiled, and took in preference to the sturgeon we were furnished with at the fort, and which had now a very *mauvaise odeur*. Encamped alone this evening, in consequence of Messrs. Henry and M'Tavish having very good-naturedly gone on ahead, and left us to manage matters as well as we could. It was not, however, with my friend M'Tavish's consent that we were left behind; for I knew he would have preferred remaining with us, had his own wishes been consulted; but when any of the little great men of the North-West obtain a command, they imagine they have no legitimate method of showing their temporary superiority, but by leaving their subordinate officers as far *en arrière* as possible.

[4] Henry McKenzie (1781?–1832) was born in Scotland and came to Canada about 1800. He was a younger brother of Roderick McKenzie and during the Selkirk troubles of 1814–18 was in charge of the publicity campaign in behalf of the North West Company. See Wallace, *Documents,* 477.

I derived much pleasure from the conversation of my two new *compagnons de voyage*, Messrs. Wentzel and M'Neill. The former had been upwards of sixteen years in the Indian country, principally in the department of Athabasca, and had obtained a thorough knowledge of the manners, customs, and language of the natives of that quarter. He was an active enterprising trader, but, having no family connexions to place his claims in the prominent point of view which they ought to occupy, and being moreover of an honest unbending disposition, his name was struck out of the house-list of favourite clerks intended for proprietors, and he had the vexation to see many young men promoted over his head, several of whom had never slept a night with a hungry stomach, or seen a shot fired in anger. Disgust followed disappointment, and he was now proceeding to Canada, determined, if justice were not rendered him by the directors, to quit the service of the Company for ever.[5]

M'Neill belonged to a highly respectable family in the north of Ireland, and had at an early age entered the ———— regiment of foot as an ensign. Owing, however, to a serious quarrel with his commanding officer, he was obliged to quit the service; and being too proud to seek any assistance from his relatives, whom he had reason to suspect were displeased at his conduct, he re-entered the army as a private soldier. He was quickly appointed a serjeant, and behaved with distinguished bravery throughout the peninsular campaigns, in which he was twice wounded.

After the battle of the Pyrenees he was promoted to the rank of serjeant-major; and upon the termination of hostilities in the south of France, his regiment with others were ordered from Bourdeaux to Canada. His American services were of short duration. Peace speedily followed Sir George Prevost's disgraceful retreat from Plattsburg, and the battalion to which M'Neill belonged was ordered to be disbanded. This unwelcome intelligence reached him at a period when he had every reason to hope that he would have been speedily restored to his former rank. Not wishing to return home, he preferred accepting his discharge in Canada, where he was shortly after introduced to one of the agents of the North-West Company, which then stood in need of a few fighting characters to make a stand against the encroachments of their rivals.

[5] This gentleman is the same whose name so frequently occurs in Captain Franklin's journal.—R. C.

M'Neill's face was in itself a letter of recommendation. His countenance was a ruddy bronze, with a noble nose of the Nassau cut, a superb pair of full-blown cossack whiskers, and an interesting transverse sabre-wound over his right eye. Valour was then at a premium, and M'Neill's character, joined to his warlike visage, at once secured him a handsome engagement. On his arrival in the interior, an opportunity quickly offered for trying his hand at his old profession. He was dispatched with a few men to intercept a party of Indians who were loaded with furs, in order to prevent them falling into the hands of the Hudson's Bay Company. He found, however, that he had been anticipated by a clerk of the latter establishment. Warm words took place between them, and a duel was the consequence. M'Neill drove a ball through his adversary's hat, and there the affair ended. Some time after he was engaged in two broadsword encounters, in which he wounded one of his opponents, and disarmed the other. His fame soon became established; and wherever he appeared opposition vanished.

A year of inactivity followed his first campaign; and as no fighting reinforcement appeared among the ranks of the enemy, he became dissatisfied with his situation. A quarrel occurred between him and the proprietors. He alleged that he was badly treated, and did not experience the attention to which he considered himself justly entitled; while the latter stated that his unruly conduct was a terrible example of insubordination to all the younger clerks in the establishment; and that in his bearing to his superiors, he showed more of the *major,* than of the *serjeant-major.*

Without stopping to inquire upon whom the greater share of the blame rested, it is sufficient to say, that the gentlemen of the interior were *graciously* pleased to dispense with his services a year before the termination of his engagement, and generously allowed him the full amount of his salary for the entire period. He was now on his way to Canada, uncertain as to his future course of life, but so strongly imbued with a dislike of the Indian country, that he swore he would rather carry a halbert all his life, than roll in a coach and four, obtained by cheating the poor Indians.

August 9th. Embarked at half-past three A. M. Made four portages during the day, and passed a few Sotoes in canoes. Embarked at eight o'clock in Lac d'Eturgeon. The scenery, since we left Lac la Pluie, is much more diversified with woods and rising grounds, than below that establishment. Weather very warm for the last three days.

AUGUST 10TH. At eight A. M. made the Portage des Deux Rivières,[6] and at nine, that of Les Morts, at which we breakfasted. Arrived at the Portage des Français at half-past one P. M., and owing to its length, and bad pathway, did not finish it until half-past seven. Encamped, at dusk, at the entrance of Rivière des Français. Had a great deal of thunder and heavy rain during the afternoon.

AUGUST 11TH. Made the Portage de la Pente at ten A. M. At noon passed the Portage des Barrils, and entered Mille Lac with a fair breeze. At five P. M. passed an uninhabited house, built last year for a trading post by order of Lord Selkirk. Encamped, at eight, in a handsome savannah, close to a river which takes its name from the place (La Savanne.)

AUGUST 12TH. Started at day-break. At ten, met an old guide, named Joseph Paul, in charge of a brigade of seven loaded canoes destined for English River. At eleven, arrived at Savannah portage, which we did not finish until three P. M. At five passed the Portage de Milieu; at which we met a single canoe heavily laden, destined for the Red River. At dusk we made the Portage de la Prairie, and encamped on the shores of another Lac Froid, a small body of clear water, so called from its extreme frigidity.

AUGUST 13TH. Found the air very chilly during the night, which some of our Canadian *Savans* attributed to the proximity of Lac Froid. A heavy dew also fell. Embarked at half-past four; and at half-past five made the Portage de l'Eau Froide, the air round which we found extremely cold. We continued down a chain of small rapids, in one of which we were obliged to unload. After this we descended a small river, with low banks, and a smooth current; in which, at three P. M., we met Messrs. John George M'Tavish and J. Thompson,[7]

[6] Cox is following the regular North West Company route across the height of land between Rainy Lake and Lake Superior. He traversed the first-named lake, following the international boundary as far as Lac la Croix, then went up Sturgeon River, across French Portage to Sand Lake and Thousand Lakes. Then he crossed Meadow Portage near the present railroad station of Savanne to Dog Lake. For detail see the map in the end pocket of Simpson, *Journal of Occurrences.*

[7] John Thompson (d. 1828) was of Scandinavian origin. He joined the North West Company before 1789 and served at various posts as a clerk. In 1800, he built "Old Rocky Mountain House" on the Mackenzie River. In 1804, he became a partner in the company. From 1806 to 1810 he was in the Athabaska department and from 1810 to 1821 on the English River. In 1821, he became a chief factor in the merged company but apparently retired from the fur trade in the same year. See Wallace, *Documents,* 503.

on their way to the interior. Encamped at seven, at Lac des Chiens, where we were joined by a Mr. Conolly,[8] a senior clerk for many years in charge of one of the principal trading posts in the interior. We encamped together; and he invited us to his tent, where we made a sensible impression on the contents of a well-stocked garde-vin. This gentleman left Ireland when a boy, with his family, who settled in Canada. He had at this period been seventeen years in the Company's service, and was to be elected a partner the following year. He was *un véritable bon garçon,* and an Emeralder of the first water.

AUGUST 14TH. At four A. M. parted from our worthy host of the tent, when each pursued his different route. At six, met Mr. Duncan M'Dougall, proceeding to Winepic River in a loaded canoe. We stopped a couple of hours with him, and breakfasted together. This gentleman had been one of the directors of the late Pacific Fur Company, and had subsequently joined the North-West. He was one of our party crossing the mountains; but at the English River, he set off in a light canoe with Mr. Bethune for Fort William, from which place he was now returning to his winter quarters.

Came to the termination of the lake about eleven o'clock, and finished the Portage des Chiens[9] at noon. The country about this place is very handsome, and the view from the rising grounds about the portage highly picturesque and diversified. At one, passed another portage, called Le Petit Chien; and in the course of the evening passed several rapids, at six of which we were obliged to unload and let the canoes down with the line. Encamped at dusk at the Portage des Cédres. From Lac des Chiens the country assumes quite a hilly, and in some places a mountainous, appearance. The timber, too, particularly the pine and spruce, becomes much larger, and nearly approaches the magnitude of the trees on the Columbia.

AUGUST 15TH. At five P. M. made the Portage de l'Ile; previous to

8 William Connolly (1787?–1849) was born at Lachine, near Montreal, and about 1801 became associated with the North West Company. He became a partner in 1818 and the next year at Cumberland House entertained Sir John Franklin, during the latter's first expedition to the Arctic. As a member of the Hudson's Bay Company he was in charge of New Caledonia from 1824 to 1831. An earlier "fur trade marriage" to a Cree Indian woman was disregarded when he later married a white woman in Montreal, which after his death led to considerable litigation over his estate by the various children involved. See Wallace, *Documents,* 433.

9 Dog Portage leads over the divide which separates the waters of Hudson Bay from the Lake Superior system. It is about a mile in length. For the origin of the name see Franchère, *Narrative,* 385 n.

which we were obliged to unload at two rapids. At eight, made the Portage Ecarté; and soon after, a loud and roaring noise announced our approach to the great falls of Portage de la Montagne,[10] which we reached a little before ten o'clock.

This stupendous cataract is second only to Niagara. It is 156 feet in height, and upwards of 200 in breadth. The river, in its advance to the fall, moves slowly and majestically forward until its course is interrupted by an enormous mass of rough craggy rocks, over whose dark grey front it rushes with a tremendous noise resembling distant thunder.

We stopped to breakfast at the foot of the cataract, the spray from which dashed over us. It was a melancholy-looking spot. The morning was dark and cloudy, and not a ray of sunshine appeared to enliven the dread abyss; owing to which circumstance, and the banks on each side being high, rocky, and thickly wooded, we were deprived of seeing that beautiful phenomenon of the prismatic rainbow, so often observed at Niagara and other great falls. The scene was one of sombre grandeur; and, however it might have been relished by a philosopher, or an embryo Demosthenes, was well calculated to damp the animal spirits of the most vivacious disciple of Momus.

For six leagues below this cataract there is a chain of shallow rapids,[11] down which we had to pass the canoes with the cod-lines. Encamped late at the foot of the last rapid, without a mouthful of any substance for dinner or supper; indeed we had been in a starving state for the last four days, having had only a scanty meal per diem. In the course of the day we met a brigade of loaded canoes, bound for Forts des Prairies, and another for Lac la Pluie.

AUGUST 16TH. Embarked at day-break; and at six passed Point Meuron, one of Lord Selkirk's establishments, so called from a number of De Meuron's regiment having been employed in building it. The situation is handsome; but the settlement consists of a few straggling huts, miserably provided with the common necessaries of life.

---

[10] This mountain portage is around Kakabeka Falls in the Kaministikwia River. The name is said to come from the Indian term for "cleft rock." See Franchère, *Narrative,* 385 n.

[11] Below the falls there is a series of shallow rapids extending to the mouth of the stream. The name of the river is said to mean "difficult entrance." See Franchère, *Narrative,* 385 n.

At eight o'clock we arrived at Fort William,[12] as the welcome sound of the breakfast-bell was summoning the inmates to their morning's repast. We instantly repaired to the *salle à manger,* and over a bowl of coffee, fresh eggs, excellent hot cakes, and prime cold venison, quickly forgot our late privations.

Fort William is the great emporium for the interior. An extensive assortment of merchandise is annually brought hither from Montreal, by large canoes, or the Company's vessels on the lakes, which, in return, bring down the produce of the wintering posts to Canada, from whence it is shipped for England. A number of the partners and clerks, whose turn of rotation has not arrived for going to Montreal, assemble here every summer, and deposit the furs which they purchase during the winter, when they obtain a fresh supply of trading goods for the ensuing season. Those on their way to Canada also remain some time previous to their final departure. In addition to these, one or two of the principal directors, and several clerks, come up every spring from Montreal to make the necessary changes, and superintend the distribution of the merchandise for the wintering parties. Fort William may therefore be looked upon as the metropolitan post of the interior, and its fashionable season generally continues from the latter end of May to the latter end of August. During this period, good living and festivity predominate; and the luxuries of the dinner-table compensate in some degree for the long fasts and short commons experienced by those who are stationed in the remote posts. The voyageurs too enjoy their carnival, and between rum and baubles the hard-earned wages of years are often dissipated in a few weeks.

We arrived too late to see Fort William in its prime. A great portion of the interior aristocracy had departed for their winter destinations; and most of those outward-bound had set off before our arrival. A small portion of respectability, however, remained; and during the two days that we stopped, our time was passed agreeably enough.

The following is a list of the company who assembled at the dinner-table; viz. Messrs. John M'Donald[13] (le Borgne[14]), Haldane,[15] Ron-

[12] Fort William, on Lake Superior, was constructed in the years between 1802 and 1805 but was not named until 1807. The name was in honor of William McGillivray. The site was a favorite one of the gentry of the fur trade, having been occupied as early as 1678 by the French. It was headquarters for the North West Company and in 1817 was captured by Lord Selkirk's forces. After the coalition of the two companies it was abandoned and soon fell into ruin.

ald Cameron,[16] James Grant (le Borgne),[17] and Doctor M'Loughlin.[18] The above comprised all the members of the proprietory present, the doctor having two shares in consequence of long services, and being resident physician at the fort.

Among the clerks were, Captain R. Mackenzie, nearly fifty years of age, twenty-five of which he had spent in the Indian country; Mr. Crebassâ, also a North-Wester of twenty-five years' standing, who was now on his way to Canada to abide his trial, on certain charges preferred against him by some of Lord Selkirk's agents; Mr. Wentzel, my travelling companion, of whom I have already spoken; Mr. Cummings, thirteen years in the Company's Service, and presumptive heir to a partnership; Mr. Alexander M'Tavish, from the Columbia, going to Canada from ill health; Mr. Hector M'Neill, from Athabasca, quitting the country in consequence of having no one to fight with. There were also from the establishment in Montreal, Messrs. Grant, M'Robb, Cowie, M'Lean, and Robinson; and at the end of the table a long list of worthies, consisting of hieroglyphic clerks, interpreters,

[13] John McDonald, *le Borgne*, (1770–1828) was born in Scotland but came to Canada in 1786 with his family. He first joined the XY Company and then the North West Company. In 1816, he was arrested by Lord Selkirk's men at Fort William but was later acquitted of the charges against him. At the time of the merger he became a chief factor in the new company. See Wallace, *Documents,* 463–64.

[14] So called by the Canadians, owing to the gentleman having lost one eye.—R. C.

[15] John Haldane (d. 1857) was of Scotch birth but came to Canada at an early age. Originally a member of the XY Company, he joined the Northwesters in 1804 and served at various posts as a wintering partner. In 1821, he became a chief factor and was assigned to the Columbia River district, but in 1823, he was brought east to Lake Superior. See Wallace, *Documents,* 453.

[16] Ronald Cameron (fl. 1793–1817) entered the fur trade in opposition to the North West Company but joined the latter concern in 1797. In 1808, he became a partner. He was at Fort William in 1817 and died some time between then and the year 1821. See Wallace, *Documents,* 430.

[17] James Grant (fl. 1805–1827) was a clerk at Fond du Lac from 1805 to 1813. The next year he was at the Pic but the year following was back at Fond du Lac, where he was arrested by Selkirk's forces. In 1818, he retired from the fur trade. See Wallace, *Documents,* 450.

[18] John McLoughlin (1784–1857) was born in Canada but studied medicine at the University of Edinburgh and became a qualified physician. In 1806, he entered the North West Company. In 1814, he became a partner and was in charge at Rainy Lake, where he was involved in the Selkirk troubles. In 1820, he and Angus Bethune were North West Company representatives at the merger negotiations in London, but owing to trouble over credentials, the merger was arranged by others. In 1821, he became a chief factor and two years later was sent to the Columbia River, where he remained until 1846, practically the uncrowned King of Oregon. See Wallace, *Documents,* 482. A good biography is that by Richard G. Montgomery, *The White-Headed Eagle* (New York, The Macmillan Company, 1934).

and guides, who are looked upon as warrant officers, and at head quarters are permitted to dine with the mess.

The dining-hall is a noble apartment, and sufficiently capacious to entertain two hundred. A finely executed bust of the late Simon M'Tavish is placed in it, with portraits of various proprietors. A full-length likeness of Nelson, together with a splendid painting of the battle of the Nile, also decorate the walls, and were presented by the Hon. William M'Gillivray to the Company. At the upper end of the hall there is a very large map of the Indian country, drawn with great accuracy by Mr. David Thompson, astronomer to the Company, and comprising all their trading posts, from Hudson's Bay to the Pacific Ocean, and from Lake Superior to Athabasca and Great Slave Lake.

This immense territory is very little known, except to those connected with the Company; and if it did not interfere with their interests, the publication of Mr. Thompson's map would prove a most valuable addition to our geographical knowledge of the interior of that great continent.

The buildings at Fort William consist of a large house, in which the dining-hall is situated, and in which the gentleman in charge resides; the council-house; a range of snug buildings for the accomodation of the people from the interior; a large counting-house; the doctor's residence; extensive stores for the merchandise and furs; a forge; various workshops, with apartments for the mechanics, a number of whom are always stationed here. There is also a prison for refractory *voyageurs*. The whole is surrounded by wooden fortifications, flanked by bastions, and is sufficiently strong to withstand any attack from the natives. Outside the fort is a ship-yard, in which the Company's vessels on the lake are built and repaired. The kitchen-garden is well stocked, and there are extensive fields of Indian corn and potatoes. There are also several head of cattle, with sheep, hogs, poultry, &c., and a few horses for domestic use.

The country about the fort is low, with a rich moist soil. The air is damp, owing to frequent rains, and the constant exhalation from Lake Superior. This produces agues; and numbers of the people who have wintered here, have been more or less afflicted with that troublesome disorder.

In addition to the persons whose names I have already mentioned, we also found at Fort William, Captain Miles M'Donnell,[19] a gentleman connected with Lord Selkirk's establishment, in the custody of a constable named Fitzpatrick, on certain charges preferred against him by some members of the North-West Company, and for which he was about to be conducted to Canada. There was also a Mr. Joillette, a notary from Assomption, who came up as secretary to the commissioners, Messrs. Coltman and Fletcher; by the latter of whom he was discharged from his functions, and was now waiting for a passage to Montreal. Besides the above, there was a subaltern's detachment of the 70th Foot, and a number of disbanded soldiers, who had belonged to de Meuron's regiment, and who were ready and willing to cut the throats of all persons opposed to the interest of their employers.

Most part of the *voyageurs,* soldiers, Indians, half-breeds, &c., were encamped outside the fort in tents, leathern lodges, mat covered huts, or wigwams. On inquiry, I ascertained that the aggregate number of the persons in and about the establishment was composed of natives of the following countries; viz. England, Ireland, Scotland, France, Germany, Italy, Denmark, Sweden, Holland, Switzerland, United States of America, the Gold Coast of Africa, the Sandwich Islands, Bengal, Canada, with various tribes of Indians, and a mixed progeny of Creoles, or half-breeds. What a strange medley! Here were assembled, on the shores of this inland sea, Episcopalians, Presbyterians, Methodists, Sunworshippers, men from all parts of the world, and whose creeds were "wide as the poles asunder," united in one common object, and bowing down before the same idol.[20]

An observatory (rather a crazy structure) stands in the court-yard of the fort. From it the eye takes in an extensive view of flat country, thickly wooded, with the bold shores of Thunder Island at a distance, rising abruptly out of Lake Superior; while immediately around the fort the scene was enlivened by animating groups of women, soldiers, *voyageurs,* and Indians, dancing, singing, drinking, and gambling; in their features comprising all the shades of the human species, and in their dress, all the varied hues of the rainbow.

[19] Miles Macdonell (1769–1828) was born in Scotland. After migrating to Canada, he became a lieutenant and then captain in the Royal Canadian Volunteers. He was a brother of a Northwester. In 1811, Lord Selkirk made him his agent at the Red River establishment and the Hudson's Bay Company made him the first governor of Assiniboia. In 1814, he issued a proclamation forbidding the export of provisions for a year. In 1815, he was arrested by the North West Company men and taken to Montreal as a prisoner. In 1817, he returned to Red River with Lord Selkirk but remained only a short time. See Wallace, *Documents,* 466.

[20] We had one East-Indian from Bengal, two Negroes, and the De Meurons were a mixture of nearly every nation in Europe.—R. C.

Chapter 28

Enter Lake Superior—St. Mary's Falls—Sketch of Mr. Johnston—Lake Huron—French River—Lake Nipising—Arrive on the Ottawa—A backwoodsman—Chaudière Falls—Hull—Long Sault—Mr. Grant—Laughable mistake—Mr. M'Donald Le Pêtre—Mr. M'Gillis—Snyder's tavern—Lake of the Two Mountains—La Chine—Arrival at Montreal

AUGUST 18TH. Received our sailing orders and provisions for our voyage last night; and at six A. M. this morning took our departure from Fort William in company with a brigade of loaded canoes. Messrs. Wentzel, M'Neill, and I travelled in the same canoe. The day was remarkably warm and calm. Our route lay along the northern shore of Lake Superior, and we encamped at P. M. on a stony beach. The country appeared to be generally high and rocky. Some handsome open spots were visible at intervals along shore; and other parts were thickly wooded.

AUGUST 19TH. This day was also calm, and we continued on with the paddle until dusk, when we put ashore in a small bay. The general appearance of the land was rocky, diversified however by several beautiful situations admirably calculated for settlements.

AUGUST 20TH. Embarked at day-break. The shores appeared higher, and were indented with larger bays than we had yet seen. We had several slight showers. About noon it came on to blow rather fresh, and at two P. M. we were obliged to put ashore from the violence of the gale, which kept us stationary the remainder of the day.

AUGUST 21ST. Started at three A. M. At six a hard breeze sprung up, accompanied by heavy rain; and as the lowering appearance of the clouds portended no favourable change, we put ashore at ten o'clock at one of the Company's trading posts, called *Le Pic*.[1] The house is handsomely situated on the shores of a small bay. A proprietor was in charge. He was on the beach when we approached in shore; and on seeing us disembark, he turned on his heel and retreated into the fort. This movement forboded any thing but a hospitable reception; and we therefore pitched our tent, and prepared for breakfast. As Wentzel had formerly known him, he paid him a visit; but M'Neill and I preferred remaining in the tent, from which no friendly invitation offered to dislodge us.

Between one and two P. M. the rain ceased, and enabled us to quit the dominions of the surly landlord of the Pic. A stiff breeze wafted us on rapidly the remainder of the day, and we encamped late in a small bay. After leaving the Pic the shores appeared quite rocky, with little timber, and the interior mountainous.

AUGUST 22ND. Had a strong breeze all day, which at half-past four P. M. brought us to the River de la Chienne, close to the great bay of *Michipicoten*,[2] to cross which in stormy weather is rather hazardous. We therefore encamped at the river, where we remained all night. During the day we passed several islands, which, like the northern shore of the lake, are rocky; they are also thinly wooded, and, as the *voyageurs* told me, possess a very unproductive soil.

AUGUST 23RD. Rose at three; but the threatening aspect of the clouds deterred us from embarking until half-past four A. M., when we commenced crossing the bay, or as the *voyageurs* called it, the *Grande Traverse de Michipicoten*. We made use of the paddle and the sail by turns, and finished the traverse in five hours. At noon arrived at a point called *Gargue en trois,* from which a strong breeze brought us, at half-past four, to Montreal Island, on which we encamped. The northern coast more rocky and mountainous than yesterday.

AUGUST 24TH. Embarked at four, in calm weather, which about seven increased to a breeze, that brought us on rapidly till ten, when it obliged us to land at Point Mamas. Here we overtook Mr. Fletcher, a barrister, and superintendent of the police at Quebec. This gentleman had been appointed, by the Governor-General, joint commissioner with Mr. Coltman, to inquire into the causes of the various

[1] Le Pic was at the mouth of the Pic River, which was an Indian word meaning "mud." The stream was of a reddish-yellow color owing to the fact that its flow was through banks of clay. See Franchère, *Narrative,* 392 n.

[2] Michipicoten Bay was seventy-five miles by canoe from Le Pic. See Franchère, *Narrative,* 392 n.

affrays between the two companies, and was now on his way to Canada with the result of his mission. We remained wind-bound at this place until three P. M., when, the gale moderating, we continued on in company with Mr. Fletcher. Encamped at dusk at the opening of the bay of Batchiwina,[3] one of the most extensive inlets on the northern shores of Lake Superior. Mr. Fletcher invited us to his tent, which was plentifully stocked with *toutes les bonnes choses* calculated to render travelling in such a country very agreeable; and as our Fort William supply of luxuries was rather in a consumptive state, this gentleman in the kindest manner helped us most liberally from his store.

From Point Mamas to this place the shore is rather low, and much less rugged than any part we had hitherto seen.

AUGUST 25TH. Embarked at day-break with a fair breeze, and made the traverse of the Batchiwina without using a paddle.[4] At one P. M. doubled a cape called by the Canadians *Le Gros Cap*, at which place the lake suddenly narrows to little better than a mile in breadth. The country on both sides is low and well wooded.

At five P. M. arrived at St. Mary's Falls, or, as the Canadians name the place, Le Saut de Sainte Marie,[5] at which Lake Superior terminates, and discharges its waters into Lake Huron. The North-West Company had extensive stores at this place, of which a Mr. Kennedy had charge. Mr. Fletcher stopped with us at the Company's house, where we had an excellent dinner of fish, wild fowl, and deer.

The southern side of St. Mary's forms part of the territory of the United States; the northern belongs to Great Britain. On the American side there are several settlements, in consequence of which

[3] Batchawana Bay was referred to by Franchère as "a poor little post, situated at the bottom of a sandy cove, which offers nothing agreeable to the eye." It was forty-five miles from Sault Ste Marie. See *Narrative*, 393.

[4] This is a dangerous traverse. The year before, as Mr. Kenneth Mackenzie and fourteen men were crossing it in a gale of wind under heavy sail, their canoe upset, and that gentleman and ten of the *voyageurs* were unfortunately drowned.—R. C. (Kenneth McKenzie (d. 1817) was probably a relative of Roderick McKenzie. The date of his birth and of his joining the North West Company are unknown, but he became a partner in 1805. From 1806 to 1816 he was at Fort William, where he was arrested in the latter year. It was while still a prisoner that he was drowned in Lake Superior in 1817. He is not to be confused with the Kenneth McKenzie who was later active in the American fur trade on the Missouri River, although he, too, had served briefly with the North West Company. See Wallace, *Documents*, 478.—eds.)

[5] Sault Ste Marie was a rapid at the outlet of Lake Superior where the water falls about twenty feet in less than a mile. See Franchère, *Narrative*, 394.

the North-Westers regard this place as the commencement of civilisation. We crossed over in the evening in company with Mr. Fletcher, from the stern of whose canoe a British jack was flying. On landing, we were received in the kindest manner by Mr. Johnston,[6] the principal inhabitant of the place, who politely invited us to his house, where we spent a few hours. He returned with us to the Company's establishment, and the night was far advanced before we separated.

AUGUST 26TH. In consequence of the canoes requiring some repairs, we remained at St. Mary's Falls this day, which we passed in the most agreeable manner at the residence of Mr. Johnston.

The history of this gentleman is remarkable. He was a member of a highly respectable family in the county Antrim, and in early life moved in the most fashionable circles in Ireland. A circumstance, however, which blasted his early hopes of happiness, induced him to abandon his native country, and about twenty-eight years before this period he arrived in America. After wandering for some time about the continent, he made his way to St. Mary's Falls, where he shortly became a great favourite with the Indians, and entered extensively into the fur-trade. The chief had only one child, a daughter. She was a beautiful and interesting girl, and, although sought for as a wife by many of the youthful warriors, she declined all their offers. Her father was old and infirm, and wished her to marry before his death; but still his affection for his daughter was so great, that he would not exercise his parental authority in compelling her to choose. It soon, however, became apparent that Mr. Johnston was the object of her choice. For some time previous, as he told me himself, he began to experience the truth of St. Pierre's opinion, that "man without woman, and woman without man, are imperfect beings in the order of nature." On learning, therefore, that he had found favour in the sight of this youthful Indian, he at once came to the resolution of rendering both himself and her perfect. Her father consented, and they were married according to the rites and ceremonies of the tribe. Death shortly after deprived the old man of his command; and Mr. Johnston, whose wisdom and courage were highly admired by the Indians, was unanimously elected his successor.

[6] This was John Johnston, who was born in Ireland in 1763 and came to Canada in 1792. He joined the North West Company and married the daughter of an Indian chief. In 1794, he moved to Sault Ste Marie, and in the War of 1812, despite the fact that his establishment was on American soil, he cast his lot with the British. For the American attack there see Franchère, *Narrative*, 393–94.

Some years after his union with the chief's daughter, an extensive property fell to him in the north of Ireland, to which place he repaired in order to take possession. While there, offers of a tempting nature were made to induce him to reside in the country of his nativity, but his fealty to the "lady of the lake" could not be shaken; and the moment he had finished his business he hastened back to St. Mary's. His family consisted of two sons and two daughters, and a Miss Campbell, an interesting girl, whose father had a few years before been shot in a duel by a Mr. Crawford. One son was employed in a public department in Canada, and the other was an officer in a local corps. The mother received us in a friendly manner at the door, but did not join us at the breakfast or dinner table.

Mr. Johnston had extensive plantations of corn, potatoes, &c., with a beautifully arranged and well-stocked fruit and flower garden. During the late short war with America, he induced one thousand Indian warriors (of whom he took the command) to join the British forces, and rendered important services while so employed.

He suffered severely for his loyalty; for, during his absence with the army, a predatory party of Americans attacked his place in the hope of obtaining a large quantity of valuable furs, which they were informed he had in his stores, but which a short time before his departure he had fortunately removed. Disappointed in their hopes of plunder, they burned his house, out-offices, &c., destroyed the greater part of his valuable stock, and carried away every portable article they could find.[7] At the period, therefore, of our visit the buildings were quite new, and were constructed with much taste. The furniture was elegant, and the library select and excellent.

Mr. Johnston possessed a highly cultivated mind, much improved by extensive reading. He had made many excursions round the shores of Lake Superior, and along the banks of its tributary streams, in which scientific researches imparted a pleasing variety to the business of an Indian trader. His collections of specimens were varied and well selected; and if the result of his inquiries be published, they will, I have no doubt, prove a valuable addition to our geological knowledge of interior America.

Mr. Johnston was an enthusiastic admirer of Indian manners and

[7] I met Mr. Johnston a few years afterwards in England, and was happy to learn that he succeeded in obtaining from Government compensation for the losses he sustained on the above occasion.—R. C.

customs; and if a word were uttered condemnatory of their morals, he poured forth a torrent of eloquent, but vituperative satire against the fashionable follies of the civilised world; which, as it was felt he spoke *jure uxoris,* if it failed to establish the superior morality of Indian manners, silenced at least all opposition.

Two retired traders, named Nolin and Ermantinger,[8] also resided on the same side with Mr. Johnston, a short distance below his house. They had Indian wives, and large families, and appeared to be in comfortable circumstances.

Mr. Johnston has plenty of cattle, hogs, sheep, domestic fowl, &c., and has also a very good windmill close to his dwelling-house. Fish is found in great abundance, particularly trout. They are of enormous size—sixty pounds is not uncommon; and Mr. Johnston assured me he saw one caught, in Lake Superior, which weighed ninety pounds!

He treated us to an excellent dinner, fine wine, and a few tumblers of *Irish mountain dew,* which had never seen the face of an exciseman. We left Mr. Johnston's at dusk; but he crossed over with us, and we spent together another night of social and intellectual enjoyment.

AUGUST 27TH. Embarked at seven P. M., and bid adieu to the worthy Hibernian chieftain of St. Mary's. Entered Lake Huron with a stiff breeze, which kept up during the greater part of the day, with rain at intervals. We were obliged to land at five P. M., owing to the increasing violence of the gale. Passed a number of islands, for every one of which the Canadians have peculiar names. The part of the lake through which we passed this day was rather narrow, the shores on each side being visible. Country low, and thickly wooded.

AUGUST 28TH. Left our encampment at day-break with a fair wind, shortly after which the lake suddenly widens, and we quickly lost sight of the southern shore. At noon passed the traverse opposite Michillimackana,[9] and at two passed the River de Tresallons. Encamped late on an island. Several smart showers during the day. Country low and woody.

AUGUST 29TH. Set off at five A. M. Passed a number of islands during the day. They were generally rocky, and covered with pine, birch, dwarf oak, and immense quantities of the Indian weed called Sacacommis. Encamped at six P. M. on an island, in company with

---

[8] For Nolin and Ermatinger see Franchère, *Narrative,* 395 n.; and also the index to *Henry-Thompson Journals,* III, 990.

[9] Mackinaw.

a brigade of loaded canoes, under the charge of a guide named Guillaume d'Eau. Weather excessively sultry, with slight rain.

AUGUST 30TH. Started at four A. M. Passed nearly as many islands as yesterday, and much of the same appearance. The shore of the main land still low and rocky, with a few handsome spots. Sultry weather and light breezes. Encamped on an island at seven P. M.

AUGUST 31ST. Embarked at four. Charming weather all day. Some of the islands we passed were rather long and fertile. The north shore of the lake still low, but during the day we observed a few ridges of rather high hills some distance in the interior. Encamped at half-past five at the entrance of Rivière des Français;[10] at which place we quitted Lake Huron, on our way to the Ottawa. The country about the mouth of the river is rather low and swampy.

SEPTEMBER 1ST. At half-past four A. M. commenced ascending the Rivière des Français; and at seven passed a rapid called La Petite Faucille, at which we were obliged to carry the greater part of the lading. At half-past three P. M. came to a small cascade a few feet perpendicular, called the Portage de Rècollet,[11] previous to which we passed several small rapids. The Canadians say this portage obtained its present name in consequence of a Franciscan friar having made his way to it as a missionary, for the purpose of converting the Indians, during the period that the French had possession of Canada. He lived to an old age, and during his last illness was attended by the natives; who, after his death, deposited his remains in a grave behind his solitary hut. During the remainder of the day the river was uninterrupted by any rapids; and we encamped, at six P. M., close to a few lodges of Indians. Weather very sultry all day.

SEPTEMBER 2ND. Embarked at half-past three. Passed several small rapids in the morning. At eight made the Portage de Parisien, and at eleven passed the three discharges of La Grande Faucille, Les Pins, and Portage des Pins, all short. The banks of the river thickly wooded, with a rocky soil. At four P. M. made the Portage de Chaudière, at the head of the river, where it takes its rise from Lake Nipising. Encamped at five, a short distance in the lake. Passed a free trader named La Ronde, on his way to Montreal, in a canoe with fourteen packs of beaver, and nearly as many children.

[10] The French River, which received its name from serving as the early waterway from Lower Canada to the upper country. See Franchère, *Narrative,* 397.
[11] Recollet Falls are about twenty miles from Lake Nipissing.

SEPTEMBER 3RD. Started at two A. M., with calm weather, which continued until we got about half-way over the Grande Traverse, when we were struck by a hard squall, which nearly filled our canoes. At ten A. M. arrived at a snug house belonging to Mr. La Ronde's son, at which we breakfasted. Here we left Lake Nipising, and entered a small stream which falls into it, and which is called La Petite Rivière.[12] Its banks are low, with a rich soil, and well wooded. About two miles up the river made rather a long portage called La Vase, above which a dam has been constructed, for the purpose of keeping some water in the channel, which at this place is little better than a ditch. We floated the canoes through this canal about two miles, when we were compelled to stop and make another pretty long portage, named the Middle Vase, at the end of which we encamped.

SEPTEMBER 4TH. Rose at five A. M., after suffering the most dreadful torments all night from the combined attacks of the musquitoes and sandflies, which insinuated themselves through the smallest aperture of the tent, and fastened their infernal fangs on every part of our bodies, the neck, cheeks, and forehead in particular. At nine A. M. made another portage, called the Last Vase. It is a mile and a half in length, full of fine trees, with an excellent road, and a rich black soil. From the Middle Vase to this there is a narrow communication by water, sufficiently large to float a canoe, and no more. Remained encamped at the end of the portage all day in consequence of heavy rain, and the canoes wanting repairs.

SEPTEMBER 5TH. Embarked at half-past four A. M., and crossed a small lake about four hundred yards wide, at the end of which we made the Décharge de Sable. From this we had a clear navigation of four leagues, which brought us to the Décharge de la Tortue. At half-past ten, made a portage called Mauvaise de la Musique, the road of which is extremely awkward and dangerous. A few years before, a man while carrying a canoe fell against a large rock, by which his head was completely severed from his body. His grave is in the middle of the pathway. At half-past twelve, made the portage des Pins de La Musique; and at half-past four made another portage called Les Talons, the road in which is bad and rocky, and we were obliged to repair the canoes after crossing it. Within a few minutes of six, made the Décharge de la Carpe; and at half-past seven, passed another décharge named La Prairie, at the end of which we encamped.

[12] Probably the present Rivière de Vase.

341

The banks of this river[13] are generally high, rocky, and thickly wooded with pine, ash, beech, and poplar. The stream itself is narrow, and, except where it is interrupted by cascades or rapids, the current moves on very sluggishly. The reflection of the dark foliage of the trees gives the place a gloomy appearance, which is unenlivened by the sight of game, or the warbling of a single bird.

SEPTEMBER 6TH. Remained until half-past six repairing the canoes, after which we embarked. At nine arrived at a pretty high fall, called the Portage des Paresseux, the view from which is highly picturesque. At half-past ten, passed a small décharge, called Les Epingles, and at noon made the Décharge des Grosses Roches. At two, passed the Décharge du Campion; at three the Décharge des Roses; and at seven, the Portage du Plein Champ, at the end of which we encamped. The river this day appeared a little wider, but the general aspect of the country did not differ from that described yesterday.

SEPTEMBER 7TH. Embarked at six A. M.; passed a few rapids, and at seven arrived at the termination of the river where it falls into the Ottawa, called by the Canadians La Grande Rivière. Remained here the rest of the day, for the loaded canoes behind. A range of high hills are visible on the north side of the Ottawa, which extend down to the Labrador coast.

SEPTEMBER 8TH. Mr. Fletcher took the sun's altitude at noon, and determined this place to be in latitude 46° 19′ N., exactly the same as the mouth of the Columbia; and the longitude about 80° West. Did not embark until four P. M. Passed two rapids, in one of which we partly unloaded, and encamped at five to wait for the canoes. The banks of the Ottawa, as far as we have proceeded, are high, and the soil gravelly, and the wood principally pine and birch. Had very fine weather all day.

SEPTEMBER 9TH. Set off at half-past five A. M. Unloaded part of our packages at Les Batteries de Matawan and L'Eveillée; and took out all our loading at the Trou and Les Deux Rivières, at the foot of which latter place we encamped. These are all large rapids, and the two latter are dangerous. During the day we passed some very fine low bottoms, admirably adapted for building on, and completely sheltered by the hills in their rear. Wood and soil same as yesterday, and the current of the river generally rapid.

[13] The Mattawa, a tributary of the Ottawa. Its headwaters are divided from those of the Rivière de Vase by a height of land about three-fourths of a mile across.

SEPTEMBER 10TH. It rained hard all night. Remained until eight A. M. repairing the canoes. At half-past ten arrived at the great rapid called Le Rocher Capitaine, at which we were obliged to unload, and carry the goods by a long portage. Encamped, at five, at a handsome spot called the Pointe aux Chênes, from the great quantity of oak trees growing on it. It is one of the prettiest situations I have ever seen for a village.

SEPTEMBER 11TH. Embarked at five A. M., in a thick fog. At seven arrived at a dangerous rapid called the Joachim,[14] at which we were obliged to unload and carry the canoes and packs over a very bad portage, which we finished at half-past eight. About an hour after came to another equally dangerous rapid called the Second Joachim, where we also unloaded, and finished the portage at a quarter-past eleven. Here we breakfasted, and stopped to gum and repair the canoes. We walked between the two portages, and passed a small inland lake about a furlong in breadth. Continued on at one P. M., and had no farther obstructions in the river during the day. Encamped at seven in a pretty little bay. The banks of the Ottawa this day appeared to be well supplied with excellent pine, birch, and other trees. The oak had a dwarfish appearance, and very little underwood was visible; a circumstance which must materially facilitate the location of new settlers.

SEPTEMBER 12TH. Embarked at half-past two A. M. At seven passed a rapid called the Culbute, at which we partly unloaded. Within a few minutes of nine passed another, called Les Allumettes, where also we were obliged to carry part of our lading. At two P. M. arrived at a trading post called Fort Coulonge, in charge of a worthy substantial old soul, called, from his age and weight, Alderman Godin. He gave us a repast of the best he had, which was no great things; but as he was unable to supply us with any provisions for the use of the men, we took our leave of him at sun-set, and drove down the current all night, which, being free from rapids, exposed us to no great danger. The poor *voyageurs,* who were in a starving condition, kept up *les chansons à l'aviron* until day-break, to divert their hunger.

SEPTEMBER 13TH. At six A. M. arrived at the rapid of the Grand Calumet, where we had to make a portage of our canoes and baggage, which was not completed until a quarter past eleven. This portage is

---

[14] The Joachim Rapids are low cascades about three-fourths of a mile long. See Franchère, *Narrative,* 397 n.

very long, but the pathway is excellent. At twelve passed a rapid called Tergir, at which we partly unloaded; and in less than an hour afterwards came to the Portage de la Montagne, which we finished at half-past one. Road excellent. Some time after we shot down a very dangerous rapid called Du Sable, without unloading. Our canoes touched the rocks several times, and sustained considerable injury. At half-past four made Portage du Fort, rather short; and at six encamped at the entrance of Lac des Chats. We walked several miles on each bank during the day, and observed the predominant timber to be stately pine, and very fine cedar.

SEPTEMBER 14TH. The Ottawa here forms a lake, which the Canadians, as I have already mentioned, called Lac des Chats, but why I could not learn. The shores of the lake are rather low, and the trees much smaller than those higher up. We embarked at four A. M., and crossed the lake at half-past ten; after which we entered a number of dangerous and intricate channels formed by several rocky islands, through which we had the greatest difficulty in passing, from a combination of rocks, snags, &c. On extricating ourselves from this labyrinth, we arrived at Portage des Chats, which we passed at noon. At the end of this portage we found a Mr. Hodgeson settled, who had formerly been a clerk in the service of the Hudson's Bay Company. The only refreshment he could afford to our half-starved men, was a meal of potatoes and butter. Finding nothing very attractive about this solitary settlement, we lost no time in resuming our journey.

Encountered no other rapids during the day, and at nine P. M. arrived at the house of an American back-woodsman, who with his family had retired to rest. It was a miserable smoky dwelling, and it was no easy task to rouse them from a loft in which their dormitory was situated. The master of the family at length made his appearance, which was highly unprepossessing. On his head he wore an old bear-skin cap, and over his shoulders was thrown a kind of half-worn deer-skin covering. He was upwards of six feet in height, with square shoulders, piercing grey eyes, large bushy whiskers, a smoke-dried countenance, and a beard which for months had not felt a razor.

The salutation of this uncouth savage gave us no favourable idea of his hospitality. On opening the door he roared out in a sharp nasal accent, "D——n and b——t ye, what do you want? Why do ye make sich a d——n noise at this hour of the night, ye d——d French rascals?"

"We are hungry, and want something to eat."

"I have none to give, —so be off."

"But we will pay you for it in hard dollars."[15]

"B——t me if I care. —I have nothing, —so don't trouble me any more.

The Canadians however having assured us that he was generally well supplied with provisions, we told him we should forthwith institute a search, and take by force that which he refused for money. This threat induced the boor to dislodge from a large cupboard, some cold meat, dried fish, and Indian corn, which with a mess of potatoes served to blunt the keen edge of our appetite for the night.

SEPTEMBER 15TH. Started at day-break. At half-past seven passed a large log-house occupied by several Americans, from whom the men obtained corn and fish enough for a meal. At half-past nine arrived at Portage des Chênes, where we obtained an excellent breakfast at two shillings a head in the house of Mr. M'Collum, a native of Prince Edward's Island, from which place he had lately removed to the banks of the Ottawa, where he set up a small tavern, the first I had seen for six years.

A short distance below this portage the navigation is interrupted by the great falls of La Chaudière,[16] at which the village of Hull is situated. We walked thither from M'Collum's. This settlement appeared to be in a thriving condition, and, under the superintendence of its enterprising proprietor Mr. Wright,[17] bids fair to be a place of considerable importance. We observed a few comfortable houses; and his shop, the only one in the village of any respectability, was tastefully ornamented by a handsome steeple. No provisions could be obtained for love or money, and, with the exception of some bad rum, our men could procure no refreshment of any description. The crops promised to be very abundant, but a premature frost had in a great degree injured them. The potatoes were very large, but quite moist,

[15] M'Neill, Wentzel and I obtained, a couple of days before, sixty dollars from Mr. Fletcher, who had gone on ahead for Montreal.—R. C.

[16] La Chaudière, or Caldron Falls are described by Franchère as a rock that extended from shore to shore and that so completely cut off the course of the river that no water "was seen falling over, but sinking by subterranean channels, or fissures in the rock, it boiled up below, from seven or eight different openings, not unlike water in a huge caldron. . . ." See *Narrative*, 398.

[17] Philemon Wright, the "father of the town of Hull," who came from Woburn, Massachusetts. Opposite Hull is the site of the city of Ottawa. See Franchère, *Narrative*, 398.

which, some of the inhabitants told me, is their general characteristic both on the banks of the St. Lawrence and the Ottawa. The soil near the shore is rocky and barren, but a short distance in the interior it is rich and highly productive. Rafting is the principal business of the settlers, and white oak, red and white pine, the chief timber sent downwards. Notwithstanding the immense distance these rafts have to descend, and the number of hands employed in hewing the timber, the business is tolerably profitable.

Twenty-two families of emigrants, chiefly Irish and Scotch, had reached Hull a short time previous to our arrival. They were stationed in a range of small miserable huts, and appeared to be in a state of great destitution. The portion of land which each expected had not been yet allocated, and the poor creatures complained with apparent justice of the gross want of attention on the part of those whose duty it was to superintend their location. A few lodges of Indians were also here. The men assisted our *voyageurs* in carrying the packs across the portage; and their squaws, who were poor and dirty, made certain advances, which, to judge by their amatory glances, some of the Canadians perfectly understood without any lingual explanation.

The navigation of the Ottawa, at this place, is obstructed by a line of bold, dark-looking rocks, which stretch across the river, and over which the descending torrent, after rushing with headlong fury, and forming a beautifully extended prismatic curtain, falls into a foaming cauldron, the frightful ebullition of which requires no small degree of nerve to survey with composure.

We remained this evening at Hull, and but for the hospitable attention we received from a Mr. Downes, who was in the employment of Mr. Wright, we should not have imagined ourselves within the precincts of civilisation.

SEPTEMBER 16TH. It rained hard during the morning, which delayed our departure until nine o'clock. Passed a number of poor straggling huts some distance below Hull, inhabited by some of the newly arrived settlers. At eleven P. M. passed the River Rideau, which falls into the Ottawa over a high perpendicular rock, and forms a beautiful and picturesque cascade. This river, I understand, runs through a fruitful district, which is thickly settled, chiefly by Scotch emigrants. A few miles lower down passed another stream called La Rivière Blanche, near the mouth of which there is a thriving village. During the day we observed several farms thinly scattered along the banks, the occupants of which were very reluctant in parting with any of their provisions. Had a smooth steady current all day, uninterrupted by rapids. The appearance of the country was low, and tolerably well wooded; but the Canadians say, that in high water, some of the flat bottoms are inundated. At nine P. M. put ashore at a farm-house, where we procured a little addition to our scanty supply for supper. As the weather was fine, and the navigation free from danger, we re-embarked at eleven P. M., and drove gently down the current all night.

SEPTEMBER 17TH. At half-past eight A. M. we arrived at the great rapid called Le Long Sault,[18] the navigation of which is so dangerous, that guides reside at the place for the special purpose of conducting the canoes through it. While we were waiting for our pilot, we asked one of the *habitans* where we could obtain a good breakfast? He pointed to a handsome house on an eminence above the rapid, and merely said *"là!"* A few seconds brought us to the door, which was opened by a ruddy blue-eyed damsel, who conducted us to the parlour. We told her we wished to see her master or mistress immediately, upon which she curtsied obedience and withdrew.

From the windows of this apartment we had an extensive and picturesque view of hills, forests, corn-fields, farm-houses, and gardens; while close to the foot of the hill the majestic Ottawa rolled its turbulent waters over a mass of large detached rocks upwards of two miles in extent. The parlour itself was the *beau idéal* of elegance and comfort. The breakfast-table was partly laid, and a polished copper tea-kettle simpered most harmoniously on a bright brass footman, which was suspended from the shining bars of a Rumford grate.

While we were indulging by anticipation in the pleasures of a substantial *déjeûné*, the door opened, and a female *en déshabille,* of prepossessing appearance entered. A large bunch of keys in her hand announced her domestic supremacy. She saluted us in the most cordial and friendly manner, and begged to know if we had come from the interior? Having replied in the affirmative, she added—

"You are Nor-Westers I presume, gentlemen?"

"Yes, Madam," said Wentzel, "and have been travelling all night in search of a breakfast, which one of the *habitans* told us we could get here."

---

[18] The Long Sault Rapids are "nine miles long, and full of islets, rocky bars, and narrow passages." They are about sixty miles below Ottawa. See Franchère, *Narrative,* 399 n.

"You shall have the best the house affords," was the reply.

"Hot rolls?—"Yes."

"Fresh eggs?"—"Most decidedly."

"A broiled chop?"—"I'll try."

"And do you hear me, landlady," said M'Neill, as she was quitting the room, "This is a sharp morning, —could we get a whet out of Boniface's own bottle?" To this a favourable answer was also returned, and away she flew to comply with our various requisitions.

In a few minutes Marguerite made her appearance, carrying a large tray furnished with the hot rolls, fresh eggs, broiled chops, and the *whet*. She was followed by her mistress, who was accompanied by a middle-aged gentleman in his dressing-gown.

"You are welcome, gentlemen," said he; "Ha! my dear Wentzel, is this you?" I'm delighted to see you. How did you find me out?"

"Find you out," replied Wentzel, "Why, my dear Grant, can this be your house?" "Certainly," said he; "and permit me to introduce you, gentlemen, to Mrs. Grant."

We all began to stammer out excuses for our apparent rudeness, and explained the trick which the Tony Lumpkin of the village had played on us. Mrs. Grant laughed heartily at our confusion, and graciously sealed our pardon by pledging us in a flowing bowl of refreshing Hyson.

Mr. Grant[19] had been formerly a member of the North-West Company, and while in the Indian country, had been associated with Wentzel in many hazardous excursions. In short, they were old friends, and were naturally overjoyed at their unexpected meeting, the pleasure of which was much heightened by the ludicrous mistake that led to it. At 11 o'clock we took leave of our worthy host and his amiable lady; and in less than two hours arrived at the foot of Le Long Sault, which is one of the longest and most dangerous rapids in the interior. Here we met another retired partner of the North-West Company, Mr. John M'Donald,[20] who insisted on our visiting his

[19] This was probably Peter Grant (1764–1845), who was a Scot by birth but in 1784 came to Canada and joined the North West Company. Later he was in opposition to the company but rejoined it in 1795. In 1799, he was at Rainy Lake and for several years was in charge of the Red River department. He retired from the fur trade in 1807 and settled at Ste Anne. He died at Lachine in July, 1848. There was also a John Grant, probably a relative, who died at Lachine on August 23, 1817, which would have been shortly before Cox's arrival. See Wallace, *Documents,* 450–51.

[20] Possibly John McDonald of Garth, for whom see note 2, Chap. XIII. He had retired from the fur trade and was then living near Montreal.

house. An excellent dinner was quickly prepared, during the demolition of which we cracked half a dozen of Mr. Mac's prime Madeira. This gentleman was a strict Roman Catholic, and, during his residence in the Indian country, was distinguished by the Canadians from others of the same name by the title of *Le Prêtre* (Priest), owing to the rigid manner in which he made his men adhere to the various fasts of the Catholic church; a proof of orthodoxy with which the great majority of them would have gladly dispensed. From this circumstance, joined to his general character among the *voyageurs,* I was led to expect in Mr. M'Donald a second St. Francis; but in lieu of the austere monk, we saw in the retired trader a cheerful, healthy, and contented old man—a proof, if any were wanting, that true piety and social gaiety are not incompatible.

At five P. M. we took our leave of the hospitable *Prêtre,* who anxiously pressed us to spend the night at his house; an invitation which our arrangements precluded us from accepting. Passed several handsome farms during the evening; and after nightfall had set in, we arrived at the entrance of Rivière à la Graisse, on the banks of which a long straggling village is situated. Having seen the men properly accommodated, we left them at the mouth of the river, and proceeded towards the village, in which, after some inquiry, I found an old Columbian friend, named Donald M'Gillis, comfortably settled. He quickly collected a few rustic *bon vivans* to greet our arrival, and the night was far advanced in festive mirth before our good-natured host permitted us to throw our jaded bodies on a bed.

SEPT. 18TH. We did not rise till ten this morning, at which time some of the men insisted on awakening us. They told us that two of the loaded canoes which stopped to repair below the *Sault* the evening before, had not yet arrived. We therefore told them to wait a couple of hours longer, at the expiration of which, if they did not arrive, we should proceed. Took a late breakfast, shortly after which we bade farewell to my friend M'Gillis, who accompanied us to the beach. Seeing no appearance of the two canoes, we ordered our men to make little use of the paddles; and as the day was remarkably fine, after descending a few miles, Wentzel, M'Neill, and I landed, and proceeded seven or eight miles on a good road running parallel with the river, until we arrived at an excellent tavern kept by a curious and eccentric person named Snyder, a German by birth, at which place we determined to pass the night. We therefore sent orders to

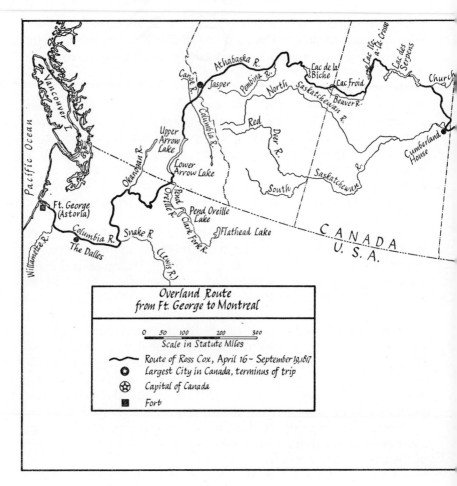

Overland Route
from Ft. George to Montreal

0   50   100   200   300
Scale in Statute Miles

Route of Ross Cox, April 16 – September 19, 1817
Largest City in Canada, terminus of trip
Capital of Canada
Fort

the canoes to encamp before the tavern; and, having inquired what we could obtain for dinner, were presented with a bill of fare that would not have derogated from the credit of the first inn in England. It was not, however, like many of those documents—all show and no substance: the German put nothing on paper, that he was not prepared to put on the table; and in less than an hour after our orders were given, the dinner was served up in a style of neatness and even elegance which I have seldom seen surpassd in any house of public entertainment.

350

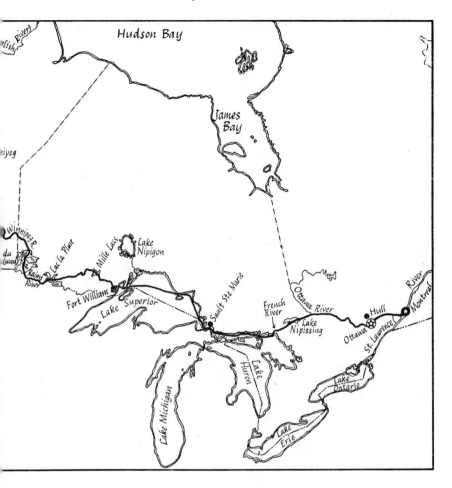

After dinner we invited the old man to join us. He was a most entertaining companion. Fame had celebrated him as a first-rate narrator of anecdotes, and the report we found was not exaggerated. His conversation was a complete antidote to *ennui,* and effectually checked any propensities we might have had to sleep. The North-Westers, he said, were the founders of his fortune: they always stopped at his house in their journeys to and from the interior, and, no matter how other customers might fare, a Nor-Wester should always have the best bed and bottle in his house. He kept his word, —but we could

351

not keep our beds. Five months continued sleeping on the hard ground had so vitiated our taste for comfort, that we in vain endeavoured to compose ourselves to rest; and, after suffering the torments of luxury for a couple of hours, were obliged to order the beds to be removed, after which we slept tolerably well on the mattrasses.

SEPTEMBER 19TH. Partook of an early breakfast with the worthy old Rhinelander, immediately after which we embarked. Some distance below Snyder's we entered the Lake of the Two Mountains, which is formed by the extension of the Ottawa.[21] Stopped at a village on the western shore of the lake, from which it derives its name. The principal inhabitants of this place are Iroquois Indians, a small remnant of that once powerful tribe. They are all Roman Catholics, and have a plain neat church. Here I also found another old friend from the Columbia, Mr. Pillet, with whom we stopped a couple of hours. He had a snug farm, a comfortable house, a handsome wife, and two pretty children, and altogether appeared to be in happy circumstances.

The two canoes which had been so long in the rear overtook us here, and we continued on together the remainder of the day. On passing the village of St. Anne's we were hailed by Mr. Daniel Mackenzie,[22] one of the senior proprietors of the North-West Company, for whom I had some letters. We therefore put ashore, and found with him Messrs. Cameron[23] and Sayers,[24] against whom certain charges had been preferred by some members of the Hudson's Bay Company, relative to the outrages in the interior, the result of which it was

[21] This lake, which is about twenty miles long, is at the base of the Long Sault Rapids.

[22] Daniel McKenzie (1769–1832) was probably born in Scotland. About 1790, he joined the North West Company and six years later became a partner. He served in the Athabaska and Red River departments and at Fond du Lac. He was arrested in 1816 by Lord Selkirk but was released, and in 1817, he was at Ste Anne. He retired from the fur trade about a year later. See Wallace, *Documents,* 476.

[23] Possibly Duncan Cameron (1764?–1848), who was born in Scotland and whose parents migrated to America and then at the outbreak of the American Revolution moved to Canada. He entered the North West Company in 1784 and in 1800 became a partner. After serving at various posts, he was in charge at Red River in 1814 and faced with the task of dealing with the Selkirk troubles. In 1816, he was taken prisoner by Lord Selkirk's men and sent to England, where he was released. He later returned to Canada and may have been the person that Cox met. See Wallace, *Documents,* 430.

[24] John Sayer (1750?–1818) had been an independent trader, trading under license before joining the North West Company. He retired about 1806 and went to live at Ste Anne on the island of Montreal. He was probably the father of John Charles Sayer, a half-blood who was involved in the Selkirk troubles in 1815, and who is probably the person to whom Cox refers. See Wallace, *Documents,* 497.

deemed prudent they should abide at this retired village. Remained a few hours with those gentlemen, with whom we took a luncheon; after which we resumed our voyage.

The country from Rivière à la Graisse to Snyder's, and from thence to St. Anne's, is highly cultivated, well stocked with farms and thriving villages, and is rich in scenery of the most beautiful and romantic description.

At four P. M. arrived at the termination of the Ottawa, where it forms a junction with the Great St. Lawrence, down which we continued until six, when we arrived at the village of La Chine, at which place canoe-voyaging terminates with the parties homeward-bound, and commences with those destined for the interior.

After some delay we procured a *caleche* sufficiently large to hold Wentzel, M'Neill, and myself. We next purchased, at a neighbouring *auberge,* a keg of rum, which we presented as a valedictory allowance to our *voyageurs,* and, having shook each man cordially by the hand, drove off amidst their benedictions, for Montreal, in which city we arrived at half past nine P. M. at Clamp's Coffee-House in Capital Street, after a journey of five months and three days from the Pacific Ocean.

Chapter 29

Sketches of the Canadian voyageurs—*Anecdote of La Liberté—The freemen, or trappers—The half-breeds—Anecdote—Retired partners—Josephine— Française—Amusing letter—Iroquois Indians—Anecdote*

There are three descriptions of men in the Company's employment, namely: the white Canadians, the half-breeds, and the Iroquois Indians. A few words respecting each class may not be uninteresting to the general reader. The first are the descendants of the original French settlers. They are generally engaged for five years; and, at the period I speak of, the foreman and steersman of each canoe received one thousand livres per annum, the middlemen six hundred, with an equipment, which means a suit of clothes and a large carrot of tobacco annually. The number of men in each canoe varies, according to its size, from six to ten. The strongest and most expert are employed in the bow and stern; for upon their skilful management in conducting the vessel through the dangerous rapids, the safety of the crew chiefly depends. Their rations at first view may appear enormous. Each man is allowed eight pounds of solid meat per diem, such as buffalo, deer, horse, &c., and ten pounds if there be bone in it. In the autumnal months, in lieu of meat, each man receives two large geese, or four ducks. They are supplied with fish in the same proportion. It must, however, be recollected that these rations are unaccompanied by bread, biscuit, potatoes, or, in fact, by vegetables of any description. In some of our journeys up the Columbia they were allowed pork and rice; and on particular occasions, such as wet weather, or making a long portage, they received a glass of rum.

At Christmas and New Year they are served out with flour to make cakes or puddings, each man receives half a pint of rum. This they call a *régale,* and they are particularly grateful for it.

Sketches of the Canadian Voyageurs

With no rent to pay, or provisions to purchase, it may be thought these men save the greater part of their wages. Such, however, is not the fact. There is not perhaps in the world a more thoughtless or improvident race of people than the Canadian *voyageurs*. Every article of extra clothing or finery which they want must be obtained from the Company's stores; and as there is no second shop at which to apply, prices immeasurably beyond the value are charged for the various articles they purchase.[1] In this manner, between the expenses attending their Indian wives, and children, the purchasing of horses, gambling, &c., the wages of years are dissipated.

I know of no people capable of enduring so much hard labour as the Canadians, or so submissive to superiors. In voyages of six months' duration, during which

Sunday shines, no Sabbath day to them,

they commence at day-break, and from thence to night-fall hard paddling and carrying goods occupy the time without intermission. They are remarkably good-natured and affectionate to each other, and it is no uncommon thing to hear one man address his comrade as *"mon frère,"* or *"mon cousin,"* without any degree of consanguinity existing between them. The enlivening anecdote, or *la chanson à l'aviron,* by turns softens down the severity of their laborious duties, in the midst of which they uniformly display the same elasticity of spirits and *gaieté de coeur* by which their vivacious French ancestors were so much distinguished. It is laughable to hear the nominal distinctions they are obliged to adopt in reference to many of the partners and clerks, who have the same surname. There are Mr. Mackenzie, *le rouge;* Mr. Mackenzie, *le blanc;* Mr. Mackenzie, *le borgne;* Mr. Mackenzie, *le picoté;* Mr. M'Donald, *le grand;* Mr. M'Donald, *le prêtre;* Mr. M'Donald, *le bras croche;* and so on, according to the colour of their hair, the size, or other personal peculiarity of each individual.

Mr. Shaw,[2] one of the agents, had passed many years in the in-

[1] The prices of goods charged the Canadians was 300 per cent above prime cost. See Simpson, *Journal of Occurrences,* 7 n.

[2] Angus Shaw (d. 1832) was a native of Scotland who had entered the North West Company before 1787 and had become a partner between the years 1795 and 1799. He had served at many posts in the interior and in 1810–11 was at Fort William. In 1819, he was one of the partners arrested by the Selkirk forces. He had had an Indian wife but later married a sister of William McGillivray. He died in 1832. See Wallace, *Documents,* 497–98.

terior, and was by the *voyageurs* called *Monsieur Le Chat*. On quitting the Indian country he married a Canadian lady, by whom he had several children. Some years after this event, one of his old foremen, named Louis La Liberté, went to Montreal to spend the winter. He had heard of his old *bourgeois'* marriage, and was anxious to see him. Mr. Shaw was walking on the Champ de Mars with a couple of officers, when La Liberté spied him. He immediately ran up, and seizing him by both hands, began as follows: *Ah, mon cher Monsieur le Chat, comment vous portez-vous?" "Très bien, Louison." "Et comment se porte Madame la Chatte?" "Bien, bien; Louison, elle est très bien." "Et tous les petits Chatons?"* This was too much for Mr. Shaw, who answered shortly that *kittens* and all were well, and, telling him to call at his house, turned sharply away with his military friends, leaving the *Cate*chetical Louison quite astonished at the abruptness of his departure.

La Liberté was an extraordinary old man; he had several fine daughters by an Indian wife, and became father-in-law to three proprietors. He was therefore proud of his connexions, and, feeling indignant at Mr. Shaw's supposed cavalier treatment, adopted an eccentric method of manifesting his resentment. He ordered a coat to be made of fine green cloth, with silver buttons, a waistcoat of crimson velvet, back and front (like the sailor at Portsmouth), with cornelian buttons, braided sky-blue pantaloons, Hessian boots with gold tassels and *silver heels*, a hat, feather, and silk sash; and thus accoutred, with a long calumet in his right hand, and a splendidly ornamented smoking-bag in his left, he proceeded to the Champ de Mars, during a regimental parade, and observing Mr. Shaw walking in company with some ladies and gentlemen, he vociferated, *"Ha, ha, Monsieur le Chat, voyez ma veste, voilà les boutons! En avez-vous de même? Ha, ha, Monsieur le Chat, regardez mes bottes—je suis ferré d'argent. Je suis le beau père de Monsieur M'Dinnill; —Monsieur Mackenzie est mon gendre; et je me sacre de tous les Chats, et de toutes les Chattes!"* Some of his friends, who previous to his leaving home observed him drinking a quantity of rum, followed him to the parade ground, and with much difficulty at length succeeded in forcing him away, while the poor old man every now and then lifted up a leg, and dared any Shaw, or officer on the ground, to show silver heels to his boots!

The dress of a *voyageur* generally consists of a capot made out of a blanket, with leather or cloth trowsers, mocassins, a striped cotton shirt, and a hat or fur cap. They seldom annoy themselves with a waistcoat; and in summer season their necks are generally exposed. They all wear belts of variegated worsted, from which their knives, smoking-bags, &c., are suspended. They enjoy good health, and with the exception of occasional attacks of rheumatism, are seldom afflicted with disease. The principal trading establishments are supplied with well-assorted medicine-chests, containing books of directions, lancets, &c. An assortment of the more simple medicines is made up for each outpost; and as each clerk must learn how to bleed, we generally manage, between low diet, salts, castor-oil, opodeldoc, friar's balsom, and phlebotomy, to preserve their health unimpaired, and cure any common accident which may befall them.

The Canadians are not much inclined to Indian warfare. This, however, does not proceed from any want of courage; for in the late short war with the United States they conducted themselves with eminent bravery. A local corps, composed of the officers and men of the North-West Company, was raised by the Honourable William M'Gillivray. His son Mr. Joseph M'Gillivray, as I have mentioned elsewhere, was an officer in it; and he gave us some laughable details relative to the conduct of the privates in the campaign in which he was engaged. When on duty in company with the regular forces or the militia they were guilty of much insubordination, and it was quite impossible to make them amenable to military law. They generally came on parade with a pipe in their mouths and their rations of pork and bread stuck on their bayonets. On seeing an officer, whether general, colonel, or subaltern, they took off their hats and made a low bow, with the common salutation of *Bon jour, Monsieur le Général,* or *le Colonel,* as the case might be, and, if they happened to know that the officer was married, never failed to inquire after the health of *Madame et les enfans.* On parade they talked incessantly, called each other "pork eaters," quarrelled about their rations, wished they were back in the Indian country again, &c., and when called to order by their officers and told to hold their tongues, one or more would reply, "Ah, dear captain, let us off as quick as you can; some of us have not yet breakfasted, and it's upwards of an hour since I had a smoke." If the officer was a North-Wester, he generally told them to have patience, and he would give them their *congé tout de suite.* In moments when danger ought to have produced a little steadiness, they completely set discipline at defiance, and the volatile volunteer broke out into all the unrestrained mirth and antimilitary familiarity of the thoughtless *voyageur*. In vain the subaltern winked, in vain the captain threatened, in vain the colonel frowned; neither winks, or threats, or frowns, could restrain the vivacious laugh, silence the noisy tongue, or compose the ever changing features into any thing like military seriousness.

These repeated infractions of the *code militaire* subjected many of them to temporary confinement; but as night approached, if the sentinel was a *voyageur,* he told the prisoner to *"aller coucher avec sa femme, et retourner le lendemain de bonne heure."* This friendly advice was immediately followed, and they had always the honour to return according to promise. They could not be got to wear stocks; and such as did not use cravats came on parade with naked necks, and very often with rough beards. In this condition they presented a curious contrast to the unchangeable countenances and well-drilled movements of the British soldiery, with whom they occasionally did duty. Notwithstanding these peculiarities the *voyageurs* were excellent partisans, and, from their superior knowledge of the country, were able to render material service during the war. They had great confidence in their officers, particularly their colonel, Mr. M'Gillivray, whose influence frequently saved them from the punishment to which their repeated breaches of discipline subjected them.

There are scattered throughout the north-west territories a few dozen Canadian trappers called freemen. These individuals were formerly engaged as *voyageurs* in the Company's service, and preferred, after the termination of their respective engagements, to remain in the Indian country rather than return to Canada. They have generally Indian families, and from their peculiar occupation lead a wandering life.

They must bring the produce of their hunts to the Company's posts, when they receive payment in goods according to a regular tariff, or the value in money is placed to their credit, and paid on their arrival in Montreal. From their constant exposure to the sun, these men are as irretrievably bronzed as the native Indians, from whom, owing to their long separation from their countrymen, they differ but little either in their habits or modes of living. Some of them have large bands of horses; and, I understand, a plurality of wives is not unfrequent among them!

THE HALF-BREEDS

This race is now numerous throughout the Indian country, particularly on the east side of the Rocky Mountains. Owing to the recent arrival of white people at the Columbia, they are comparatively few on the western side. The sons of the *voyageurs,* on attaining a proper age, are generally engaged in the Company's service. They are called Les Bois Brûlés—but why, it is difficult to ascertain. While they are taught to despise the traditions of their mothers' tribe, no one busies himself in unfolding to them the divine truths of Christianity, and the loose manners of their fathers are but ill calculated to impress them with any great respect for the ties of morality. It is therefore not surprising, that when precept is silent, and parental example vicious, they should exhibit conduct at variance with the relations of civilised life. They are fond of ardent spirits, and are much addicted to swearing; while the abominable custom of Indian mothers in talking in the most undisguised manner before their children of sexual intercourse creates a grossness of ideas with regard to female purity, which may account in a great degree for their carelessness on that head.

They are good canoe-men, and excellent hunters, remarkably active either on horseback or on foot; brave, daring, rather passionate, and, while they possess all the vivacity of their father, they at times manifest a slight symptom of Indian ferocity; this however is only evinced when any insulting allusion is made to their mixed origin. They are open-hearted and generous, practise little cunning, detest hypocrisy; and while they are determined not to submit quietly to a wrong, are extremely cautious against giving any unnecessary cause of offence.

The proprietors generally send their sons to Canada or England for education. They have a wonderful aptitude for learning, and in a short time attain a facility in writing and speaking both French and English that is quite astonishing. Their manners are naturally and unaffectedly polite, and their conversation displays a degree of pure, easy, yet impassioned eloquence, seldom heard in the most refined societies.

On finishing their studies, those intended for the Company's service enter as apprentice clerks, and in course of time, according to their talents and seniority, become proprietors.

The half-breed women are excellent wives and mothers, and instances of improper conduct are rare among them. They are very expert at the needle, and make coats, trowsers, vests, gowns, shirts, shoes, &c., in a manner that would astonish our English fashioners. They are kept in great subjection by their respective lords, to whom they are slavishly submissive. They are not allowed to sit at the same table, or indeed at any table, for they still continue the savage fashion of squatting on the ground at their meals, at which their fingers supply the place of forks. They wear no caps in the house; but in travelling hats are used instead of bonnets. With the exception of the head, their dress resembles that worn by the Bavarian broom-girls, who of late years visit our shores.

A gentleman whose name frequently occurs in these pages, but which it is here unnecessary to repeat, had, a few years after his arrival in the Indian country, taken a half-breed girl as a partner. She was the daughter of a Canadian by a Cree mother, and was very young, handsome, and possessed such amiable and engaging manners that he determined to bring her with him on his first visit to Canada, and legalize their union by the seal of marriage. She had made some progress in reading, and had two fine boys whom he sent to Scotland for their education. In short, no man was more happy than young ————, no woman was judged more perfect than his interesting wife. He was obliged one year to conduct a brigade of loaded canoes from his wintering-post to Fort William, and during his absence, which occupied about four months, left his wife behind him.

He returned sooner than was expected, and, leaving the canoes some distance below the fort, arrived there about midnight. The dogs knew his signal, and he proceeded without any noise or obstruction to his bed-room, in which he found his guilty partner in the arms of another. He instantly drew his dagger, with which he nearly destroyed the paramour, while she fled to one of the married men's apartments, in which she remained concealed during the night. Next morning, when his passion had cooled, he sent for her, and addressed her feelingly on her base and ungrateful conduct. He declared he could not think of living again with her; that he should send her to her father (who was a free trapper), and give her all her clothes, trinkets, &c.; and, should her future life prove correct, promised that her usual supply of clothes and provisions should be regularly furnished her. She retired weeping, and deeply affected. Her misconduct preyed heavily on her mind; and in less than four months after joining her father, she was numbered with the dead. Her seducer quitted the Company's service, and Mr. ——— never after took a wife. Instances of this nature are however of rare occurrence among the half-breed women; and taking their numbers and want of education into consideration, perhaps fewer cases of infidelity occur among them than among any equal portion of females in the civilised world.

When a young trader becomes united to an Indian or half-breed woman he seldom calculates on a family, and foolishly imagines he can easily dissolve a connexion which is unsanctioned by the ceremony of marriage. He is however much deceived. When the period which he had originally fixed for quitting the Indian country arrives, he finds that the woman who had been for many years a faithful partner cannot in a moment be "whistled off," and "let down the wind to prey at fortune." Children have grown up about him; the natural affection of the father despises the laws of civilised society—the patriot sinks in the parent—each succeeding year weakens the recollection of home, and of—

> *The pleasant fields, travelled so oft*
> *In life's morning march, when his bosom was young;*

and in most cases the temporary *liaison* ends in a permanent union. Those so circumstanced, on quitting the Company bring their families to Canada, where they purchase estates, on which they live in a kind of half-Indian, half-civilised manner, constantly smoking their calumet and railing at the fashionable frivolities of the great world.

When a trader wishes to separate from his Indian wife he generally allows her an annuity, or gets her comfortably married to one of the *voyageurs,* who, for a handsome sum, is happy to become the husband of *la Dame d'un Bourgeois.* A retired partner, thus disembarrassed, arrives in Canada determined to enjoy the pleasures of matrimony with an educated female. His arrival is quickly known, his object buzzed about. The ladies of Montreal and Quebec are immediately on the *qui vive;* invitations are numerous, the wealthy North-Wester is universally admired; bronzed features, Oxford-grey hairs, and a *dégagé tout ensemble* impart peculiar interest to his appearance. When he speaks, every tongue is silent;

> *Each moving accident by flood and field*

361

is listened to with breathless attention, and many a fair auditor unconsciously wishes that

Heaven had made her such a man.

Music follows, then a song; dancing succeeds; and he retires bewildered in joy, and cursing the fortune that so long debarred him from the enjoyment of such happiness. His selection is quickly made, and he at length becomes a legal Benedict.

I believe such unions are generally happy; but the censorious, particularly those who remain faithful to their Indian wives, assert that many of their old associates have been sadly duped in their matrimonial speculations.

These envious scandal-mongers allege that the unfortunate husband too quickly discovers that a bright eye, a fair face, a sweet voice, or a tune on the piano, is rather an empty compensation for the waste of a hard-earned fortune; while, if he attempts to remonstrate against his wife's extravagance, his interesting bronze is compared to copper, the Oxford-grey assumes a white hue, the *air dégagé* degenerates to the air slovenly; and an English tongue, quite at variance with his ideas of conjugal submission, reminds him that when all the officers of the garrison were dying for her, she was thrown away upon a weather-beaten, rheumatic, dog-eating, moss-chewing barbarian, whose habits were better adapted to the savage society of Indian squaws, than to that of ladies of education. The latter gentlemen, however, retaliate on the former by alleging that all their ill-natured reports are caused by the refusal of the white ladies to visit or associate with those brought down from the interior, whom they regard as little better than savages. There may be some truth on each side; but on which it preponderates I am unable to determine.

Very few men wish to have any offspring by their Indian wives; a sterile woman is therefore invaluable. They are however scarce, and happy is the man who succeeds in obtaining one.

One of the clerks on the Columbia, Mr. J——, was particularly cautioned by his father, who was an old proprietor, against taking an Indian wife, lest he should be burdened with children during his clerkship. The son promised obedience; but being stationed at Kamloops, he learned that an Indian recently drowned had been married five years, during which period his wife never had a child. This was a prize not to be lost; and as he knew the parental prohibition was more levelled against children than a wife, he lost no time in proposing for the young widow. His offers were liberal, and were gladly accepted by her relations. From a fancied resemblance to a late celebrated empress he called her *Josephine*. The resemblance however was imperfect, for nine months had scarcely elapsed when *his* Josephine brought forth a thumping swarthy pet. He was in despair—immediately dissolved the connexion, gave the boy to one of the men's wives to nurse, and sent home the mother with a plentiful stock of clothes and presents, which quickly obtained her another husband.

Mr. J—— was transferred that autumn from the Columbia to the Athabasca department, to replace a Mr. C—— who was about quitting the country, and leaving behind him a handsome half-breed wife. J—— succeed him both in bed and board, with what results will appear from the following extract of a letter which I subsequently received from him:

You are aware of the cause which obliged me to repudiate my Columbian wife, Josephine. *Another* great man repudiated his Josephine for the opposite cause; but, *n'importe,* I divorced myself, and resolved thenceforth never to run the risk of having another child in the *pays sauvage.* On my arrival here I found my friend C—— on the point of quitting Athabasca, and bidding adieu to his wife, *la belle Française,* one of the finest women in the department. Her history is rather *hors du commun.* Her father was a Canadian guide, and at the age of fourteen gave her in marriage to an interpreter with whom she lived three years without children, when she became a widow in consequence of her husband having been killed by some of the Blood Indians. Mr. C—— shortly after became her husband, and brought her to Athabasca, where she lived with him eight years *sans enfans.*

She had lived eleven years, with two husbands, and her character therefore was firmly established. She was besides a fine woman, good tempered, and remarkably ingenious. I therefore determined to secure such a prize, and made my proposals in due form. She was her own mistress; and, happy at catching such a respectable successor to her late lord, she at once consented to become mine.

Ere a few months passed, symptoms of a most suspicious nature began to appear; but I could not imagine my Française would turn mother; it might be dropsy—any thing in fact but pregnancy—but "list, oh list." On the 1st of April we became *one* (the day was ominous), and on that day nine months precisely (it is a melancholy coincidence of dates) she presented me with a New-Year's gift in the shape of a man-child! But the cup of my misfortune is not yet full. Owing to some mamillary malformation,

363

she was unable to supply the *brass* bantling with milk, which obliged me to give it to nurse to one of the men's wives. Apprehensive of having another, I resolved on a separation, but I knew not how to break my intention to her. The newborn delight of a mother seemed to absorb all her faculties. The child is continually in her hands, she says he's my picture, and, to do the little rascal justice, I think there is a likeness; but to my story: —while I was deliberating as to the least painful mode of conveying my resolution to her, I received a few days since the astounding intelligence of her being *encore enceinte!!* Murder! murder! isn't this too bad? Still I can't blame her, knowing that I am a *particeps criminis*. But, what will the governor say? Ay, that's the question. In two years two copper grand-children; three I mean, for I understand my Columbian pet is thriving apace. Why the old gentleman will destroy me. Was ever a man so tricked? There's the fruits of striving to cheat Nature; but I must send him a long, explanatory, apologetical letter, introduce morality, &c. Française may now as well remain until I hear from him; and if he interposes no objection, I do not intend to change her, I have called my last *Hector*. Adieu!

The third description of men in the Company's service are the Iroquois, Nipisings, and others of the native tribes of Canada. These Indians have been all nearly reclaimed from their original state of barbarism, and now profess the Roman Catholic religion. They engage for limited periods in the Company's service as canoe-men and hunters, but on lower terms than are usually allowed to the French Canadians. They are strong, able-bodied men, good hunters, and well acquainted with the management of canoes. They are immoderately attached to the use of ardent spirits,[3] are rather quarrelsome, revengeful, and sometimes insubordinate; and during their periods of intoxication the utmost prudence and firmness are necessary to check their ferocious propensities, and confine them within proper bounds. They are generally employed on the east side of the mountains, but we had a few of them on the Columbia. One, named George Teewhattahownie, was a powerful man about six feet high. On one occasion, during our voyage to the sea, we had a stiff breeze, and George, who was foreman of my canoe, kept up a heavy press of sail. I requested him repeatedly to take in a reef, and pointed out the danger to which we were exposed in the event of an accident. He appeared to pay no attention to my request, and I was at length obliged to use peremp-

[3] The Iroquois, in particular, had a general reputation as troublemakers. McKenzie, Ross, and Ogden, in their conduct of the Snake River brigade, had all had trouble with their Iroquois.

tory and threatening language, which produced a forced and sulky obedience. A few days after our arrival at Fort George he came into my room in a state of intoxication, and ungovernable rage, with a vessel containing rum in his left hand, and in his right his *couteau de chasse;* in short his whole appearance was wild and savage, and I at once guessed his visit was not of a friendly nature. His opening speech realised my suspicions.

"Cox, you toad, prepare for death! you abused me, and I must have my revenge."

"You're not sober, George; go sleep awhile, and we'll talk on this subject tomorrow."

"No; you insulted me before the men, and I must have satisfaction; but as you're a young man, I will now only take one of your ears!"

I became a little easy on finding he had lowered his demands; but as I had an equal affection for both lugs, and as "the prejudice ran in favour of two," I had no wish, like Jack Absolute, to affect singularity in that respect. After some further parley, and finding he was determined to try his knife on my auricular cartilages, I told him to retire, or I should be obliged to order him into confinement. "Ha crapaud!" said he, "do you threaten Teewhattahownie?" and at the same instant rushed on me like a grizzly bear. I was now forced to draw my dagger in self-defence, and in parrying off his thrust gave him a severe wound across the fingers of the right hand. He dropped the knife, but instantly seized it with the left hand, and at the same time attempted to catch me, which I avoided by running under his arm, and as he turned round was compelled to give him a severe cut, which nearly laid open one side of his head. He now became quite furious, roared like a buffalo, and with the blood streaming down his face appeared more like a demon than a human being. I thought to fly, but in the attempt he seized the skirt of my coat, and I was obliged once more to give him another wound across the left hand, which obliged him to drop the knife. A desperate struggle then followed for the dagger, which, from his great strength, he must have wrested from me, had not the noise occasioned by his bellowing and my cries for assistance brought Mr. Montour and some of the men into the room. With much difficulty they succeeded in binding him hand and foot, and lodging him in the guardroom. He tore off the dressings that were applied to his wounds, refused every assistance, and the greater part of the night was spent in wild yells and ferocious threats against me. Nature at last became exhausted, and he fell asleep, in which state his wounds were dressed. None of them were dangerous. Between the loss of blood and a long fast he became quite cool on the following day, and when told of what had occurred he could scarcely believe it, cursed the rum as the cause, and made a solemn promise never again to drink to intoxication. At the end of a couple of days I interceded and had him liberated. He appeared most grateful, acknowledged that he deserved what he got, expressed his surprise that I did not kill him, and declared if he ever heard a man say a bad word of me for wounding him he would knock him down. I believe his regret was sincere, and from that period until the following year, when I quitted the Columbia, I never saw him in a state of inebriety.

Conclusion

Coalition of the two Companies—New Caledonia—Description of the Chil-cotins, Talkotins, &c.—Soil, produce, lakes, rivers, animals, climates—Pe-culiarities of the natives—Suicides—Cruelty to relatives—Horrible treat-ment of prisoners—Sanguinary quarrels—Extraordinary ceremonies attend-ing the dead—Barbarities practised on widows, &.—Table of population

It will be seen from a perusal of the foregoing pages that they contain simply a detail of such events as occurred under my own observation, or were cotemporaneous with my residence in the interior. I thought it better to follow this course, than, by the introduction of new matter, to break in on the regular chronological order of the narrative. Since I left the Indian country I have maintained a correspondence with many of my old associates there, particularly Mr. Joseph M'Gillivray, from whose friendly communications the information contained in the following pages is chiefly extracted.

It will, I have no doubt, be found highly interesting; and his de-scription of New Caledonia furnishes the only information we possess of a portion of the American continent respecting which we have been heretofore perfectly ignorant.

A few years subsequent to my quitting the Columbia the Company abandoned Fort George (of which I have made such frequent men-tion), and erected another on a larger scale in a beautiful situation at Bellevue Point on the northern shore, and about eighty miles from the entrance of the river. This point was so named by Lieutenant Brough-ton, who had been sent up the Columbia by Vancouver, and in honour of the latter the Company has called the new establishment "Fort Vancouver."

The long and violent opposition between the Hudson's Bay and

367

North-West companies ceased in the year 1821 by their coalition. The ruinous rivalship that so long existed between them must have ultimately proved destructive to both, had not a few sensible men come forward, and by their united exertions succeeded in forming a junction. The preliminaries were signed in London, in March, 1821, and confirmed at Fort William by the wintering partners in the July following. The particulars of the treaty would be uninteresting to the general reader; and I shall here only remark that the old North-Westers are by no means pleased with it, and loudly complain of some of its minor arrangements, &c.

New Caledonia

This district extends from 51° 30′ north lat. to about 56°. Its extreme western boundary is 124° 10′. Its principal trading post is called Alexandria, after the celebrated traveller Six Alexander Mackenzie. It is built on the banks of Fraser's River, in about lat. 53° N. The country in its immediate vicinity presents a beautiful and picturesque appearance. The banks of the river are rather low; but a little distance inland some rising grounds are visible, partially diversified by groves of fir and poplar.

Six Alexander Mackenzie, in his voyage of discovery across the continent in 1793, came to the spot on which the fort is built, and was dissuaded by the Indians from following the course of the river to its mouth. On quitting this place he proceeded to the West Road River,[1] from whence by an overland journey he succeeded in reaching the shores of the Pacific Ocean.

This country is full of small lakes, rivers, and marshes. It extends about ten days' march in a north and north-east direction. To the south and south-east the Atnah, or Chin Indian country, extends about one hundred miles; on the east there is a chain of lakes, and the mountains bordering Thompson's River; while to the westward and northwest lie the lands of the Naskotins and Clinches.

The principal rivers are Fraser's, Quesnel's, Rough Poplar, Chilcotin, and West Road. Of these Fraser's River only is navigable.[2] It

[1] The West Road River is a tributary of the Blackwater, which in turn is a tributary of the Fraser. Mackenzie went up the Blackwater and then up the West Road on his way to the ocean.

[2] The Fraser River is not navigable. It was for that reason that Mackenzie turned back and took the Blackwater route.

receives the waters of Quesnel's, and West Poplar rivers, which issue from small lakes to the eastward.

The lakes are numerous, and some of them tolerably large: one, two, and even three days are at times required to cross some of them. They abound in a plentiful variety of fish, such as trout, sucker, &c.; and the natives assert that white-fish are sometimes taken. These lakes are generally fed by mountain streams, and many of them spread out, and are lost in the surrounding marshes.

In visiting the Naskotin and Chin Indians our conveyance is by canoes on Fraser's River; but our journeys to Bear Lake, Kloukins, and Chilcotins, must be performed on foot.

The trading goods are now obtained from the Columbia department, to which the returns of furs are forwarded. Horses are used for conveying the goods, and the journey generally occupies six weeks. The roads are extremely bad, and in every direction we encounter numerous rivulets, small lakes, and marshes.

The soil is poor: an indifferent mould, not exceeding eight inches in depth, covers a bed of gravel and sand. All the vegetables we planted, notwithstanding the utmost care and precaution, nearly failed; and the last crop of potatoes did not yield one-fourth of the seed planted.

On the banks of the river, and in the interior, the trees consist of poplar, cypress, alder, cedar, birch, and different species of fir, spruce, and willow. There is not the same variety of wild fruit as on the Columbia; and this year (1827) the berries generally failed. Service-berries, choke-cherries, gooseberries, strawberries, and red whortle-berries, are gathered; but among the Indians the service-berry is the great favourite. There are various kinds of roots, which the natives preserve and dry for periods of scarcity. There is only one kind which we can eat. It is called *Tza-chin,* has a bitter taste, but when eaten with salmon imparts an agreeable zest, and effectually destroys the disagreeable smell of that fish, when smoke-dried. St. John's wort is very common, and has been successfully applied as a fomentation in topical inflammations. A kind of weed, which the natives convert into a species of flax, is in general demand. An evergreen similar to that we found at the mouth of the Columbia (and before described), with small berries growing in clusters like grapes, also flourishes in this district. Sarsaparilla and bear-root are found in abundance. A strong decoction of the two latter with the berries last mentioned has been repeatedly tried by our men in venereal cases, and has always proved successful.

White earth abounds in the vicinity of the fort; and one description of it, mixed with oil and lime, might be converted into excellent soap. Coal in considerable quantities has been discovered; and in many places we observed a species of red earth, much resembling lava, and which appeared to be of volcanic origin.

We also found in different parts of New Caledonia quartz, rock crystal, cobalt, granite, fuller's earth, some beautiful specimens of black marble, and limestone in small quantities, which appeared to have been forced down the beds of the rivers from the mountains.

The jumping deer, or chevreuil, together with the rein- and red-deer, frequent the vicinity of the mountains in considerable numbers, and in the summer season they oftentimes descend to the banks of the rivers and the adjacent flat country.

The marmot and wood-rat also abound. The flesh of the former is exquisite, and capital robes are made out of its skin; but the latter is a very destructive animal.

Their dogs are of diminutive size, and strongly resemble those of the Esquimaux, with the curled-up tail, small ears, and pointed nose. We purchased numbers of them for the kettle, their flesh constituting the chief article of food in our holiday feasts for Christmas and New Year.

The fur-bearing animals consist of beavers; bears, black, brown, and grizzly; otters, fishers, lynxes, martins; foxes, red, cross, and silver; minks, musquash, wolverines, and ermines. Rabbits also are so numerous that the natives manage to subsist on them during the periods that salmon is scarce.

Under the head of ornithology we have the bustard, or Canadian *outarde* (wildgoose), swans, ducks of various descriptions, hawks, plovers, cranes, white-headed eagles, magpies, crows, vultures, wood-thrush, red-breasted thrush, or robin, woodpeckers, gulls, pelicans, hawks, partridges, pheasants, and snow-birds.

The spring commences in April, when the wild flowers begin to bud, and from thence to the latter end of May the weather is delightful. In June it rains incessantly, with strong southerly and easterly winds. During the months of July and August the heat is intolerable; and in September the fogs are so dense, that it is quite impossible to distinguish the opposite side of the river any morning before ten o'clock. Colds and rheumatisms are prevalent among the natives during this period; nor are our people exempt from them. In October the falling of the leaves and occasional frost announce the beginning winter. The lakes and parts of the rivers are frozen in November. The snow seldom exceeds twenty-four inches in depth. The mercury in Fahrenheit's thermometer falls in January to 15° below 0; but this does not continue many days. In general, I may say, the climate is neither unhealthy nor unpleasant; and if the natives used common prudence, they would undoubtedly live to an advanced age.

The salmon-fishery commences about the middle of July, and ceases in October. This is a busy period for the natives; for upon their industry in saving a sufficiency of salmon for the winter depends their chief support. Their method of catching the salmon is ingenious, and does not differ much from that practised by the upper natives of the Columbia. A certain part of the river is enclosed by a number of stakes about twelve feet high, and extending about thirty feet from the shore. A netting of rods is attached to the stakes, to prevent the salmon running through. A conical machine, called a *vorveau,* is next formed; it is eighteen feet long, and five feet high, and is made of rods about one inch and a quarter asunder, and lashed to hoops with whattap.[3] One end is formed like a funnel to admit the fish. Two smaller machines of nearly equal length are joined to it. It requires a number of hands to attach these *vorveaux* to the stakes. They are raised a little out of the water; and the salmon in their ascent leap into the *boot* or broad part, and fall into the enclosed space, where they are easily killed with spears. This contrivance is admirably calculated to catch fish; and when salmon is abundant, the natives take from eight to nine hundred daily.

The salmon fishery this year (1827) completely failed, which obliged us to send to Kamloops, a post belonging to the Columbia department, for a supply. We got thence 2,500, and subsequently 1,500 from Mr. Connolly, which, with some of our old stock and thirty-five kegs of potatoes, kept us from starvation.

Jub, suckers, trout, and white-fish are caught in the lakes; and in the month of October, towards the close of the salmon fishery, we

[3] A tough fibrous root used in sewing bark canoes. It is split into various lengths, quite flat and flexible, and seldom exceeding one-eighth of an inch in breadth.—R. C.

catch trout of a most exquisite flavour. Large-sized sturgeon are occasionally taken in the *vorveaux*, but they are not relished by the natives.

In consequence of several of the Chilcotin[4] tribe having represented that beaver was plentiful in their country, some of our people visited it, whose statements fully corroborated those of the Indians; and the northern council of Rupert's Land therefore determined about two years ago to establish a trading post in that quarter. A circumstance, however, shortly after occurred, which has hitherto prevented the Company from carrying their intention into effect.

The Talkotins,[5] who inhabit the banks of Fraser's River, in the vicinity of Alexandria, were formerly on the most friendly terms with the Chilcotins, and when salmon failed among the latter they were always permitted to fish in Fraser's River.

In the winter of 1826 four young men of the Talkotins proceeded on a hunting excursion to the Chilcotin lands. A quarrel, the cause of which we could never ascertain, occurred between them, and three of the young men were butchered. The fourth, who escaped dangerously wounded, arrived at the fort on the 19th March, and immediately communicated the disastrous intelligence to his countrymen. One Chilcotin, who was at the fort, would have fallen a victim to their revenge had we not interfered, and with much difficulty concealed him until an opportunity offered for his escape; which, notwithstanding the vigilance of his enemies, he effected.[6] A sanguinary war followed, and in some skirmishes the Talkotin chief lost three nephews. This determined him to carry hostilities into the enemy's camp; and, having selected a chosen band of warriors, twenty-four in number, they departed on the 19th of April, and on the 20th of June returned with five prisoners, and the scalps of twelve men, women, and children, whom they had surprised and killed.

A large party of Chilcotins, who were quite ignorant of the rival chief's successful expedition, appeared on the 21st of June on the banks of the river opposite the fort. They killed one stray Talkotin, but retired without coming to a general engagement. A few weeks afterwards a party, consisting of twenty-seven, made their appearance, and their chief made an oration, which, owing to a strong wind,

[4] The Chilkotins are Athapascan and related to the Carriers.
[5] The Talkotins, or Tautins, are another branch of the Carriers.
[6] This poor fellow was subsequently murdered by a Talkotin.—R. C.

we could not understand. They encountered some of our people who were attending the gardens on the opposite bank of the river, but did not injure them. They also retired without coming to blows. During the summer the Talkotins were constantly kept on the *qui vive* by various rumours of intended attacks; and at length, on the morning of the 24th of September, a formidable party of Chilcotins, amounting to eighty warriors, appeared on the banks of the river. The Talkotins were lodged in a log-house, surrounded by rows of strong palisades, with numerous loop-holes between. The battle commenced a little after day-break; but, owing to the manner in which the latter were protected, their loss was trifling—say one man and one old woman killed; while that of the Chilcotins amounted to six killed and many dangerously wounded. Still they pressed on, and might have been ultimately successful, had we not forwarded to the Talkotins a supply of arms and ammunition, which effectually checked their advances on the log-house. A woman of the Chilcotin tribe, who happened to be at the fort, observing the assistance we had given the enemy, stole away unperceived and communicated to her countrymen the circumstance; on learning which, they at once determined to retreat. On their departure they pronounced vengeance against us, and threatened to cut off all white men that might thereafter fall in their way.

No friendly overture has been since made by either tribe; and although we sent word repeatedly to the Chilcotins that we should feel happy in bringing about a reconciliation, we have not as yet received an answer, and none of them have been seen in our neighbourhood since Sept. 1826. Notwithstanding this apparent disinclination on their part to renew relations of friendship, we determined in the autumn of 1827 to establish a trading post in their country; but were prevented from doing so by the total failure of salmon.

I herewith subjoin a brief sketch of the district. The Chilcotin River takes its rise in a lake of the same name; its course from Alexandria is S.S.E.; its length, including its meanderings, about 180 miles; and its breadth varies from forty to sixty yards; it is quite shallow, and full of rapids. The lake is about half a mile in breadth, and 60 miles in length, and is surrounded by lofty mountains, from which a number of small rivulets descend. It contains abundance of sucker, trout, and white-fish. Salmon however is the favourite fish; but as it does not regularly ascend their river, they are often obliged

373

to content themselves with the produce of the lake. They are poor hunters, otherwise they might chiefly subsist on animal food; for the rein-deer, with the red- and moose-deer, are found in great numbers in the mountains; and in the autumnal months the black-tail and jumping deer are plentiful. Beaver must be abundant; for men, women, and children are clad in robes of the fur of that animal.

It is impossible to ascertain with accuracy the number of the tribe; but I conceive the men capable of bearing arms cannot be under 180. They are cleanly in their persons, and remarkably hospitable.

The Chilcotins speak the Carrier language, but many of their words bear a strong affinity to the Slave Indian dialect.

They are extremely fond of iron-works, and appear to be well acquainted with the use of fire-arms. We saw one excellent gun in their possession, marked "Barret, 1808." The owner said he purchased it from Indians who came from the sea coast. According to their accounts, travellers may in six days, from the end of Chilcotin Lake, after crossing a range of mountains, reach a river in a southerly direction which discharges its waters into the ocean, at a place where the Indians carry on a traffic with Europeans. From their general behaviour we were led to imagine they must have had frequent intercourse with the whites; and a peculiar kind of blanket, resembling a rug, which was in common use amongst them, we supposed had been obtained from Russian traders. The journey from Alexandria to the Chilcotin Lake occupies eighteen days; and as proof of the richness of the country in fur-bearing animals, I have only to state that the small experimental party sent thither in December 1825 purchased from the natives between three and four hundred excellent beaver skins.

The Indians on the upper part of Fraser's River are divided into various tribes, under the following names; viz. Slowercuss, Dinais, Nascud, Dinnee, and Talkotin. They are evidently sprung from one common origin. Their manners and customs are the same; and there is no variation in their language, which bears a close affinity to that spoken by the Chepewyans and Beaver Indians.

Several families generally club together and build a house, the size of which is proportioned to the number of inhabitants, and is partitioned off into several divisions. The building has one long ridge pole, which in several places is uncovered, for the free egress of the smoke. They are supremely dirty and lazy, and full of vermin, which they take great pleasure in eating. They never bathe or wash their bodies, which, with the interior of their dwellings, and the surrounding neighbourhood, present a shockingly repulsive appearance of filthy nastiness, which we never observed among any other tribe. When reproached with their want of cleanliness they replied, that the dirt preserved them from the intense cold of winter, and protected them equally from the scorching sun of summer!

The women are, if possible, worse than the men; and when they wish to appear very fine they saturate their hair with salmon oil, after which it is powdered over with the down of birds, and painted with red ochre mixed with oil. Such another preparation for the head is certainly not used by any other portion of his majesty's copper-coloured subjects. While in this oleaginous state they are quite unapproachable near a fire; and even the *voyageur,* whose sense of smelling is not over-refined, cannot bring his nasal organ into a warm apartment with one of those bedizened beauties.

It is quite common to see six or eight of the men during the summer, while their wives and children are digging roots for their subsistence, stretch their filthy covering on branches, and expose their naked bodies to the sun, changing their position as it revolves in its course.

Independently of the starvation to which their incurable indolence subjects them, it also entails on them diseases which often prove fatal to numbers; and asthma, with rheumatic and pulmonary complaints, are quite common among them.

They are generally about the middle size, and few of them reach to the height of five feet nine inches. Their colour is a light copper, with the same long lank hair and black eyes which distinguish the other aborigines of America. Their features are good, and, were it not for the barbarous incrustation which surrounds them, might be called prepossessing. The women are stouter than the men, but inferior to them in beauty. The dress of both consists of a robe made of marmot, or rabbit skin, tied round the neck and reaching to the knees, with a small slip of leather or cloth covering underneath. In the summer months the men dispense even with this slight covering, and wander about in a complete state of nudity. They are fond of European clothing; and such of them as were enabled to purchase a coat, trousers, and shirt, took great pride in appearing in them at the fort.

They are much addicted to gambling, and umpires are chosen to see that each party plays fairly; still their games seldom terminate without a quarrel. They will gamble their guns, robes, and even their shoes. One of them, who had been out three months on a hunting excursion, returned with a large lot of prime beaver, with which he intended to purchase a gun for himself, and other articles for his wife and children. His evil genius induced him to play; and in a short time he lost half his stock. He then desisted, and was about retiring to the fort; but in the mean time several of the gamblers collected about him and upbraided him with want of spirit. His resolution was overcome, and he recommenced; fortune was still unpropitious, and in less than an hour he lost the remainder of his furs. The following day he came to us with tears in his eyes, and having related his misfortune, and promised never to run so great a risk again, we gave him goods on credit to the amount of twenty beavers.

They are fond of feasting, and on particular occasions invite their friends from villages thirty or forty miles distant. When the entertainment is over, the guest has nothing more to expect; and no matter how long he may remain, there is no renewal of hospitality. Gambling is carried on to a dreadful extreme at these assemblages.

Polygamy is practised, but is not very general, few of them being able to support more than one wife. There are no marriage ceremonies. The choice of each party is kept unfettered; and it frequently happens that if their tempers do not agree, the union is dissolved by mutual consent. The women are unfruitful, which may be attributed to the many laborious avocations to which they are condemned, particularly that of digging for roots; and abortions are also frequent among them.

Prostitution is notoriously practised among unmarried females, and is productive of disease to a deplorable extent. Few escape the consequences resulting from this general depravity, and many fall victims to it. Leprosy is also common among the young people of both sexes, and proceeds from the same demoralising cause. Sickness or excessive labour produces a depression of spirits among the females, many of whom while in that state commit suicide. We saw the bodies of several of these wretched beings who had hanged themselves from trees in sequestered parts of the wood.

Their doctor, or man of medicine, differs little from the same personage on the Columbia, except that the profession here is rather dangerous.

The same mode of throwing the patient on his back, beating the parts affected, singing in a loud voice to drown his cries, &c., is practised here; but in the event of his death, his relatives generally sacrifice the quack or some one of his connexions. This summary way of punishment is admirably calculated to keep the profession free from intruders; and their medical practitioners, I am happy to state, are becoming every day less numerous.

The affectionate regard for friends and relatives, which, more or less, characterises other tribes, appears to be unknown amongst these savages. A few instances, which came under our personal knowledge, may be sufficient to prove their total want of all the finer feelings of humanity.

In December, 1826, an elderly man, nearly related to the Talkotin chief, fell short of provisions, and although he was surrounded by numbers who had abundance of dried salmon, he was actually allowed to die of starvation in the midst of plenty. The day after his death the corpse was burned, and no one seemed to mourn his loss.

One night during the same winter a young woman nearly naked, her body covered with bruises, and dreadfully frost-bitten, came to the fort, and begged for admission. This was readily granted. She alleged she had been in a starving condition, and had asked her husband for a little dried salmon, which he refused to give, although he had plenty in his lodge; that she watched an opportunity during his absence to take a small piece, which he discovered her in the act of eating; and that without any other cause he gave her a dreadful beating, and then turned her out, declaring she should no longer live with him. She added, that all her friends refused her assistance, and that she would have inevitably perished from the inclemency of the weather but for the protection and relief we afforded her. During her narrative her uncle entered, and, on learning the particulars, he declared he would make up the quarrel, and went away, promising to return shortly with some rabbits. With much difficulty we succeeded in restoring her to health; but neither husband, uncle, nor any other relation ever after troubled us with inquiries concerning her, but she still remains at the fort living on our bounty.

Another instance, and I shall have done: In January, 1827, two stout young men, brothers, with their wives and children, and a grey-headed, infirm old man, their father, encamped for a few days close to the fort.

Late in the evening of the second day after their departure we were surprised at seeing the unfortunate old man crawling towards the house, and crying out piteously for "fire and salmon." His hands and feet were frost-bitten, and he was scarcely able to move. A piece of salmon and a glass of rum quickly revived him, when he told us that on that morning his sons abandoned him at the place they had slept at the night before, and on going away, told him he might take care of himself as well as he could, as they would not any longer be encumbered with him!

These cases establish a degree of barbarism I believe unparalled in any country; and I know of no redeeming feature to counterbalance them. We have repeatedly afforded relief to numbers who were dying from starvation or disease, and who, but for our assistance, would have perished; yet ingratitude is so strongly implanted in their savage nature, that these very individuals in periods of plenty have been the first to prevent us from taking a salmon; and whenever a dispute or misunderstanding arose between our people and the natives, these scoundrels have been seen brandishing their weapons and urging their countrymen to exterminate us.

They are also incorrigible thieves and liars. No *chevalier d'industrie* could excel them in skilful operations; and it required our utmost vigilance to guard against their felonious propensities; while their disregard of truth is so glaring, that we have actually heard them contradict facts of which we ourselves had been eye-witnesses.

During the severity of winter they make excavations in the ground sufficiently capacious to contain a number of persons; and in these holes they burrow until the warm weather once more permits them to venture above ground. They preserve their dry salmon rolled up on baskets of birch bark in holes of a similar description, but somewhat smaller. The smell from these subterranean dwellings while thus occupied, is horribly offensive, and no white man could stand within its influence. Men, women, and children, dogs, fleas, &c., all live together in this filthy state.

It has been already mentioned that in the battle of September, 1827, they killed some Chilcotins, and took others prisoners. Their treatment of both dead and living was in perfect accordance with their general character. After having taken off the scalps, they raised the bodies of the deceased on stumps of trees, and exhibited them to the Atnahs, a band of whom had been specially invited to witness

378

these trophies of their valour. One would then plunge his knife into the corpse, a second hack the skull with his axe, and a third perforate the body with arrows. Women and children equally participated in this savage amusement, and all washed their hands and faces in the blood of their victims, which they did not remove until it dried and fell off.

Among the prisoners was one woman with a child at her breast. A Talkotin ruffian instantly cut its throat, and, holding the infant on the point of his knife, asked the mother, with a degree of horrible exultation, if it "smelt good." She replied "No." He repeated the question, but still received the same answer. Irritated at her obstinacy, he seized her violently by the neck, and asked her a third time if it "smelt good." The wretched woman, knowing that death awaited her, in the event of another refusal, at length faltered out an affirmative. "Is it very good?" repeated the savage. "Yes," she replied, "very good"; upon which, flinging her from him, and dashing the lifeless remains of her infant on the ground, he walked away.

The war-dance next commenced; and the unfortunate prisoners were introduced into the middle of the circle, and compelled to join in the dancing and singing, while at intervals their inhuman conquerors displayed the scalps of their fathers, brothers, or husbands, and rubbing them across their faces, asked with ferocious joy if they "smelled good?"

We endeavoured to purchase some young children which were among the captives, with a view of returning them to their friends; but they refused all our offers. They, however, promised that none of them should be injured; but their habitual perfidy was manifested in this as in all their other transactions; for we learned that on the same night a child was killed, and the body burned; a few days afterwards another was thrown alive into a large fire, and consumed; in the course of the winter our people discovered the remains of three others, with scarcely any flesh on their bones; and we had good reason to believe they had been starved to death.

Inhumanity to prisoners, however, is a vice which these Indians practice in common with all the savage tribes of America; but in their domestic quarrels the Talkotins evince the same brutal and sanguinary disposition; a remarkable instance of which occurred in the year 1826. A young man who had killed a rein-deer, determined to give a treat to his friends, and having concealed it, as he thought, in a place of security, proceeded to their various dwellings for the purpose of inviting them to the feast. In the interim, however, some of the tribe discovered the hidden treasure, the greater part of which they made away with. He became highly exasperated at his disappointment, and in his passion slew one man whom he found sitting at a fire broiling part of the animal. The friends of the deceased instantly armed themselves, and having surrounded the lodge in which the owner of the deer resided, butchered all his relations, amounting to seven individuals. He however escaped, and being a person of some influence, quickly collected a number of his friends, determined on revenge; but the murderers in the mean time fled to the mountains, where they have lurked about since, occasionally obtaining relief by stealth either from our people, or from some of their own countrymen.

Since the battle of September, 1827, the Talkotins have, as a measure of security, established their village within pistol-shot of our fort. They are by no means pleasant neighbours. They are in a constant state of apprehension from the Chilcotins, and pass the nights up to two or three o'clock each morning singing, screaming, and howling in a most disagreeable manner. It is almost impossible to sleep. The slightest rustling in the branches, or the barking of a dog, turns out the whole population; and if a strange Indian appears, he is immediately magnified into a host of warriors, coming to destroy both them and the white men.

The ceremonies attending the dead are very singular, and quite peculiar to this tribe. The body of the deceased is kept nine days laid out in his lodge, and on the tenth it is burned. For this purpose a rising ground is selected, on which are laid a number of sticks about seven feet long, of cyprus neatly split, and in the interstices is placed a quantity of gummy wood. During these operations invitations are dispatched to the natives of the neighbouring villages requesting their attendance at the ceremony. When the preparations are perfected the corpse is placed on the pile, which is immediately ignited, and during the process of burning the by-standers appear to be in a high state of merriment. If a stranger happen to be present they invariably plunder him; but if that pleasure be denied them, they never separate without quarreling among themselves. Whatever property the deceased possessed is placed about the corpse; and if he happened to be a person of consequence, his friends generally purchase a capot, a shirt, a pair of trousers, &c., which articles are also laid round the pile. If the doctor who attended him has escaped uninjured, he is obliged to be present at the ceremony, and for the last time tries his skill in restoring the defunct to animation. Failing in this, he throws on the body a piece of leather, or some other article, as a present, which in some measure appeases the resentment of his relations, and preserves the unfortunate quack from being maltreated. During the nine days the corpse is laid out, the widow of the deceased is obliged to sleep alongside it from sun-set to sun-rise; and from this custom there is no relaxation, even during the hottest days of summer! While the doctor is performing his last operation she must lie on the pile; and after the fire is applied to it, she cannot stir until the doctor orders her to be removed; which, however, is never done until her body is completely covered with blisters. After being placed on her legs, she is obliged to pass her hands gently through the flames, and collect some of the liquid fat which issues from the corpse, with which she is permitted to rub on her face and body! When the friends of the deceased observe the sinews of the legs and arms beginning to contract, they compel the unfortunate widow to go again on the pile, and by dint of hard pressing to straighten those members.

If during her husband's lifetime she had been known to have committed any act of infidelity, or omitted administering to him savoury food, or neglected his clothing, &c., she is now made to suffer severely for such lapses of duty by his relations, who frequently fling her on the funeral pile, from which she is dragged by her friends; and thus, between alternate scorching and cooling, she is dragged backwards and forwards until she falls into a state of insensibility.

After the process of burning the corpse has terminated the widow collects the larger bones, which she rolls up in an envelope of birch bark, and which she is obliged for some years afterwards to carry on her back! She is now considered and treated as a slave; all the laborious duties of cooking, collecting fuel, &c., devolve on her. She must obey the orders of all the women, and even of the children belonging to the village, and the slightest mistake or disobedience subjects her to the infliction of a heavy punishment. The ashes of her husband are carefully collected and deposited in a grave, which it is her duty to keep free from weeds; and should any such appear, she is obliged to root them out with her *fingers!* During this operation her husband's relatives stand by and beat her in a cruel manner until the task is completed, or she falls a victim to their brutality. The wretched widows, to avoid this complicated cruelty, frequently commit suicide. Should she, however, linger on for three or four years, the friends of her husband agree to relieve her from her painful mourning. This is a ceremony of much consequence, and the preparations for it occupy a considerable time, generally from six to eight months. The hunters proceed to the various districts in which deer and beaver abound, and after collecting large quantities of meat and fur, return to the village. The skins are immediately bartered for guns, ammunition, clothing, trinkets, &c. Invitations are then sent to the inhabitants of the various friendly villages, and when they have all assembled the feast commences, and presents are distributed to each visitor. The object of their meeting is then explained, and the woman is brought forward, still carrying on her back the bones of her late husband, which are now removed, and placed in a carved box, which is nailed or otherwise fastened to a post twelve feet high. Her conduct as a faithful widow is next highly eulogised, and the ceremony of her manumission is completed by one man powdering on her head the down of birds, and another pouring on it the contents of a bladder of oil! She is then at liberty to marry again, or lead a life of single blessedness; but few of them I believe wish to encounter the risk of attending a second widowhood.

The men are condemned to a similar ordeal, but they do not bear it with equal fortitude; and numbers fly to distant quarters to avoid the brutal treatment which custom has established as a kind of religious rite.

Mr. M'Gillivray here concludes his remarks on the various tribes about Fraser's River by a table, which he formed from the most authentic sources of information, and which will show their relative numbers of married and unmarried men, women, &c.

Table of Population

Names of Tribes	Chiefs	H'ds. families	Married		Unmarried				Children		Total	Remarks
			Men	Women	Widowers	Widows	Young Men	Young Women	Boys	Girls		
Those Kuz Lake	1	2	12	15	0	1	16	15	8	6	76	This tribe hunts on the Chilcotin Mountains. The lake, on the shores of which they reside, supplies the water of the north branch of West River. A. Mackenzie places the latitude in 53° 4′ 30″ N.
Naskotins in various villages	4	15	53	75	4	4	47	17	21	20	260	The Naskotins hunt with the above, but the greater number generally hunt towards Bear Lake, and the range of mountains to the N.E., where beaver is plentiful.
Talkotins at Alexandria	2	2	30	36	8	6	34	16	17	15	166	The lands of the Talkotins are poor. They hunt chiefly about the mountains of the N. E.; but are afraid to venture far, from the dread of the Chilcotins. They are very bad hunters, and their limits are much circumscribed.
Atnahs in various villages	4	20	100	142	1	19	91	50	43	40	510	The Atnahs do not bring much beaver to Alexandria, owing to the exorbitant tariff of that department, and they resort principally to our establishment at Thompson's River, where they procure better prices for their furs.
	11	39	195	268	13	30	188	98	89	81	1012	With the exception of the Atnahs, the same language is spoken in a direct line from the N.E. head of Deserter's River, in lat. 53° 30′ to Hudson's Bay; so that a Chipewyan leaving Churchill River, and following a N.W. direction, would make himself perfectly well understood.

Our census of the Chilcotins is imperfect; but we reckoned two chiefs, 52 heads of families, and 130 married men between the age of twenty and forty. Their country abounds in beaver; but we are not yet acquainted with their hunting grounds.

Appendix

Extract of a Letter From the Interior, Dated July, 1829

The intelligence from this country is by no means of a pleasant nature. The number of lives lost last winter is incredible, particularly in your old department, the Columbia.

The Company's ship, after a tolerably quick passage from England, was lost on the bar, and the entire crew, twenty-six in number, were inhumanly butchered by the Clatsops.[1]

Your friend Ogden,[2] in a hunting excursion, was attacked by a party of the Black-feet, who killed four of his men; and six of the people stationed at New Caledonia were murdered by the Carriers during the winter.

Two American parties, under the command of Messrs. Smith[3] and Tulloch,[4] were completely cut off; not a soul escaped; and property to a considerable amount fell into the hands of the savages.

These misfortunes have considerably weakened our influence with the Indians on the Columbia, whose behaviour, in consequence, has become very bold and daring, and we greatly fear the ensuing winter may be productive of more disasters.

We shall have much difficulty in filling up the appointments for

[1] The *William and Anne* was the supply ship of the Hudson's Bay Company post at Fort Vancouver. It was wrecked just inside the entrance to the Columbia River early in 1829. While there is no doubt that the vessel was pillaged by the Indians, there is not a shred of valid historical evidence that the crew was massacred by the natives.

[2] Ogden led his fifth and last expedition into the Snake River country this year. He had had many adventures, and it is difficult to tell to which of these Cox refers.

[3] Jedediah Smith was not massacred. He and three of his men escaped, although the others met their death at the hands of the natives near the present Umpqua River.

[4] Tulloch was not massacred. In 1832, he established Fort Cass at the confluence of the Big Horn and Yellowstone rivers.

384

that district next spring; in fact, symptoms of rebellion have already begun to manifest themselves, and several of our gentlemen have been heard to declare, that in the event of their being nominated to the Columbia, they will retire from the service sooner than risk their lives among such sanguinary barbarians. God speed them! I say. Numbers of them have been long enough enjoying idleness and luxury on the east side of the mountains, and it is only fair they should experience some of our Columbian privations. I have had my full share of them, and am therefore under no apprehensions of being ordered there in a hurry.

Extract of Another Letter

In your last you expressed a wish to know the population of the new colony at the Red River, and how they are getting on. I have not been there lately, but I enclose you the last census taken about two years ago, since which period it has scarcely increased. Besides men, women, boys, and girls, I give you a list of the most useful animals in possession of the settlers, in order that my statistics may be perfect so far as regards the animal world.

189	married men
37	unmarried do
193	married women and widows
96	young women
237	girls
90	young men
210	boys
1052	souls

178	houses	33	barns
126	stables	164	horses
87	mares	27	bulls
295	cows	76	oxen
147	calves	20	swine
96	carts	31	ploughs
39	arrows	13	boats
173	canoes		

There are 672½ acres of land in a state of cultivation; 144,105 acres of prairie, and 21,901 acres of woodland. The total extent of lands measured amounts to 170,135 acres three roods.

The population would have been double the above number were it not for the falling off of the Swiss and the de Meurons,[5] most of whom have abandoned the colony, and proceeded to St. Louis and the banks of the Mississippi, and their places have not been supplied by any fresh arrivals from England.

Extract of a Letter from Churchill, or Prince of Wales' Fort, 1829

After spending several years among our new establishments on the north-west side of this great continent, behold me now in one of our most ancient settlements on the north-east side. Any thing in the shape of antiquity is a novelty in the *pays sauvage;* and as I know you are fond of novelty, I must give you a sketch of this redoubtable fortress. Churchill was erected in 1733, under the superintendence of Mr. James Robson, chief architect to the Hudson's Bay Company. It was well fortified with a raveline and four bastions, and the walls measure twenty-seven feet in breadth. Forty pieces of cannon were mounted on the walls; in fact the place was deemed impregnable; yet, notwithstanding all this apparent strength, it was captured by La Peyrouse, without any trouble, and nearly all rased to the ground. Had the Company's servants done their duty at the time, they might have bid defiance to any force; but *de mortuis nil,* &c. About the fort are now to be seen decayed carriages without guns, rust-eaten guns without carriages, groups of unappropriated balls of various calibre, broken down walls, and dilapidated stores. The governor's old house is the only place any way inhabitable! and even it will require immense repairs to make it tolerably tenantable. I assure you I would prefer residing in one of our snug square-built little boxes on the Columbia to this melancholy remnant of departed greatness.

The following names are cut out in large characters in the wall in front of the fort: RICHARD NORTON, 1752; GUILFORD LONG OF ROTH-ERHITHE, 1754; JOHN NEWTON, 1752.[6]

In the year 1800 Mr. Atkinson found the following inscription

---

[5] De Meuron's regiment was disbanded in Canada at the late peace, and numbers of the men proceeded to Lord Selkirk's colony at the Red River.—R. C.

[6] Churchill is in lat. 58° 44′ N., and long. 95° 30′ W.—R. C.

written in a piece of cedar wood, about a foot square and five feet above the ground, on Old Factory Island in James' Bay, about thirty miles to the northward of East Main Factory. All the letters were quite visible.

In the year 1692 wintered three ships at this island, with one hundred and twenty-seven men, under the government of Captain James Knight. Then we erected this monument in remembrance of it.

Three different tribes occasionally visit us. They belong to the Crees, Chipewyans, and Esquimaux, and we purchase from them beaver, otter, martin, red, silver, and white foxes, &c. The Crees who have visited us have never exceeded twelve men, young and old. The Chipewyans vary considerably in their numbers. From twenty to fifty occasionally come, and the total number who have visited the fort does not exceed one hundred. Our Esquimaux customers reside at and about Chesterfield Inlet. They do not muster more than one hundred and twenty full-grown men, about forty of whom visit us annually. They are all quiet, well-behaved people, and tolerably honest.

About two-thirds of our provisions consist of country produce; the remaining one-third, namely, flour and oatmeal, we procure from England. Among the former we have fresh and salt geese, partridges, venison, and fish. The geese are principally procured in the spring from the Crees and Chipewyans, and numbers are salted by our people. The latter tribe chiefly supply us with the venison, which they bring in a half-dried state, nearly a distance of seventeen days' march. During the summer season we occasionally kill a chance deer. In the winter we are well supplied with partridges, the chief part of which our men take in nets.

Our principal fish is the salmon and jack-fish; the former is taken during the summer season in nets at a place called Cuckold's Point, between two and three miles from the fort; and the Jack is taken in October and November at Deer's River, distant about twenty-five miles from Churchill. Neither however is plentiful.

It was from this place that Hearne set out on his arctic ocean hunting expedition; and as I think he says enough about the climate, soil, production, &c., I shall not tire you by alluding to these subjects. Suffice it to say, that Churchill is a rascally, disagreeable, cold, unsocial, out-of-the-way, melancholy spot, —and I don't care how soon

I am changed. No hunting, horse-racing, or any other of the sports which we enjoyed on the Columbia, which I once thought bad enough; but, talking of Indian trading posts, I may truly say, "bad is the best." So, wishing you all manner of good things, with plenty of *white boys*, and abundance to feed them, I remain *ton tendre ami à la mort*.

Index

Index

Index

THE AMERICAN EXPLORATION
AND TRAVEL SERIES

of which *The Columbia River* is Number 24, was started in 1939 by the University of Oklahoma Press. It follows rather logically the Press's program of regional exploration. Behind the story of the gradual and inevitable recession of the American frontier lie the accounts of explorers, traders, and travelers, which individually and in the aggregate present one of the most romantic and fascinating chapters in the development of the American domain. The following list is complete as of the date of publication of this volume.

1. Captain Randolph B. Marcy and Captain George B. McClellan. *Adventure on Red River*: Report on the Exploration of the Headwaters of the Red River. Edited by Grant Foreman.

2. Grant Foreman. *Marcy and the Gold Seekers*: The Journal of Captain R. B. Marcy, with an account of the Gold Rush over the Southern Route.

3. Pierre-Antoine Tabeau. *Tabeau's Narrative of Loisel's Expedition to the Upper Missouri*. Edited by Annie Heloise Abel. Translated from the French by Rose Abel Wright.

4. Victor Tixier. *Tixier's Travels on the Osage Prairies*. Edited by John Francis McDermott. Translated from the French by Albert J. Salvan.

5. Teodoro de Croix. *Teodoro de Croix and the Northern Frontier of New Spain, 1776–1783*. Translated from the Spanish and edited by Alfred Barnaby Thomas.

6. A. W. Whipple. *A Pathfinder in the Southwest*: The Itinerary of Lieutenant A. W. Whipple During His Explorations for a Railway Route from Fort Smith to Los Angeles in the Years 1853 & 1854. Edited and annotated by Grant Foreman.

7. Josiah Gregg. *Diary & Letters*. Two volumes. Edited by Maurice Garland Fulton. Introductions by Paul Horgan. Out of print.

8. Washington Irving. *The Western Journals of Washington Irving*. Edited and annotated by John Francis McDermott. Out of print.

9. Edward Dumbauld. *Thomas Jefferson, American Tourist*: Being an Account of His Journeys in the United States of America, England, France, Italy, the Low Countries, and Germany.

10. Victor Wolfgang von Hagen. *Maya Explorer*: John Lloyd Stephens and the Lost Cities of Central America and Yucatán.

11. E. Merton Coulter. *Travels in the Confederate States*: A Bibliography.

12. W. Eugene Hollon. *The Lost Pathfinder*: Zebulon Montgomery Pike.

13. George Frederick Ruxton. *Ruxton of the Rockies*. Collected by Clyde and Mae Reed Porter. Edited by LeRoy R. Hafen.

14. George Frederick Ruxton. *Life in the Far West*. Edited by Le-Roy R. Hafen. Foreword by Mae Reed Porter.

15. Edward Harris. *Up the Missouri with Audubon*: *The Journal of Edward Harris*. Edited by John Francis McDermott.

16. Robert Stuart. *On the Oregon Trail*: Robert Stuart's Journey of Discovery (1812–1831). Edited by Kenneth A. Spaulding.

17. Josiah Gregg. *Commerce of the Prairies*. Edited by Max L. Moorhead.

18. John Treat Irving, Jr. *Indian Sketches*, Taken During an Expedition to the Pawnee Tribes (1833). Edited and annotated by John Francis McDermott.

19. Thomas D. Clark (ed.). *Travels in the Old South, 1527–1825*: A Bibliography. Two volumes.

20. Alexander Ross. *The Fur Hunters of the Far West*. Edited by Kenneth A. Spaulding.

21. William Bollaert. *William Bollaert's Texas*. Edited by W. Eu-

22. Daniel Ellis Conner. *Joseph Reddeford Walker and the Arizona Adventure*. Edited by Donald J. Berthrong and Odessa Davenport.

23. Matthew C. Field. *Prairie and Mountain Sketches*. Collected by Clyde and Mae Reed Porter. Edited by Kate L. Gregg and John Francis McDermott.

24. Ross Cox. *The Columbia River*: Scenes and Adventures During a Residence of Six Years on the Western Side of the Rocky Mountains Among Various Tribes of Indians Hitherto Unknown, Together with a Journey Across the American Continent. Edited by Edgar I. and Jane R. Stewart.